Field Theory
in Social Science

hARPER 🔥 τORCHBOOKS

EDITORS' NOTE: *A check-list of Harper Torchbooks, clas-*
sified by subjects, is printed at the end of this volume.

RESEARCHES IN THE SOCIAL, CULTURAL AND BEHAVIORAL SCIENCES

EDITED BY
BENJAMIN NELSON

ADLER, ALFRED: Problems of Neurosis: *A Book of Case Histories*. Edited by P. Mairet, Introduction by H. L. Ansbacher. TB/1145

BURRIDGE, KENELM: *Mambu: A Melanesian Millennium*.

CANTRIL, HADLEY: The Invasion from Mars: *A Study in the Psychology of Panic*. New Introduction by the author. TB/1282

DAVIS, ALLISON and DOLLARD, JOHN: Children of Bondage: *The personality development of Negro youth in the Urban South*. TB/3049

DURKHEIM, EMILE, et al.: Essays on Sociology and Philosophy, *with appraisals of Durkheim's life and work*. Edited by Kurt H. Wolff. TB/1151

FESTINGER, LEON, RIECKEN, HENRY W. and SCHACHTER, STANLEY: When Prophecy Fails: *A social and psychological study of a modern group that predicted the destruction of the world*. TB/1132

FINGARETTE, HERBERT: The Self in Transformation: *Psychoanalysis, Philosophy and the Life of the Spirit*. TB/1177

GOULDNER, ALVIN W.: Wildcat Strike: *A Study in Worker-Management Relationships*. TB/1176

GRAÑA, CÉSAR: Modernity and Its Discontents: French Society and the French Man of Letters in the Nineteenth Century. TB/1318

HAMMOND, J. L.: *The Rise of Modern Industry*. Introduction by Max Hartwell

HAMMOND, J. L. and BARBARA: *The Village Labourer*. Introduction by H. J. Habakkuk. *The Skilled Labourer*.

HEGEL, G. W. F.: The Phenomenology of Mind. Introduction by George Lichtheim. TB/1303

LANDY, DAVID: Tropical Childhood: *Cultural Transmission and Learning in a Puerto Rican Village*. TB/1235

LEWIN, KURT: Field Theory in Social Science: *Selected Theoretical Papers*, edited by Dorwin Cartwright. TB/1135

LOCKWOOD, DAVID: *The Black-Coated Worker*. Introduction by Ralf Dahrendorf

MERTON, ROBERT K.; BROOM, LEONARD; COTTRELL, LEONARD S. JR., editors: Sociology Today: *Problems and Prospects*, Vol. I, TB/1173; Vol. II, TB/1174

MICHELS, ROBERTO: First Lectures in Political Sociology. Translated with an Introduction by Alfred de Grazia. TB/1224

MOORE, BARRINGTON JR.: Political Power and Social Theory: *Seven Studies*. TB/1221

MOORE, BARRINGTON JR.: Soviet Politics—The Dilemma of Power: *The Role of Ideas in Social Change*. New Introduction by the author. TB/1222

MOORE, BARRINGTON JR.: Terror and Progress—USSR. TB/1266

ROSEN, GEORGE: Madness in Society: *Chapters in the Historical Sociology of Mental Illness*. TB/1337

SAINT-SIMON, HENRI DE: Social Organization, the Science of Man, *and other writings*, edited by Felix Markham. TB/1152

SAMUELSSON, KURT: Religion and Economic Action: *A Critique of Max Weber's* The Protestant Ethic and The Spirit of Capitalism TB/1131

SCHAAR, JOHN H.: Escape from Authority: *The Perspectives of Erich Fromm*. TB/1155

SHERIF, MUZAFER: The Psychology of Social Norms. TB/3072. *Group Relations at the Crossroads.

SIMMEL, GEORG, et al.: Essays on Sociology, Philosophy and Aesthetics, edited by Kurt H. Wolff. TB/1234

THOMAS, W. I.: The Unadjusted Girl. Introduction by Michael Parenti. TB/1319

TIRYAKIAN, EDWARD A., editor: Sociological Theory, Values and Sociocultural Change. TB/1316

WARNER, W. LLOYD: A Black Civilization: *A Study of an Australian Tribe*. TB/3056

WARNER, W. LLOYD and ASSOCIATES: Democracy in Jonesville: *A Study in Quality and Inequality*. TB/1129

ZNANIECKI, FLORIAN: *The Social Role of the Man of Knowledge. Introduction by Lewis Coser.

* *In Preparation*

Field Theory in Social Science

SELECTED THEORETICAL PAPERS

by

Kurt Lewin

Late Director, Research Center for Group Dynamics
Massachusetts Institute of Technology

Edited by
DORWIN CARTWRIGHT

HARPER TORCHBOOKS ❦ The Academy Library
Harper & Row, Publishers
New York, Evanston and London

FIELD THEORY IN SOCIAL SCIENCE

Copyright, 1951, by Harper & Row, Publishers, Incorporated.

Printed in the United States of America.

This book was originally published in 1951 by
Harper & Brothers.

Harper & Row, Publishers, Incorporated
49 East 33rd Street
New York 16, N. Y.

First HARPER TORCHBOOK edition published 1964 by
Harper & Row, Publishers, Incorporated
New York, Evanston and London

Contents

Foreword

When the intellectual history of the twentieth century is written, Kurt Lewin will surely be counted as one of those few men whose work changed fundamentally the course of social science in its most critical period of development. During his professional life of only about thirty years, the social sciences grew from the stage of speculative system building, through a period of excessive empiricism in which facts were gathered simply for their intrinsic interest, to a more mature development in which empirical data are sought for the significance they can have for systematic theories. Although the social sciences are only barely into this third stage of development, Lewin's work has accelerated greatly the rate of development. Though he was primarily a psychologist and made his major contributions in that field, the influence of his work has extended well beyond the bounds of traditional psychology.

One reason for this breadth of influence is that much of his work concerned itself with determining the methodological and conceptual prerequisites for a mature science of human behavior. His earliest work in Berlin dealt with the comparative theory of science, an enterprise which permitted him as a young man to get clear what the formal properties of a developed human science must be. He then proceeded throughout the rest of his life to work systematically toward establishing such a science. As a consequence of this early concern with the necessary conditions for scientific progress, his subsequent work on a broad range of special topics in psychology and sociology had a consistent orientation and a pointed impact upon social science generally.

The influence Lewin exerted upon social science is remarkable in that a fully systematic statement of his work was never drawn together in readily accessible form during his life. Most English-speaking social scientists knew him through his *Dynamic Theory of Personality* and his *Principles of Topological Psychology*. While these volumes brilliantly propounded the broad outlines of his work, they merely alluded to the more systematic type of development presented in such lesser known publications as *Der Begriff der Genese in Physik, Biologie, und Entwicklungsgeschichte,* the *Conceptual Representation and the Measurement of Psychological Forces,* the several introductions and appendixes to series of publications of his co-workers, and papers scattered throughout various journals. Moreover, these two more widely known books contain none of the results of his highly productive years of work after he came to America. Many of the controversies that grew up in regard to his systematic position stemmed from the fact that his work was only partially known.

The writings brought together in this book should help greatly to clarify the systematic nature of Lewin's contributions to psychology and the social sciences. Although they were written during a relatively short span of his life (approximately the last ten years), they add up to a remarkably comprehensive statement of his major contributions. Even those familiar with the individual chapters will find that rereading them together and in sequence provides new insights and a deeper understanding of the full significance of this monumental work.

It is possible to state the theme of this volume as a thorough and careful answer to the question: What is field theory in social science? This question is concisely answered in Chapter 3: "Field theory is probably best characterized as a method: namely, a method of analyzing causal relations and of building scientific constructs." (P. 45.) The answer to this question, however, is treated throughout the book in many different ways with particular illustrations from many different fields. It is stated in terms of what the field theorist does as well as what he believes. It makes clear that field theory is more an approach to the scientific task than a theory about a realm of data.

In a broader sense, then, Lewin analyzes in this volume the major attributes that will characterize the working methods of any productive social scientist, regardless of his theoretical orientation. Or, to put the matter differently, he discusses many basic problems of scientific method which all social scientists must face and he proposes solutions not so much on a basis of absolute "right or wrong" as in terms of what will make the scientist most productive. He believes strongly that science is a continuous enterprise in which advance is made by successive approximations to "the truth" and by a never-ending series of small excursions into the unknown. It is more than a coincidence that so productive a scientist should be greatly concerned with the problems of scientific productivity. It is significant, too, that, although his own personal experiences dramatized all too emphatically the political and social influences upon scientific productivity, he felt especially constrained to plead for a recognition of the pervasive influences on productivity that stem from the scientist's own beliefs in the realm of the philosophy of science. He saw clearly that even the most empirical scientist cannot avoid making assumptions of a metaphysical and epistemological sort and that these assumptions shape inevitably the nature of the descriptive concepts he uses, the phenomena he observes, and the way he collects his data.

Although the papers in this volume touch on many topics, throughout all the discussions certain principles guide the development, sometimes quite explicitly but sometimes less obviously. It may be useful to examine briefly Lewin's treatment of three of these more basic issues. The first deals with the nature of constructs in social science and the process of conceptualizing. The second concerns the definition of the fundamental concept, "field." The third opens up problems of strategy concerning the proper balance, at any stage of scientific development, between the construction of rigorous, formal systems and the use of less exact, more popular concepts.

THE PLACE OF CONSTRUCTS IN SOCIAL SCIENCE

To Lewin the essential nature of the work of the scientist consists of making a proper translation from phenomena to concepts. This process of *conceptualizing*, he believes, contains within it some of the most crucial problems faced by the scientist. In order to develop a satisfactory system of concepts, the scientist has to be particularly careful about the way in which he develops his concepts. Before a system can be fully useful the concepts in it have to be defined in a way that (1) permits the treatment of both the "qualitative" and "quantitative" aspects of phenomena in a single system, (2) adequately represents the conditional-genetic (or causal) attributes of phenomena, (3) facilitates the measurement (or operational definition) of these attributes, and (4) allows both generalization to universal laws and concrete treatment of the individual case.

How can such powerful concepts be generated? Lewin found a guide in the "method of construction" first developed in mathematics:

To consider qualitatively different geometrical entities (such as circle, square, parabola) as the product of a certain combination of certain "elements of construction" (such as points and movements) has since the time of the Greeks been the secret of this method. It is sometimes called the method of "genetic definition." It is able, at the same time, to link and to separate; it does not minimize qualitative differences and still lays open their relation to general quantitative variables. Cassirer has shown how the same method proved to be fruitful in empirical sciences where the "elements of construction" are mathematically described empirical entities (such as forces, ions, atoms). [Chapter 2, page 32.]

In psychology and the social sciences it is necessary similarly to develop appropriate "elements of construction" and ways of combining these elements into a system of concepts. In Chapter 2 Lewin presents a penetrating discussion of the problems involved in this process. Of especial help to those working toward the development of a system of concepts is the treatment in this chapter of the *conceptual dimensions* of constructs, for it is the dimensional characteristic of a construct that determines how it may be combined with other constructs and how it may be measured. The significance and practical value of this discussion have yet to be fully utilized by most theorists in the human sciences.

This analysis of the nature of conceptualizing, though highly abstract, is important for an understanding of Lewin's work, because it was in the concrete application of these principles that he made some of his most significant contributions. The essence of much of his most brilliant work consists of a conceptual analysis of the "nature" of phenomena which previously had had only popular labels. Time and again Lewin took some popular notion, such as conflict, frustration, or learning, and subjected it to a conceptual analysis which consisted of ascertaining its elements of construction. Once these were determined, phenomena which had long been thought inaccessible to scientific treatment became fruitful topics of experimental research. And, as Lewin points out in Chapter 9, even the "reality" attributed to them by scientists changed as a result of a successful conceptual analysis of their nature. Examples of this process recur throughout this volume, but especially noteworthy are the treatment of "intention" (Chapter 1), "frustration" (Chapter 2), "learning" (Chapter 4), "regression" (Chapter 5), "adolescence" (Chapter 6), "resistance to change" (Chapter 9), and the classic analysis of "conflict" (reproduced in Chapter 10).

DEFINITION OF "FIELD"

The most fundamental construct for Lewin is, of course, that of "field." All behavior (including action, thinking, wishing, striving, valuing, achieving, etc.) is conceived of as a change of some state of a field in a given unit of time, $\left(\dfrac{dx}{dt} \right)$. In treating individual psychology, the field with which the scientist must deal is the "life space" of the individual. This life space consists of the person and the psychological environment as it exists for him. In dealing with group psychology or sociology, a similar formulation is proposed. One may speak of the field in which a group or institution exists with precisely the same meaning as one speaks of the individual life space in individual psychology. The life space of a group, therefore, consists of the group and its environment as it exists for the group. It is the task of the scientist to develop constructs and techniques of observation and measurement adequate to characterize the properties of any given life space at any given time and to state the laws governing changes of these properties.

In carrying out this task, it is necessary to determine specifically what things are to be included in the representation of any given life space at any particular time. This problem is equivalent to that of determining criteria for attributing scientific "existence" or "reality" to phenomena. It is also closely related to the problem of defining the boundaries of a specific science, for it raises such questions as "What is a psychological fact, an economic fact, a political fact, etc.?" In defining a given field, or life space, it is also important to characterize it so that the interdependence of its parts may be treated satisfactorily. Finally, there is the problem of specifying its location and depth in time.

Existence. The life space is defined so that at any given time it includes all facts that have existence and excludes those that do not have existence *for the individual or group under study.* "Existence for the individual or group" is given a pragmatic definition. Lewin chose to attribute existence to anything having demonstrable effects. In individual psychology, the environment and the person as consciously perceived by the person are ordinarily included in the life space. But, in addition, unconscious states are also included to the extent that by direct observation or inference the scientist can determine that they have effects. It is interesting to note that many of the great "discoveries" of psychology have consisted essentially of a demonstration of the existence in the life space of influences previously not included. A notable example would be Freud's "discovery" of unconscious influences.

In Chapters 3, 8, and 9 Lewin examines in some detail what should be included within the life space of an individual. He indicates that it is reasonably easy to decide to include many things, such as needs, goals, cognitive structure, and the like, and to exclude many others, such as physical and social events occurring at a remote distance and having no direct effect on the individual. There is, however, a boundary zone of events and processes which are ordinarily thought of as physical, economic, political, legal, etc., which, nonetheless, do have direct effects upon individual behavior. Such events and processes must be included within the life space of the individual. Many of Lewin's contributions to the understanding of human behavior consisted of showing that a wider and wider realm of determinants must be treated as part of a single, interdependent field and that phenomena traditionally parceled out to separate "disciplines" must be treated in a single coherent system of constructs. In the last few months of his life, he was coming to recast considerably his conception of motivation to emphasize "needs" less and to stress more such determinants as group membership, personal ability, economic and political resources, social channels, and other influences usually omitted from psychological theories of motivation.

Interdependence. It is a basic assertion of field theory, and here its close relation to Gestalt psychology is apparent, that the various parts of a given life space are to some degree interdependent. It is probable that nothing satisfying the criterion of existence in a given life space can be completely independent of anything else in the same life space. This interdependence of parts poses many special problems in relation both to research methods and to conceptualizing. Problems of both types interested Lewin immensely. In the Appendix to this volume is presented his careful treatment in formal mathematical terms of the concept of interdependence. He believed strongly that a set of interdependent facts can be adequately handled conceptually only with the mathematical concept of space and the dynamic concepts of tension and force. These points are developed to some degree in virtually every chapter in this book. The methodological consequences of the interdependence of parts of the life space are elaborated in Chapter 3 (where the interdependence of the size of unit observed and the length of a unit of time is explored), in Chapter 7 (where the problems of observation and analysis of social events are discussed), and in Chapter 10 (where many phenomena which must be viewed as properties of an interdependent whole are described in detail).

Contemporaneity. Lewin's assertion that the only determinants of behavior at a given time are the properties of the field at the same time has caused more controversy than any of his other systematic principles. This principle asserts that the life space endures through time, is modified by events, and is a product of history, *but only the contemporaneous system can have effects at any time.* The principle of contemporaneity of causation seemed to many to be an attack upon psychoanalytic theory, which asserts the extreme importance of early childhood for later personality, and a denial of the efficacy of learning. In fact, neither of these implications was intended. The discussion in Chapter 3 shows that the essential problem is twofold: one of keeping concepts rigorous and the other of designing appropriate research techniques. The discussion of regression in Chapter 5 provides an excellent example of the gains to be derived from conceptual rigor in regard to the time dimension. The useful distinction made there between regression and retrogression is a result of this concern. The methodological consequences of the principle of contemporaneity are evident in the abstract discussion of anamnesis as a method of determining an individual's present state (Chapter 3) and in the more detailed treatment of the problems of conducting research on group culture and history (Chapter 7).

FORMALIZATION AND PROGRESS

The great emphasis placed by Lewin upon the formal properties of scientific constructs and his insistence that the determinants of human behavior can be represented in rigorous mathematical terms have led some to exaggerate and misinterpret the significance that he attached to formalization in the human sciences. It is true that he devoted great energy to such work as the development of "hodological" space (presented in *The Conceptual Representation and the Measurement of Psychological Forces*) and to the mathematical treatment of differentiated wholes (presented in the Appendix to this volume). It is also true that he believed that these parts of his work would have a more lasting significance than many of his more empirically related studies. And yet his most basic attitude toward science was a practical one, full of common sense, and he was fearful that an enthusiasm for formal systems might lead to a substitution of mere verbalisms for empirically descriptive theories.

In Chapter 1, where he discusses the place of formalization in scientific progress, there is revealed most vividly a man who views his job mainly as that of taking the next possible step in solving the puzzles that nature presents to him. His comparison of the scientific enterprise to that of building "highways and superhighways" across an undeveloped continent is compelling because it is so evident that it was written by an expert builder who had tried out the whole variety of possible tools of building and who therefore knew the value and function of each. Formalization and mathematization, if prematurely done, he asserts, may lead us to the building of a logical superhighway which turns out to be a "dead end leading nowhere." The essential wisdom of an experienced and productive scientist is revealed in his summary statement: "Enthusiasm for Theory? Yes! Psychology can use much of it. However, we will produce but an empty formalism, if we forget that mathematization and formalization should be done only to the degree that the maturity of the material under investigation permits at a given time." (Chapter 1, p. 1.)

The method of successive approximation, he maintains, is the key to scientific productivity. He rarely gave advice to his students, but he never hesitated to advise a young researcher, "Only ask the questions in your research that you can answer with the techniques you can use. If you can't learn to ignore the questions you are not prepared to answer definitely, you will never answer any."

This attitude resulted in his introduction of many "semipopular" concepts which represented only modest steps toward rigorous conceptualization, but which inspired much research. Examples of this sort are the concepts of level of aspiration, group decision, and gate-keeper. Other terms of a similar nature he borrowed from Freud (among others) and proceeded to refine to a next higher level of precision. Examples of this sort are his treatment of substitution, conflict, and regression.

To those who worked closely with him it was repeatedly dramatized how easily and spontaneously he moved from the practical, empirical, and intuitive, to the abstract, rigorous, and formal. I recall vividly a conversation with him shortly before his death in which we were discussing technical problems of constructing an interview for an action-research project on intergroup relations. Suddenly, in the midst of phrasing a question, he interrupted himself with great enthusiasm to say, "Within the next year we'll be able really to measure psychological forces." He was always striving for rigor and precision and he made constant use of the formal constructs available, but he refused to let formalization become an end in itself.

Many people who knew Kurt Lewin have asked how much his rich productivity derived from his theories and beliefs, and how much it resulted simply from his keen sensitivity and clinical insight. That he possessed unusual sensitivity cannot be denied. That his warm and receptive personality contributed to his productivity is also without question. It is my own conclusion, however, from a number of years of close association with him that he was unusually productive because he took seriously and practiced continuously the principles of scientific thinking and methodology which he advocated in the publications contained in this volume.

Kurt Lewin's basic attitude toward science building is perhaps best revealed in a passage where he describes the work of Ernst Cassirer, a man to whom he felt a great intellectual indebtedness:

He discloses the basic character of science as the eternal attempt to go beyond what is regarded scientifically accessible at any specific time. To proceed beyond the limitations of a given level of knowledge the researcher, as a rule, has to break down methodological taboos which condemn as "unscientific" or "illogical" the very methods or concepts which later on prove to be basic for the next major progress.[1]

D. C.

[1] Kurt Lewin: Cassirer's Philosophy of Science and the Social Sciences, in Paul Arthur Schilpp (Ed.): *The Philosophy of Ernst Cassirer*, p. 275. Evanston, Ill.: Library of Living Philosophers, 1949.

Preface

This is the second of two volumes of collected writings by Kurt Lewin which are intended to bring together for convenient reading a number of papers he published during the fifteen years he lived in the United States. The two volumes are integrally related parts of Lewin's total work and yet they contrast in their emphasis. While the first, *Resolving Social Conflicts,* is oriented toward practical problems of society, this second volume deals with more theoretical issues. While in the first volume the emphasis is placed upon the building of a better world, in this volume the concern is that of a scientist attempting to construct a scientific system for understanding man and society. More particularly the papers presented here discuss the working problems of the social scientist. His conceptual and methodological tools are the object of study.

This volume divides rather naturally into three major parts. The first three chapters, together with the Appendix, constitute an examination of several basic problems in the philosophy of science. They set up certain guiding principles which serve as a basis for understanding why the more specific problems in the following chapters are treated as they are. The six following chapters take up these principles and demonstrate their application to research in the fields of learning, development and regression, social psychology and group dynamics, and to research on selected problems of cultural anthropology, sociology, and economics. The final chapter constitutes an excellent, though concise, summary of the major theoretical and substantive findings derived from the research carried out under his immediate supervision.

These two volumes, together with *A Dynamic Theory of Personality, Principles of Topological Psychology,* and *The Conceptual Representation and the Measurement of Psychological Forces,* now make readily available to the English reader a good coverage of the major writings of Kurt Lewin. There remain untranslated, however, several important contributions which appeared in German, and it is to be hoped that these may soon be made available. In a real sense, too, much of his work remains scattered throughout the many journals and monographs where his students and colleagues published research in which his contribution was unmistakable. His modest insistence that he not be listed as a co-author of these publications resulted in an imperfect reflection of his role in most of this research. Those wishing to study fully Lewin's work are referred to the bibliographical references at the end of the various chapters (especially Chapter 10), to the long series of studies that he edited for the *Psychologische Forschung*, and to the series of monographs, *Studies in Topological and Vector Psychology*, contained in the University of Iowa Studies in Child Welfare.

Editing this volume has been a gratifying task. It has been a rare intellectual experience to discover the essential coherence that the various papers collected here possess. It has been literally thrilling to see the systematic and integrated structure emerge from the mere bringing together of long familiar publications not before read in immediate sequence. For the most part it has been possible to leave the single papers without editorial modification. Certain duplication had to be omitted here and there and certain transitional paragraphs had to be supplied, but the material was written almost as though it had been intended for publication in a single volume. The only substantial modification of form is found in respect to Chapters 2, 7, and 8. In Chapter 7, "Problems of Research in Social Psychology," are presented excerpts from Lewin's presidential address before the Society for the Psychological Study of Social Issues and a section from the paper, "Constructs in Psychology and Psychological Ecology" (the bulk of which appears as Chapter 2). In Chapter 8, "Psychological Ecology," Lewin's theory of social channels is presented. Since he developed this theory in three separate places, the editorial problem consisted of bringing together from these sources a single and complete statement of this theory. It proved to be possible to extract a coherent presentation from the much longer treatment, "Forces behind food habits and methods of change." Certain brief sections are also included from "Constructs in psychology and psychological ecology" and from "Frontiers in group dynamics, II." (More specific reference to these sources is given below.)

We are greatly indebted to the publishers of the original papers for permission to print them here. Below are listed the original sources of each of the chapters.

Chapter 1. Formalization and progress in psychology, *University of Iowa Studies in Child Welfare*, 1940, *16*, No. 3, 9-42. Reprinted by permission of Iowa Child Welfare Research Station.

Chapter 2. Constructs in psychology and psychological ecology, *University of Iowa Studies in Child Welfare*, 1944, *20*, 1-29. Reprinted by permission of Iowa Child Welfare Research Station.

Chapter 3. Defining the "field at a given time," *Psychological Review*, 1943, *50*, 292-310. Reprinted by permission of the *Psychological Review* and of the American Psychological Association.

Chapter 4. Field theory of learning, *Yearbook of the National Society for the Study of Education*, 1942, *41*, part II, 215-242. Reprinted by permission of the Society.

Chapter 5. Regression, Retrogression, and Development (Chapter 1), *Frustration and Regression* by Roger Barker, Tamara Dembo, and Kurt Lewin. *University of Iowa Studies in Child Welfare*, 1941, *18*, No. 1, 1-43. Reprinted by permission of Iowa Child Welfare Research Station. The co-authors have informed the editor that Dr. Lewin was the author of this chapter and of the appendix.

Chapter 6. Field theory and experiment in social psychology: concepts and methods, *American Journal of Sociology*, 1939, *44*, 868-897. Reprinted by permission of the University of Chicago Press.

Chapter 7. Psychology and the process of group living, *Journal of Social Psychology*, 1943, *17*, 113-131. Reprinted by permission of The Journal Press. Constructs in psychology and psychological ecology, *University of Iowa Studies in Child Welfare*, 1944, *20*, 23-27. Reprinted by permission of the Iowa Child Welfare Research Station.

Chapter 8. Forces behind food habits and methods of change, *Bulletin of the National Research Council*, 1943, *108*, 35-65. Reprinted by permission of the National Research Council. Constructs in psychology and psychological ecology, *University of Iowa Studies in Child Welfare*, 1944, *20*, 17-20. Reprinted by permission of the Iowa Child Welfare Research Station. Frontiers in group dynamics, II, *Human Relations*, 1947, *1*, 143-153. Reprinted by permission of *Human Relations*.

Chapter 9. Frontiers in group dynamics, *Human Relations*, 1947, *1*, 2-38. Reprinted by permission of *Human Relations*.

Chapter 10. Behavior and development as a function of the total situation. Reprinted by permission from *Manual of Child Psychology*, by L. Carmichael, published by John Wiley & Sons, Inc., copyright 1946.

Appendix. Analysis of the concepts whole, differentiation, and unity, *University of Iowa Studies in Child Welfare*, 1941, *18*, No. 1, 226-261. Reprinted by permission of the Iowa Child Welfare Research Station.

I wish to express here my great debt to Dr. Albert Pepitone who helped immeasurably in all phases of editing this volume.

DORWIN CARTWRIGHT

Ann Arbor, Michigan
June 15, 1950

I

Formalization and Progress
in Psychology
(1940)

ᒐᒐᒐᒐᒐᒐᒐᒐᒐᒐᒐᒐᒐᒐᒐᒐᒐᒐᒐᒐᒐᒐᒐᒐᒐᒐᒐᒐᒐᒐᒐᒐᒐᒐ

I

IN RECENT years there has been a very marked change in the attitude of American psychology. During the 1920's and early 1930's psychologists were, on the whole, rather adverse to theory. Governed by a naive metaphysical belief, they were apt to consider "fact finding" the only task of "scientific" psychology, and were particularly skeptical of the idea of psychological laws in the fields of needs, will, and emotion, that is, in fields other than perception and memory.

Today, a definite interest in psychological theory has emerged, due partly to the efforts of a few psychologists (particularly Tolman and Hull in animal psychology). The need for a closer fusion of the various branches of psychology demands tools which permit better integration. The practical tasks of mental hygiene and education demand conceptual tools which permit prediction. Neither demand can be met without theory.

Now, however, it seems necessary to point to certain dangers of theorizing. Enthusiasm for Theory? Yes! Psychology can use much of it. However, we will produce but an empty formalism, if we forget that mathematization and formalization should be done only to the degree that the maturity of the material under investigation permits at a given time.

Philosophically, there seems to exist only an "either-or": if scientific "facts" and particularly all so-called dynamic facts are not merely "given data," but inseparably interwoven with theoretical assumptions, there seems to be no choice other than to base every statement in psychology on theoretical assumptions.

For the psychologist, as an empirical scientist, the situation looks rather different. He finds himself in the midst of a rich and vast land full of strange happenings: there are men killing themselves; a child playing; a child forming his lips trying to say his first word; a person who having fallen in love and being caught in an unhappy situation is not willing or not able to find a way out; there is the mystical state called hypnosis, where the will of one person seems to govern another person; there is the reaching out for higher, and more difficult goals; loyalty to a group; dreaming; planning; exploring the world; and so on without end. It is an immense continent full of fascination and power and full of stretches of land where no one ever has set foot.

Psychology is out to conquer this continent, to find out where its treasures are hidden, to investigate its danger spots, to master its vast forces, and to utilize its energies.

How can one reach this goal? At first, in what might be called the "speculative epoch," the attempt was made to dig down deep into the ground. A peculiar something was reported to lie underground as the hidden source of energy. One gave it the name "association." New investigators drove their shafts down at somewhat different places. They found something different which they called "instinct." A third group of explorers reported a different entity, "libido." And all claimed to have found *the* foundation on which the land rested. By this time, psychologists had become rather tired of the various claims. It had become clear that the continent was much larger than was suspected at first. Perhaps there was more than one source of energy. The whole depth-sounding process had become rather open to suspicion, particularly since no explorer seemed able to bring his material up to the surface for inspection in broad daylight. How was one ever to prove a real connection between the entities supposedly existing underground and what was going on at the surface? There, open to all eyes, and unquestionable, interesting phenomena presented themselves. The psychologist now turned to extensive traveling over the surface of the continent, eager to find new phenomena, to describe them exactly, to count and to measure them, to register their growth.

This procedure, however, did not prove altogether satisfactory either. After all, what the psychologist observed were human beings. Children needed help and education; delinquent people needed guidance; people in distress wanted cure. Counting, measuring, and classifying their sorrows did not help matters much. Obviously one had to go to the facts "behind," "below the surface." How to accomplish this without the fallacies of the speculative epoch? That is the dominant methodological question of psychology today, at the beginning of its "Galilean period."

The answer is something like this: to make oneself master of the forces of this vast scientific continent one has to fulfill a rather peculiar task. The ultimate goal is to establish a network of highways and superhighways, so that any important point may be linked easily with any other. This network of highways will have to be adapted to the natural topography of the country and will thus itself be a mirror of its structure and of the position of its resources.

The construction of the highway system will have to be based partly upon assumptions which cannot be expected to be fully correct. The test drilling in exploring the deposits will not always lead to reliable results. Besides, there is a peculiar paradox in the conquering of a new continent, and even more so in that of a new scientific field. To make the proper tests, some machinery has to be transported, and such transportation presupposes more or less the same road, the construction of which is contingent upon the outcome of the test. In other words, to find out what one would like to know one should, in some way or other, already know it.

What should science do to resolve this paradox? If it is wise, it follows the same procedure used in a systematic exploration of the resources of a new land: small paths are pushed out through the unknown; with simple and primitive instruments, measurements are made; much is left to assumption and to lucky intuition. Slowly certain paths are widened; guess and luck are gradually replaced by experience and systematic exploration with more elaborate instruments. Finally highways are built over which the streamlined vehicles of a highly mechanized logic, fast and efficient, can reach every important point on fixed tracks.

By and large, the actual development of a science seems to follow this general pattern. Yet frequently somebody, thinking he knows where an important treasure lies, tries to build a superhighway straight to this point without regard for the natural structure of the country. Much enthusiasm and work are put into such roadbuilding, but after some time it becomes apparent that this superhighway is a dead end leading nowhere.

Formalization and mathematization in psychology, if prematurely done, may lead us to the building of such logical superhighways. Formalization will have to be achieved if psychology is to become an acceptable science, and psychology can and must take definite steps in that direction now. However, the promising beginning and the growing interest for such undertaking will soon turn into disappointment if certain dangers, arising partly from recent trends in philosophy and logic, are not frankly discussed and avoided.

I feel somewhat obliged to take this matter up, because two of my books[1] deal mainly with the conceptual tools of psychology. Some of the critics, who did not realize that these conceptual tools have been used for several years in a great number of investigations in a variety of fields, seem to have concluded that my main interest in psychology is formalization or mathematization. Nothing can be more erroneous. As psychologists we are interested in finding new knowledge about, and deeper insight into, psychological processes. That is, and always has been, the guiding principle. Theory, mathematization, and formalization are tools for this purpose. Their value for psychology exists only in so far as they serve as a means to fruitful progress in its subject matter, and they should be applied, as complex tools always should, only when and where they help and do not hinder progress.

II

Some psychologists interested in "strict logical derivations" have criticized our experimental work for not being written in the form: (a) definition, (b) assumption, (c) conclusion. On the other hand, French[2] writes:

In the course of fifty years [psychoanalysis] has developed an extensive system of scientific concepts but the concepts have grown step by step as a necessary and inevitable product of Freud's attempt to orient himself in

[1] *Principles of Topological Psychology* (New York: McGraw-Hill Book Co., 1936); The conceptual representation and the measurement of psychological forces, *Contr. psychol. theor.*, 1938, *1*, No. 4, Duke University Press.

[2] Thomas M. French: A review of *A Dynamic Theory of Personality* and *The Principles of Topological Psychology*, by Kurt Lewin. In *Psychoanalytic Quarterly*, 1937, *6*, 122-128.

a bewildering chaos of psychological facts that no one previously had been able to understand. Due to close contact of these new concepts with the facts, one set of concepts was devised to explain one set of facts and a new problem would give rise to an entirely new set of concepts. . . . Topological psychology on the other hand starts with a self-consistent mathematical discipline and then goes to look for facts to fit it. [P. 127.]

As an answer I may be permitted to survey the actual historical development. My work in psychology began with experiments on association and the *determinierende Tendenz*.[3] The intention was not to criticize associationism but rather to refine the measurement of the "strength of the will" as developed by Ach. His work at that time, I believe, was the most precise theoretically in the field of will and association. After three years of experimentation with hundreds of series of nonsense syllables, and after thousands of measurements of reaction times (at that time one had to measure in $1/1000$ seconds) I became convinced that there was no point in trying to improve the exactness of this measurement. The attempts were all based on the assumption of the classical law of association as stated, e.g., by G. E. Müller. The experiments however seemed to prove conclusively, contrary to my expectation, that this assumption had to be abandoned or decidedly modified. It was necessary to distinguish two rather different types of habits (associations): "need habits" (like alcoholism) and "execution habits" (like pulling a lever up rather than down). The first type represents a "tension" (source of energy), a need such as hunger, which demands satisfaction either directly or through substitution. The execution habit, on the other hand, is in itself no source of action. It is equivalent to a pattern of restraining forces determining a certain path. Without a need or quasi-need the execution habit does not lead to action.

After an interruption due to the first World War, a systematic attempt was made to test the positive assumption growing out of this criticism of the law of association. The first step was an attempt to achieve a more precise conceptual analysis. Dynamically, an "association" is something like a link in a chain, i.e., a pattern of restraining forces without intrinsic tendency to create a change. On the other hand, the tendency to bring about action is basic to a need. This property of a need or quasi-need can be represented by coordinating

[3] Kurt Lewin. Die psychische Tätigkeit bei der Hemmung von Willensorgängen und das Grundgesetz der Assoziation, *Ztschr. f. Psychol.*, 1917, 77, 212-247.

6 *Field Theory in Social Science*

it to a "system in tension." By taking this construct seriously and using certain operational definitions, particularly by correlating the "release of tension" to a "satisfaction of the need" (or the "reaching of the goal") and the "setting up of tension" to an "intention" or to a "need in a state of hunger," a great number of testable conclusions were made possible.

After these basic conclusions had been proved valid, mainly through the experiments of Zeigarnik[4] and Ovsiankina,[5] the theory was expanded to include problems like psychological satiation, substitution on the reality and irreality level and in play situations, the measurement of substitute value, the level of aspiration, its shift after success and failure, the effect of distance from the goal upon the strength of psychological forces; in short, the pattern of goals and needs, their interrelation, and the ways of satisfying them, were studied. Today, a multitude of problems including personality and personality development, cognitive structure, social and cultural relations are being attacked with a set of related concepts.

If one looks through our publications in the order that they have been published one will, I think, agree that the various theoretical assumptions and constructs have been developed rather slowly step by step. The assumptions were made rather tentatively at first and with a fair amount of hesitation. Only to the degree that more and more empirical facts could be brought together experimentally, the theory gained in firmness and more specific statements emerged.

This gradual elaboration based on empirical facts and a great variety of experiments holds true particularly for the mathematical aspects of the theory. The application of topological and vector concepts was first made in a way which left it open whether we had to deal merely with a pedagogical device or rather with a real scientific representation. Only to the extent that these conceptual tools proved to be valuable in formulating problems, and permitting derivations which could be tested experimentally, did they become essential parts of the theory and of its dynamic constructs.

French's criticisms of the *Principles of Topological Psychology*

[4] B. Zeigarnik: Über das behalten von erledigten und unerledigten Handlungen, *Psychol. Forsch.*, 1927, 9, 1-85.

[5] M. Ovsiankina: Die Wiederaufnahme von unterbrochenen Handlungen, *Psychol. Forsch.*, 1928, 11, 302-389.

overlook the fact that this first attempt at a systematic survey of the conceptual tools used in our research was not made till after many years of empirical work with them. What French says about the gradual growth of psychoanalytic concepts out of psychological facts can as well be said in regard to the use of topological and vector concepts in field theory. As a matter of fact, the feeling for the necessity of rather slow and careful theorization was the main reason which restrained us from using strict, so-called formalistic derivations in those early experimental studies. That does not mean that I considered those derivations to be not fully stringent or that I did not esteem the value of a mathematical logical language which I had found very helpful when treating problems of comparative theory of science.[6] However, it would have been premature to present certain ideas "*more geometrico*," i.e., by setting forth so-called formal definitions, assumptions, and deductions without being able to do so in well-defined mathematical symbols, in the form of equations or similar representations of functional dependence. If one uses terms of everyday language such as "frustration," "need," "learning" without being able to coordinate mathematical entities to them, one might as well use the normal form of reasoning. To present statements employing amathematical constructs "*more geometrico*" suggests a degree of exactness of derivation which, I am afraid, cannot generally be reached with those types of constructs. This holds true even when these conceptually rather vague constructs are operationally well defined. We will come back to this point later.

One can go even one step further. The dynamic constructs used for example in the study of Zeigarnik may be said to be already of that type which readily lends itself to a strict mathematical representation. However, we felt that it would be wiser to wait with the formalistic representation until these constructs had proved more thoroughly to be empirically fruitful. A too high degree of formalization is likely to endanger this plasticity.

Psychology cannot try to explain everything with a single construct, such as association, instinct, or gestalt. A variety of constructs has to be used. These should be interrelated, however, in a logically precise manner. Moreover, every theoretical statement brought forth

[6] Kurt Lewin: *Der Begriff der Genese in Physik, Biologie, und Entwicklungsgeschichte* (Berlin: Springer, 1922).

to explain certain empirical data should be carefully examined not only in the light of these data but in the light of the totality of empirical data and theoretical statements of psychology. In other words *ad hoc* theories should be avoided. Bringing together the total field of psychology and doing that in a logically consistent manner might well be viewed as one of the basic purposes of our approach. The demand for a new level of precision in regard to the conceptual properties of the constructs, with a view to an ultimately strictly mathematical representation, is but a means to this end. On the other hand, it has been realized that without such mathematization the development of a consistent scientific psychology is impossible in the long run.

III

Occasionally criticisms have been made that the number of subjects in some of our experiments was not sufficiently large. It is probable that, in one or the other experiment, a greater number of cases would have added to the reliability; and, of course, additional confirmation is always desirable. But, where other investigators have repeated our experiments in a competent manner, our results have stood up very well on the whole. Besides, different types of confirmation are most desirable for different types of questions. For instance, if one wishes to find out how the frequency of resumption depends upon the point at which an activity has been interrupted one will have to use a relatively great number of cases to get reliable results, for the problem involved is how within one situation a gradual quantitative change of one factor changes another factor quantitatively. In such cases the problem of the exactness of measurement is paramount and therefore a great number of cases is important.

Take, on the other hand, such questions as whether the effect of an intention is that of a link (association) or the creation of a quasi-need (equivalent to a tension system). If the latter theory is correct, one should expect a fair number of resumptions after interruption. The study of about one hundred interruptions by Ovsiankina shows indeed 80 per cent of resumption. There is some merit in trying another group of one hundred interruptions. If, however, this group again shows about 80 per cent of resumption, one can follow two lines. Either one tries to determine the actual percentage of resumption as accurately as possible, or one is mainly interested in the question whether the effect of an intention can be adequately understood as the creation of a tension system. For the latter question it is at present of minor importance whether the percentage of resumption is 75, 80, or 85, because any of these figures would be in line with the general assumption. To prove or disprove the theory of tension systems, it seems much more important to find a variety of derivations from this theory which should be as different as possible from each other, and to test as many as possible of these derivations, even if this test should be rather crude quantitatively at the beginning.

IV

It might be well to illustrate this point by reviewing in detail the first experimental study of the above-mentioned series, viz., the experiments of Zeigarnik, which were carried out in the years 1924 to 1926 about the recall of finished and unfinished actions. Let us repeat some of Zeigarnik's derivations making use, however, of the formal apparatus of symbols and equations which has been developed in the meantime.

THE BASIC ASSUMPTIONS AND THE MAIN DERIVATION

The critical experiments about association and "the measurement of will power" mentioned above had suggested the theory that the effect of an intention was equivalent to the creation of an inner personal tension. The purpose of Zeigarnik's experiment was to provide a first experimental test of this theory. The theory contains two basic assumptions.

(A1) *Assumption 1:* The intention to reach a certain goal G (to carry out an action leading to G) corresponds to a tension (t) in a certain system (S^G) within the person so that $t(S^G) > 0$. This assumption co-ordinates a dynamic construct (system in tension) with the observable syndrome popularly called "intention."

(A2) *Assumption 2:* The tension $t(S^G)$ is released if the goal G is reached.

$$t(S^G) = 0 \text{ if } P \subset G$$

Zeigarnik uses as a symptom for the existence of the tension the tendency to recall activities corresponding to the system in tension. The expectation of the existence of such a system is based on the following:

(A3) *Assumption 3:* To a need for G corresponds a force $f_{P,G}$ acting upon the person and causing a tendency of locomotion toward G.

$$\text{if } t(S^G) > 0 \quad f_{P,G} > 0$$

This assumption determines the relation between need and locomotion. In other words it means a construct of tension in the person and the construct of force for locomotion in the environment.

Assumptions (A1), (A2), and (A3) are rather general in nature and have been used as basic assumptions for a great variety of deductions and experimentation. [It may be possible to eliminate (A3) to a certain degree and to replace it by a combination of (A1) and (A2). One could say without formally introducing the construct of force for locomotion that if $t(S^G) > 0$ there should result according to (A2) a tendency to change the life space so that $t(S^G) = 0$. We prefer, however, to state (A3) as a separate assumption.]

(A3a) *Assumption 3a:* A need leads not only to a tendency of actual locomotion towards the goal region but also to thinking about this type of activity; in other words the force $f_{P,G}$ exists not only on the level of doing (reality) but also on the level of thinking (irreality);

$$\text{if } t(S^G) > 0 \quad f_{P,R} > 0$$

where R means recall.

This last assumption of Zeigarnik is more specific in character. It can be viewed as a specialization of (A3). For the derivations of Zeigarnik this specific form (A3a) rather than (A3) is needed.

From the three assumptions (A1), (A2), and (A3a) follows:

(D1) *Derivation 1:* The tendency to recall interrupted activities should be greater than the tendency to recall finished ones. This derivation can be made as follows. We indicate the completed task by C, the unfinished one by U, and the corresponding systems by S^o and S^u respectively. We can then state

    (a) $t(S^u) > 0$ according to (A1)
    (b) $t(S^o) = 0$ according to (A2)

    Hence (c) $f_{P,U} > f_{P,C}$ according to (A3a), on the level of thinking. In other words: there is a greater tendency to recall spontaneously unfinished tasks than finished tasks.

Experimental Proof: The first objective of Zeigarnik was to test experimentally this conclusion and it was found to be correct, the quotient $\frac{\text{recalled unfinished tasks} = \text{RU}}{\text{recalled completed tasks} = \text{RC}}$ being 1.9 approximately. Experiments where certain tasks were first interrupted but later on allowed to be finished served to prove that it is not the experiences connected with the interruption itself which are the cause of this result but the reaching or not reaching of the goal. In this experiment the recall was not more frequent than in the case of tasks completed without interruption.

After this main conclusion has been found to be true two procedures are open. One can feel that one has done enough for the proof of the main assumption and can go into more exact quantitative measurements, or one can try to find new independent derivations from the basic assumptions and test these experimentally with the purpose of corroborating them. Zeigarnik embarked mainly upon the second alternative.

FIELD THEORETICAL IMPLICATIONS OF THE CONSTRUCT "TENSION"

Using the construct of a "system in tension" for representing psychological needs definitely presupposes a field theory. Conceptually, tension refers to the state of one system relative to the state of surrounding systems. The essence and the purpose of this construct is to include a tendency for change in the direction of equalization of the state of neighboring systems. The construct, therefore, presupposes a geometric representation of the person and a distinction of functional subparts or "systems" within the person, with a definite position in regard to each other. This is but an elaboration of the conceptual properties already implied in the construct tension. Formalistically, one can express the basic relation between neighboring tension systems in the following way:

(C1) If $t(S^1) \neq t(S^2)$ and $b_{s1} \cdot b_{s2} \neq 0$, a tendency exists to change so that $t(S^1) = t(S^2)$. In this formula b_{s1} and b_{s2} indicate the boundaries of the systems S^1 and S^2, $b_{s1} \cdot b_{s2}$ their common part.

The construct tension furthermore presupposes definite assumptions as to the dynamic character of this field, e.g., if the systems corresponding to different needs or quasi-needs should be able to maintain different amounts of tension during a certain period, one will have to assume that this field is not too fluid. If it should be a very fluid field, any differences between the tension levels of the various systems would be found to disappear in a very short time because of the fact that the tendency of equalization resulting from the local tensions would not meet any resistance; in other words, if a quasi-need is coordinated to a tension system which may show its effect even over a considerable time interval, one has to assume that dynamically the person cannot be considered as entirely fluid. On the other hand, a person cannot be regarded as entirely rigid. Otherwise, the effect which one need has on other needs and on the tension level of the person as a whole could not be accounted for. A person, therefore, has to be conceived of as having a medium degree of fluidity in regard to the intercommunication of his tension systems. It is clear that this degree of fluidity may vary from person to person and from situation to situation for a single person. Assuming the constancy of the structural relations of a given set of systems (and assuming a temporarily impermeable boundary surrounding the set as a whole), one can express this statement in the following way:

(C2) Let us indicate the absolute difference between the tension $t(S^1)$ and the tension $t(S^2)$ of two neighboring systems S^1 and S^2 at the time the tensions are being built up by $|t(S^1) - t(S^2)|^0$, the time since then elapsed by Ti, the tension difference at this time by $|t(S^1) - t(S^2)|^{Ti}$, and the fluidity by fl. Then we can state

$$|t(S^1) - t(S^2)|^0 - |t(S^1) - t(S^2)|^{Ti} = F(Ti, fl)$$

where F symbolizes a monotonously increasing function.

This means: the change in the tension difference of neighboring systems depends upon the time interval and the fluidity. Of course, this holds true only if the tensions of these systems are not changed by other factors such as e.g. release of tension by reaching the goal.

As far as I can see, (C1) and (C2) are necessary conceptual elements of the construct tension. The coordination of needs and quasi-needs to this construct tension, therefore, makes it possible to derive a number of facts which may seem rather remote from the problem primarily investigated. These predictions could hardly be made without this specific dynamic theory, and therefore if they can be proved they are of particular value for the confirmation of the theory.

DERIVATIONS IN REGARD TO THE FLUIDITY OF THE FIELD AND THE COMMUNICATION BETWEEN TENSION SYSTEMS

(D2) The difference in tension between systems corresponding to unfinished and finished tasks decreases with the time interval elapsed since the creation of the tension system.

Derivation: Follows immediately from the right side of the equation (C2) by means of (A1) and (A3a).

Experimental Proof: The Zeigarnik quotient decreases from about 1.9 to about 1.2 if the recall test has been postponed one day.

If we are correct in assuming that the maintenance of a tension difference between the partial systems of an individual depends upon a sufficient rigidity of the medium, a quicker decrease of tension could occur if the person is more fluid. To prove this conclusion experimentally, Zeigarnik had to find a state which could reasonably be characterized as increased fluidity (fl). The general symptoms of fatigue seem to justify

(A4) *Assumption 4:* fl (P tired) $>$ fl (P nontired).

(D3) The Zeigarnik quotient $\dfrac{RU}{RC}$ is smaller for tired than for nontired subjects.

Derivation: It follows immediately from the denominator in (C2) by means of (A1), (A3a), and (A4).

Experimental Proof: Subjects who were tired during performance and recall yielded a quotient of .7; those tired during performance but not during recall, a quotient of .6; those not tired during performance but tired during recall, 1.0. This threefold variation was made because a fluid state of a person might prevent the building up of any considerable tension difference. The last variation shows that even if the tension has been built up in a nontired state, the quotient becomes smaller if the subject is tired during recall. (The problem of the quotient being smaller than 1 is accounted for by factors not discussed here; they are discussed by Zeigarnik in her paper.)

Several experimental data and other observations suggest that the levels of greater irreality (levels of wishes and dreams) have to be considered as more fluid than the level of reality (level of action). From this it would follow that needs and quasi-needs related to these more irreal levels should show a quicker diffused discharge of tension.

(A5) *Assumption 5:* $fl = F$ (degree of irreality).

(D4) The rate of decrease of the Zeigarnik quotient, within a given time interval, increases with the degree of irreality of activities involved.

$$\left(\frac{RU}{RC}\right)^{o} - \left(\frac{RU}{RC}\right)^{Tl} = F \text{ (degree of irreality)}.$$

Derivation: (D4) follows immediately from (C2) in connection with (A1), (A3a), and (A5).

Experimental Proof: Brown[7] has shown that the ability to recall interrupted "irreal" activities decreases faster than the ability to recall the more "real" ones. (It is possible that the experiment of Brown does not deal with differences in the degree of reality but rather with differences between more peripheral activities as against more central ones on approximately the same level of reality. In this case, his experiment would show that the more peripheral region of a person has to be regarded as more fluid.)

One way to destroy the differences of tension in the various systems of the inner personal region seems to be the creation of a high emotional tension or, more specifically, a quick shift up and down of strong emotional tension. The bringing up of the general emotional tension within a person to a magnitude of a different order than that corresponding to the relatively weak quasi-needs created in these experiments would, one might expect, equalize these tensions or at least make their differences practically negligible. A sudden change up and down of such a magnitude might well destroy quite a number of walls between the systems or bring about another process equivalent to their dedifferentiation and equalize the tensions in this way. As the constructs of "permeability" and "elasticity" are not elaborate enough at present to warrant a formalistic representation we prefer to give this statement in verbal form:

(A6) *Assumption 6:* Strong waves of emotional tension destroy tension differences corresponding to relatively superficial needs.

(D5) The Zeigarnik quotient $\frac{RU}{RC}$ after an emotional excitement and "let down" is smaller than without such a process intervening between performance and recall.

[7] J. F. Brown: Über die dynamische Eigenshaften der Realitäts und Irrealitätsschichten, *Psychol. Forsch.*, 1933, *18*, 143–190.

Derivation: It follows from (A6), (A1), and (A3a).

Experimental Proof: After experimentally created emotional waves the Zeigarnik quotient decreases to .6. A similarly low quotient of .75 is shown by those subjects who have been emotionally excited during the experiments as a result of their general life situation.

As a last example in this group of derivations which are based mainly on the spatial relations between the various systems and on their amount of communication, we mention the following: A condition for a difference between the systems corresponding to finished and unfinished tasks is that the systems corresponding to each individual task in the experiment are set up from the beginning as sufficiently separated within the person. For if these various systems are subparts of one comprehensive unit without much separation no great difference in tension can persist. In this case there may be differences in the tension levels of those greater units but no differences between the various subsystems within the larger units. That sufficiently strong boundaries between the systems are a prerequisite for the persistence of tension is already contained in (C1) and (C2).

(D6) The Zeigarnik quotient $\dfrac{RU}{RC}$ should be about 1 if S^u and S^c are not sufficiently separated.

Derivation: Follows directly from (C1) and (C2) in connection with (A1) and (A3a).

Experimental Proof: A larger unit in which the single tasks, no matter whether finished or unfinished, are not much separated, can be created by the setting up of a cognitive structure at the beginning of the experiment, according to which the single tasks appear as parts of a more highly unified series. In such settings the quotient was found to be about .97.

DERIVATION IN REGARD TO INTENSITY OF QUASI-NEEDS

One can elaborate our basic assumption (A1) about the relation between psychological needs and tension systems by correlating the intensity of the tension to the intensity of the need.

(A1a) *Assumption (A1a):* $t(S^G) = F(n^G)$ where n^G means the intensity of the need correlated to the goal G.

Correspondingly, we can elaborate the basic assumption (A3)

and (A3a) concerning the relation between tension and force for locomotion and recall into a quantitative relation.

(A3b) *Assumption (A3b):* $|f_{P, G}| = F|t(S^G)|$ where $|f_{P, G}|$ means the strength of the force in the direction of locomotion or recall.

(D7) $$\frac{RU}{RC} = F(n^u)$$

Derivation: (D7) follows from (A1a), (A3a), and (A3b).

Experimental Proof: It is to be expected that subjects who are particularly ambitious will show quasi-needs of a greater intensity than the average subject, whereas subjects whose involvement in the activities is particularly weak should have particularly weak quasi-needs. Zeigarnik has grouped separately those subjects who according to their general behavior in the experiment could be characterized as "ambitious" (without regard to the Zeigarnik quotient.) She found that their quotient showed a value of 2.75 as against 1.9 for the average kind of subject. On the other hand, a group of subjects who merely did "what the experimenter told them" without getting personally involved showed a quotient of 1.03, much less than the average. According to Zeigarnik the most seriously involved group of subjects were children. Indeed, their quotient shows a value of 2.5. It may be that there are other factors which contribute to this result. Marrow[8] has attacked the problem of the relation between the intensity of the need and the Zeigarnik quotient in a particularly careful way. He compares the control group of subjects with another group in a situation of competition. He still further sharpens this competition either by praise or by blame. Although he uses a different type of activity, the Zeigarnik quotient of the control group was again 1.9, whereas in the situation of competition, where the need of the subject is very much intensified, the Zeigarnik quotient went up decidedly, in the case of encouragement to 2.17, in the case of blame to 2.10. Marrow showed that the Zeigarnik quotient was particularly high for those tasks which directly followed after the experience of praise or blame by the experimenter.

DERIVATIONS IN REGARD TO PSYCHOLOGICAL AS AGAINST NON-PSYCHOLOGICAL CHARACTERIZATION OF TASKS

It is a general presupposition of psychological field theory that one has to be careful to use psychological rather than "objective" sociological or physical categories. There are cases where an activity

[8] A. J. Marrow: Goal tensions and recall (I & II), *J. Gen. Psychol.*, 1938, *19*, 3–35; 37–64.

might be finished from the subject's point of view although it might be classified as interrupted by the experimenter. On the other hand, there are outwardly finished activities which psychologically are unfinished for the subject.

According to (A2) the release of tension is coordinated to the reaching of the goal and this reaching of the goal has to be understood psychologically. From this follows:

(D8) $\dfrac{RU}{RC} = 1$ if $P \supset G$ at the time of "interruption."

Derivation: This follows directly from (A2) in connection with (A1) and (A3a).

Experimental Proof: Zeigarnik reports a number of specific cases of outwardly unfinished, psychologically finished activities where the quotient was about 1. Marrow used a special experimental setup where the subject was told that the experimenter was merely interested in finding out whether or not the subject was able to carry out the task and that he would interrupt as soon as he had received this impression. Thus, the interrupted task here psychologically appears finished. Marrow found indeed that the Zeigarnik quotient in this case was .74.

We might mention here the difference between continuous and end tasks. The end tasks such as making a chair out of plasticine or writing a poem have a rather well-defined end, so that in the case of interruption the subject has definitely not reached the goal, whereas by finishing he has reached it. In this case the Zeigarnik quotient is decidedly greater than 1, viz., 1.8. In the case of a continuous task, however, such as putting beads on a string, the subject does not reach a definite goal after "finishing" nor does he definitely get outside the goal region if "interrupted." Therefore the tension in those cases should not be very much different. Indeed, the Zeigarnik quotient is 1.1. (The low values of both R_u and R_c found by Zeigarnik show that the continuous task, no matter whether outwardly interrupted or finished, is psychologically finished.)

(D9) $\dfrac{RU}{RC} = 1$ if $P \quad G$ at the time of "finishing."

Derivation: In this case a tension $t > 0$ remains both in the systems S^u and S^c because none of the tasks is psychologically finished. (D9) follows directly from (A2) in connection with (A1) and (A3a).

Experimental Proof: For interesting tasks the Zeigarnik quotient was

SUMMARY AND VERIFICATION OF SOME OF ZEIGARNIK'S CONSTRUCTS, ASSUMPTIONS, AND DERIVATIONS

Term	Constructs Operational Definition (C)	Conceptual Properties (C)	Basic Theorems Assumptions (A)	Derived Theorems (D)	Verification
Psychological tension (t)	Empirical syndrome indicating a "need"	Tendency of spreading to neighboring systems (C1)	Relation between intention and need (tension) (A1), (A1a), (A2)	Zeigarnik quotient = $\dfrac{RU}{RC} > 1$ (D1) from (A1), (A2), (A3a)	Predicted
				Decrease of Zeigarnik quotient with time elapsed since creation of need (D2) from (A1), (A3a), (C2)	Predicted
Psychological force (f)	Psychological locomotion	Vector (C3)	Relation between tension and force: $\|f_{P,G} = F\|t(S^G)\|$ (A3), (A3b)	Zeigarnik quotient smaller for tired subjects (D3) from (A1), (A3a), (A4), (C2)	Predicted
			Relation between tension and force on the level of thinking (tendency to recall): $\|f_{P,R} = F\|t(S^G)\|$ (A3a)	Zeigarnik quotient smaller for more peripheral systems (D4) from (A1), (A3a), (A5), (C2)	Predicted by J. F. Brown
Fluidity (fl)	Factor determining the velocity of equalization of tension with neighboring systems (C2)	Fluidity as a function of tiredness (A4)		Zeigarnik quotient=1, if the systems corresponding to finished and unfinished tasks are not separated (D6) from (C1), (C2), (A1), (A3a)	Explained
		Fluidity as a function of degree of irreality (inverse centrality) (A5)		Decrease of Zeigarnik quotient after emotional shake-up (D5) from (A1), (A3a), (A6)	Predicted
		Leveling of tensions in different systems by emotional waves (A6)		Zeigarnik quotient increases with intensity of need (D7) from (A1a), (A3b)	Explained; predicted by Marrow
				Zeigarnik quotient=1, if "unfinished" task is psychologically finished (D8) from (A1), (A3a)	Explained; predicted by Marrow
				Zeigarnik quotient=1, if "finished" task is psychologically unfinished (D9) from (A1), (A3a)	Explained
				Zeigarnik quotient decreased with added tendency created by instruction to recall in definite order (D10) from (A1), (A2), (A3a)	

found to be equal to 1. In the case of an interesting task, there is still a need to go back to this type of activity even if the special example has been solved.

DERIVATION IN REGARD TO ADDITIONAL FIELD FORCES

According to general field theory the actual behavior is related to the resulting force acting on the person at that time. It is therefore always important to know which other forces might influence behavior aside from those specifically established in the experiment. In Zeigarnik's experiments the forces in the direction of recall are due to two sources: the instruction to recall given by the experimenter sets up a quasi-need, and the corresponding tension $t(S^R)$ and force $if_{P,R}$. (The symbol if designates an "induced" force rather than a force corresponding to one's "own" need.) This is but a further application of (A1) and (A3) in regard to the activity of recalling. In addition, there is a force in the direction of spontaneous recall $f_{P,R}$ due to the tension $t(S^u)$ corresponding to the interrupted task according to (A3a).

The recall of a finished task is therefore due to the force $if_{P,R}$ whereas the recall of the unfinished task is due to $if_{P,R} + f_{P,R}$.

From this follows:

(D10) The more the recall loses its spontaneity and becomes the result of the experimenter's instruction, the more the Zeigarnik quotient approaches 1:

$$\frac{RU}{RC} \to 1$$

Derivation: One can assume that on the average

$$|if_{P,RU}| = |if_{P,RC}|$$

From (A1), (A3), and (A3a) it follows that

$$f_{P,RU} > 0; \; f_{P,RC} = 0$$

Although we do not know the general laws governing the addition of forces, it seems safe to deduce from these relations that

$$|if_{P,RU} + f_{P,RU}| > |if_{P,RC} + f_{P,RC}|$$

Hence we can write

$$\frac{RU}{RC} = F\left(\frac{if_{P,RU} + f_{P,RU}}{if_{P,RC} + f_{P,RC}}\right)$$

and this fraction converges towards 1, if the spontaneous forces remain constant and the induced forces are increased.

Experimental Proof: Zeigarnik found that the quotient of those subjects who experienced the experiment as a memory test and therefore had a relatively high $if_{P,R}$ was 1.5 (as against the average of the whole group of 1.9); whereas those subjects who performed the recall in a spontaneous mood of "telling about" had the very high quotient of 2.8.

V

Psychologists agree that the value of constructs and theories in an empirical science depends in the last analysis on their fruitfulness in "explaining" known facts and predicting unknown ones. Not infrequently it has been stated that theories which merely explain known facts are of no particular value. I cannot agree with this view. Particularly if the theory combines into one logical system known facts which previously had to be treated by separate theories; it would have a definite advantage as an organizational device. Besides, agreement with the known facts proves the adequacy of this theory at least to a certain degree. It is true, however, that it is a clearer test of the adequacy of the theory if one can make predictions from it and prove these predictions experimentally. The reason for this difference seems to be that empirical data generally allow for quite a range of different interpretations and classifications and that therefore it is usually easy to invent a variety of theories covering them.

The table (p. 18) indicates that most of the proofs used in the study of Zeigarnik have had the character of predicting unknown facts. These facts are generally not of a nature which one would have expected from everyday experience. As a matter of fact, at the time the experiments were carried out one would have had to predict the opposite results for the main experiment according to the laws of association and emotion accepted at that time. And these predictions are the more significant as they deal with a wide range of psychological data: they link problems of memory with problems of fatigue; with momentary emotional states; with attitudes such as ambition, which are generally considered to belong to the field of personality; with perceptual structurization (seeing the tasks separately or as one series); with problems of development and personality constancy. In what single experimental study do a few constructs and theorems allow for a greater manifold of experimentally testable predictions in different fields of psychology? Zeigarnik's study, to my mind, sufficiently demonstrated the fruitfulness of constructs and theories to warrant continued investigation. There have since been a great number of studies about satiation, level of aspiration, success and failure, substitution, habits, emotion, environmental structure and forces, social power fields, social pressure, feeblemindedness, development and regression—all of which have been based on this field theoretical approach. They have been carried out partly by my co-workers, but to a considerable extent by independent investigators. They have confirmed and elaborated these results and thus indirectly shown the value of the constructs used. Nearly all of this experimentation was quantitative in character in the sense that this is used in psychology today. Of course, difficulties have arisen, and more serious difficulties may still arise later. Until now, however, the contradictions have been minor ones and generally could be clarified quite simply. To hold that all these results could have been predicted without these constructs and theorems might be logically possible; actually, it was these constructs which first led to the predictions. Besides, to my knowledge, there is not yet any other theory formulated which actually would account for the totality of these results.

The attempt to develop a field theory on the basis of mathematically defined constructs and theorems is, however, very much at an early stage. Thus, in spite of what seems to be an astonishingly wide range of consistent applications, one will have to be ready for major changes. As Hull[9] most appropriately points out, it should be the virtue of an empirical theory not to refrain from making definite assumptions which might later turn out to be wrong. That no major change has had to be made until now I mainly attribute to one aspect of our methodological procedure, viz., the method of gradual approximation. We have tried to avoid developing elaborate "models"; instead, we have tried to represent the dynamic relations between the psychological facts by mathematical constructs at a sufficient level of generality. Only gradually, and hand in hand with experimental work, was the specification of the constructs attempted.

To my mind, such a method of gradual approximation, both in regard to the constructs used and the technical measurement in exper-

[9] C. Hull: The problem of intervening variables in molar behavior theory, *Psychol. Rev.*, 1943, *50*, 273–291.

iments, is by far the most cautious and "empirical." In this way a minimum of assumption is made.

The mathematician too easily forgets that the problem of mathematics in psychology is one of applied mathematics. It cannot be the task of the psychologist to develop new mathematical propositions, nor to look for particularly complicated mathematical laws. Instead, he will have to be interested in using as simple mathematical tools as possible. The mathematician will have to realize, in addition, that to apply a system of mathematical concepts in an empirical field one does not necessarily have to prove directly the adequacy of the basic mathematical axioms of this system one by one. It is as well to prove the fruitfulness of some of the derived propositions of this mathematical system for the representation of the empirical properties of the field in question. If the representation of spatial relations in physics by Euclidean geometry had not been permitted until its axioms (such as the divisibility *ad infinitum* of any part of the space) were proved one by one to hold also for the physical space, physics could never have used Euclidean geometry. All one can say is this: if one coordinates certain physical processes to certain geometrical entities one can make certain physical predictions. Such a fruitfulness of coordinating certain physical processes to entities of one rather than of another kind of geometry is all that one can mean by saying that a certain type of geometry holds or does not hold for the physical space. Exactly the same procedure is followed if certain psychological processes (such as social locomotion) are coordinated to certain entities of topological or hodological geometry (such as path). There can be no other meaning and no other proof of the applicability of these geometries to psychology than the fruitfulness of predictions based on such coordination.

The nonmathematician, on the other hand, has accused us of using highbrow mathematical or physical concepts. In several places it has been explained that using spatial geometrical concepts does not necessarily mean using physical concepts. In regard to logico-mathematical deduction there is no difference in principle between numerical and geometrical concepts. It seems necessary to emphasize two points which should warn us against a too early formalization and may be helpful in describing with greater precision the purpose of mathematization in an empirical science like psychology.

VI

In recent years it has been much emphasized, particularly by Hull and his students, that a psychological theory should be presented in the form of definitions, assumptions, and conclusions. This argumentation should be carried out step by step so that its logical stringency can be easily checked. We, too, have emphasized for quite a while that psychology will have to depend on strictly logical derivations and that a step in this direction is at present one of the most urgent tasks. Hull has attempted to fulfill this task, as far as I can see, mainly by retaining the traditional concepts of conditioned reflex and by elaborating them and presenting them in the order of definitions, assumptions, and conclusions.

One should recognize the value of a presentation of psychological argumentation in the form of such a strict scheme because it might help to discover shortcomings of a less formal reasoning. I feel, however, that we are not dealing here with the most essential aspect of the development of psychology towards a science which uses logical derivations based on well-defined constructs. The terms conditioned reflex, inhibition, excitatory tendency, frustrations, etc., as used in such derivations, are operationally more or less well defined. However, little attempt has been made to clarify the conceptual properties of those constructs. One does not ask whether any of these constructs has mathematically the properties of a vector, or a scalar, or a tensor, whether it is a region in a field, a pattern of regions, or a change occurring within a region. No attempt is made to approach what is called in physics the dimension of a construct. In short, the conceptual properties of the constructs, i.e., their logical interdependence as opposed to their empirical interdependence as discovered by experiments, are left entirely vague. An outstanding example is the construct *intelligence* which is very well defined operationally but so poorly defined conceptually that practically no logical derivation seems possible. In the long run, it seems hopeless to approach a satisfactory logical level in psychology and, at the same time, to leave conceptually vague the dynamic constructs which play an outstanding part within the framework of derivation.

The necessary conceptualization of psychology cannot be reached by merely repeating, in a more formalistic manner, the statements of an existing psychological school like that of conditioned reflex or of psychoanalysis. Logical form and content are closely interwoven in any empirical science. Formalization should include the development of constructs every one of which is considered from the start both as a carrier of formal implication and as an adequate representation of empirical data. This implies that the operational and the conceptual definitions are not arbitrarily related but show an internal coherence (e. g., the possibility of coordinating psychological force operationally to locomotion and conceptually to a vector is mainly based on their common feature of directedness). It further implies that the various constructs should be built up in such a way as to be parts of one logically consistent and empirically adequate system.

Without the development of such a type of dynamic constructs the mere formalization of the traditional constructs might hamper progress in psychology, in spite of a possible gain in precision. One psychologist believes that association is something real, libido or gestalt but a magic word; another is equally convinced that libido or instinct is something real. Which psychological constructs are accepted and which are repudiated depends mainly upon the system-language in which the individual psychologist has been taught to think. It is clear that the formalization of such a language into an elaborate system is apt to have a freezing effect. Even after conceptually well-defined concepts have been found, it may be well to postpone formalization until their empirical fruitfulness has been well established.

This is the reason why the original presentation of Zeigarnik's derivations and results was not given in a formalistic system. Similar caution is advisable in new psychological fields such as experimental social psychology. The further the conceptual development proceeds in psychology as a whole, the quicker will it be possible to apply formalistic representation even to new fields.

VII

What is accomplished in regard to representing psychological relations by means of topological and vector concepts, and what should be the next objectives? If I may express my own feeling about this question, which will be answered properly, of course, only by the future development of psychology, I would stress the following points:

1. The possibilities of a field theory in the realm of action,

emotion, and personality are firmly established. The basic statements of a field theory are that (a) behavior has to be derived from a totality of coexisting facts, (b) these coexisting facts have the character of a "dynamic field" in so far as the state of any part of this field depends on every other part of the field. The proposition (a) includes the statement that we have to deal in psychology, too, with a manifold, the interrelations of which cannot be represented without the concept of space.[10] In fact all psychological schools implicitly agree with this statement by using concepts like approach or withdrawal, social position, and so forth in their descriptions. It is more and more recognized, although there are still some exceptions, that the spatial relations of psychological data cannot be adequately represented by means of the physical space, but have to be treated, at least for the time being, as a psychological space. It is everywhere accepted that this "life space" includes the person and the psychological environment.

In regard to proposition (b) the situation is similar. Even theories originally based on a coordination of isolated stimuli to isolated reactions have developed in a direction which brings them at least very close to (b). A good example for this is the theory of Hull, which does not correlate a reaction to a single stimulus such as an optical one, but to a "pattern of stimuli" which includes goal and drive stimuli. In principle it is everywhere accepted that behavior *(B)* is a function of the person *(P)* and the environment *(E)*, $B = F\,(P,E)$, and that P and E in this formula are interdependent variables.

2. The first prerequisite for a scientific representation of the psychological field is the finding of a geometry adequate to represent the spatial relations of psychological facts. We know from the history of physics that an empirical space might be represented by different geometries: at first physics used Euclidean, more recently Riemannian geometry. It is to be expected that for psychology, too, more than one geometry might be found useful. Today, one will be satisfied to find at least one geometry which permits a mathematical interpretation of terms like "approach" and "withdrawal" without being psychologically meaningless. The hodological space[11] is sup-

---

[10] See Chapter VI.

[11] Kurt Lewin: The conceptual representation and the measurement of psychological forces, *Contr. Psychol. Theor.*, 1938, *1*, No. 4, Duke University Press.

posed to be such a geometry. The hodological space is a finitely structured space, that is, its parts are not infinitely divisible but are composed of certain units or regions. Direction and distance are defined by "distinguished paths," which can easily be coordinated to psychological locomotion. Such a geometry permits an adequate representation of the step-by-step character of most psychological processes. It permits furthermore an adequate answer to the puzzling necessity to ascribe different psychological directions to locomotions in the same physical direction if the goal of those locomotions is different. This is particularly important for the problem of the roundabout route. The hodological space permits the description of the structural relations within the person as well as in his psychological environment. For instance, the degree of differentiation of the person and the peripheral and central layers can thus be defined. Hodological space is no less useful for describing the structure of groups and their changes. Its greatest value, however, becomes apparent when we deal with problems of dynamics.

3. During the latter part of the last century the development of dynamic concepts in scientific psychology was governed by the fear of slipping into the "metaphysics of teleology." The idea that not the future but the past has to be considered as the "cause" of behavior was one of the major motives in developing associationism. At that time anything connected with the concept of direction was considered to be a teleological approach. The concept of goal was suspect and had to be replaced by something which did not imply the concept of direction. Other aspects of teleology looked upon with no less suspicion were: "foresight," which permits the avoiding of obstacles, and "consciousness," which takes into account the total setting. Associationism tried hard to avoid these allegedly unscientific elements. It tried to develop a concept of association devoid of the logical element of direction. Association should be "blind" and based entirely on the past (that meant that the theory of association had to be based on the concept of repetition).

Of course the facts of goals, needs, and will were too important simply to be neglected. With psychology under the spell of the dichotomy "teleology" or "causation by the past," nothing else seemed to be left for those psychologists who were impressed by the importance of goal-seeking and directedness than to resort to a definite teleological theory. McDougall is a classic representative of this approach. The associationists, too, could not entirely neglect goal-directed and meaningful behavior. They tried to take goals, intentions, and will into their system, and it is interesting to see how by doing this the character of the associationistic theory was changed. Thorndike's law of effect and Ach's concept of *determinierende Tendenz* ascribe to those types of repetition which are connected with certain aspects of a goal (reaching the goal, or setting up an intention) the creation of particularly strong associations. Hull recognized the importance of goals and needs by including goal- and need-stimuli as important elements into those "stimulus patterns," which are assumed as the cause of a reaction. More and more, the theory of associationism (conditioned reflex) has been influenced by the attempt to derive directed activities without assuming directed dynamic factors.

According to field theory, behavior depends neither on the past nor on the future but on the present field. (This present field has a certain time-depth. It includes the "psychological past," "psychological present," and "psychological future" which constitute one of the dimensions of the life space existing at a given time.) This is in contrast both to the belief of teleology that the future is the cause of behavior, and that of associationism that the past is the cause of behavior. Furthermore, it is an error to consider the assumption of directed factors as characteristic of teleology. The causal explanations in physics certainly do not avoid such assumptions: physical force is a directed entity, a vector. Psychology, too, becomes in no way metaphysical by resorting to constructs of vectorial character such as psychological forces. This permits a direct attack on the problems of directed action. In addition, by defining direction in terms of hodological space, an adequate representation is possible of what has been meaningful in some of the other claims of teleology. The puzzling relation between knowledge and dynamics which had a mystical character in teleology is made understandable at least in one fundamental point: it becomes clear why lack of knowledge has the effect of a barrier. The mysterious ability of animals to make roundabout routes can be rationally related to the fact that equilibria in the hodological space depend upon the totality of relations in the field.

4. A variety of psychological processes, I feel, can be treated with relative adequacy with the conceptual tools at hand.[12] These include the basic *characteristics of needs* and the various ways of their gratification, including substitution. The *substitute value* of one activity for another can be measured, and the general conditions for substitute value can be derived. Substitution involves the basic problems of *setting up new goals* and of the *level of aspiration.* In this field an important step forward has been made by the derivation of the somewhat paradoxical tendency to prefer difficult goals to easy ones (a tendency which seems to contradict the "law of parsimony"). We have already mentioned that many problems related to the process of *striving for a given goal* can be attacked, particularly the relation between the *cognitive structure* (learning, insight, roundabout route) and the direction and the strength of the psychological forces. The same holds for many problems connected with *conflict situations.* The treatment of problems of *atmospheres* might be specifically mentioned. It is possible to derive the effect of pressure of different degrees upon the degree of the momentary *personality differentiation.* The predictions concerning the effect of *frustration* upon *productivity* and *regression* have been borne out by experiment. The degree of *rigidity* or dynamic communication between the subparts of the person (one of the basic factors in personality besides its degree of differentiation) has been measured. Finally, one result which seems to me of great consequence: the size of those regions which, at a given time, have the character of undifferentiated *units in the life space* has become measurable, at least in certain cases.[13] A number of predictions about the effect of the size of these units on animal behavior have been verified.[14]

As to the next tasks, it is hoped that the quantitative measurement of psychological forces will be accomplished soon. This will provide the answer for the laws of the composition of forces (resultant forces) and aid in the measurement of tension. One of the fields which most urgently requires improvements is that of social psy-

[12] For a more detailed description of the research mentioned here, see Chapter X.

[13] Dorwin Cartwright: Relation of decision-time to the categories of response, *Am. J. Psychol.,* 1941, *54,* 174-196.

[14] Claude Buxton: Latent learning and the goal gradient hypothesis, *Contr. Psychol. Theor.,* 1940, *2,* No. 2. Duke University Press.

chology. To my mind, it is possible today to define *groups* and group goals operationally and with the type of constructs referred to. With their help predictions have been made, and experimentally confirmed, about the effect of certain *social atmospheres* on group life. However, a number of basic constructs in social psychology, including that of inducing fields (*power fields*), need refinement.

The progress thus far made in the conceptual development of psychology warrants much optimism. The idea that such phenomena as hope or friendship could ever be represented by geometrical or other mathematical concepts would have seemed beyond any realistic expectation a few years ago. Today such representation is possible and of great help in dealing with these phenomena. I have no doubt that the concepts of topology and hodological space, or concepts of a similar nature, will prove fruitful for representation and prediction in every field of psychology. On the other hand, one of the most important factors for steady progress in any science is good judgment in deciding which problems are ready for attack and which are better delayed until a more mature state of that science has been reached.

II

Constructs in Field Theory
(1944)

⎣⎤⎣⎤⎣⎤⎣⎤⎣⎤⎣⎤⎣⎤⎣⎤⎣⎤⎣⎤⎣⎤⎣⎤⎣⎤⎣⎤⎣⎤⎣⎤⎣⎤⎣⎤⎣⎤

QUALITY AND QUANTITY IN PSYCHOLOGY

EVER since the time of Weber and Fechner there has been a trend in psychology toward quantification and mathematization. This trend has become increasingly stronger. There has been much controversy, however, as to how mathematization can be achieved. In the beginning there was much opposition in "principle" that psychology is a qualitative science and that quantification was to be limited to the narrow field of psychology of perception. Today it is accepted that many of the previously excluded areas such as the psychology of motivation have to be treated mathematically, too.

E. Cassirer[1] has given a detailed historical description of controversies between qualitative and quantitative approaches in the ·development of physics and chemistry. Some of the present-day theoretical problems in psychology show great methodological similarities to these controversies although they are historically separated by centuries. According to Cassirer, the basic idea which has led to the solution of these controversies in mathematics itself and in the mathematical treatment of physical data has been: quantitative and qualitative approaches are not opposites but necessary complements of each other.

Cassirer points out again and again that mathematization is not identical with quantification. Mathematics handles quantity *and*

[1] E. Cassirer: *Substanzbegriff und Functionbegriff, Untersuchungen über die Grundfragen der Erkenntniskritik* (Berlin: B. Cassirer, 1910).

30

quality. This is particularly apparent in those branches of geometry which make nonquantitative but still mathematically "exact" statements in regard to position and other geometrical relations.

Psychology, too, might gain much if it were more aware of the fact that mathematics is able to handle quantitative and qualitative problems. That correct qualitative analysis is a prerequisite for adequate quantitative treatment is well recognized in psychological statistics. What seems less clear is that the qualitative differences themselves can and should be approached mathematically.

Psychologists who think in field-theoretical terms and those who think in stimulus-response terms agree that psychological explanations have to use "constructs" and that psychological theory has to be mathematical in nature. There are still differences, it seems, in regard to what mathematization means and how to ·proceed in developing theories.

We may use the conceptual development of the problem of frustration as an example.

EVERYDAY CONCEPTS AND SCIENTIFIC CONSTRUCTS

The concept of frustration has been brought to the fore by Freud. He links frustration with basic problems of sex, culture, sublimation, dreams, and the whole area of psychopathology. These concepts were not designed to serve as a basis for strict experimentation or for quantitative procedures. They were taken from everyday language. Still their placement in the psychoanalytical system has somewhat sharpened and specified their meaning.

Up to 1920 academic psychology, breathing the "pure scientific air" of sensory perception and memory, did not deem it appropriate for a scientist to consider these "darker and mystical aspects of life." Whenever these questions arose, they were handled gingerly. To speak about frustration, substitution, aggression, or love in experimental psychology appeared at that time as symptomatic of a discussion outside the realm of science, as to some psychologists today the very term "group atmosphere" seems to be symptomatic of a nonscientific approach.

From the beginning, the field-theoretical discussion of frustration was highly analytical. A variety of situations was distinguished, such as: frustration in a setting of reward as compared with frustration under threat of punishment; frustration of desire to move toward as against moving away from an area of activities; frustration where only a circumscribed area is inaccessible as against a prisonlike setting where a barrier surrounds the person on all sides.

These distinctions can be said to be qualitative in nature. However, they can be represented through topological and vector concepts in a way which (a) makes each situation open for quantitative treatment, (b) does not handle these qualitatively different situations as entirely separate entities but conceives of them as a result of certain quantitative variations or of variations in the distribution of forces.

This seemingly paradoxical feat can be achieved by a "method of construction," which has been first developed in mathematics itself. To consider qualitatively different geometrical entities (such as circle, square, parabola) as the product of a certain combination of certain "elements of construction" (such as points and movements) has since the time of the Greeks been the secret of this method. It is sometimes called the method of "genetic definition." It is able, at the same time, to link and to separate; it does not minimize qualitative differences and still lays open their relation to general quantitative variables. Cassirer has shown how the same method proved to be fruitful in empirical sciences where the "elements of construction" are mathematically described empirical entities (such as forces, ions, atoms).

The field-theoretical analysis of frustration achieves a similar qualitative *and* quantitative characterization, a conceptual separation *and* linkage through such constructs as "psychological force," "psychological region," "power field." With the help of these conceptual means certain derivations were made, such as: under what conditions frustration would lead to a roundabout route and when to a leaving of the field, under what conditions social aggression would result, and what the form of restless movements would be. These predictions are partly made in regard to different types of setting and partly linked to quantitative conditions (such as the relative strength of forces) within one setting.

These predictions were the basis for planning and analyzing a number of experiments.[2] In a setting of frustration, relatively strong

[2] For a more detailed discussion of these experiments, see Chapter X.

emotions and aggression were produced; persistence, at various age levels and under conditions of repeated frustration, was studied; the substitute value of various types of play and nonplay behavior was measured in settings of goal frustration; the effect of different intensities of frustration on constructiveness in play was studied and the degree of regression measured with single children and with pairs of friends; factors which determine the effect of frustration in a prison were investigated; experiments on group atmosphere and studies of organized and unorganized groups deal with the effect of social frustration in a group setting, particularly with the effect on aggression, cooperation, and passivity.

These investigations of the causes and effects of frustration include quite a variety of divergent topics, such as: hope and time perspective, type of activity and group organization, security and shyness, productivity, emotional tension, friendship and fight, cooperation and aggression, development and regression, reward and punishment, tools and obstacles, leadership, degree of acceptance of other persons' goals. Yet this variety of phenomena is approached with relatively few basic concepts (such as force field, power field, tension, simple and organizational dependence). These few concepts, used as "elements of construction," permit the analytical treatment and "genetic definition" of a vast realm of qualitative phenomena and quantitative problems in a concrete fashion. That this can be done shows, so it seems to me, the power of the method and the fruitfulness of the concepts.

SR(stimulus–response) theories, too, follow something like a method of conceptual construction. More recently this approach has widened its area of application from the problems of rote learning to such general problems as frustration.[3] One might ask: What is similar and what is different between the field-theoretical approach and the SR approach in this area of problems?

WHAT "IS" FRUSTRATION

One of the standard criticisms made by SR theory has been that field theory is not sticking to a physical definition of the conditions.

[3] J. Dollard, *et al.*: *Frustration and Aggression* (New Haven: Yale University Press, 1939).

The term "expectation," for instance, has been taboo, as much as terms like "degree of acceptance," or "feeling of belonging." Even today some veterans of SR theory seem to hold to the idea that scientific psychology means definition in terms of physics.[4] The study of frustration and aggression, on the other hand, seemed to be a clear departure from this position. Most of the terms, like frustration or cooperation, are defined in psychological terms. In other words, the trend away from physicalistic definitions toward psychological definitions (which was apparent ever since the concept of "goal" was accepted as legitimate) seems to prevail and to lead to a happy union with the aspects expressed in field theory.

There seems to be no difference in regard to the tendency toward a quantitative approach to frustration. There is, of course, no difference in regard to problems of reliability or similar methodological questions of a technical nature. There is no difference of opinion in regard to the necessity of an operational definition of psychological concepts nor a difference of opinion in regard to the desirability of strict theories and derivations.

An important difference seems to lie in the following direction: In SR theory "frustration" is treated as a "concept," as an "element of construction." The attempt is made to define this concept operationally and to proceed from there to a quantitative theory, for instance, about the relation between frustration and aggression. When the psychologist who follows field-theoretical lines speaks about frustration, learning, hope, friendship, aggression he is conscious of the fact that he is using "popular terms." These terms are quite helpful, even necessary, in the beginning. However, they are not considered, within field theory, as psychological concepts in the sense of scientific "elements of construction." The reason for this is that a term like "frustration" (a) lacks a conceptual definition through coordination to mathematical concepts, (b) refers in a vague way to a multitude of different settings rather than to *one* conceptually definable type of situation.[5]

---

[4] C. Hull: The problem of intervening variables in molar behavior theory, *Psychol. Rev.*, 1943, 50, 273–291.

[5] Some studies use the term "frustration" as a name for the incident which interrupts a goal-directed activity. In this case the term "frustration" does not refer to a structure of a "situation" but to an "event," that is, something which has the same conceptual dimension (see later) as "behavior." The conclusion that several

If this is correct, it would be scientifically meaningless to attempt, for instance, to link the intensity of frustration lawfully with any specific effect (such as aggression); for one would have to know the type of frustration and the detailed setting in order to make any definite derivations. Indeed, the experiments show that it is as correct to say "frustration leads to increased friendship and nonaggression"[6] as it is to say "frustration leads to aggression." It is correct to say that frustration leads to increased as well as to decreased productivity, that it leads to new efforts as well as to passivity.[7]

It is interesting to note that the more recent publications of the Yale group increasingly recognize the necessity of differentiating between the various setups, and that they, too, are becoming more analytical. However, the attempt to keep "frustration" as one definable psychological entity and to link it lawfully with certain effects, such as aggression, seems not yet to have been given up. Cases of nonaggression are treated as the result of "additional factors" which bring about, in the particular case, phenomena which are only apparently different from what is expected by the general law.

The field-theoretical approach in this point is more radical. Its higher demands on concepts can be formulated in the following way: Psychology should be as much concerned with the question of what frustration "is" psychologically, as with the effect of frustration. In fact, field theory considers it impossible to investigate the laws of frustration, hope, friendship, or autocracy without investigating at the same time what frustration, hope, friendship, or autocracy "is" psychologically.

I am well aware that questions about the "nature" of objects or events have been much abused and have been asked in a scientifically meaningless, metaphysical way. When psychology departed from its early "philosophical" speculations it banned, very understandably

---

types of frustration should be distinguished and defined analytically before definite laws can be formulated would hold in this case, also. As a rule, it is impossible to link such phenotypically defined events consistently to the same concept, independent of the situation in which the event occurs. This is one of the basic methodological axioms and a main reason for the development of "constructs" in a science.

[6] M. E. Wright: Constructiveness of play as affected by group organization and frustration, *Charact. and Pers.*, 1942, *11*, 40–49.

[7] R. Barker, T. Dembo, K. Lewin: Frustration and regression, *Univ. Iowa Stud. Child Welf.*, 1941, *18*, No. 1.

and correctly, questions about what a psychological phenomenon like intelligence is. The only answer permitted was an "operational definition," as, for instance, "Intelligence is what is measured by intelligence tests."

Unfortunately, in this way the child has been thrown out with the bath. There is one meaning behind the question about the "nature" of things which is as essential for psychology as it is for science in general. If a chemist finds a certain material he may be able to define it operationally by pointing out where it can be found and by specifying its color and weight. In studying this material, the first question of the chemist will be: "What is this material chemically?" He might find that it is an element or a compound, or he might find that the chemical constitution of this material varied from piece to piece (as much as the psychological nature of frustration varied from occasion to occasion). In this case, the material, in spite of its being well-defined operationally, does not represent "*one* type" from the point of view of the chemist. The criterion for this oneness is the possibility of representing it by *one* chemical formula, through one combination of "elements of conceptual construction" (such as ions, atoms). What an object is is now determined by the possibility of characterizing it by one combination of conceptual constructs.

The history of chemistry and physics shows a slow change from such popular distinctions as "fire, water, and earth"—which are related to easily observable "obvious" but "superficial" properties—to classifications based on the method of conceptual construction. This method frequently overrules the testimony of the "common appearance"; it calls different what appears to be one, and calls one what appears different. The chemist follows this method because he is interested in the chemical behavior of the material rather than its appearance. He therefore will not attempt to look for common laws or common effects if he knows that—from the point of view of conceptual construction—the material at hand is an arbitrary conglomeration of types.

Doubtlessly "empirical laws of the descriptive type" can be established (on the basis of operational definitions alone) in the psychology of "learning" and "frustration" as well as in the physics of "water, fire, and earth."

Many valuable data can be and have been gathered with the scientific tools available on this level. Wherever psychology reaches out into a new area, groundwork has to be laid with these tools. Conceptual refinement should not be regarded as the only aspect of progress in psychology. It is, however, of greatest importance that psychology, too, can in its own way proceed from the "water and fire" level to a more advanced level of concepts. For no part of psychology or its applications can progress beyond very definite limitations if it cannot reach the level where the "psychological nature" of an event is characterized by the conceptual construction which represents it.

Conceptual Dimensions of Psychological Constructs

One of the symptoms of scientific constructs above the water and fire level is the possibility of defining their "conceptual type" or ultimately their "conceptual dimension." To give a simple example from physics: "Speed" and "acceleration" do not have the same conceptual dimension because speed is distance over time (d/t), whereas acceleration is distance over the square of time (d/t^2). On the other hand, everything which can be expressed as speed has the *same* conceptual dimension. Similarly, every physical phenomenon which can be expressed as a physical force (that is, mathematically as a vector) has the same conceptual dimension. Force, however, has not the same dimension as energy.

To know what the conceptual dimension of a construct is is of great methodological importance. (1) Only those entities which have the same conceptual dimension can be compared as to their magnitude. (2) Everything which has the same conceptual dimension can be compared quantitatively; its magnitude can be measured, in principle, with the same yardstick (units of measurement).

It seems to be necessary and possible to apply the idea of conceptual dimension also to the constructs in psychology. This can be done by relating each construct to a few basic psychological elements of conceptual construction.

Obviously, the state of development of psychology is not such that a *systematic linking of every construct with any other* by a system of quantitative equations can be realized. On the other hand, I am inclined to think that psychology is not far away from a level where a good number of the basic constructs can be linked in a precise manner. (Both SR and field theory have actually established such explicit relations for some of the constructs.) But we have not yet become accustomed to think in terms of conceptual dimensions or—to use a more general and for the present state more appropriate term—"conceptual types."

It would be a mistake to delay using this approach until psychology has reached a stage where each construct designates phenomena which can be measured quantitatively. For to reach a point where all psychological laws can be expressed in *quantitative equations,* we have to recognize that such equations presuppose that both sides of them have psychologically the same conceptual dimension. Working toward such objectives will be much facilitated if we become aware of the importance of these aspects and, at least, learn carefully to distinguish different conceptual types.

Whenever the problem of psychological *measurement* arises we should ask: What is the conceptual type of the phenomenon we want to measure, and how is the measuring procedure related to this particular type? A concern with this aspect of measurement should do much to clarify the frequently obscure relations between the conceptual definition of a psychological construct and its operational definition (symptoms, measurements); it should facilitate the development of methods to measure not yet measured constructs.

There are indications that certain types of questions can be answered only by certain types of constructs. For instance, it seems that a "prediction of the behavior of an individual in a specific situation" has to be based on a "force field" or a conceptually equivalent construct. If it is correct that no other conceptual type (such as power field, position, tension, force) suffices for such a prediction, important positive and negative methodological implications are obvious.

On the whole, then, we may say that the problem of conceptual types is closely related to the problems of psychological measurement and of mathematical equations expressing psychological laws, and to the task of interrelating systematically all psychological constructs. This relation makes the issue timely; it indicates, too, that we have to deal here with one of the basic permanent questions of scientific psychology.

We shall not attempt here to develop the idea of conceptual dimensions in detail. This task demands much thought and careful elaboration. However, we should like to give as illustrations a few examples of dynamic and nondynamic constructs of different and of equal "conceptual type."

1. One of the basic psychological concepts is that of psychological *position*. Position is a "spacial relation of regions"; for instance, the position of a region A can be characterized by its lying in B. Examples of psychological concepts which have the conceptual dimension of position are: group belongingness of an individual, his occupational position, involvement in an activity.

2. *Locomotion* has a different dimension from position. It refers to a "relation of positions at different times." Any psychological phenomenon that can be represented as a locomotion—and that holds for most "behavior"—would have the same conceptual dimension.

3. *Cognitive structure* might be regarded as having the same dimension as position because it refers to the relative position of different parts of a field. Structure does not refer, however, to the position of one point but to the position of a multitude of points or regions.

4. *Force* or "tendency to locomotion" has conceptually a different character from actual locomotion, although locomotion is one of the symptoms (operational definition) for a constellation of forces where the resultant force is greater than zero. It has sometimes been stated that the term force is equivalent to "strength of drive" in the SR theory. This would be correct if by strength of drive a psychological entity is meant which mathematically has the character of a vector. Such a "strength of drive" would have to be distinguished from the strength of "need" if need refers to tension (tension has a different dimension from force). SR theory will have to specify whether strength of drive should be understood to be a vector before the question can be decided.

5. *Goal*. This concept does not have the dimension of a force, in spite of the fact that there is a close relation between goals and forces. A goal has the conceptual dimension of a *"force field"*—that is, of a distribution of forces in space. Goal (or in field-theoretical terminology, a positive valence) is a force field of a special structure,

namely, a force field where all forces point toward the same region. To conceive of a goal in this way gives it a definite place within the totality of possible patterns of force fields. The counterpart of a distribution of forces toward one region is the distribution away from one region. This is equivalent to the concept of "aversion." Other types of force fields are equivalent to what is called a "difficulty" or "barrier." The transformation of such everyday concepts as goals, difficulties, aversions into force fields of different types makes it possible to link these qualitatively very different entities in a way which lays open their functional similarity and differences.

6. *Conflict* refers not to one force field but to the *overlapping of at least two force fields.* "Frustration" has the same dimension as conflict. A systematic survey of the possible types of frustration or conflict should, therefore, inquire how force fields can overlap in such a way that equally strong but opposite forces result at some points of the field. Such analysis permits a systematic treatment of the conditions and the effects of conflicts. The concept *equilibrium* has the same dimension as conflict; it refers to certain constellations of overlapping force fields.

7. *Fear* may seem to have the same dimension as aversion. However, in most cases fear is related to the psychological future. It has to deal with some aspect of "time perspective." In this respect it is similar to concepts like hope, plan, expectation. *Expectation* refers to the psychological structure and the distribution of forces on the reality level of the psychological future. *Hope* refers to a relation between the structure of the reality level and of the wish level of the psychological future. *Guilt* refers to the relation between the structure of the reality and the wish level of the psychological past.

8. *Power* does not have the same dimension as psychological force. That the power of *A* is greater than the power of *B* does not imply that *A* actually exerts pressure on *B*. The concept of power refers to a "possibility of inducing forces" of a certain magnitude on another person. The concept of *power field*, therefore, does not have the same conceptual dimension as that of a force field. In using concepts like attack, defense, aggression, friendship, one has to be aware of the different dimensions of the concepts: power field, force field, force and behavior.

9. *Values.* Like the term *ideology*, the term value is a rather unclear

concept in psychology. Values influence behavior but do not have the character of a goal (that is, of a force field). For example, the individual does not try to "reach" the value of fairness but fairness is "guiding" his behavior. It is probably correct to say that values determine which types of activity have a positive and which have a negative valence for an individual in a given situation. In other words, values are not force fields but they "induce" force fields. That means values are constructs which have the same psychological dimension as *power fields*. It is interesting to consider from this point of view the psychoanalytical theory that values are "internalized" parents. Independent of whether this statement in regard to the genesis of values is or is not correct we can at least say that values and persons are equivalent in so far as both can be represented by power fields.

SUMMARY

It is not necessary to discuss here the relations between the different conceptual types, that is, the problem of conceptual "dimension" in the narrower sense of the term, although that seems to be possible for some of the concepts. The examples may suffice to illustrate at least some of the points which make the problem of conceptual types or dimensions of constructs very important for psychology today. In my experience, we have here one of the most helpful methodological tools for approaching new areas of problems in psychology. A major difficulty in setting up worthwhile experiments in a new field is the inability to formulate intelligently and adequately experimental and theoretical questions. An investigation into the conceptual types is one of the most helpful first steps toward the formulation of such questions.

To state, for instance, that the conceptual types of a value are those of a power field means raising the problem of a systematic survey of all kinds of power fields. It relates values in a precise manner to the rest of the psychological constructs (such as "forces" or "behavior"). It indicates, at least in a general way, along what lines a measurement of the effects of values should proceed. It opens up a wealth of experimental problems. For instance, if a value is equivalent to a power field any change of values would have to be conceived of as a process which depends on the totality of power fields, including social, political, and personal power fields, existing in that situation. On this basis a systematic experimental attack on the relation between ideological changes and power relations within a group might well be outlined.

Finally, the idea of conceptual types or dimensions gives scientific meaning to the question of what a psychological phenomenon "is." It helps determine whether a psychological term designates a conglomeration of phenomena which can be conceived of as a unit only on the "fire and water level" of concepts or whether it is worth being retained in a psychology built with constructs that have clearly defined conceptual dimensions.

III

Defining the "Field at a Given Time"
(1943)

⊔⊓⊔⊔⊓⊔⊓⊔

FIELD THEORY AND THE PHASE SPACE

THE history of acceptance of new theories frequently shows the following steps: At first the new idea is treated as pure nonsense, not worth looking at. Then comes a time when a multitude of contradictory objections are raised, such as: the new theory is too fancy, or merely a new terminology; it is not fruitful, or simply wrong. Finally a state is reached when everyone seems to claim that he had always followed this theory. This usually marks the last state before general acceptance.

The increasing trend toward field theory in psychology is apparent in recent variations of psychoanalysis (Kardiner, Horney) and also within the theory of the conditioned reflex. This trend makes the clarification of the meaning of field theory only the more important because those psychologists who, like myself, have been in favor of field theory for many years have not been very successful in making the essence of this theory clear. The only excuse I know of is that this matter is not very simple. Physics and philosophy do not seem to have done much analytical work about the meaning of field theory that could be helpful to the psychologist. In addition, methods like field theory can really be understood and mastered only in the same way as methods in a handcraft, namely, by learning them through practice.

Hilgard and Marquis[1] quote from a letter of Clark Hull the

[1] E. R. Hilgard and D. G. Marquis: *Conditioning and Learning* (New York: D. Appleton-Century, Co., 1940).

following sentence: "As I see it, the moment one expresses in any very general manner the various potentialities of behavior as dependent upon the simultaneous status of one or more variables, he has the substance of what is currently called field theory."

It is correct that field theory emphasizes the importance of the fact that any event is a resultant of a multitude of factors. The recognition of the necessity of a fair representation of this multitude of interdependent factors is a step in the direction toward field theory. However, this does not suffice. Field theory is something more specific.

To use an illustration: Success in a certain sport may depend upon a combination of muscular strength, velocity of movement, ability to make quick decisions, and precise perception of direction and distance. A change in any one of these five variables might alter the result to a certain degree. One can represent these variables as five dimensions of a diagram. The resultant of any possible constellation of these factors for the amount of success can be marked as a point in the diagram. The totality of these points then is a diagrammatic representation of this dependence, in other words, of an empirical law.

Physics frequently makes use of such representation of a multitude of factors influencing an event. To each of certain properties, such as temperature, pressure, time, spacial position, one dimension is coordinated. Such a representation in physics is called "phase space." Such a phase space may have twenty dimensions if twenty factors have to be considered. A phase space is something definitely different from that three-dimensional "physical space" within which physical objects are moving. In the same way the psychological space, the life space or psychological field, in which psychological locomotion or structural changes take place, is something different from those diagrams where dimensions mean merely gradations of properties.

In discussing these questions with a leading theoretical physicist, we agreed that the recognition of a multitude of factors as determining an event, and even their representation as a phase space, does not presuppose field theory. In psychology, Thurstone's factor analysis deals with such relations of various factors. Any character profile recognizes the multitude of factors. Field theorists and non-field theorists can both avail themselves of these useful devices, but not everybody who uses them is therefore a field theorist.

What is field theory? Is it a kind of very general theory? If one proceeds in physics from a special law or theory (such as the law of the free-falling body) to more general theories (such as the Newtonian laws) or still more general theories (such as the equations of Maxwell), one does *not* finally come to field theory. In other words, field theory can hardly be called a theory in the usual sense.

This fact becomes still more apparent when we consider the relation between the correctness or incorrectness of a theory and its character as a field theory. A special theory in physics or psychology may be a field theory, but nevertheless wrong. On the other hand, a description of what Hans Feigl calls an "empirical theory on the lowest level" may be correct without being field theory (although I do not believe that a theory on the higher levels of constructs can be correct in psychology without being field theory).

Field theory, therefore, can hardly be called correct or incorrect in the same way as a theory in the usual sense of the term. *Field theory is probably best characterized as a method:* namely, a method *of analyzing causal relations and of building scientific constructs.* This method of analyzing causal relations can be expressed in the form of certain general statements about the "nature" of the conditions of change. To what degree such a statement has an "analytical" (logical, *a priori*) and to what degree it has an "empirical" character do not need to be discussed here.

THE PRINCIPLE OF CONTEMPORANEITY AND THE EFFECT OF PAST AND FUTURE

One of the basic statements of psychological field theory can be formulated as follows: Any behavior or any other change in a psychological field depends only upon the psychological field *at that time*.

This principle has been stressed by the field theorists from the beginning. It has been frequently misunderstood and interpreted to mean that field theorists are not interested in historical problems or in the effect of previous experiences. Nothing can be more mistaken. In fact, field theorists are most interested in developmental and historical problems and have certainly done their share to enlarge the temporal scope of the psychological experiment from that of the classic reaction-time experiment, which lasts only a few seconds, to experimental situations, which contain a systematically created history through hours or weeks.

If a clarification of the field-theoretical principle of contemporaneity could be achieved, it would, I feel, be most helpful for an understanding among the various schools in psychology.

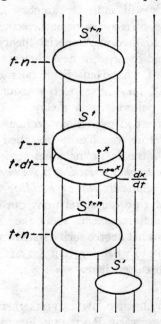

FIGURE 1. *S* during $t-n$ until $t+n$ is a "closed system"; but *S* is not genidentic with *S'*. $\frac{dx}{dt}$ indicates the velocity of *x*.

The meaning of this far-reaching principle can be expressed rather easily by referring to its application in classical physics.

A change at the point x in the physical world is customarily characterized as $\frac{dx}{dt}$; that is to say, as a differential change in the position of x during a differential time-period dt. Field theory states that the change $\dfrac{dx}{dt}$ at the time t depends only on the situation S^t at that time t (Figure 1).

$$(1) \qquad\qquad \frac{dx}{dt} = F(S^t)$$

It does not depend, in addition, on past or future situations. In other words, the formula (1) is correct, but not the formula (1a):

$$(1a) \qquad dx = F(S^t) + F^1(S^{t-1}) + \cdots + F^2(S^{t+1}) + \cdots$$

Of course, there are cases in physics where one can state the relation between a change and a past situation S^{t-n} (where $t - n$ is a time not immediately preceding t; $|t - n| > dt$). In other words, there are occasions where it is technically possible to write:

$$(2) \qquad\qquad \frac{dx}{dt} = F(S^{t-n})$$

However, this is possible only if it is known how the later situation S^t depends on the previous situation S^{t-n}; in other words, if the function F in the equation

$$(3) \qquad\qquad S^t = F(S^{t-n})$$

is known. Such knowledge presupposes usually (a) that both situations are "closed systems" which are genidentic[2]; (b) that the laws are known which deal with the change of all points of the previous situation S^{t-n} and also the laws dealing with the changes in the situations between the previous situation S^{t-n} and the latter situation S.

The meaning of linking a change to a past situation by formula (2) might be clarified best by pointing out that it is possible in a similar way to link a present change to a future situation S^{t+n} and to write:

$$(2a) \qquad\qquad \frac{dx}{dt} = F(S^{t+n})$$

This is possible whenever we have to deal with a "closed system" during the time-period t until $t + n$, and if the laws of the on-going changes during this period are known.

The possibility of writing this functional equation does not mean that the future situation S^{t+1} is conceived of as a "condition" of the

[2] K. Lewin: *Der Begriff der Genese in Physik, Biologie und Entwicklungsgeschichte* (Berlin: Springer, 1922).

present change $\frac{dx}{dt}$. In fact, the same $\frac{dx}{dt}$ would occur if the closed system were destroyed before the time $(t + n)$. In other words, the change $\frac{dx}{dt}$ depends on the situation (S^t) at that time only (in line with formula $\{1\}$). The technical possibility of expressing this change mathematically as a function of a future or a past time does not change this fact.[3]

The equivalent to $\frac{dx}{dt}$ in physics is the concept "behavior" in psychology, if we understand the term behavior to cover any change in the psychological field. The field-theoretical principle of contemporaneity in psychology then means that the behavior b at the time t is a function of the situation S at the time t only (S is meant to include both the person and his psychological environment),

$$(4) \qquad b^t = F(S^t)$$

and not, in addition, a function of past or future situations S^{t-n} or S^{t+n} (Figure 2). Again, it is possible to relate the behavior b indirectly to either a past situation (S^{t-n}) or a future situation (S^{t+n}); but again, this can be done only if these situations are closed systems, and if the changes in the intermediate periods can be accounted for by known laws. It seems that psychologists are increasingly aware of the importance of this formula.

HOW TO DETERMINE THE PROPERTIES OF A FIELD AT A GIVEN TIME

If one has to derive behavior from the situation at that time, a way has to be found to *determine* the character of the "situation at a given time." This determination implies a number of questions which are, I think, interesting both psychologically and philosophically.

To determine the properties of a present situation or—to use medical terminology—to make a diagnosis, one can follow two dif-

---

[3] Frequently an occurrence is said to be caused by the "preceding conditions." This term seems to have been misunderstood by psychologists to refer to a distant past situation (S^{t-n}), although it should refer to the present situation, or at least to the immediately preceding situation" (S^{t-dt}). We will come back to this question.

ferent procedures: One may base one's statement on conclusions from history (*anamnesis*), or one may use diagnostic *tests of the present*.

To use a simple example: I wish to know whether the floor of the attic is sufficiently strong to carry a certain weight. I might try to gain this knowledge by finding out what material was used when the house was built ten years ago. As I get reliable reports that good material has been used, and that the architect was a dependable man, I might conclude that the load probably would be safe. If I can find the original blueprints, I might be able to do some exact figuring and feel still more safe.

Of course, there is always a chance that the workmen have actually not followed the blueprints, or that insects have weakened the wood-work, or that some rebuilding has been done during the last ten years. Therefore, I might decide to avoid these uncertain conclusions from past data and to determine the present strength of the floor by testing its strength now. Such a diagnostic test will not yield data which are absolutely certain; how reliable they are depends upon the quality of the available test and the carefulness of testing. However, the value of a present test is, from the point of view of methodology, superior to that of an *anamnesis*. An *anamnesis* includes logically two steps: namely, the testing of certain properties in the past (of the quality, size, and structure of the woodwork) and the proof that nothing unknown has interfered in the meantime; in other words that we have to deal with a "closed system." Even if a system is left untouched by the outside, inner changes occur. Therefore, in addition, the laws governing these inner changes have to be known if the properties of a situation are to be determined through an *anamnesis*.

Medicine, engineering, physics, biology are accustomed to using both methods, an inquiry into the past and a test of the present. But they prefer the latter whenever possible.[4]

Psychology has used diagnosis by *anamnesis* rather excessively,

---

[4] There are cases where a historical procedure is preferable. For instance, the hunger of a rat can probably be better determined by the duration of starvation than by a physiological or psychological test of the hunger at the time t. This conclusion from the past to the present can be made, however, only during periods and in settings where a "closed system" (no interference from outside) can be enforced; e.g., for animals which during this period do the same amount of work, which have been on a known diet, etc. The difficulties of this type of control have led Skinner to link the problem of drive strength to properties of present consumption.

particularly in classic psychoanalysis and other clinical approaches to problems of personality. Psychology of perception and psychology of memory have been relatively free from the historical type of diagnosis. Experimental psychology, on the whole, has shown a progressive trend toward testing the present situation.

The method of determining the properties of a situation (S^t) by testing them at that time t avoids the uncertainties of historical conclusions. It does not follow, however, that this method eliminates considerations of time-periods altogether. A "situation at a given time" actually does not refer to a moment without time extension, but to a certain time-period. This fact is of great theoretical and methodological importance for psychology.

It may be helpful to go back for a moment to the procedure in physics. If the vertical lines in Figure 1 represent the so-called physical "world-lines," a "situation" means a cut through these lines at a given time t. A description of such a situation has to include (1) the relative position of the parts of the field at that time; (2) the direction and the velocity of the changes going on at that time. The first task is fulfilled by ascribing certain scalar values to the different entities; the second, by ascribing certain vectors to them. The second task contains a difficulty which I would like to discuss.

To describe the direction and velocity of a change going on at a given moment, it is necessary to refer to a certain period of events. Ideally, a time-differential should suffice for such determination. Actually, one has to observe a macroscopic time-interval or at least the position at the beginning and at the end of such an interval to determine that time-differential. In the simplest case the velocity at a given time is assumed to equal the average velocity during that macroscopic time-interval. I will not attempt to follow up the details of this procedure in physics. If sufficient laws are known, certain indirect methods like those based on the Dopler effect permit different procedures.

However, it remains a basic fact that an adequate description of a situation at a moment is impossible without observation of a certain time-period. This observation has to be interpreted (according to the "most plausible" assumption and our knowledge of the physical laws) in a way which permits its transformation into a statement of the "state of affairs at the time t."

In psychology a similar problem exists. The person at a given time

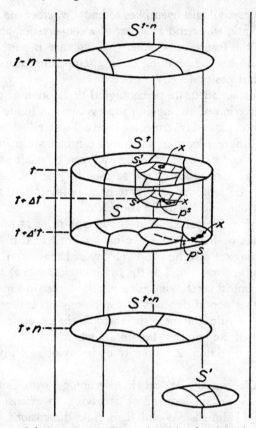

FIGURE 2. S during $t - n$ until $t + n$ is a "closed system"; but S is not genidentic with S'. $s^{t,t+\Delta t}$ is a small time-field-unit which extends over a relatively small area and includes the relatively small time-period t until $t + \Delta t$. $S^{t,t+\Delta't}$ is a larger time-field-unit covering a larger area and including the longer period t until $t + \Delta't$. p' and p^s indicate the change in position of x during the small and the large time unit.

may be in the midst of saying "a." Actually such a statement implies already that a certain time-interval is observed. Otherwise, only a certain position of mouth and body could be recorded. Usually the psychologist will not be satisfied with such a characterization of the on-going process. He likes to know whether this "a" belongs to the word "can" or "apple" or to what word it does belong. If the word was "can," the psychologist wants to know whether the person was going to say: "I cannot come back" or "I can stand on my head if

I have to." The psychologist even likes to know whether the sentence is spoken to an intimate friend as a part of a conversation about personal plans for the future or whether this sentence is part of a political address and has the meaning of an attempt to retreat from an untenable political position.

In other words, an adequate psychological description of the character and the direction of an ongoing process can and has to be done on various microscopic and macroscopic levels. To each "size of a unit of behavior" a different "size of situation" can be coordinated. That the individual in our example is saying "a," can be made sure without taking into account much of the surrounding of the individual. To characterize the sentence as a part of a political retreat, much more of the surrounding has to be considered.

Without altering the principle of contemporaneity as one of the basic propositions of field theory, we have to realize that to determine the psychological direction and velocity of behavior (i. e., what is usually called the "meaning" of the psychological event), we have to take into account in psychology as in physics a certain time-period. The length of this period depends in psychology upon the scope of the situation. As a rule, the more macroscopic the situation is which has to be described the longer is the period which has to be observed to determine the direction and velocity of behavior at a given time (Figure 2).

In other words, we are dealing in psychology with "situational units" which have to be conceived of as having an extension in regard to their field dimensions and their time dimensions. If I am not mistaken, the problem of time-space-quanta, which is so important for modern quantum theory in physics, is methodologically parallel (although, of course, on a more advanced level) to the problem of "time-field-units" in psychology.

The concept of situations of different scope has proved to be very helpful in solving a number of otherwise rather puzzling problems. Tolman,[5] Muenzinger,[6] and Floyd Allport[7] have stressed that a psy-

[5] E. C. Tolman: *Purposive Behavior in Animals and Men* (New York: D. Appleton-Century Co., 1932).

[6] K. F. Muenzinger: *Psychology: the Science of Behavior* (Denver: World Press, 1939).

[7] F. H. Allport. Methods in the study of collective action phenomena, *J. Social Psychol.*, 1942, *15*, 165–185.

chological description has to include the macroscopic as well as the microscopic events. Barker, Dembo, and Lewin[8] distinguish and treat mathematically three sizes of units of processes and corresponding sizes of situations. They have handled certain problems of measuring the strength of frustration during extended periods by referring to overlapping situations in regard to two different sizes of time-field-units. Lippitt and White,[9] in their study of social atmosphere, distinguish still larger periods of events. They have shown that the beginning and end of these macroscopic units can be determined rather precisely and with very satisfactory reliability. However, I will not discuss these questions here, where we are interested in methodological problems only.

THE PSYCHOLOGICAL PAST, PRESENT, AND FUTURE AS PARTS OF A PSYCHOLOGICAL FIELD AT A GIVEN TIME

The clarification of the problem of past and future has been much delayed by the fact that the psychological field which exists at a given time contains also the views of that individual about his future and past. The individual sees not only his present situation; he has certain expectations, wishes, fears, daydreams for his future. His views about his own past and that of the rest of the physical and social world are often incorrect but nevertheless constitute, in his life space, the "reality-level" of the past. In addition, a wish-level in regard to the past can frequently be observed. The discrepancy between the structure of this wish- or irreality-level of the psychological past and the reality-level plays an important role in the phenomenon of guilt. The structure of the psychological future is closely related, for instance, to hope and planning.

Following a terminology of L. K. Frank,[10] we speak of "time perspective" which includes the psychological past and psychological future on the reality-level and on the various irreality-levels. The time perspective existing at a given time has been shown to be very im-

[8] R. Barker, T. Dembo, K. Lewin: Frustration and regression, *Univ. Iowa Stud. Child Welf.*, 1941, *18*, 1–314.

[9] R. Lippitt: An experimental study of the effect of democratic and authoritarian group atmospheres, *Univ. Iowa Stud. Child Welf.*, 1940, *16*, No. 3, 44–195.

[10] L. K. Frank: Time perspectives, *J. Social Phil.*, 1939, *4*, 293–312.

portant for many problems such as the level of aspiration, the mood, the constructiveness, and the initiative of the individual. Farber[11] has shown, for instance, that the amount of suffering of a prisoner depends more on his expectation in regard to his release, which may be five years ahead, than on the pleasantness or unpleasantness of his present occupation.

It is important to realize that the psychological past and the psychological future are simultaneous parts of the psychological field existing at a given time t. The time perspective is continually changing. According to field theory, any type of behavior depends upon the total field, including the time perspective at that time, but not, in addition, upon any past or future field and its time perspectives.

It may be illustrative to consider briefly from this field-theoretical point of view the methodological problems connected with one of the basic concepts of the conditioned reflex theory, namely, the concept of "extinction." An individual has experienced that after a certain stimulus, let us say the ringing of a bell, food will appear. Being hungry, the individual eats. After a number of such experiences, the individual will show certain preparatory actions for eating as soon as the eating bell rings. The individual is then said to be "conditioned." Now, the situation is secretly changed by the experimenter and the eating bell is not followed by food. After a while the individual catches on and does not show the preparatory action for food when the bell rings. This process is called "extinction."

"Habits" of a person at a given time can and have to be treated as parts of the present field. Whether they should be represented partly as cognitive structure or resistance to change of cognitive structure, partly as a building up or fixation of valences, or whether they have to be conceptualized in other ways is not a problem here. Habits of action, as well as of thinking, are dealt with in field-theoretical research.

As Tolman, Hilgard and Marquis, and others have correctly pointed out, conditioning as well as extinction are both related to changes in the reality-level of the psychological future. Field theorists have to distinguish, in regard to conditioning and extinction, two types of problems. The one type deals with a question such as how

---

[11] M. L. Farber: Suffering and time perspective of the prisoner, *Univ. Iowa Stud. Child Welf.*, 1944, 20, 155-227.

expectation is affected by perception on the one hand, and memory on the other. What changes in the perceived structure of the psychological present lead to a change in the structure of the psychological future, and what are the laws governing the interdependence of these two parts of the psychological field? The studies on level of aspiration have provided some knowledge about the factors which influence the structure of the future reality-level. Korsch-Escalona[12] has made a step toward a mathematical treatment of the effect of the future reality-level on the forces which govern present behavior. Study of the level of aspiration has also given us considerable insight into the effect of the psychological past (namely of previous success or failure) on the psychological future. This question is obviously closely related to extinction.

The methodological position of these types of problems is clear: They deal with the interdependence of various parts of the psychological field existing at a given time t. In other words, they are legitimate field-theoretical questions of the type $b^t = F(S^t)$.

The second type of questions, treated in the theory of conditioned reflex, tries to relate a later situation S^4 (for instance, during extinction) to a previous situation S^1 during learning or to a number of similar or different previous situations S^1, S^2, S^3, $\cdots$: it relates behavior to the number of repetitions. In other words, these questions have the form $b^t = F(S^{t-n})$ or $b^t = F(S^{t-n}, S^{t-m}, \cdots)$. Here field theory demands a more critical and more analytical type of thinking. One should distinguish at least two types of problems:

a. How the perceived psychological situation will look at the time S^4 depends obviously upon whether or not the experimenter will provide food and on similar external physical or social conditions. Everybody will agree, I suppose, that these factors cannot possibly be derived from the psychological field of the individual at the previous time, even if all the psychological laws were known. These factors are alien to psychology.

b. There remain, however, legitimate psychological questions in this second type of problem. We can keep the boundary conditions of a life space constant or change them in a known way during a certain period and investigate what would happen under those conditions. These prob-

[12] S. Korsch-Escalona: The effect of success and failure upon the level of aspiration and behavior in manic-depressive psychoses, *Univ. Iowa Stud. Child Welf.*, 1939, *16*, No. 3, 199–303.

lems lie definitely within the domain of psychology. An example is the problem of restructurization of memory traces. We know that these processes depend on the state of the individual during the total period S^{t-n} until S^t (Figure 2) and are different, for instance, during sleep and while being awake. Doubtless the experiments on conditioned reflex have given us a wealth of material in regard to this type of problem. They will have to be treated finally in the way which we discussed in the beginning, namely, as a sequence of relations between a situation S^t and the immediately following situation S^{t+dt}.

On the whole, I think the psychological trend is definitely going in this direction. For instance, the goal gradient theory was formulated originally as a relation between behavior and past situations. Straight, analytical thinking demands that such a statement should be broken into several propositions, one of which has to do with the intensity of goal striving as a function of the distance between individual and goal. This is identical with a statement about certain force fields and is probably correct. A second proposition implied in the goal gradient theory links the present behavior to the past situation S^{t-n}. The specific form is, to my mind, unsatisfactory. But even if it should be correct, it should be treated as an independent theory. Hull's formulation of a "Gradient of Reinforcement Hypothesis" is a step in this direction.

PSYCHOLOGICAL ECOLOGY

As an elaboration of our considerations, I would like to discuss some aspects of Brunswik's treatment of the role of statistics.[13] I do not expect ever to live down the misunderstandings created by my attack on some ways in which statistics have been used in psychology. I have been always aware that quantitative measurement demands statistics. That statement holds also for "pure cases"; i. e., situations where it is possible to link theory and observable facts in a definite way. Since psychology is increasingly abandoning the inadequate objectives of statistics, further discussion might have little pragmatic value.

However, Brunswik has brought into the open new and important

[13] E. Brunswik: Organismic achievement and environmental probability, *Psychol. Rev.*, 1943, 50, 255–272.

aspects, and I feel that their clarification may be helpful for psychological methodology in general.

Within the realm of facts existing at a given time one can distinguish three areas in which changes are or might be of interest to psychology:

1. The "life space"; i. e., the person and the psychological environment as it exists for him. We usually have this field in mind if we refer to needs, motivation, mood, goals, anxiety, ideals.

2. A multitude of processes in the physical or social world, which do not affect the life space of the individual at that time.

3. A "boundary zone" of the life space: certain parts of the physical or social world do affect the state of the life space at that time. The process of perception, for instance, is intimately linked with this boundary zone because what is perceived is partly determined by the physical "stimuli"; i. e., that part of the physical world which affects the sensory organs at that time. Another process located in the boundary zone is the "execution" of an action.

Brunswik states correctly: "The 'field' within which Lewin is able to predict, in the strict sense of the word, is the person in his life space." Then he proceeds, "But the life space is not to be confused with geographic environment of physical stimuli, nor with actually achieved results in the environment. It is post-perceptual, and pre-behavioral." This statement is partly incorrect, namely, in so far as perception and behavior, to my mind, are legitimate problems of psychology. This view is a necessary consequence of the field-theoretical approach according to which the boundary conditions of a field are essential characteristics of that field. For instance, processes of perception which should be related to the boundary zone depend partly on the state of the inner part of the psychological field; i. e., upon the character of the person, his motivation, his cognitive structure, his way of perceiving, etc., and partly on the "stimulus distribution" on the retina or other receptors as enforced by physical processes outside the organism. For the same reasons, the problems of physical or social action are legitimate parts of psychology proper.

Brunswik, however, is correct in assuming that I do not consider as a part of the psychological field at a given time those sections of the physical or social world which do not affect the life space of the person at that time. The food that lies behind doors at the end of a maze so that neither smell nor sight can reach it is not a part of the life space of the animal. If the individual knows that food lies there this *knowledge,* of course, has to be represented in his life space, because this knowledge affects behavior. It is also necessary to take into account the subjective probability with which the individual views the present or future state of affairs because the degree of certainty of expectation also influences his behavior.

The principle of representing within the life space all that affects behavior at that time, but nothing else, prevents the inclusion of physical food which is not perceived. This food cannot possibly in-fluence his behavior at that time under the conditions mentioned. Indeed, the individual will start his journey if he thinks the food is there even if it is actually not there, and he will not move toward the food which actually is at the end of the maze if he does not know it is there.

According to Brunswik, it is possible to think in terms of laws rather than mere statistical rules if one limits the psychological field in the way described. However, he claims that for this gain one has to pay "the price of an encapsulation" into a realm of problems which actually leaves out the most dynamic aspects of psychology. He wishes to include in the psychological field those parts of the physical and sociological world which, to my mind, have to be ex-cluded. These parts, he states, have to be studied in a statistical way, and the probability of the occurrence of events calculated.

To my mind, the main issue is what the term "probability" refers to. Does Brunswik want to study the ideas of the driver of a car about the probability of being killed or does he want to study the accident statistics which tell the "objective probability" of such an event. If an individual sits in a room trusting that the ceiling will not come down, should only his "subjective probability" be taken into account for predicting behavior or should we also consider the "objective probability" of the ceiling's coming down as determined by the engineers. To my mind, only the first has to be taken into account.

I can see why psychology should be interested even in those areas of the physical and social world which are not part of the life space or which do not affect its boundary zone at present. If one wishes to safeguard a child's education during the next years, if one wishes to predict in what situation an individual will find himself as a result of a certain action, one will have to calculate this future. Obviously, such forecast has to be based partly on statistical considerations about nonpsychological data.

Theoretically, we can characterize this task as discovering what part of the physical or social world will determine during a given period the "boundary zone" of the life space. This task is worth the interest of the psychologists. I would suggest calling it "psychological ecology."[14]

Some problems of the "life history" of an individual have their places here. The boundary conditions of the life space during long as well as short time-periods depend partly on the action of the individual himself. To this degree they should be linked to the psychological dynamics of the life space. The rest of the calculation has to be done, however, with other than psychological means.

The essence of explaining or predicting any change in a certain area is the linkage of that change with the conditions of the field at that time. This basic principle makes the subjective probability of an event a part of the life space of that individual. But it excludes the objective probability of alien factors that cannot be derived from the life space.

[14] For further elaboration of this concept, see Chapter VIII.

IV

Field Theory and Learning
(1942)

FIELD THEORY

I AM often asked to characterize those essential features of the field-theoretical approach which distinguish it most clearly from other theoretical orientations. What are the principal attributes of field theory? The following characteristics of this theory seem to me particularly important: the use of a constructive rather than classificatory method; an interest in the dynamic aspects of events; a psychological rather than physical approach; an analysis which starts with the situation as a whole; a distinction between systematic and historical problems; a mathematical representation of the field.

1. CONSTRUCTIVE METHOD

Like any science, psychology is in a dilemma when it tries to develop "general" concepts and laws. If one "abstracts from individual differences," there is no logical way back from these generalities to the individual case. Such a generalization leads from individual children to children of a certain age or certain economic level and from there to children of all ages and all economic levels; it leads from a psychopathic individual to similar pathological types and from there to the general category "abnormal person." However, there is no logical way back from the concept "child" or "abnormal person" to the individual case (38).[1] What is the value of general concepts if they do not permit predictions for the individual case? Certainly, such a procedure is of little avail for the teacher or the psychotherapist.

---

[1] Numbers in parentheses refer to publications listed at the end of this chapter.

This problem has been acute in other sciences. In the time of the Greeks, geometry shifted from a "classificatory" method (which groups geometric figures according to "similarities") to a "constructive" or "genetic" method (which groups figures according to the way they can be produced or derived from each other). Ever since, the "genetic definition" has dominated mathematics. In physics, a similar development occurred at the time of Galileo (45). Biology tried to take a major step in this direction when the system of Linnee was superseded by that of Darwin.

The essence of the constructive method is the representation of an individual case with the help of a few "elements" of construction. In psychology, one can use psychological "position," psychological "forces," and similar concepts as elements. The general laws of psychology are statements of the empirical relations between these constructive elements or certain properties of them. It is possible to construct an infinite number of constellations in line with those laws; each of those constellations corresponds to an individual case at a given time. In this way, the gap between generalities and specificities, between laws and individual differences, can be bridged.

2. DYNAMIC APPROACH

Psychoanalysis has probably been the outstanding example of a psychological approach which attempts to reach the depths rather than the superficial layers of behavior. In this respect, it has followed the novelists of all periods. Psychoanalysis has not always kept in line with the requirements of scientific method when making its interpretations of behavior. What is needed are scientific constructs and methods which deal with the underlying forces of behavior but do so in a methodologically sound manner. (The term "dynamic" here refers to the concept "dynamis" = force, to an interpretation of changes as the result of psychological forces.)

The points mentioned under the above headings are at least to some degree recognized by other theories. The next two points, however, are more specific to field theory.

3. PSYCHOLOGICAL APPROACH

Field theory, as any scientific approach to psychology, is "behavioristic," if this means the tendency to provide "operational definitions" (testable symptoms) for the concepts used (49). Many psychologists, particularly those who followed the theory of conditioned reflex, have confused this requirement for operational definitions with a demand for eliminating psychological descriptions. They insisted on defining "stimuli" superficially in terms of physics. One of the basic characteristics of field theory in psychology, as I see it, is the demand that the field which influences an individual should be described not in "objective physicalistic" terms, but in the way in which it exists for that person at that time (cf. the concept "behavioral environment" of Koffka, 32). A teacher will never succeed in giving proper guidance to a child if he does not learn to understand the psychological world in which that individual child lives. To describe a situation "objectively" in psychology actually means to describe the situation as a totality of those facts and of only those facts which make up the field of that individual. To substitute for that world of the individual the world of the teacher, of the physicist, or of anybody else is to be, not objective, but wrong.

One of the basic tasks of psychology is to find scientific constructs which permit adequate representation of psychological constellations in such a way that the behavior of the individual can be derived. This does not weaken the demand for operational definitions of the terms used in psychology, but it emphasizes the right and necessity of using psychological concepts in psychology.

The properties of the "life space" of the individual depend partly upon the state of that individual as a product of his history, partly upon the nonpsychologic—physical and social—surroundings. The latter have a relation to the life space similar to that which "boundary conditions" have to a dynamic system. Gestalt theory has much emphasized (perhaps overemphasized in the beginning) certain similarities between the perceived structure and the objective structure of the stimuli. This does not mean, however, that it is permissible to treat stimuli as if they were inner parts of the life space (rather than boundary conditions), a common mistake of physicalistic behaviorism.

4. ANALYSIS BEGINNING WITH THE SITUATION AS A WHOLE

It has been said frequently that field theory and Gestalt theory are against analysis. Nothing could be more erroneous. In fact, field theory criticizes many physicalistic theories for their lack of a thorough psychological analysis (see example later); a great number of situations have been dealt with much more analytically by the field-theoretical approach than by any other approach.

What is important in field theory is the way the analysis proceeds. Instead of picking out one or another isolated element within a situation, the importance of which cannot be judged without consideration of the situation as a whole, field theory finds it advantageous, as a rule, to start with a characterization of the situation as a whole. After this first approximation, the various aspects and parts of the situation undergo a more and more specific and detailed analysis. It is obvious that such a method is the best safeguard against being misled by one or another element of the situation.

Of course, such a method presupposes that there exists something like properties of the field as a whole (30), and that even macroscopic situations, covering hours or years, can be seen under certain circumstances as a unit (3). Some of these general properties—for instance, the amount of "space of free movement" or the "atmosphere of friendliness"—are characterized by terms which might sound very unscientific to the ear of a person accustomed to think in terms of physics. However, if that person will consider for a moment the fundamental importance which the field of gravity, the electrical field, or the amount of pressure has for physical events, he will find it less surprising to discover a similar importance in the problems of atmosphere in psychology. In fact, it is possible to determine and to measure psychological atmospheres quite accurately (42). Every child is sensitive, even to small changes in social atmosphere, such as the degree of friendliness or security. The teacher knows that success in teaching French, or any subject, depends largely on the atmosphere he is able to create. That these problems have not been properly dealt with in psychology until now is due neither to their unimportance nor to any specific difficulty in the empirical determination of atmosphere, but mainly to certain philosophical prejudices in the direction of physicalistic behaviorism.

5. BEHAVIOR AS A FUNCTION OF THE FIELD AT THE TIME IT OCCURS

It has been accepted by most psychologists that the teleological derivation of behavior from the future is not permissible. Field theory insists that the derivation of behavior from the past is not less metaphysical, because past events do not exist now and therefore cannot have effect now. The effect of the past on behavior can be only an indirect one; the past psychological field is one of the "origins" of the present field and this in turn affects behavior. To link behavior with a past field therefore presupposes that one knows sufficiently how the past event has changed the field at that time, and whether or not in the meantime other events have modified the field again. Field theory is interested in historical or developmental problems, but it demands a much sharper analytical treatment of these problems than is customary, particularly in the theory of associationism.

6. MATHEMATICAL REPRESENTATIONS OF PSYCHOLOGICAL SITUATIONS

To permit scientific derivations, psychology must use a language which is logically strict and at the same time in line with constructive methods. As late as 1900, much argument was going on as to whether the use of numbers should be permitted in such a "qualitative" science as psychology. Many philosophers argued against such use on the grounds that numbers are characteristics of the physical sciences. Today, the use of numbers in psychological statistics is well accepted. However, there is some opposition to the use of geometry in representing psychological situations on the same ground. Actually, geometry is a branch of mathematics and as such is eligible as a tool in any science. Certain types of geometry, like topology, are most useful in representing the structure of psychological situations (39, 40). Topological and vectorial concepts combine power of analysis, conceptual precision, usefulness for derivation, and fitness for the total range of psychological problems in a way which, in my opinion, makes them superior to any other known conceptual tool in psychology.

At the moment, field theory is accepted probably by only a minority of psychologists. However, there are increasing signs that practically all branches of psychology—such as perception psychology, psychology of motivation, social psychology, child psychology, animal psychology, and abnormal psychology—are moving in the direction of field theory much faster than one would have expected a few years ago.

LEARNING: A TERM WITH MANY MEANINGS
AND A DISTURBING HISTORY

The term *learning* is a popular one which refers in a more or less vague way to some kind of betterment. Around 1910, students of psychology were taught to explain any change in behavior by learning (which meant improvement in speed or quality), by fatigue (which meant decrease in speed or quality), or by a combination of the two. Actually, the term *learning* refers to a multitude of different phenomena. The statement, "Democracy, one has to learn; autocracy is imposed upon the person," refers to one type of learning. If one says that the "spastic child has to learn to relax," one is speaking of a different type of learning. Both types probably have very little to do with "learning French vocabulary," and this type again has little to do with "learning to like spinach."

Have we any right to classify the learning to high-jump, to get along without alcohol, and to be friendly with other people under the same term, and to expect identical laws to hold for any of these processes?

The theory of association and its successor, the conditioned reflex theory, speaks of association in regard to any type of psychological processes and assumes the laws of association independent of psychological content. This practice has strengthened the tendency toward a broad usage of the term *learning*. Some psychologists identify learning with any change. Sometime, we hope, psychological theory will be so advanced that, as in modern physics, a few very general formulas will permit the derivation of most psychological phenomena. However, a science cannot reach this state without first having developed more specific laws, each representing the nature of certain types of processes.

Today, attempting to find the laws of learning in that broad sense seems comparable to an attempt by the chemist to develop *one* chemical formula for all the material contained in a building instead of grouping these different materials according to their chemical nature and finding the properties for each type of material separately. Similarly, the term *learning,* in the broad sense of "doing something better than before," is a "practical" term referring to a variety of processes which the psychologist will have to group and treat according to their psychological nature.

Within what is called learning, we have to distinguish at least the following types of changes: (1) learning as a change in cognitive structure (knowledge), (2) learning as a change in motivation (learning to like or to dislike), (3) learning as a change in group belongingness or ideology (this is an important aspect of growing into a culture), (4) learning in the meaning of voluntary control of the body musculature (this is one important aspect of acquiring skills, such as speech and self-control).

The history of psychology has done much to confuse rather than to clarify this situation. The classic theory of association, as stated by such an excellent experimentalist as G. E. Mueller, is based on the following theorem. If two experiences (or actions) *a* and *b* occur frequently together or in direct contiguity, an association between them is established. This association is operationally defined as the probability of producing *b* if *a* occurs alone. The strength of this association is a function of the number of repetitions. Originally, associationism was concerned with the connection between "ideas"; in other words, with knowledge or intellectual processes. However, associationism reached out further and further until it prided itself on explaining with one law not only the process of rote learning but any kind of intellectual process, behavior habits, values, and particularly directed actions. In other words, association was supposed to explain both motivation and cognition.

The explanation, following closely Darwinistic ideas of directed actions as the result of factors which do not contain the concept of directedness, was considered a particularly important achievement because at that time the controversy between the teleological and causal explanations of behavior was acute. The outstanding characteristic of a scientific causal explanation was incorrectly seen as requiring the avoidance of the concept of direction. This view was held in spite of the fact that one of the basic concepts in physics, the concept of physical force, refers to a directed entity (a vector, in terms of mathematics). The development of associationism can well be viewed as a struggle with this very problem. Ach's theory of "determining tendency" and Thorndike's "law of effect" were attempts to recognize the particular role which goals, needs, or other "directed" factors play in behavior without giving up the basic position of associationism. Both have singled out one special type of experience (reaching the goal, getting what is called a "reward," or setting up an intention) as particularly important for the formation of associations. Ever since,· leading representatives of the theory of associationism and conditioned reflex have given goals an increasingly dominant role in their derivations.

It is probably fair to say today that, in regard to questions of motivation, the original position of associationism is all but abandoned. One is tempted to say that a theory of needs very similar to that accepted in field theory has been taken over, although a somewhat peculiar type of terminology makes this fact less apparent. Instead of speaking, for instance, of "consumption," conditioned reflex theory speaks of "goal response." This goal response is not defined, as one might expect, as any reaction to a goal stimulus; rather, the other way around, all behavior which reduces need tension, and only such behavior, is called goal response (8, p. 6). In two other respects also, a change in the direction toward field theory is apparent.

a. The theory of conditioned reflex had tried to be behavioristic in the sense of physicalism and had shied away from all psychological terms as being unscientific. After heated discussion, the concept "goal" (53) was finally accepted in spite of its psychological character. Today, even terms like "expectation" are admitted to the vocabulary of the conditioned reflex psychologists (19, 23). In other words, a trend toward psychological concepts is visible, and it seems that classic physicalistic behaviorism is slowly being reduced to an approach which demands the correct technical requirements of operational definition.

b. All approaches to psychology are apparently becoming more and more aware that the theory has to include the particular pattern of factors existing at a given time. Such a leading conditioned reflex theorist as Hull (22) recognizes this point. On the whole, however, this recognition has led toward a complication rather than a clarification of the theory of the conditioned reflex.

In general, one might say that the history of associationism and its attempt to cover all types of psychological processes by one law has been much influenced by philosophical considerations (any such attempt is necessarily metaphysical in character). It was a correct fight against the teleological attempt to derive present behavior from the *future*. The desire to replace such an explanation by causal explanations led to the tendency to derive behavior from the past. This emphasis on the *past* has contributed much to the overemphasis on the problem of learning.

Looking back over the history of the experimental studies of the psychology of learning, the distinction of two main lines of development may help to clarify the still very unclear picture. One line deals with learning as related to motivation; the other, with learning as related to cognition.

a. The term *habit* can be used as a prototype of a concept in which the classic law of association is linked with action rather than cognition and is interpreted as a psychological force of a character similar to motivational forces. In my view, the most sincere attempt to follow up the implications of this aspect of associationism was made by Ach (1). He argued correctly that if repetition creates habits, it should be possible to measure the strength of the will by measuring the number of repetitions necessary to overthrow the effect of an intention to act in a different direction. His positive results have not been able, however, to stand up. It has been shown (36, 37, 46) that even an extreme number of repetitions does not form a measurable obstacle to carrying through a differently directed intention. To understand the various phenomena, it is necessary to distinguish "executive habits," which do not have the character of motivational forces, from "need habits," which imply the existence of a need (or quasi-need) or its fixation on certain valences. In other words, it is necessary to distinguish the motivational from the cognitive problems, and to study the laws of each of them in detail. Then the special role of each type of factor has to be determined for the different constellations.

Unfortunately, the fact that many learning experiments have been done with animals has made a clear separation of motivational and cognitive problems very difficult (2, 34, 50). Adams, Tolman, and others have stressed this point strongly. The work on latent learning (7, 53) has been one of the important results of this better conceptual analysis. However, even today, it is probably more difficult to distinguish these aspects properly in experiments with animals than in those with humans.

b. The second line of development deals with the specific laws which govern learning in the sense of change in cognitive structure. It becomes more and more apparent that even in this, its original realm, associationism is much too primitive a theory. The problems of insight, of acquiring knowledge, and of other kinds of change in cognitive structure seem to be closely related to those laws which govern perception (27, 30, 32) and determine the structure of the perceived field. Doubtlessly, great progress has been made in the study of these problems.

The lack of clarity in the discussions of learning in relation to motivation and cognition seems to be connected mainly with the term *memory*. It may mean the individual's views of his own past. The problems of memory in this regard are part of the problems of time perspective. On the other hand, speaking about memory processes, one may refer to the structural similarities and differences between life spaces of an individual existing at different times. The problems of plasticity of the psychological field and of the forces which create changes are of prime importance for this question. The relation between memory and learning is highly complex. Following the experiences of the past is one way of learning from experience. However, frequently one has to learn *not* to follow the same procedure one used previously; one must learn to be guided instead by something like a theoretical analysis of the present situation. One of the reasons for slow progress in social life is that, in the field of politics, people are more apt to go by the way of tradition than to follow the second procedure.

LEARNING AS CHANGE IN KNOWLEDGE
(Cognitive Structure)

I. DIFFERENTIATION OF UNSTRUCTURED AREAS

An individual moves to a new town. Slowly he learns to find his way around geographically and socially. What are the psychological changes called *learning* in this case? The individual arrives at the depot as a stranger. He may have secured an apartment in advance. He knows his house number, but standing at the station and failing to have a map of the town, he does not know how to get there. The situation corresponds to Figure 3. There is an area corresponding to the station *(ST)* where the person *(P)* is located. There exists another area in his life space corresponding to the apartment *(A)*. Between these two areas lies a region which has psychologically the character of being unstructured *(U)*, that is, the stranger does not know how to go from the station to his apartment, how far it is, and how the area around his apartment looks.

This unclearness is of decisive importance for his behavior. He does not know which streets around the station lead to, and which

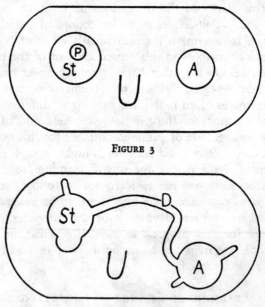

FIGURE 3

FIGURE 4

lead away from, the apartment. In other words, it is not defined what "direction" from the station to the apartment means.

The stranger inquires and learns that streetcar *D* will bring him directly to his apartment. As the result of his first trip from the station to his home, some structuralization takes place: "Direction from the station to the apartment" has become defined as using the streetcar *D*; the newcomer has acquired an impression of the distance between these points in the city. The streetcar made a number of turns. As a result, the newcomer is not very clear about the geographical position of both points. Still, he knows the direction in the sense of the "path which can be taken" (Figure 4).

It may be that he has to start to work the very next morning. In this case, he might learn in a similar way the "functional" relations between his home and the place of his work. But there will still be great areas of the city which are unstructured. Probably, at first an area geographically close to his home will become better known to him, and slowly the degree of cognitive structuralization will increase so that finally he will know not only one path from his home to his work *(W)* or to the station, but several (Figure 5). He will know

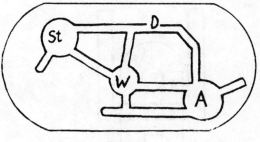

FIGURE 5

what is the direct route and finally he will be able to determine quite well the direction from any one place to any other in the city. He will know what the shortest route is for walking or for using an automobile or the subway.

A similar process of differentiating previously undifferentiated areas will occur in regard to the social life of the city. In the beginning, it will be unclear in what direction socially the stranger moves in approaching a particular person. But more and more he will know who is who, how the social life of the city is made up, what are the direct and indirect ways, which social paths are easy and which are difficult to use. It is probably not necessary to elaborate the similar process of differentiation which occurs for the student who studies Greek history. Again, a previously vague and unstructured area becomes cognitively structured and specific.

Another example of this type of learning is the cognitive change of a psychological world as a whole during development. From all that we know, the newborn cannot distinguish between himself and his environment; slowly certain areas, for instance, those connected with eating, take on a specific character, become more and more differentiated; the parts of his own body become differentiated from each other and from the rest of the world; social relations develop and become differentiated; needs, emotions, language go through a similar process of differentiation (3, 6, 31, 53).

The concept of differentiation is a basic biological concept related to such fundamental and familiar biological processes as the sub-division of the egg into smaller units of more specific character. A shift from the theory of association or conditioned reflex to a theory

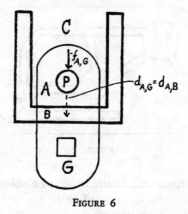

FIGURE 6

of differentiation (or similar changes in structure) means a change from a physical analogy (namely that of links in a chain) to a more biological approach. In addition, it seems to be easier to represent differentiation and other changes in structure in a mathematically precise way (3) than by the concepts used in the older theories. Associations, so far as they refer to changes in knowledge, may well be reinterpreted as relatively simple cases of change in structure.

2. RESTRUCTURIZATION, PSYCHOLOGICAL SOCIAL DIRECTIONS, MEANING

Not all changes of cognitive structure which we call learning have the character of differentiation in the sense of a subdividing of regions into smaller units. Sometimes a change in cognitive structure occurs without increase or decrease in the degree of differentiation. Classic examples are the detour problems (29). What is the difference between the psychological situation of the one-year-old child who cannot find the way to his goal when he stands within a U-shaped barrier (Figure 6) and the four-year-old child who has no difficulty whatever? To state this question in a different form: What psychological change occurs at the moment when the child has "insight" into the solution for the first time?

The difference can partly be described as follows (38.): Before the solution, the direction $(d_{A, G})$ from the region A where the child (P)

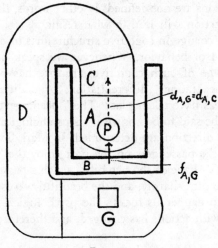

FIGURE 7

is located toward the goal G is the same as the direction $(d_{A, B})$ to the barrier B $(d_{A, B} = d_{A, G})$. Moving in the direction C would at that time mean for the child going in the direction $(d_{A, -G})$ "away from the goal" $(d_{A, C} = d_{A, -G})$. The force $f_{A, G}$ acting on the child in the direction toward this goal leads, in this constellation, to a tendency to locomote in the direction $d_{A, B}$. As the restraining forces of the barrier B are too great, the child is unable to reach his goal.

After the insight (or when the child is old enough), the cognitive structure of the situation is changed (Figure 7). The areas A and G, which previously had the character of separated areas, are now connected as part of the area A, C, D, G. A locomotion from A to C may be seen as the first part of the path $W_{A, C, D, G}$. Correspondingly, the direction toward C $(d_{A, C})$ is now equal to the direction toward the goal G $(d_{A, G})$ rather than away from G $(d_{A, C} = d_{A, G}; d_{A, C} = d_{A, -G})$ The force $f_{A, G}$ leads now to locomotion from A to C, in line with this changed meaning of the direction.

This example illustrates how a psychological direction depends on the cognitive structure of a given situation. Behavior results from forces which have direction. Therefore, all behavior depends to a large degree on the cognitive structure of the life space. In an unstructured, or new, situation the person feels insecure because the psychological directions are not defined; in other words, the person does not know what action will lead to what result.

Learning, as a change in cognitive structure, has to deal with practically every field of behavior. Whenever we speak of a change in meaning, a change of such cognitive structure has occurred. New connections or separations, differentiations or dedifferentiations, of psychological areas have taken place. The "meaning" of an event in psychology may be said to be known if its psychological position and its psychological direction are determined. In Mark Twain's *Life on the Mississippi*, the passengers on the boat enjoy the "scenery," but for the pilot the V-shape of the two hills, which a passenger admires, means a signal to turn sharply, and the beautiful waves in the middle of the river mean dangerous rocks. The psychological connection of these "stimuli" with actions has changed, and therefore the meaning has changed.

One word about the problem of learning and repetition. One should be careful to distinguish the effect of repetition on motivation (see below) and on change in cognitive structure. It is correct that a change in cognitive structure may occur on the occasion of repeated experience. However, it is important to realize that it is not the repetition itself but the change in cognitive structure which is essential for learning. If the newcomer has a map of the city, the number of trips from the individual's home to his place of work which is necessary for the creation of an adequate cognitive structure may be reduced to a few. According to Krechevsky (33) and others, even animals learn a maze by a series of changes in cognitive structure, called "hypotheses." The above analysis makes it understandable why gaining sufficient psychological distance from the problem and getting an over-all view of a broader area (29) are usually more helpful for creating that change of cognitive structure which corresponds to the solution of a task than repeating over and over again the same attempts. Recent experiments show that even in rote learning the number of repetitions is of secondary importance (19). Mere repetition, if carried on frequently enough, has a definite opposite effect on learning. It leads to disorganization and dedifferentiation which are typical symptoms of what has been called psychological satiation (see below). As the result of the satiation, the meaningful will become meaningless and what has been known may be unlearned.

3. TIME PERSPECTIVE, PSYCHOLOGICAL REALITY AND IRREALITY

The behavior of an individual does not depend entirely on his present situation. His mood is deeply affected by his hopes and wishes and by his views of his own past. The morale and happiness of an individual seem to depend more on what he expects of the future than on the pleasantness or unpleasantness of the present situation.

The totality of the individual's views of his psychological future and his psychological past existing at a given time can be called "time perspective" (15). In addition, one has to distinguish the dimension of reality-irreality within the psychological life space. The reality level of the psychological past, present, and future corresponds to the situation as they actually existed, exist, and will exist according to the individual's belief.

During development, an enlargement of the time perspective takes place. The small child lives in the present; his time perspective includes only the immediate past and the immediate future. This smallness of time perspective is characteristic of what is usually called "primitive behavior." The time dimension of the life space of the child grows with increasing age; more and more distant future and past events affect present behavior.

Normal development brings with it, in addition, an increased differentiation in the reality-irreality dimensions of the life space. The young child does not clearly distinguish wishes from facts, hopes from expectations (44). The older person is said to be better able to distinguish between daydream wishes and reality, although wishful thinking is certainly very common in adults, too.

Teachers and educators have been aware of the importance of time perspective as one of the fundamental aspects of development. "Broadening the pupil's view" has always been considered one of the main purposes of education. Such an increase in time perspective can be viewed as one type of change in cognitive structure. There seem to be no experimental data available on ways in which such a change can be achieved other than through normal development. This also holds for the differentiation of the life space in regard to its reality-irreality dimension.

Some experimental studies indicate several conditions under which time perspective is narrowed and the difference between reality and irreality is blurred. An outstanding example is the "primitivation" under emotional stress. It has been shown (3) that, in an insecure or frustrated situation, the productivity of a five-and-one-half-year-old child may regress to the level of a three-and-one-half-year old. This regression is partly caused by the decreased time perspective under those circumstances. Orphan children living under great social restrictions and meager opportunities show a much slower increase in mental age (and, as a result, a decrease in IQ) than children living under better conditions (48).

LEARNING AS CHANGE IN VALENCES AND VALUES

In discussing the multitude of meanings attached to the term *learning*, we mentioned the following example: Autocracy is imposed upon the individual; democracy, he has to learn. It may be clarifying to discuss the meaning of the term *learning* in this sentence in more detail.

Learning democracy means, first, that the person has to do something himself instead of being passively moved by forces imposed on him. Second, learning democracy means to establish certain likes and dislikes, that is, certain valences, values, and ideologies. Third, learning democracy means to get acquainted with certain techniques, such as those of group decision.

The last point does not need to be elaborated here because the problem of learning of techniques (in case one wants to have democracy) is practically identical with the problem of acquiring knowledge (i. e., change in cognitive structure, which we have already discussed) in combination with the problem of execution. The other two points will now be discussed.

I. LEARNING AND FORCES IMPOSED ON THE PERSON

Progressive education is accustomed to speak of "child-driven activities" as opposed to those activities which the child is compelled to do. This points to a basic difference in motivation. Teacher, parent, or society frequently has to face the problem of an individual's having certain goals which he should not have or of lacking certain goals he should have.

There are two principal ways to bring about the desired change. The one implies a change of the person's own needs or interests; the other leaves needs or interests more or less untouched, and compels the individual to do the undesired action either by direct force or by setting up a constellation where other stronger needs overbalance the effect of the first need.

Mere force plays a considerable role in all education. The baby is not asked by the mother when it is to be taken out of the crib and when it is to be fed. The students are not asked for their consent in taking final examinations. We shall mention but a few aspects of this basic question. (1) A great deal of difference exists in how gently or how forcefully mothers pick up their babies, and in how sensitively they observe those small indications of the babies' needs and desires. This question is closely related to the problem of the age at which education for democracy should start (35). (2) "Learning" by force might take place when an individual is pushed into a situation and then "adapts" himself to this situation. These methods are frequently used in politics and in education. To make a person behave in a way which he would resent, a step-by-step method is frequently applied—a procedure ingeniously employed by Hitler. The individual is pushed into a situation which is not sufficiently different from the previous one to create great resistance. After he has adapted himself, the next step is taken. Jerome Frank (14), in a study with students, has shown that such a step-by-step method is considerably more efficient in breaking resistance than the all-at-once method.

A method frequently used as motivation in learning is reward or punishment. The theory of association, or the law of effect, treats reward and punishment essentially as a linkage between a certain activity and a pleasant or unpleasant tone. To predict the actual behavior, one has to see that reward and punishment are psychologically something more specific. An analytical treatment of the typical situation of the threat of punishment, for instance, shows the following constellation. The individual dislikes the activity T (Figure 8). To make him carry out this activity, a second even more disagreeable possibility is set up in such a way that the individual has to face one of them. In other words, the individual is in a particular type of conflict situation, namely, in a conflict between two forces ($f_{P, -T}$ and $f_{P, -Pu}$) away from two disagreeable areas. It can be shown (38, 40) that such conflicts lead to a tendency to "leave the field" (1), to run away from both activities. To make the threat of punishment effective, barriers (B) against this way out have to be established—

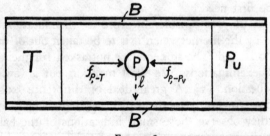

FIGURE 8

barriers strong enough to keep the individual within the conflict area. These barriers usually consist of social forces imposed upon the individual by an authority. By detailed analysis of the field in case of threat of punishment, one can derive the tension resulting from the conflict, the tendency to fight the authority, and a variety of other factors. It can also be shown that the space of free movement has to be sufficiently narrowed down, that a somewhat prisonlike situation has to be created if the threat of punishment is to be effective.

Neither the promise of reward nor the threat of punishment creates the same constellation of psychological forces as a change of interest in the demanded activity itself. Nor is the difference between reward and punishment merely that of attaching a pleasant or unpleasant tone to an activity. The promise of reward does not require a prisonlike situation and this permits more freedom to the individual (38) in other directions. Still, a barrier has to be kept up around the reward in such a way that the goal cannot be reached save by the way of the disliked but requested activity. Reward in the end may lead to an actual change in interest, so that the originally disliked activity may become liked. The repetition of punishment usually makes the demanded activity only more hated. However, a state of apathy and giving-in may be reached, as shown by experiments on social climates (42).

2. CHANGES IN VALENCES AND VALUES

a. Changes in Needs and Meaning. Anyone who wishes to influence likes and dislikes has to be aware of the changes of valences which take place with the changes of needs in the process of satiation or during development. The individual may be attracted by an activity like drawing or dancing or going to the movies. If he follows this desire long enough, a change in attractiveness results. As in physical consumption, the psychological "consumption" of the activity satiates the underlying need. Experiments have shown that repetitions beyond the satiation point lead to variation, inattentiveness, mistakes, fatigue, and finally to a complete disorganization; in other words, to an "un-learning" in the sense of inability to carry out an activity previously mastered (26).

Frequently, "learning" to like or dislike certain activities is the result of the long-range change of needs which takes place during development and seems particularly marked during the so-called crises, such as adolescence. Oversatiation, too, may lead to a permanent dislike for an activity.

It has been one of the fallacies of classic behaviorism to describe the character of an activity by its physical aspects only and to neglect the great effect of the psychological setting. The experiments on satiation clearly indicate that moving the arm in an identical way by making certain lines may have different psychological and physiological effects, according to the meaning of this activity. For instance, making a pattern of four lines may have become disintegrated and the arm fatigued as a result of oversatiation. A change to a different pattern of lines, or to making a picture from these lines, suffices to wipe out the bodily symptoms of fatigue and to bring about reorganization of the activity. To write a paper containing hundreds of letters does not mean repetition and therefore does not lead as quickly to satiation. This is one of the reasons why the method of writing and reading by learning sentences or words is superior to the older method of learning letters. The modern primer uses stories which "progress" although they are composed of relatively few words and elements. In this way, positive motivation for learning to read is created or set up.

The valence of an activity depends partly on its meaning and therefore on the cognitive structure. For instance, a child who dislikes a certain food at home may show no such dislike when getting the same food at a friend's party. The most frequent method of changing valences in education is based on this relation to cognitive structure. For instance, the mother may try to eliminate a certain behavior by remarking that only "bad children do that"; she may induce the unwilling child to eat by saying, "One bite for papa, one bite for mamma, and one bite for baby." Food preferences in children can be changed by telling a story in which the disliked food is a favorite for the hero of the story (9).

The relation between cognitive structure and valence is less obvious in cases like those where children continue to dislike food when eating it at home even though they do not mind eating the same food at the nursery school. For these children, coming to the dinner table at home has acquired the meaning of going to a fight with mother. These old "habits" can be changed from one day to another if it is possible to change the meaning of the activity (52). It is easy to make an adult do something in a medical setting or as a subject in a psychological experiment (14) which he would definitely refuse to do outside of the experimental situation.

The relation between cognitive structure and valence is particularly striking in what is called "cultural differences." Cultures are not only different in regard to what values are recognized; at least as important is the way different activities are seen as linked. For Mennonite children in Iowa, for instance, work and religion are much more closely related than for non-Mennonite children in comparable rural areas (25). Much of advertising and most of propaganda are effective not by changing needs and values as such but by changing the cognitive structure in a way which makes the propagandized activity appear to be a part of, or a means to, an area which has high value for that individual.

"Learning" of new ideologies, or in other words, conversions, is usually difficult to bring about partly because of the way in which needs and cognitive structure are interwoven. An example of a successful change in ideology and social behavior is the retraining of relatively autocratic recreation leaders into excellent democratic leaders, as carried out by Bavelas (4). These leaders had followed their method of handling groups for five to seven years. The change took place within three weeks. It was brought about partly by observation of other leaders and a detailed discussion of the various possibilities of the leaders' reactions to a multitude of situations arising from group life. In this way, the cognitive structure of the field "leader behavior" became much more finely differentiated; the individual became sensitized. The motivational change from skepticism to enthusiasm for democratic procedure cannot be discussed here in detail. It came about, in part, through the thrill of experiencing what a democratic group-life can do to children, and through the realization that one is able to create such an atmosphere. The preceding years had been for these people a period of low morale, of dissatisfaction with the insecure position of the W.P.A. recreation worker and the carrying through of their work as a matter of routine. The new experience could change the ideology and morale of these people so suddenly and deeply because it provided worth-while goals and a long-range outlook to individuals who previously had lived with a time perspective which was composed of a disagreeable past, unsatisfactory present, and no positive outlook for the future. In other words, the retraining was achieved, not in spite of the long-standing bad habits but, partly, because of them.

The problem of time perspective is closely related to certain changes in valences or goals which depend on the level of aspiration.

b. Learning and the Level of Aspiration. The level of aspiration is defined as the degree of difficulty of the goal toward which a person is striving. Whether or not a person will learn a certain activity is deeply influenced by his trying or not trying to do so. Therefore, the factors which determine the level of aspiration are of basic importance for learning.

The level of aspiration is influenced partly by the ability of the individual as manifested in his past and present successes and failures (17, 21, 24), partly by certain group standards (12, 17, 20, 43). By and large, the experience of success and failure occurs only in a relatively limited area of difficulties which is close to the boundary level of ability of the individual. Success and failure influence the expectation for the outcome of the future action and raise or lower the level of aspiration accordingly. However, this "rational" factor is by no means the only one determining the level of aspiration. A child below or above the average of the group may permanently keep his level of aspiration too high or too low for his ability. It has been shown (12) that the knowledge of one's own or others' group standards affects the reality- and the wish-level, depending on the degree to which these group standards are accepted.

Good students tend to keep their level of aspiration slightly above their past achievement, whereas poor students tend to show, relative to their ability, excessively high or excessively low levels of aspiration (47). In other words, the poor students have not learned to be "realistic" in evaluating success and failure for their goal-setting. Failure frequently leads to rationalization, emotional outbreak, over-persistency, or rapid discontinuance (17, 28). It has been shown that children who had the tendency to react to failure by quitting, by rationalization, or by emotional outbreak can learn to react more maturely to such failure (28). This "learning to take it" is certainly one of the most important aspects of learning as a part of the character development of the individual.

SUMMARY

This brief survey of problems related to learning has not attempted to deal with the difficult questions of learning in the sense of voluntary control of the motoric (which would include such matters as self-control, handling of mechanical or social "tools," such as speech, and "action through a distance"). An important approach to the latter is contained in Heider's theory of "thing and medium" (18). The dynamics of these processes seem to be guided by a type of "organizational interdependence" (3) similar to the relation between leader and led or between the so-called higher and lower nerve centers.

Summarizing our discussion from a more dynamic view, we might say: We have distinguished learning in the sense of change in cognitive structure from learning in the sense of change in motivation.

I. CHANGE IN COGNITIVE STRUCTURE

A change in cognitive structure may occur in any part of the individual's life space, including the psychological future, the psychological present, or the psychological past. It may occur on the reality-level or on the irreality-level (wish- and fear-level) of each of these sections of the life space.

Establishment or severance of the linkage between two regions of the life space, with which the theory of association or conditioned reflex is mainly concerned, is only one type of structural change. A basic change in structure, both for learning and for long-range development, is the differentiation of previously undifferentiated regions.

According to field theory, all changes are due to certain forces (directed entities). In regard to the forces which bring about a change in cognitive structure, it is convenient to distinguish two types: one resulting from the structure of the cognitive field itself, and the other from certain valences (needs or motivations).

a. The first type of forces leading to change in cognitive structure is very similar to, if not identical with, those forces which govern the perceptual fields. They must be considered when discussing problems of figure and ground, of specific patterns and their internal equilibria (54). We should get accustomed to include within perception psychology also the perception of the character of other persons and of social facts. There are a number of indications that the laws which determine the patterning in perception are more or less the same as those in thinking and memory. (One should, however, be warned against too simple an approach. For instance, three developmental types of cognition are distinguished by Vigotsky [51]: situational thinking, classification, and thinking in theoretical terms. Similar distinctions are much emphasized in psychopathology [16].)

b. In addition to the forces resulting from the cognitive structure as such, the cognitive structure is deeply influenced by the needs of the individual, his valences, values, and hopes. These forces play an important role in the solution of any intellectual task. In fact, a psychological force corresponding to a need can be said to have two basic results. It leads either to locomotion of the individual in the direction of the psychological force or to a change of his cognitive structure in a way which corresponds to such a locomotion or which facilitates it. Therefore, all intellectual processes are deeply affected by the goals of the individual. We have seen that intellectual processes, which can be viewed as one type of productive activity of the individual, depend upon his emotional state, that is, the tension, the degree of differentiation, the size, and the fluidity of the life space as a whole. It is a corollary of the relation between cognitive structure and perception that perception, too, is dependent on the needs and emotions of the individual. The "projective" techniques of studying personality are making use of this relation.

2. CHANGE IN MOTIVATION

Learning as related to change in motivation deals either with a change in needs or a change in the means of their satisfaction. To these processes belong not only such examples as becoming addicted to or breaking away from a drug habit, and any ideological conversion, but also the normal process of acculturation during childhood or after entering a new social group. Obviously, forces governing this type of learning are related to the total area of factors which determine motivation and personality development. We have mentioned here but a few—the basic laws of needs and satiation, goal structures, the level of aspiration, and the problem of group belongingness.

REFERENCES

1. ACH, N.: *Über den Willensakt und das Temperament: Eine experimentelle Untersuchung* (Leipzig: Quelle und Meyer, 1910).
2. ADAMS, DONALD K.: A restatement of the problem of learning, *Brit. J. Psychol.*, 1931, 22, 150–178.
3. BARKER, R., DEMBO, T., and LEWIN, K.: Frustration and regression: An experiment with young children, *Univ. Iowa Stud. Child Welf.*, 1941, *18*, No. 1.
4. BAVELAS, ALEX.: Morale and training of leaders. In Watson, G. (ed.): *Civilian Morale* (Boston: Houghton Mifflin Company, 1942).
5. BERGMANN, G., and SPENCE, K.: Operationism and theory in psychology, *Psychol. Rev.*, 1941, 48, 1–14.
6. BROOKS, F. D.: *Child Psychology* (Boston: Houghton Mifflin Company, 1937).
7. BUXTON, C. E.: Latent learning and the goal-gradient hypothesis, *Contr. Psychol. Theor.*, 1940, 2, No. 2.
8. DOLLARD, J., MILLER, N. E., DOOR, L. W., ET. AL.: *Frustration and Aggression* (New Haven: Yale University Press, 1939).

9. DUNCKER, K.: Experimental modification of children's food preferences through social suggestion, *J. Abnorm. & Social Psychol.*, 1938, *33*, 489–507.

10. FARBER, M. L.: Suffering and time perspective of the prisoner, *Univ. Iowa Stud. Child Welf.*, 1944, *20*, 153–228.

11. FESTINGER, LEON: A theoretical interpretation of shifts in level of aspiration, *Psychol. Rev.*, 1942, *49*, 235–250.

12. FESTINGER, LEON: Wish, expectation, and group standards as factors influencing level of aspiration, *J. Abnorm. & Social Psychol.*, 1942, 37, 184–200.

13. FRANK, J. D. Some psychological determinants of the level of aspiration. *Am. J. Psychol.*, 1935, 47, 285–293.

14. FRANK, J. D.: Experimental studies of personal pressure and resistance, *J. Gen. Psychol.*, 1944, *30*, 23–64.

15. FRANK, L. K.: Time perspectives, *J. Social Philos.*, 1939, *4*, 293–312.

16. GOLDSTEIN, KURT.: *The Organism* (New York: The Macmillan Company, 1939).

17. GOULD, ROSALIND.: An experimental analysis of the "level of aspiration," *Genet. Psychol. Monogr.*, 1939, *21*, 3–115.

18. HEIDER, FRITZ.: Environmental determinants in psychological theories, *Psychol. Rev.*, 1939, *46*, 383–410.

19. HILGARD, E. R., and MARQUIS, D. G.: *Conditioning and Learning* (New York: D. Appleton-Century Co., 1940).

20. HILGARD, E. R., SAIT, E. M., and MAGARET, G. A.: Level of aspiration as affected by relative standing in an experimental group, *J. Exper. Psychol.*, 1940, 27, 411–421.

21. HOPPE, FERDINAND: Erfolg und Misserfolg, *Psychol. Forsch.*, 1930, *14*, 1–62.

22. HULL, C. L.: The problem of stimulus equivalence in behavior theory, *Psychol. Rev.*, 1939, *46*, 9–30.

23. HUMPHREYS, L. G.: The effect of random alternation of reinforcement on the acquisition and extinction of conditioned eyelid reactions, *J. Exper. Psychol.*, 1939, *25*, 141–158.

24. JUCKNAT, MARGARET: Leistung, Anspruchsniveau und Selbstbewusstein, *Psychol. Forsch.*, 1937, *22*, 89–179.

25. KALHORN, JOAN: Values and sources of authority among rural children, *Univ. Iowa Stud. Child Welf.*, 1944, *20*, 99–151.

26. KARSTEN, A: Psychische Sattigung, *Psychol. Forsch.*, 1928, *10*, 142–254.

27. KATONA, GEORGE: *Organizing and Memorizing* (New York: Columbia University Press, 1940).

28. KEISTER, M. E.: The behavior of young children in failure: An experimental attempt to discover and to modify undesirable responses of preschool children to failure, *Univ. Iowa Stud. Child Welf.*, 1937, *14*, 28–82.

29. KOEHLER, WOLFGANG: *The Mentality of Apes* (New York: Harcourt, Brace & Co., 1925).

30. KOEHLER, WOLFGANG: *Dynamics in Psychology* (New York: Liveright Publishing Corporation, 1940).

31. KOFFKA, KURT: *The Growth of the Mind* (New York: Harcourt, Brace & Co., 1925).

32. KOFFKA, KURT: *Principles of Gestalt Psychology* (New York: Harcourt, Brace & Co., 1935).

33. KRECHEVSKY, I.: Brain mechanisms and variability I, II, III, *J. Comp. Psychol.*, 1937, *23*, 121–138, 139–163, 351–364.

34. LASHLEY, K. S.: Learning I: Nervous mechanisms in learning. In Murchison, Carl (ed.): *Foundations of Experimental Psychology* (Worcester: Clark University Press, 1929).

35. LEWIN, GERTRUD, and LEWIN, KURT: Democracy and the school, *Understanding the Child*, 1941, *10*, 7–10.

36. LEWIN, KURT: Die psychische Tätigkeit bei der Hemmung von Willensvorgängen und das Grundgesetz der Assoziation, *Ztschr. Psychol.*, 1917, 77, 212–247.

37. LEWIN, KURT: Das Problem der Willensmessung und das Grundgesetz der Assoziation, *Psychol. Forsch.*, 1922, *1*, 65–140, 191–302.

38. LEWIN, KURT: *A Dynamic Theory of Personality* (New York: McGraw-Hill Book Co., 1935).

39. LEWIN, KURT: *Principles of Topological Psychology* (New York: McGraw-Hill Book Co., 1936).

40. LEWIN, KURT: The conceptual representation and measurement of psychological forces, *Contrib. Psychol. Theor.*, 1938, *1*, No. 4.

41. LEWIN, KURT, and LIPPITT, RONALD: An experimental approach to the study of autocracy and democracy: A preliminary note, *Sociometry*, 1938, *1*, 292–300.

42. LEWIN, K., LIPPITT, R., and WHITE, R. K.: Patterns of aggressive behavior in experimentally created "social climates," *J. Social Psychol.*, 1939, *10*, 271–299.

43. LEWIS, H. B.: Studies in the principles of judgments and attitudes: II. The influence of political attitude on the organization and stability of judgments, *J. Social Psychol.*, 1940, *11*, 121–146.

44. PIAGET, JEAN: *The Child's Conception of the World* (New York: Harcourt, Brace & Co., 1929).

45. REICHENBACH, HANS: *Experience and Prediction: An Analysis of the Foundations and the Structure of Knowledge* (Chicago: University of Chicago Press, 1938).

46. SCHWARZ, GEORG: über Rückfälligkeit bei Umgewöhnung, I & II, *Psychol. Forsch.*, 1927, 9, 86–158; 1933, *18*, 143–190.

47. SEARS, P. S.: Levels of aspiration in academically successful and unsuccessful children, *J. Abnorm. Social Psychol.*, 1940, *35*, 489–536.

48. SKEELS, H. M., UPDEGRAFF, R., WELLMAN, B. L., and WILLIAMS, H. M.: A study of environmental stimulation, *Univ. Iowa Stud. Child Welf.*, 1938, *15*, No. 4.

49. STEVENS, S. S.: Psychology and the science of science, *Psychol. Bull.*, 1939, *36*, 221–263.

50. TOLMAN, E. C.: *Purposive Behavior in Animals and Man* (New York: D. Appleton-Century Co., 1932).

51. VIGOTSKY, L. S.: Thought and speech, *Psychiatry*, 1939, 2, 29–54.

52. WARING, E. B.: Guidance and punishment: Some contrasts, *Cornell Bull. Homemakers*, 1935, No. 334.

53. WERNER, HEINZ: *Comparative Psychology of Mental Development* (New York: Harper & Brothers, 1940).

54. WERTHEIMER, MAX: Untersuchungen zur Lehre von der Gestalt: I. Prinzipielle Bemerkungen, *Psychol. Forsch.*, 1922, *1*, 47–65.

V

Regression, Retrogression, and Development
(1941)

┗┛┛

IN PSYCHOLOGY the term *regression* refers to a primitivation of behavior, a "going back" to a less mature state which the individual has already outgrown. A temporary regression frequently occurs in tense emotional situations with normal adults and children, particularly if these emotions are unpleasant. Intense joy, too, may lead to certain primitive actions. Fatigue, oversatiation, and sickness often cause temporary regression. A more or less permanent type of regression can be observed in certain cases of senility, in a great variety of neuroses, and in functional and organic psychoses. Regression, therefore, has to be considered a common phenomenon which is related to many situations and problems, and concerns the total behavior of the person rather fundamentally.

The relation between regression and development is another reason why psychology should regard regression as an important topic. Knowledge of the process of psychological development has greatly increased in recent years. We have learned particularly that the varieties of possible developments are much greater than might have been expected. However, our knowledge of the factors determining development, its dynamics and laws, is extremely meager. Regression can be said to be a negative development. The experimental study of regression seems to be technically somewhat easier than that of development. Therefore, the indirect way of studying the dynamics of development by studying regression may prove to be fruitful for the whole theory of development.

DEFINITION OF REGRESSION

The concept of regression was brought to the fore by Freud and has been widely used in psychoanalytical literature. Freud saw from the beginning how important the problem of regression is for the theory of development. His theory of the stages of libidinal organization which marks the development of a person is to a large degree based on his observations of regression in psychopathology (10, p. 285-299).

The term regression in psychoanalysis refers to a great variety of symptoms. Freud himself uses the term regression mainly to describe "a return to the first objects invested with libido, which we know to be incestuous in character, and a return of the whole sexual organization to earlier stages" (p. 287). In addition to speaking of "regression of the libido" Freud speaks of "regression of the ego" and "object-regression" (p. 299). In other psychoanalytical and psychological literature the term regression has been used more loosely; for instance, any kind of withdrawal from reality to a fantasy-level has been called regression.

Freud himself emphasized that he used the term regression as a purely descriptive concept (p. 288) and not as a dynamic concept like repression. Nevertheless, he has brought forth certain ideas about the factors which makes for regression. According to him two main conditions for regression exist: (1) fixation of the libido to objects of a previous developmental state, and (2) difficulties in satisfying the libidinal needs at the more mature level. Frequently in the psychoanalytical literature development has been viewed as a steadily progressing libido and regression as the turning back of this flow of the libido after meeting an obstacle. A diagram by Korzybski presents this view (Figure 9). We would like to discuss this representation more in detail with the purpose of clarifying the concept of regression. The necessity of such conceptual refinement was stressed by Freud and it still seems to be needed (31).

The problems of development and of regression have their scientific place at a particular intersection of historical and dynamic problems. They point on the one hand to a unique sequence of experiences, situations, personality structures, and styles of behavior during the history of the individual. On the other hand they point to the dynamics and laws which govern the behavior in any one of these stages and the

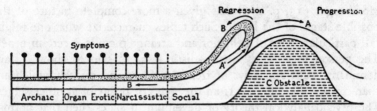

FIGURE 9. Psychoanalytical Representation of Regression. (Reprinted with the permission of the publishers from Korzybski, Alfred: *Science and Sanity: An Introduction to Non-Aristotelian Systems and General Semantics*, Lancaster, Pa.: The International Non-Aristotelian Library Publishing Co., 1933.)

transition from one stage to another. The combination of both types of questions within the problem of development or regression is entirely legitimate and necessary. However, it is important to clarify the nature of both problems and their relations.

Abraham uses the following table showing the stages of libidinal organization, stages in development of object love, and dominant point of fixation (taken from Fenichel [8, p. 379]).

Stages of Libidinal Organization	Stages of Development of Object Love	Dominant Point of Fixation in
I. Early oral (sucking)	Autoeroticism (no object) (pre-ambivalent)	Various types of schizophrenia (stupor)
II. Late oral sadistic (cannibalistic)	Narcissism; total incorporation of object	Manic-depressive
III. Early anal sadistic	Partial love with incorporation	Paranoia, paranoid
IV. Late anal sadistic	Partial love	Compulsion neurosis
V. Early genital (phallic)	Object love with exclusion of genital	Hysteria
VI. Final genital	Object love (post ambivalent)	Normality

(Stages II–V bracketed as "Ambivalent")

Homburger (15, p. 176) has given a more complete picture of the possible stages of the libido. Such tables characterize what one might call particular styles of behavior and arrange them in a certain order. The person in an early anal sadistic stage is said to show certain dominant goals, and ways of treating others and himself which are characteristically different from the styles of behavior at other stages. The psychoanalytical theory of development states then that normal development is characterized by a certain order in which styles of behavior follow each other in the life history of an individual. Sim-

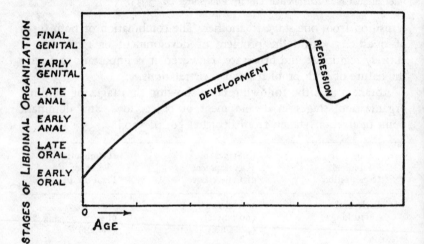

FIGURE 10.   Stages of Libidinal Organization. Schematic representation of regression by means of a system of coordinates.

ilarly the concept of regression is based on equalities or similarities between certain styles of behavior; for instance, the behavior of the paranoid is said to resemble that of the early anal sadistic stage.

If one were to represent such a life history diagrammatically, one of the coordinates of the diagram would have to represent time (age of individual). The second axis would represent the developmental stage. The actual life history, i.e., the velocity of development and the time and amount of regression, could then be indicated by a curve such as that given in Figure 10. The difference between this representation and that of the life history in Figure 9 may appear slight.

Actually the difference is methodologically rather important. In Figure 9 the libido is represented as "a turning back," like a river or, as Freud says, as a wanderer in new regions who falls back to earlier camps when he encounters obstacles. The curve representing progress and regression in Figure 10 never could "turn back" to a previous point because time never turns back, and therefore any curve representing a life history must steadily increase within the time dimension. The curve in Figure 10 connects points in an abstract system of coordinates (one of which means time) expressing relations of similarity and dissimilarity. It legitimately describes the historical sequence in the style of the behavior of the individual.[1]

However, it does not represent the concrete situation (person and environment) which determines the behavior in any one period, nor the conditions existing at the time when the regression occurs. This may suffice to make clear that Figure 10 does not refer to concrete geographical or psychological settings. The different styles of behavior existing at different times in the history of an individual cannot be treated as parts of one field of coexisting areas in which one can move about, i.e., not as a life space, because a field is a dynamic unity existing at one time.

Figure 9 would be correct if it were limited to a diagrammatic description of the type given in Figure 10. However, it represents in addition the conditions of regression at a certain moment, namely, the fact that the libido encounters an unsurmountable obstacle.

Freud approaches a field theory of regression when he states that regression is at least partly due to the inability of the libido to gain sufficient satisfaction at a more mature level. This assumption might be called a "substitute theory of regression." If one refers to the individual himself instead of his libido one can represent the situation which is said to underlie the turning back of the libido by a simple topological diagram (Figure 11). The person P tries to reach a goal $G +$ corresponding to a need which is characteristic of a certain level of maturity. This region $G +$ is at present not accessible to the individual. In other words, there exists a barrier B separating P from $G +$.

---

[1] If one uses Homburger's classification (15) of developmental stages, a system of at least three dimensions would be required because the system has to have as many coordinates as qualities are distinguished in addition to the coordinate representing time. We have to deal here with an abstract system of coordinates similar to the "phase space" in physics.

Under this condition the person turns (according to the substitute theory of regression) to another region G' which corresponds to a less mature level, because the activity G' seems to promise at least some satisfaction to the need. According to this theory regression presupposes a giving up of the attempt to overcome the barrier. Some psychoanalysts have emphasized this aspect and have called almost any kind of withdrawal from a real obstacle regression, particularly so if the person leaves the level of reality and withdraws into sickness, fantasy, or irreality. At the moment it is not important to discuss whether this theory is right or wrong. It will suffice to

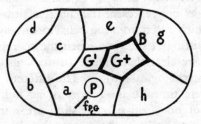

FIGURE 11.   Field Representing the Conditions of Regression (According to Freud's
Substitute Theory of Regression)

P = person; $G+$ = original goal; G' = substitute goal to which the subject regresses; B = obstacle between P and $G+$ (barrier) ; $a, b, c, \ldots$ regions of the life space; $f_{P,G}$ = force of the direction of the goal.

say that this is essentially a field theory. It is an attempt to characterize the situation at a given time and to make the topology of the life space and certain dynamic properties of its regions (attractiveness, barrier, etc.) responsible for a certain event.

In summarizing we may state: The problem of regression, like that of development, includes an historical aspect which refers to the sequence of styles of behavior in the life history, and a systematic aspect which refers to the conditions of the change occurring at a given time. Both questions are entirely legitimate and are necessarily dealt with in a psychological approach to regression. Both questions can be represented diagrammatically.

The systematic question concerning the condition of a change which occurs at a given time has to be answered partly by referring to the structure and dynamic properties of the field (life space) existing at that time. The life history can be represented by a sequence of such fields, each of which would characterize the situation at a given historical stage. However, it would destroy the meaning of the field to treat the life spaces of the newborn, of the three-, six-, and sixty-year-old person together as one dynamic unity.

When a life history is represented by one diagram we have to deal with a system of coordinates, one of which refers to time, each of the others referring to quality of the style of behavior (or the state of the person). To describe an aspect of the life history by a curve linking certain points in an abstract system of coordinates is rather common in psychology and is of course fully legitimate; any curve representing bodily growth is an example. However, it should be clearly distinguished from a field of coexisting and dynamically related facts, which represents the conditions for the change at a given time. The mixing up of historical and systematic questions, such as questions of origin and of conditions, of which Figure 9 is a typical example, has to be avoided both in diagrams and, what is more important, in thinking, if the psychology of development and regression is to make satisfactory progress.

REGRESSION AND RETROGRESSION

The question of the particular character of the substitute activity, G' (Figure 11), in cases of regression is answered in psychoanalysis by referring to the history of the individual. The character of G' is said to be determined by the kind and degree of fixation at a previous stage of development. Such a statement is logically entirely legitimate from the point of view of field theory, although it has to be specified how the present life space is affected by the fixation which happened many years ago.

This theory of the form and degree of regression touches a second conceptual aspect of the problem of regression which needs clarification.

McDougall has given a detailed account of several cases of regression from shell-shock. He describes the primitive childlike behavior of the persons and the process of recovery. McDougall expresses a certain amount of agreement with the Freudian theory but stresses two rather important points (28).

1.   He emphasizes that the regressed behavior does not need to be identical with the behavior which this individual has shown pre-

viously. Rather the regressed person shows a primitive but new kind of behavior.

2. He considers regression to be of a less "purposive" character than it appears to be in the Freudian theory.

The possibility of a new kind of behavior occurring in regression makes it necessary to distinguish two types of changes:

1. The return to a type of behavior characteristic of a previous stage of the life history of the individual. Such a change may be called "retrogression."

2. A change to a more primitive behavior, regardless of whether such behavior has actually occurred within the life history of the individual. Such a change may be called "regression."

It is frequently true that retrogression will also have the character of regression, and vice versa. However, this does not need to be the case. For instance, a child who has shown primitive behavior during a sickness will, upon recovery, return to the more mature behavior which characterized him before his sickness. One will have to call such a change a retrogression, although it cannot possibly be called a regression.

Clear distinction between retrogression and regression has become particularly important in view of recent experimental studies with animals (23, 30). These studies show that animals under certain conditions, for instance after a shock, may abandon a newly learned behavior and return to older habits. As far as we can see, none of these studies can be said to have proved that the older mode of behavior was actually more primitive than the newly learned one. Before this is done we would classify these studies as experiments in retrogression rather than in regression.

We can express the difference between the concepts regression and retrogression by the following definitions.

B^{t1}, B^{t2}, B^{t3} . . . may indicate the behavior of an individual or his state in (psychologically equivalent situations) at the time $t1$, $t2$, $t3$ . . .

Definition of Retrogression. We speak of retrogression if $B^{t2} \neq B^{t1}$ but $B^{t3} = B^{t1}$. Retrogression refers merely to differences and similarities in the time sequence without involving statements concerning "primitivity," "adaptability," etc.

Definition of Regression. We speak of regression if B^{t3} is more "primitive" than B^{t2}. This does not presuppose that $B^{t3} = B^{t1}$.

Of course one will have to discuss the definition of "primitivation" and the symptoms that can be used as its indication. It will hardly suffice to point to such vague criteria as the "less adaptive" character of behavior, particularly in view of the fact that the regression itself is frequently viewed as an attempt of the individual to adapt himself to a certain situation. The answer can be found partly in the studies in psychopathology. These suggest that there is a change from "a differentiated and pregnant pattern to a more amorphous behavior" (11, p. 31). A complicated hierarchical order within an action changes to a simple organization or to disorganization (6), from an abstract to a more concrete type of thinking, from reasoning to learning (29, 19, 29), from flexible to stereotyped behavior (19, 23). Primitivation is a change in the structure of behavior which in some respects seems to resemble the morphological dedifferentiation observable in certain primitive animals, such as under certain conditions of malnutrition (9).

Studies such as these go quite far in circumscribing more specifically what is meant by primitivation. However, they still do not seem to supply an operational definition of regression through empirically testable symptoms which is sufficiently general, and at the same time sufficiently definite, for experimental procedures. For the purpose of exploratory research one can define regression as a change of behavior from a kind typical for older normal children to that typical for younger normal children (in an equivalent psychological situation). Such an operational definition is necessarily limited to the age range before maturity, because a change from adult to senile behavior has to be regarded as regression but not as progressive development. However, within these limits it provides a definite and testable criterion for regression. Until the theory of regression is considerably more advanced it might be well to use this criterion as an operational definition.[2]

[2] One will note that this operational definition does not refer to any behavior which the individual in question has shown previously in his life history. It refers to the type of behavior which is characteristic of normal children of certain age levels.

This definition is in no sense final; it is a working definition necessitated by the current state of knowledge in the field. It has to be used with caution even within the age range up to maturity because it is at least possible that during certain periods the normal average child may actually become more primitive in one or another function. In the long run, the various developmental levels will have to be defined conceptually in terms of degree of differentiation, organization, and similar properties other than age. Eventually the age reference in the operational definition will have to be dropped entirely, and particular changes occurring under various conditions specified.

Such an operational definition evidently provides the possibility of determining the amount of regression and the level to which the person regresses. The latter can be expressed by the age level of normal children for which this behavior is typical. The amount of regression can be characterized by giving the age levels for the state of the individual before and after regression.

KINDS OF REGRESSION

Regression of Behavior and of the Person: Pseudo-Regression. A girl of two years stands before a mirror making herself small, and tries to find out how she would look if she really were small. The situation in which this behavior occurs is as follows. The girl has a baby brother of whom she is envious. She is obviously trying to make up her mind whether she should try to grow up or grow smaller. Numerous cases exist in which children in such a situation try to imitate their younger siblings and begin to show babylike behavior in their table manners, in their way of crying, or in being naughty, etc.

Is this regression? If we refer only to the face value of this behavior we may have to speak of regression in line with the definition given above. The style of behavior has been lowered from a pattern typical of a three-year level to that of a two-year level. Nevertheless, one hesitates to identify such a change with regression resulting from sickness or acute emotional tension. The girl, showing the behavior of her younger brother, may actually "play a role," although that of a younger child. This role may be played with the skill of a good actor, although not as a play but in earnest. It would probably be fairer to call it refined rather than primitive behavior.

If the child keeps up such a role for a long time he actually may become primitive. He may lose, at least to some degree, his ability to act more mature. Until such a state is reached we may speak of a "pseudo-regression of behavior" without a "regression of the person." In other words, regression of behavior may or may not be a symptom of regression of the person.

Similarities of behavior are not necessarily indications of similarities of the underlying state of the person. That the same state of the person can manifest itself in rather different symptoms has been shown in detail in regard to anger (7) and holds for all fields of psychology.

It follows from the basic formula that the behavior *(B)* is a function of the person *(P)* and the environment *(E)*, i.e., $B = F (P, E)$. This makes it necessary to distinguish the directly observable "symptoms" *(B)* from the underlying "state of the person" *(P)* which methodologically always have the position of a "construct."

In connection with developmental states it means that the maturity level of a person may actually be higher or lower than that indicated by his behavior. The girl mentioned above is an example of the former case. An example of the latter is found in the child who sticks to certain imposed rules in a way which is typical of a greater "maturity of aspiration" and shows in consequence in many respects a more adultlike behavior as a result of firm pressure from the outside; he will behave on a lower maturity level as soon as the pressure is released.

The distinction between regression of behavior and regression of the person is closely related to the necessity of referring to comparable situations if one wishes to use differences of behavior as symptoms for differences in the state of the person.

Temporary and Permanent Regression. Regression may last only a few minutes, for instance in a case of a slight shock, disturbance, or emotion, or it may last many years, for example as a result of sickness. Regression may be a slow sinking or a sudden drop. The individual may stay regressed, he may slowly or suddenly regain his previous level, or he may return to an intermediate level.

Situational and Established Regression. Under emotional stress both the behavior and the person may regress to a more primitive level. In such circumstances the individual is actually unable to behave on a higher level. Yet even in this case the primitivation may be confined to a particular situation, such as "being in prison" or "being severely frustrated." As soon as the person leaves this particular situation he may regain his previous level. In other cases the person may regress in such a way that he will not show his previous higher level even in a most favorable situation. The former case we will call *situational* regression, the latter *established* regression. There exist, of course, transitional cases.

It is important not to identify this difference with the distinction between temporary and permanent regression. A permanent regression may result from the fact that the individual is kept permanently within one specific situation; a regression may be relatively permanent and still situational. The terms situational and established regression do not refer to duration. In case of situational regression the developmental level fluctuates greatly with changes in the situation, whereas the established regression is more independent of such changes. This distinction is of practical importance for the diagnosis and treatment of cases, such as in social-psychiatric work with children. It is clear that experiments with human beings have to be limited to creating situational regression.

Partial and General Regression. Regression may affect more or less restricted areas of a person. For example, regression may affect only the motor functions, or the emotional life of a person, without much change in his intellectual capacities. Psychopathology gives many examples of different patterns of regression of specific areas of the person as well as general deterioration. Of course any regression of specific areas does, to some degree, affect all behavior of the individual.

Main Differences in Behavior at Different Age Levels

In order to understand the situations which lead to regression, it will be necessary to develop definite concepts which characterize the behavior and state of the person corresponding to different developmental levels. This should be done in such a way as to permit a logical derivation of statements in regard to forces which change a person from the state corresponding to a higher level to the state corresponding to a lower level. If this task were fulfilled one would have a full theory of regression which would permit predictions about the amount and the kind of regression of a given person under various circumstances.

It is evident that such a goal can be reached only very gradually. We will try first of all to give a survey of what one might call the main aspects of behavior differences at the different age levels. We will then proceed to discuss certain kinds of contructs which may make possible the conceptual representation of the state of the person in such a way that at least some of the behavior differences may be understood, and some conditions of regression derived.

The differences of behavior at different age levels may be classed under the following five aspects: variety of behavior, organization of behavior, extension of areas of activity, interdependence of behavior, and degree of realism.

VARIETY OF BEHAVIOR

One speaks of the increasing variety of the behavior of a child as he grows older. (This holds true despite the fact that certain types of behavior drop out during development.) The increasing variety of behavior is noticeable in many ways.

a. The *behavior* of the newborn is more or less confined to sleeping, crying, drinking, eliminating, and lying awake. The behavior of the growing child includes increasingly more types of activities: talking, walking, reading, etc. The undifferentiated behavior becomes differentiated by a branching out into a variety of species of action. For instance, an approach to a goal is at first always a direct approach. Later on, indirect ways of approach arise by means of roundabout routes and the use of physical and social tools. In addition, the direct approach shows more variety, for instance, in the degree of activeness, the amount of real or gesturelike behavior, etc. The indirect approach becomes differentiated in regard to the kind of physical and social tools used. Similar differentiation can be observed in practically all fields of activities (16). The language of the individual increases in regard to the number of words used (27, 34), the types of words used, and the grammatical construction. If one regards the activities as possibilities that the individual has, one speaks of an increase in the variety of "skills."

b. A similarly increasing variety can be observed in the field of *emotions* (3, 12). Again, primitive undifferentiated emotional expressions branch out into distinct varieties. At first joy may be difficult to distinguish from a grimace caused by stomach trouble. Later, smiling is something rather distinct in character and unmistakable. Step by step more type of smiles arise, such as friendly open smiles, happy smiles, arrogant smiles, defiant smiles and so on.

c. A similar differentiation can be observed in the field of *needs,* interests, and goals. Step by step the few needs of the infant branch out into a greater variety. This increase is very noticeable during childhood. In addition, there occurs a shift in the dominance of certain needs.

d. The process of differentiation into a great variety is particularly clear in the field of *knowledge.* The comparatively undifferentiated psychological world of the infant widens and structures itself in a process which can be described as differentiation (20). The change in knowledge includes many cognitive changes which are restructurization rather than an increase in varieties of areas. However, one of the predominant character-istics of the change of knowledge with age, both in regard to learning and insight, is its increased differentiation, its greater richness.

e. The *social behavior* and the social relations show an increasing variety. The number of persons with whom social relations exist increases as do the types of social interrelations. The relations to different individuals become more and more articulated as to specific kinds of friendship, de-pendence or leadership. A clearer distinction is made between superficial and deeper attachments.

On the whole then, we may say that the variety of behavior increases during childhood with normal development. This may be expressed by the formula:

$$(1) \quad var \ (B^{Ch}) < var \ (B^{Ad}),$$

where *var* means variety; B^{Ch} behavior of the child; B^{Ad} behavior of the adult. To simplify our formulistic representation and to indicate that we merely wish to characterize the main trends of development, we will refer in the formulas to two levels only, indicated as *Ch* and *Ad*.

ORGANIZATION OF BEHAVIOR

If development in behavior led merely to an increased variety of behavior, one might expect the conduct of an individual to become more and more chaotic or at least more and more unconnected. This is obviously not the case. Parallel to the increasing differentiation goes a development according to which an increasingly greater variety of parts is included in *one* unit of action. There are a number of ways in which different actions may become parts of a larger unit of action. Frequently the unity of a behavior which is carried through a certain period of time and containing a number of more or less different subparts is characterized by one leading idea which guides and controls the parts. This leading idea may be a governing purpose or the reaching of a goal. The subparts may be certain preparations, followed by actions which carry the individual to the goal, and finally certain consummatory actions. In this case, some of the subparts of the action have the relation of means to an end. The guiding purpose may be a precise goal, such as scaling a fence, or a more general idea, like playing house. In other cases, for instance in many recreational or play activities such as reading a book, the various parts have mainly the character of coordinated subunits.

In connection with all types of unity in behavior that are due to the guidance or steering of a governing purpose or a leading idea we will speak of the organization of behavior.[3] In these cases one can distinguish at least two levels: the guiding idea and the guided manipulation.

In development one can distinguish three aspects of the organization of behavior.

Complexity of Units. One can say that the maximum number of subparts and the variety of subparts contained in one unit of action increases with development. Instead of handling two building blocks at a time the child as he grows older uses an increasingly greater number of building blocks in making a primitive pattern. One symptom of the greater complexity is the increasing maximum duration of continuous play with increasing age (5).

Hierarchical Organization. Aside from the increasing number of manipulations which may be kept together by a guiding idea, the type of organization itself seems to become more and more complicated: a goal which steers a series of manipulations may become the subgoal of a more inclusive goal. The subgoals seem to be governed by the higher goals in much the same fashion as the actual manipulation is governed by the subgoal. For instance, the main idea of playing house may contain a number of subideas; father goes to work, mother dresses the children, does the washing, etc.,—all established in a certain sequence guided by the main idea. A subgoal such as dressing the children may contain dressing Mary and dressing George. In other words, a more inclusive unit of behavior may contain a number of hierarchical levels, each of which is ruled by the next higher level. Referring to the number of levels we will speak

[3] Frequently the term "integration" is used in this connection. We prefer to speak of organization because mathematically integration is the reverse of differentiation. However, it has been rightly emphasized that psychological "integration" does not mean dedifferentiation. It may be better to replace this term by the term "organization." This use of the term "organization" seems to be well in line with its use in embryology and also in sociology.

of different "degrees of hierarchical organization" of a behavioral unit.

The maximal degree of hierarchical organization seems to increase with age, i.e., one unit can contain more levels in older than in younger children.

Complicated Organization. An activity guided by one idea may not be carried through as a continuous action but may be interrupted by other activities and later taken up again. To carry through successfully an activity which is to be repeatedly interrupted obviously requires a relatively complicated organization. A second kind of complicated organization exists in overlapping behavior, when simultaneously two or more activities which are guided by practically unrelated ideas are carried on. An example of such behavior is secondary play, i.e., play which occurs simultaneously with other activities, such as a conversation with a second person about matters unrelated to the play. Closely related to this is the organization of behavior which has two levels of meaning. Lying, joking, showing overfriendly behavior out of hate or similar "perverted expressions" are actions on two levels which may be said to be more or less contradictory. The more overt level frequently serves to cover up the contrary meaning of the deeper level, and indicates a somewhat complicated organization of the action. Obviously, the problem of self-control is closely related to this type of organization.

Lies and jokes are rather early achievements. However, the lying of the two-year-old child is relatively overt and primitive. The ability to exhibit this type of complicated organization seems to increase with age.

It cannot be said that every action of an older child is more highly organized than every action of a younger child. The behavior of an older child frequently includes units which are less complicated than those of younger children. However, the maximum degree of organization of behavioral units seems to increase with age; in other words, we can say:

$$(2) \qquad hier\ org^{max}\ (B^{Ch}) < hier\ org^{max}\ (B^{Ad})$$

Hier org^{max} stands for the maximum degree of hierarchical organization; B^{Ch} for the behavioral unit of a child; B^{Ad} for the behavioral unit of an adult.

EXTENSION OF THE AREA OF ACTIVITIES AND INTERESTS

The psychological world which affects the behavior of the child seems to extend with age both in regard to the areas and the time span which are taken into consideration.

Scope of the Field. The three-month-old child living in a crib knows few geographical areas around him and the areas of possible activities are comparatively few. The child of one year is familiar with a much wider geographical area and a wider field of activities. He is likely to know a number of rooms in the house, the garden, and certain streets. Some of these areas are accessible to him, others are not. He may be able to crawl under the table or the couch, but he may not be able to climb on a certain chair although he would like to do so. Such areas of his life space lie outside his space of free movement (25), which is limited partly by his own ability and partly by social taboos. The child may, for instance, like to tear books. In this case tearing books is an area in his life space and may influence his behavior considerably. This is true even though the "no" of the mother keeps the child outside this area of activity. The discrepancy between the attractive areas of the life space and the space of free movement is one of the dominant factors determining the level of aspiration of an individual.

During development, both the space of free movement and the life space usually increase. The area of activity accessible to the growing child is extended because his own ability increases, and it is probable that social restrictions are removed more rapidly than they are erected as age increases, at least beyond the infant period. Certain events, like the arrival of a younger sibling, may well reverse the balance of change at a given period. However, even at times when the space of free movement is not increasing, the life space usually extends with age into new, partly accessible, partly inaccessible regions. The widening of the scope of the life space occurs sometimes gradually, sometimes in rather abrupt steps. The latter is characteristic for so-called crises in development. This process continues well into adulthood (5).

Time Perspective. A similar extension of the life space during development occurs in what may be called the "psychological time dimension." During development the scope of the psychological time dimension of the life space increases from hours to days, months, and years. In other words, the young child lives in the immediate present; with increasing age an increasingly more distant psychological past and future affect present behavior.

It may be possible to interpret the increasing extension of the life space merely as the combination of an increasing variety of behavior and of different types of organization of behavior. However, we prefer to express this change in a separate statement:

$$(3) \ L \ Sp \ (Ch) < L \ Sp \ (Ad)$$

where $L \ Sp \ (Ch)$ means the size of the life space of the child; and $L \ Sp \ (Ad)$ the size of the life space of the adult.

Also, for the space of free movement (i.e., the totality of accessible regions within the life space) it holds on the average that:

$$(4) \ SFM \ (Ch) < SFM \ (Ad)$$

where $SFM \ (Ch)$ means the size of the space of free movement of the child and $SFM \ (Ad)$ the size of the space of free movement of the adult. However, the space of free movement may be narrowed down during certain developmental periods, such as when a child is subjected to a rigid regime.

INTERDEPENDENCE OF BEHAVIOR

The statement that the individual becomes increasingly differentiated can have two meanings. It can mean that the variety of behavior increases, i.e., that the totality of behavior observable at a given age becomes less homogeneous. In this case, the term differentiation refers to relations of similarity and dissimilarity; it means "specialization" or "individualization." On the other hand, the term dfferentiation can refer to relations of dependence and independence between parts of a dynamic whole. In this case increasing differentiation means that the number of parts of the person which can function relatively independently increases; i.e., that their degree of independence increases.[4] As we have already discussed the

[4] In morphology the term "differentiation" is limited to cases where the parts become not only more independent but also different from each other. It would be advisable to use two different terms for the two concepts of differentiation. We shall speak of "specification" or "individualization" in case of increasing dissimilarity, of "differentiation" in referring to increasing independence.

increasing variety of behavior, we will now turn to the questions of dependence and independence.

The statement that the child shows a greater unity than the adult has been emphasized in psychology relatively recently. Previously, it was customary to consider that the adult exhibited the greater unity, because in childhood different needs and different areas of activity may develop more or less independently. The adult on the other hand is more likely to have these different areas of activity integrated.

Today it is generally acknowledged that the development of the child includes an increase both in differentiation and in integration. Development seems to increase the number of relatively independent subparts of the person and their degree of independence, thus decreasing the degree of unity of the individual. On the other hand, development involves integration which increases the unity of the person. As both of these processes advance at the same time, obviously, integration cannot be a process which is actually the reversal of differentiation. It does not eliminate differentiation, and it is not dedifferentiation. But, integration presupposes differentiation. To avoid misunderstandings we prefer, therefore, to use the term "organization" instead of integration.

The kind of functional interdependence which underlies the degree of organizational unity of a person must be different obviously from that kind of interdependence which underlies the degree of his differentiation. Concepts dealing with interdependence are on the level of constructs, and any attempt to determine more precisely the different types of interdependence presupposes a discussion of a number of constructs. We will approach them after surveying the empirical data referring to the individual's increasing differentiation on the one hand and his increasing organization on the other.

Decrease of Simple Interdependence. We start with those facts which indicate the increasing differentiation of the person.

Differentiation of the Motor Systems. The so-called mass action of the fetus and infant is a characteristic example of the undifferentiated reaction of the individual with his whole body rather than with certain limbs. The development of the child is characterized by an increasing differentiation of the motor functions, indicated by the increasing extent to which the different parts exhibit relatively independent actions. The development of grasping for example (13) starts with a tendency to approach the object simultaneously with eyes, legs, arms, mouth. Gradually, the other activities drop out and the child comes to use first his arms and his hands as relatively undifferentiated units and finally his fingers independently. It is probably fair to say that a young child shows a tendency to do everything with his whole body to a greater degree than an older child. The gradual decrease of the so-called involuntary accompanying movements is but another expression of the same fact. In a child the increase of tonus in one part of the muscular system is more likely to be accompanied by tonus in other parts than in an adult. In other words, the motor system shows an increasing differentiation as regards muscular tension.

Interdependence of Inner Personal and Motor Regions. A similar decrease in degree of interdependence can be observed in the way needs or emotions express themselves. The amount of muscular activity in the infant is a direct function of its hunger (17). It is probably true that for older children and adults a similar relation exists between hunger and amount of restlessness, fighting and other emotional expressions. However, this dependence is less direct. The satiated infant is whole-heartedly satiated; he is drunk; his body expresses his state in every aspect, and he is helpless against its expression. The older child is more self-controlled. His motor system does not show as openly his needs and his emotional state. In other words, with increasing age there is less direct interdependence between the motor systems and the "inner personal systems," i.e., those regions of the person which are related to his needs.

The decrease in direct dependence between these two sections of the person is apparent, also, in the effect which the state of the motor system has upon the inner personal region. With the younger child the mood and practically every sector of behavior depends more directly on bodily state, e.g., fatigue, hunger, upset stomach, etc., than with older children.

Interdependence Within the Inner Personal Regions. Certain facts indicate that the various needs may become less directly interdependent also. The cosatiation of one need through the satiation of another decreases with age (22). Experiments on substitute value (33) indicate that the satisfaction of one need is more likely to bring about a general state of satisfaction in younger than in older children. For older individuals the state of tension of the various needs is independent to a higher degree.

Interdependence of Person and Environment. The very young child is helplessly exposed to the stimuli of the momentary situation. The older child can more easily place himself above the situation. This difference has been found to be essential for the conduct of infants and older children in a conflict situation. It is partly the result of the change in time perspective, but it indicates also a greater "functional distance" between the "ego" and the psychological environment. Spencer (35, p. 316) and more recently Piaget (32, p. 360) have discussed this greater remoteness or greater "distance" between the central ego of the person and the environment (see also 1, 14). The growing child becomes differentiated into an increasing number of more central and more peripheral layers. It is also true that the "superficial" aspects of things and events in the perceived environment become increasingly distinguished from their "deeper" meaning.

The greater distance between the central layer of the ego and the psychological environment involves a greater independence, or at least a less direct interdependence between these areas of the life space, namely the psychological person and the psychological environment. It makes the child less helpless against the immediate influences of his environment, and makes the perceived environment less dependent on the mood and the momentary state of the needs of the child. We know that the adult will perceive a given physical setting as a different psychological environment if his needs, fears, wishes, etc., change. However, the dependence of the perceived environment on the needs and fears of the individual is probably more complete and more immediate in the child. Fantasy and reality, lies and truths, seem to be more interwoven in the child than in the adult and more so in a younger child than in an older one.

On the whole, then, there are a great number of facts which indicate that development brings about a differentiation within the life space of an individual so that certain parts of it become less directly interdependent. This decrease in direct interdependence is observable within the motor system of the individual, within his inner personal regions, in the relation between the inner personal and the motor regions, and finally in the relation between the inner psychological regions and the psychological environment. We may express this observation by the formula:

$$(5) \quad si \ uni \ (Ch) > si \ uni \ (Ad),$$

where *si uni (Ch)* means the degree of unity of the child as indicated by the degree of simple interdependence of certain subparts of the child's life space and *si uni (Ad)* means the degree of unity of the adult.

In addition we can state

$$(5a) \quad dif \ (Ch) < dif \ (Ad),$$

where *dif (Ch)* and *dif (Ad)* mean the degree of differentiation of the child and of the adult (see Appendix).

Change in Organizational Interdependence. The increasing differentiation of the life space into relatively separated subparts is somehow counteracted by the increasing organization of the life space. There is a wealth of material which indicates this increasing organization with age. It refers to the increasing scope of coexisting parts of the life space which can be organized as a unit and the increasingly larger sequence of actions which are unitedly governed. The latter point has already been discussed.

Organization of the Motor Systems. Psychologists have collected a great number of data which reveal the increasing organization of the motor functions in development. For example, the child's postural control of his head, and his learning to sit and to stand; the stages of the development of locomotion, such as creeping, walking, climbing, running, jumping; the development of speech; and the control of elimination can all be viewed as examples of the increasing organization of the various parts of the motor system for unified action. The organization of different muscular systems into constellations and of the constellations into sequences of constellations both show an increase to more and more complicated types. The precision of motor organization is indicated by the increasing accuracy of voluntary movements (36, 4). Talking presupposes the organization of highly complicated sequences of muscular constellations.

Organization of the Motor System by the Inner Personal Regions. The relation between the inner personal and the motor regions acquires increasingly the character of an organization in which the motor functions take the place of a tool. The following example illustrates this change. A young child who wishes to perform a manipulation, such as threading a needle, is likely to get muscularly more tense the more eager he is to succeed, even if the task is of such a nature that the muscles have to be relatively relaxed if the task is to be carried out. In other words, in a young child a greater inner personal need tension is likely to lead to a higher muscular tonus. This is in line with the direct, simple interdependence of the inner personal and motor systems discussed previously.

If the unorganized "spreading of tension" from the inner personal to the motor regions becomes too dominant, it necessarily blocks any orderly purposeful muscular action. In the "organized" dependence of the motor functions upon the inner personal regions there is not a general increase in tonus, but rather sequences of relaxation and tonus in certain groups of muscles occur and are steered in such a way that the pattern of action and the intensity of tonus is adequate for reaching the objective in the given setting. This presupposes that the pattern and intensity of muscular tonus is independent of the intensity of the tension corresponding to the need behind the action. For threading a needle, the muscles have to be relatively relaxed, even if the person is most eager to hurry; for carrying a heavy load the tonus has to be high, even if the need for doing this work is small. With increasing age the organized interdependence seems to gain in strength relative to the simple interdependence; and the position of the motoric system as a tool becomes more firmly established.

Organization of the Inner Personal Regions. In discussing the increasing differentiation of inner personal regions, we dealt with the simple interdependence of needs, i.e., the spreading of tension. The effect of the tension within one need system upon the general tension level of the need systems of an individual (2) can be understood as such a spreading. The process of cosatiation of one need by the satiation of another need (18) seems also to have the characteristics of spreading.

It seems, however, that a second type of interdependence between inner personal regions exists which has the characteristics of an organizational interdependence: one system may hold the position of a governing need, the other the position of a governed need. An individual may for instance show a great desire to join an art school. This need may be derived from and be governed by the need for doing art work. The need to enter the art school may in turn create and regulate a need for fulfilling certain requirements, such as preparing for an entrance examination; and this, in turn, the *quasi* need to buy a certain book in a certain store. In other words, there may exist a hierarchy of needs so that a more dominant need rules one or more subordinate needs which in turn dominate subordinate needs at the next lower level.

Frequently the dominated need is set up by a combination of more than one governing need. For instance, the need to enter art school may have its historical source in the need for doing art work and in the additional need to earn a living for which the school work seems to be a preparation. The derived need to enter art school may become more or less autonomous (1), that is, more or less independent of the needs to which it can be traced. We wish to stress here that the attempt to secure the satisfaction of one or more source needs in a given environmental situation may give rise to a dependent need. This type of dependence does not involve spreading of tension, but here one need is governed by another, one need is a tool of another. In other words, this is an organizational dependence similar to that between the motor systems and the inner personal regions. The hierarchy of organizational interdependence between needs seems to increase during development.

Organization of the Psychological Environment. The increasing organization of the psychological environment by the individual does not need much illustration. Simple examples of such an organization are the use of some parts of the environment as tools. The growing child becomes increasingly more able to organize parts of his physical and of his social environment in this way, and this organization becomes increasingly complicated, particularly in the social field. The approach to a goal by way of roundabout routes, instead of by direct action, also exemplifies the ability of the child to organize intelligently his actions in relation to an increasingly greater scope of his psychological environment. Such organization presupposes a decrease in the simple dependence of the person upon his immediate surroundings. For satisfying his needs the infant depends mainly on the circumstances which arise. Actually he would die if these occasions were not provided by a grownup. The growing child tries increasingly to organize his environment so that the satisfaction of his needs is not left to chance. In other words, the life space containing the psychological person and his environment tends to become a more highly organized unit. Such an organization is frequently facilitated by certain ideologies and rationalizations which bring certain otherwise contradictory facts and needs into psychological harmony with each other.

On the whole, then, the hierarchical organization of the life space increases with age. Such an increase can be observed within the motor system, within the inner psychological regions, in the relation of the motor to the inner psychological regions, and in the relation of the psychological environment to the inner personal regions. We can express this change through the formula:

$$(6) \quad hier\ org\ (Ch) < hier\ org\ (Ad)$$

where *hier org (Ch)* means the degree of hierarchical organization of parts of the child's life space, and *(Ad)* refers to the life space of the adult. Formula (6) is closely related to (2). The latter refers to the hierarchical organization of the single unit of behavior, the former to the hierarchical organization of the individual as a whole.

That the number of hierarchical strata increases during development does not necessarily mean a steady increase in the unity of the person. The older child does not always show a more harmonious

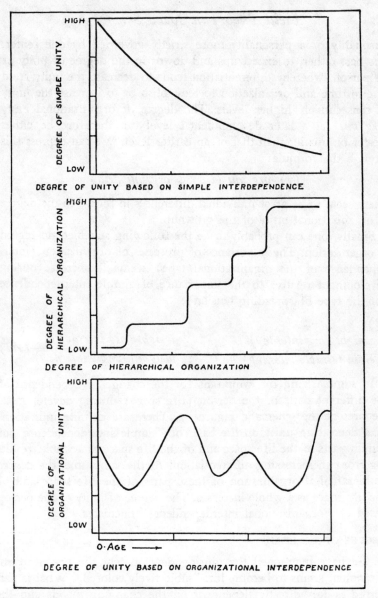

FIGURE 12. Schematic Representation of Certain Changes during Development
The degree of unity based on simple interdependence decreases with age; the degree of hierarchical organization increases stepwise; the degree of organizational unity varies.

personality or a personality more strictly governed by one center. One has, rather, to expect ups and downs in the degree of unity of the person, whereby differentiation tends to decrease the unity from time to time and organization to reestablish or to increase the unity on consecutively higher levels. The degree of organizational unity *(org uni)* at a later developmental level can therefore be either greater or smaller than that of an earlier level. We can express this through the formula:

$$(7)\ \ org\ uni\ (Ch) \lessgtr org\ uni\ (Ad)$$

There seem to be great individual differences in regard to the degree of organizational unity of the grownup.

Finally, one can probably make the following statement in regard to organization. The importance of processes of organization (interdependence of the organizational type) seems to increase during development relative to the importance of simple interdependence (of the type of spreading tension):

$$(8)$$

$$\frac{weight\ (org\ interdep)}{weight\ (simple\ interdep)}\ (Ch) < \frac{weight\ (org\ interdep)}{weight\ (simple\ interdep)}(Ad)$$

In summarizing the symptoms for the change of dependence of the different parts of the person (life space) during development, we present the schematic Figure 12. There are definite indications of a decreasing unity on the basis of "simple interdependence" of certain parts of the life space and of the life space as a whole, resulting from an increasing differentiation. At the same time, the degree of hierarchical organization of these parts of the life space and of the life space as a whole increases. The degree of unity of the person based on "organizational interdependence" fluctuates.

DEGREE OF REALISM

We have mentioned that during development the perceived environment seems to become less "subjectively colored." What is perceived is less directly dependent on the changing moods and the needs of the individual. This increasing realism of perception is particularly noticeable in the perception of social relations. In other words, reality and fantasy are more clearly distinguished. One might view this development merely as an expression of the increased differentiation of the life space, the increasing "distance" between the ego and the environment, and the increasing hierarchical organization. However, we probably have to deal here with a somewhat different dimension of change, namely, an increasing crystallization of an objective world within the life space and an increasing tendency to be realistic. The world of an insane person may be as highly differentiated and organized as that of a normal person but may lack the realism of the latter.

Piaget (32) has discussed in detail the growing realism of the child's world as shown in his various stages of thinking. A somewhat parallel process in the field of action shows one of the outstanding differences between a child's and an adult's behavior to be that the child does not "economize" his action to the same degree. To be efficient, striving to obtain a maximum result with a minimum effort, is an attitude typical of the older individual. We have to deal here with a specific organization in reference to the properties of the objective world.

One can express this change by the formula:

$$(9) \quad real\ (Ch) < real\ (Ad)$$

where *real (Ch)* means the degree of realism of the child and *real (Ad)* the degree of realism of the adult. However, we are aware that children are frequently more realistic than adults in some respects; for instance, they may be less blinded by ideologies. The statement (9) therefore is made very tentatively, with the intention mainly of pointing to an important aspect of development.

As main differences in the behavior of the child of different age levels, we have mentioned changes in the variety of behavior, in the organization of behavior, in the extension of the life space, in the unity of the person, and in the degree of realism. We do not, however, mean to suggest that these are the only behavioral changes typical of development.

Behavioral Aspects of Regression

We have defined regression as a change in a direction opposite to the changes characteristic of development. It follows that changes which are the reverse of those we have enumerated as typical of development should be typical of regression. One can ask whether this conclusion from our definition of regression and description of development is in line with the actual use of the term regression. We will see that this is the case in most, although not in all, instances.

1. If the *variety* of a person's behavior or the richness of his actions decreases considerably, one speaks of primitivation in the meaning of simplification.

2. A decrease in the degree of *organization of a behavioral unit* may mean either a decrease in the number of hierarchial levels or a disorganization. In the latter case, the parts of the action may be contradictory. In both cases the breakdown of the organization is likely to be viewed as a primitivation, as regression of behavior.

3. The same holds true for a *dedifferentiation and for a decrease of organization of the person,* i.e., those factors which are related to the unity of the person. A decrease in organization of the person, or a change from a unity based on organization toward a unity on simple interdependence (spreading of tension), is most common in those cases where one speaks about primitivation of the person. They are typical of the temporary regression observed in strong emotionality and most of the psychopathological cases of regression.

4. The decrease in the extension of the *area of activities and interest* seems to be characteristic of those cases of regression which come up, for instance, as a result of long unemployment. The unemployed man and even his children have been observed to narrow their field of activities far more than economic necessities require. Their time perspective seems to shrink so that the behavior of the person is more dependent upon the immediate situation. The shrinkage of the fantasy life seems to indicate a contraction in the reality-irreality dimension of the life space. Such a change of the life space, opposite to the extension during development, certainly represents a primitivation and regression.

We have mentioned that not only the life space as a whole, but also that part of the life space which is called the *space of free movement* usually increases during development. The space of free movement might narrow down without immediate change in the extension of the life space. This may happen when a person falls sick, or is placed in prison, or when a new sibling arrives. Such a change in the proportion of the accessible to the inaccessible areas in the life space is commonly called restriction but not regression. It might be appropriate to speak of regression only in those cases where the scope of the life space as a whole decreases. We have mentioned that this frequently happens if a decisive diminishing of the space of free movement is established for a sufficiently long time.

5. The outstanding example of a *decreasing realism* is the shift from sanity to insanity. A temporary and comparatively slight change in this direction is the "blindness" to reality, typical of high degrees of emotion. Usually, also, the "economy of action" breaks down in an emotional situation: the individual "explodes" without much concern for the efficiency and adequacy of his behavior as a means to an end.

Such decrease in realism is frequently called primitivation. Certain authors (37) seem to regard a "withdrawal from reality" as the most outstanding characteristic of regression. However, an older child may well develop elaborate fantasies without this being a symptom of primitivation. On the contrary, the older child usually has a more developed fantasy life than the younger one. Thus, a more elaborate fantasy life has generally to be considered as a symptom of differentiation, rather than of primitivity.

It seems, therefore, necessary to consider carefully the circumstances of unrealistic behavior before it is evaluated as a symptom of regression. Maybe what counts is not the actual degree of realism of behavior but the inability to be more realistic. That would mean that instead of formula (9) the following formula applies:

$$(9a)\ real^{max}\ (Ch) < real^{max}\ (Ad)$$

where $real^{max}\ (Ch)$ indicates the maximum degree of realism which the child is able to show, and this should be considered the basis for judgments of the developmental level.

The different aspects of regression, such as the decrease in variety of behavior and in organization of behavioral units, change in unity of the person, shrinking of the life space, and decreasing realism, are not linked rigidly so that a certain amount of regression in one aspect always leads to a definite amount of regression in every other aspect. The various patterns of regression observable in emotion, bodily and mental diseases, imprisonment, or senility strongly indicate that the different aspects of regression are, to a certain degree, independent of each other. On the other hand, there seems to exist some degree of interdependence so that an individual who is regressed below a certain level in one respect cannot keep his previous developmental level in regard to the other aspects.

The Representation of Developmental Levels by Means of Scientific Constructs

We have discussed some of the main behavioral properties of developmental levels. To be able to predict regression, or set forth a scientific theory of regression, one will have to characterize the different developmental levels of a person in such a way that the conditions of regression can be logically derived. Such a scientific representation of different developmental stages should also make understandable the manner in which the various characteristics of a given stage, such as variety and organization of behavior, unity of the life space, etc., are interrelated.

The psychological constructs which may be useful for such a task do not need to be invented *de nouveau*. A number of concepts (for example, differentiation) are used by practically everyone working in this field. What is needed, above all, is a conceptual clarification of these constructs. As many of these conceptual problems are highly technical in nature, the discussion of details is placed in the Appendix.

If the conceptual representation of developmental stages is to facilitate the derivation of the conditions of regression, it will have to be done in terms which include person and environment; in other words, in terms of a field theory.

THE DEGREE OF DIFFERENTIATION OF A DYNAMIC WHOLE

We will begin with the concept of differentiation. As mentioned above, the term differentiation refers either to the variety of behavior or to a dynamic construct, namely, to the degree of differentiation of the person, for which the variety of behavior is commonly said to be a symptom. We will have to consider whether this construct, i.e., this state of the person, can be represented in a conceptually more precise form.

General Characteristics of the Concept of Differentiation. Differentiation Refers to the Number of Parts of a Whole. It expresses a certain characteristic of a dynamic whole, i.e., it refers to the number of relatively separated or distinguishable parts contained in a definite whole and, perhaps, to the degree of separation of these parts. The mitosis of the egg into two, four, and eight cells, or the latter differentiation of the embryo into ectoderm, mesoderm, and endoderm, are simple examples of a differentiation which can be determined morphologically.

Differentiation Based on Independence of Parts. Unfortunately, the psychological degree of differentiation of a person cannot be determined morphologically. In psychology, the distinction of parts within the person will have to be done on the basis of a functional separation of these parts.

How, on the basis of functional independence, a part may be defined within a whole, and how the number of such parts contained in a whole may be determined so that one can speak of a definite degree of differentiation of a whole, is the task which confronts us.

Differentiation as Related to Simple Interdependence Rather than to Organizational Interdependence. The degree of functional differentiation which is to be attributed to a given whole depends upon the type and degree of independence which is being considered.

We will distinguish here but two types of interdependence of parts in a whole (see Appendix).

1. One type of dependence, which has been called *simple dependence,* has the following characteristics. First, it is based on a process which has the character of "spreading" from one part to neighboring regions according to proximity. Second, the change of the dependent part usually occurs in the direction of equalizing its state and the state of the influencing part. For instance, spreading of tension means that neighboring parts tend to change so that a state of equal tension is approached in all parts. Third, the dependence of part *a* on part *b* is essentially of the same type (although not necessarily of the same degree) as the dependence of part *b* on part *a*.

2. The dependence which has been called *organizational interdependence* shows rather different characteristics. First, it is a type of dependence between *a* and *b* similar to that between leader and led, or between someone using a tool and the tool. In such a case, the way *a* depends upon *b* is obviously rather different from the way *b* depends on *a*. Second, the organizational dependence usually does not work from neighbor to neighbor like the spreading of tension. It is a selective process: sometimes one part, sometimes another part of the system is used as a tool in a specific way. For instance, the same need may produce an organized activity in different parts of the muscular system. Third, the kind of change resulting from the organized interdependence of *a* and *b* usually does not tend

to equalize the state of *a* and *b*. The subordinate part *b* (i.e., the part which is led, the tool) changes in a way which helps *a* (the leading part) to reach its objective, but it does not lead to greater final equality between the two.

When we speak of the degree of differentiation of the person, we will refer only to the first type of dependence, i.e., the one based on simple interdependence.[5]

Determining the Number of Cells in a Dynamic Whole. Definition of the Degree of Independence of Two Regions. Two regions *a* and *b* are neither completely dependent nor independent. The question of independence, particularly of parts within a whole, is a question of degree. It is possible to define the degree of independence of region *a* from region *b* *(indep [a, b])* by referring to the amount to which the state of *b* can be changed without affecting the state of *a* (see Appendix). From this one can proceed to a definition of the degree of independence of one region from its immediate surroundings.

Differentiation Presupposes Natural Parts (Cells) Within a Whole. Within a limited homogeneous whole, e.g., a liquid in a container, one can designate arbitrarily two areas, *a* and *b*, which may be independent to a considerable degree. Nevertheless, the whole would not be called differentiated if there were no distinct natural parts. Such parts can be defined as regions with a high degree of interdependence of the subregions within one part, but a distinctly lesser degree of interdependence between the subregions of different parts.

In other words, the concept of a differentiated whole presupposes the existence of natural parts within a whole. We will call the natural parts of the whole "cells" (see Appendix).

We will indicate the degree of independence of a natural cell *c* from a neighboring cell *n* by *bo(c, n)*, to be read: the strength of the functional boundary of *c* against influences from *n* (see Appendix).

The degree to which neighboring cells are independent can be different both within the same whole and for different wholes.

[5] There is no logical reason for the different properties which we consider typical of simple interdependence (or organizational interdependence) to be always combined in this particular way. A more detailed analysis would require a study of the specific effect of each of these factors.

Wholes which do not show natural parts can be called undifferentiated.

Both psychologically and biologically, it seems to be characteristic of most organisms, and certainly it is true for a person, to be composed of natural subunits. In other words, organisms have a finite structure; a similar finite structure is characteristic for the life space as a whole.

The Degree of Differentiation. The degree of differentiation of a whole can be defined as the number of its cells.

A cell is defined by a certain degree of independence from its neighbors. The number of separated cells that are distinguishable within a given whole (W), in other words, its degree of differentiation $(dif^k [W])$, depends upon the degree of independence (k) which its cells must have to be considered two separate cells. The two values are inversely related.

$$(10) \, dif^k \, (W) = F \, (1/k)$$

However, the degree of differentiation usually does not decrease continuously with increasing k, but shows points of sudden decrease where k increases from a value just below the independence of natural neighboring cells $(bo[c,n])$ to a value just above it (see Appendix). In other words, the degree of differentiation of a whole is not an arbitrary matter; it is determined by the natural cells of the whole. This does not exclude the fact that the degree of differentiation of a whole is relative to certain arbitrarily required levels of dependence or independence.

THE UNITY AND THE DEGREE OF DIFFERENTIATION OF A WHOLE

The notion that the growing child shows an increasing differentiation is based partly on the observation that the unity of the growing child, as far as it is based on simple dependence (spreading), seems to decrease. We have discussed a variety of symptoms which indicate such a change. For a theory of regression it is essential to determine the conceptual relation between the degree of differentiation of a whole and the degree of its unity.

Definition of the Degree of Unity of a Whole. The term dynamic unity of a whole refers to the degree to which the state of one part within the whole depends upon the state of other parts of that whole.

The unity of a whole is said to be greater when the degree of interdependence of its parts is greatest.

Technically, one can define unity in a number of different ways (for instance, by referring to the average dependence of the parts). We will define the degree of unity of a whole as the *minimum* dependence of any part *x* on any other part *y*. In other words, we will measure the degree of simple unity of a whole *(si uni [W])* by the degree of dependence *(dep)* of its least dependent parts.

$$(11) \quad si \ uni \ (W) = dep^{min} \ (x, y)$$

This definition of the unity of the whole *W* implies that, if the state of any part of the whole is changed to a degree greater than that defining the unity of the whole, every part of the whole is affected.

The concept of the degree of unity can be used for undifferentiated as well as for differentiated wholes and for arbitrarily defined wholes (containing two or more not connected regions). It is, however, possible to define "natural" wholes by a method similar to that used for the definition of cells (see Appendix).

The Unity of a Whole, its Differentiation and its Diameter. What is the relation between the unity of a whole, as thus defined, and its degree of differentiation? In other words, what is the relation between the intimacy with which the state of one cell within a whole depends upon the state of any other cell of the whole and the number of cells contained in this whole?

In the following discussion we will restrict our analysis to wholes where each cell is dynamically equal to every other cell, particularly in regard to the degree of independence *(bo [c,n])* from the neighboring cells.

Given the same number of cells, and assuming that any two neighboring cells show the same degree of independence throughout the whole, the degree of unity of the whole is obviously smaller, the greater the degree of independence of the neighboring cells (see Appendix).

One might expect that the unity of the whole would decrease with differentiation, that is, with an increasing number of cells. This is, however, not entirely correct.

Even in the case of the same degree of independence of each cell from its neighbor, an increase in the number of cells does not necessarily lead to a decrease in the unity of the whole. For instance, the degree of differentiation of the whole W' in Figure 13 equals 6 while that of W'' equals 12. Nevertheless, the degree of unity of both wholes is the same. In other words, the unity of a whole depends not only on the degree of independence of each cell and the number of cells, but also upon the way these cells are grouped; that is, it depends also on the structure of the whole.

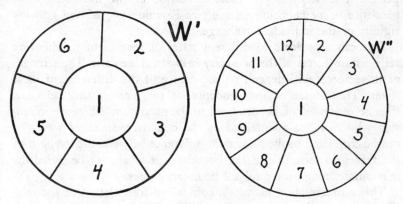

FIGURE 13. Central and Peripheral Layers of a Whole
W', whole with one central and six peripheral cells. 1, central cell; 2, 3, . . . 6, peripheral cells. W'', whole with one central and twelve peripheral cells. 1, central cell; 2, 3, . . . 12, peripheral cells W'' is more differentiated than W' but the degree of simple unity of both wholes is the same.

The more detailed discussion in the Appendix shows that the structural factor which is decisive for the unity of the whole is the maximum "hodological distance" (26) between any two cells within the whole (measured by the minimum number of steps from one cell to another). We will call this maximum distance between any two cells of the whole $(e_{x,y}^{max})$, the "diameter" of the whole.

If the cells of the whole are otherwise equal, the degree of unity of the whole is inversely related to the degree of independence of neighboring cells and the diameter of the whole.

$$(12) \quad si\ uni\ (W) = F\left(\frac{1}{bo(c,n),e_{x,y}^{max}}\right)$$

The Increasing Independence of Cells during Development. It should be possible to relate the decreasing unity of a person during development to his increasing differentiation or, more correctly, his diameter. Actually, however, a second factor seems to play a role. Kounin's study (22) on cosatiation of individuals of the same mental age, but of different chronological ages, shows that individuals of similar degrees of differentiation may nevertheless differ in regard to the degree of independence of corresponding regions within the person. This study is one more indication of the increasing independence of neighboring cells or, as Kounin says, of the growing rigidity of the individual with age.

One can coordinate to different states of tension of neighboring cells certain forces at the boundary between these cells. The strength of these forces will depend on the degree of the difference of these states. The degree of independence of two neighboring cells can then be conceived of as correlated to the maximum difference in tension which can be maintained by the boundary. In other words, it can be correlated to the maximum difference between the strength of the forces on each side of the boundary, or what may be called the maximum strength of resultant boundary forces.

This representation permits a convenient formulation of the relativity of dependence: two cells within a whole may be dependent in regard to strong resultant boundary forces and independent in regard to weaker forces. This implies that the degree of differentiation of a given whole is an inverse function of the strength of the forces relative to which the cells have to be independent (see Formula 13a). In other words, we look for dedifferentiation (regression) when the resultant forces are too great (see Appendix).

STRATIFICATION: CENTRAL AND PERIPHERAL LAYERS;
INNER AND OUTER LAYERS

In terms of the concepts discussed thus far it is possible to distinguish different layers within a whole. Psychologists have made use of the concept of layers, particularly in referring to more central and more peripheral layers. This distinction has been found to be rather important in connection with needs and in consideration of the accessibility of the person.

One can distinguish two types of layers based on different characteristics. We limit the discussion again to the simplest case where all cells have the same dynamic properties within the whole.

Central and Peripheral Layers. The maximum distance from a cell c to any other cell y within a whole $(e_{c,y}^{max})$ is usually not the same for every cell. From some cells it is possible to reach any other cell in relatively few steps. For instance, for the cell 1 in Figure 13 this maximum distance equals 1; for any other cell it equals 2. Those cells within the whole for which this distance is equal to the diameter of the whole will be called "peripheral cells," and their totality, the

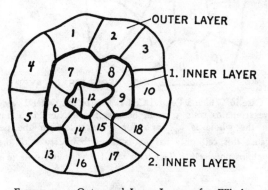

FIGURE 14. Outer and Inner Layers of a Whole
The outer layer contains cells 1, 2, 3, 10, 18, 17, 16, 13, 5, 4; the 1st inner layer contains cells 6, 7, 8, 9, 15, 14; the 2nd inner layer contains cells 11, 12.

"peripheral layer" of a whole. Starting from this peripheral layer we can distinguish more and more central layers (see Appendix). In Figure 13 the most central layer is the cell 1.

Because of its position, a central cell is relatively more influential than a peripheral cell. The minimum change of a cell necessary to affect every other cell is smaller in a central cell. In this way the state of the whole depends more on the state of the central cells.

At the same time, central cells are, on the average, more easily affected by a change anywhere in the whole. In this way they are more "sensitive" to the state of the whole.

It is obvious that these facts may be linked to some of the properties commonly attributed to psychologically more central layers. It should, however, be emphasized that we do not deal here with the relation of ruling and ruled, but rather with relative importance based on simple interdependence.

The degree of unity of the central layer taken by itself is greater than the unity of the whole (if this whole has also peripheral cells).

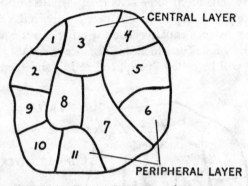

FIGURE 15. Case in Which a Central Cell is Part of the Outer Layer of the Whole
Central layer contains cells 3, 7, 8, because the maximum distance to another cell y within the whole is $e_{c,y}^{max} = 2$ for these cells. For the peripheral cells $e_{c,y}^{max} = 3$, because this cell only has no common boundary with the whole. The inner layer contains only cell 8. The cells 3 and 7 are outer cells in spite of being central.

Inner and Outer Layers. The degree of centrality of a cell deals with the question of how easily the cell is affected by changes *within* the whole. The question may be asked concerning the effect of the position of a cell on its being influenced by changes *outside* the whole. This can be answered by distinguishing inner and outer layers. Cells which have a common boundary with the boundary of the whole can be called "outer" cells, and their totality the "outer layer" of the whole (Figure 14). Starting from the outer layer one can distinguish, in a similar way, more and more inner layers (see Appendix). It is entirely possible that the increasing distance between the ego and the environment which we have mentioned above is partly related to the increasing stratification of the person during development.

Cells which are central are frequently located in an inner layer. However, this is not necessarily so; a central cell may belong to the outer layer (see Figure 15).

INHOMOGENEITY AND VARIETY OF THE STATE AS A WHOLE

One of the outstanding behavioral characteristics of development is, as we have seen, the increasing variety of behavior. Dynamically, the greater variety of behavior will have to be linked to a greater variety of patterns of states which can be realized in a given organism.

Homogeneity, Differentiation, and Unity of a Whole. A highly differentiated whole can be very homogeneous: the state of tension, for instance, of every cell may be the same throughout the whole. However, there exists a relation between the maximum difference in the state of any two cells and certain aspects of the differentiation of the whole. A more detailed discussion shows (see Appendix) that the maximum inhomogeneity within a whole, that is, the greatest difference of the state of any two parts, is closely related to its diameter and to the degree of independence of neighboring cells. The maximum inhomogeneity is an inverse function of the unity of the whole.

Variety of Patterns. The number of patterns of states which can be realized within a given whole depends upon the degree of independence of the cells, upon the diameter, and in addition, upon the number of cells, that is, the degree of differentiation of the whole (see Appendix).

Our discussion of dynamic wholes thus far has been based on rather general properties. To link these properties with the actual behavior of a person, one has to consider the more specific characteristics of an organism. It is possible with most organisms to speak of something like a normal state. Biologically and psychologically, there are limitations to the change of the state of a cell beyond which the boundary between the cells, or the cells themselves, will be destroyed and the organism will die. This fact limits the change in the state of the cells of a living whole to a relatively narrow range and to definite absolute levels. It sets very definite limitations to the variety of patterns which can be realized within an organismal whole.

If a cell or a larger part of the whole is kept on a fixed level by outside influences or such factors as a need in tension, the variety of possible patterns decreases. In other words, the flexibility and richness of behavior is reduced. The degree to which the variety of pattern decreases depends, for a given whole, mainly upon (1) the degree of centrality of the cell which is kept on a certain level, (2) the degree to which this level deviates from the normal state, and (3) the number of these cells (see Appendix). A reduction of the variety of behavior can be viewed as a regression. Therefore, these factors are of importance for the understanding of regression.

THE DEGREE OF HIERARCHICAL ORGANIZATION

We have distinguished between two types of dependence, simple dependence and organizational dependence. Having discussed differentiation, unity, and variety of pattern as a function of simple dependence between the parts of a whole, let us turn to a discussion of the properties of a whole based on the organizational dependence of its parts.

The "leader-led" relation, which is characteristic for organizational dependence, may be represented with the help of the concept "power field." This concept, which has shown its usefulness in social psychology, indicates the ability of one person to induce forces acting on another person. One can distinguish the strength and the scope of the power field. It is one important aspect of the relation between leader and led that the power field of the "leader" over the "led" is stronger than that of the "led" over the "leader."

One can apply this concept to parts of a whole and distinguish "leading" and "led" cells by referring to their power fields. For instance, the forces acting on the cells of the motor region can be said to be induced by the power field of cells belonging to the inner personal region (25).

Cells which rule other cells may themselves be ruled by a third group of cells. One can define the degree of hierarchical organization of a whole by the number of strata each of which rules a ruled stratum.

THE ORGANIZATIONAL UNITY OF A WHOLE

A conceptual clarification of what is meant by organizational unity is a necessary but rather difficult task. This term is usually linked to considerations of "harmony" or "efficiency." A well-organized unit is a whole which has one and not two or more competing "heads." One speaks of a "disorganization," or lack of unity also if the executive organs do not obey or do not readily obey the inducing power of the leading regions.

It seems to be possible to represent both aspects of organization by a relatively simple formula which refers to the strength of the power field of that part of the whole which has the function of head in relation to the strength of the power field of the rest of the whole (see Appendix).

To some degree the organizational unity of a whole depends on the properties of its "ruled" cells, the "executive" in Koffka's sense (21).[6] This would be maximal if the executive had the properties of a good medium as defined by Heider (14), i.e., if it were composed of a great number of relatively independent parts, the state of which could be easily changed. This point is important for the conditions of regression.

Probably the efficiency of the executive organs as a medium increases during childhood, at least in early childhood. But the number of heads of the hierarchical organization probably does not show a simple steady progress. In certain periods the whole person may be governed by one head and its organizational unity will be correspondingly high. The region which functions as a head may, however, differentiate into relatively independent cells and this will decrease the organizational unity of the child. Later on, a new head may emerge, and later further differentiation of the new head may follow, etc. In this way the hierarchical organization of the whole would increase, while at the same time its degree of organizational unity would periodically decrease and increase with the differentiation and organization of its head. That development of behavior frequently proceeds through periods of more harmonic and more unharmonic stages (crises) may be taken as an indication of the correctness of this view.

EXTENSION OF THE LIFE SPACE

The scope of the life space can be represented with conceptual means developed elsewhere (see Chapter 6). One may distinguish three main dimensions of extension. One deals with the scope and differentiation of that area which for the individual has the character

---

[6] By this term Koffka does not mean the "head" which leads but that part of the system which executes.

of the present reality. The second deals with increasing differentiation in the reality-irreality dimension. The third deals with the extending psychological time dimension, i.e., with the extending "psychological past" and "psychological future" which exist as parts of the life space at a given time.

Regression of behavior should result if the scope of the reality-level of the life space is narrowed down, or if its psychological time dimension or its reality-irreality dimensions are reduced. Moreover a change in behavior showing some characteristics of regression should result if the functional connection between the reality- and irreality-level is severed, i.e., if the link between fantasy and action is cut.

REFERENCES

1. ALLPORT, GORDON W.: *Personality: A Psychological Interpretation* (New York: Henry Holt & Company, 1937).
2. BIRENBAUM, GITA: Das Vergessen einer Vornahme. *Psychol. Forsch.*, 1930, *13*, 218–284.
3. BRIDGES, K. M.: *The Social and Emotional Development of the Preschool Child* (London: Kegan, Paul, Trench, Trubner, 1931).
4. BRYAN, WILLIAM L.: On the development of voluntary motor ability, *Amer. J. Psychol.*, 1892, *5*, 123–204.
5. BÜHLER, CHARLOTTE: *From Birth to Maturity: An Outline of the Psychological Development of the Child* (London: Kegan, Paul, 1935).
6. CAMERON, NORMAN: Reasoning, regression, and communication in schizophrenics, *Psychol. Monogr.*, 1938, *50*, No. 1, 1–34.
7. DEMBO, TAMARA: Der Ärger als dynamisches Problem, *Psychol. Forsch.*, 1931, *15*, 1–144.
8. FENICHEL, OTTO: *Outline of Clinical Psychoanalysis* (New York: Psychoanalytic Quarterly Press, 1934).
9. FLETCHER, JOHN M.: The wisdom of the mind, *Sigma Xi Quarterly*, 1938, *26*, 6–16.
10. FREUD, SIGMUND: *Introductory Lectures on Psychoanalysis*. Trans. by Joan Riviere. 2nd ed. (London: Allen & Unwin, 1933).
11. GOLDSTEIN, KURT: *The Organism* (New York: The Macmillan Company, 1939).
12. GOODENOUGH, FLORENCE L.: Anger in young children, *University of Minnesota, Monogr.*, Series No. 9.
13. HALVERSON, H. M.: An experimental study of prehension in infants by means of systematic cinema records, *Genet. Psychol. Monogr.*, 1931, *10*, 107–286.
14. HEIDER, FRITZ: Ding und Medium, *Symposion*, 1927, *1*, 109–157.
15. HOMBURGER, ERIK: Configurations in play: Clinical notes, *Psychoanalyt. Quart.*, 1937, *6*, 139–214.
16. IRWIN, ORVIS C.: The amount of motility of seventy-three newborn infants, *J. Comp. Psychol.*, 1932, *14*, 415–428.

17. IRWIN, ORVIS C.: The distribution of the amount of motility in young infants between two nursing periods, *J. Comp. Psychol.*, 1932, *14*, 429–445.

18. KARSTEN, ANITRA: Psychische Sättigung, *Psychol. Forsch.*, 1928, *10*, 142–254.

19. KLÜVER, HEINRICH: *Behavior Mechanisms in Monkeys* (Chicago: University of Chicago Press, 1933).

20. KOFFKA, KURT: *The Growth of the Mind: An Introduction to Child Psychology.* Trans. by Robert Morris Ogden. 2nd ed. (New York: Harcourt, Brace & Company, 1928).

21. KOFFKA, KURT: *Principles of Gestalt Psychology* (New York: Harcourt, Brace & Company, 1935).

22. KOUNIN, JACOB S.: Experimental studies of rigidity, *Character & Pers.*, 1941, *9*, 251–282.

23. KRECHEVSKY, I.: Brain mechanisms and variability I, II, III, *J. Comp. Psychol.*, 1937, *23*, 121–159; 351–364.

24. LASHLEY, K. S.: *Brain Mechanisms and Intelligence: A Quantitative Study of Injuries to the Brain.* (Chicago: University of Chicago Press, 1929).

25. LEWIN, KURT: *Principles of Topological Psychology* (New York: McGraw-Hill Book Co., 1936).

26. LEWIN, KURT: The conceptual representation and the measurement of psychological forces, *Cont. to Psychol. Theory*, 1938, *1*, No. 4.

27. McCARTHY, DOROTHEA A.: The language development of the preschool child, *University of Minnesota, Institute of Child Welfare Monograph Series*, No. 4.

28. McDOUGALL, WILLIAM: *Outline of Abnormal Psychology* (New York: The Macmillan Company, 1922).

29. MAIER, N. R. F.: The effect of cerebral destruction on reasoning and learning in rats, *J. Comp. Neurol.*, 1932, *54*, 45–75.

30. MILLER, NEAL E., and STEVENSON, STEWART S.: Agitated behavior of rats during experimental extinction and a case of spontaneous recovery, *J. Comp. Psychol.*, 1936, *21*, 205–231.

31. MOWRER, O. H.: An experimental analogue of "regression" with incidental observations on "reaction formation," *J. Abnorm. & Social Psychol.*, 1940, *35*, 56–87.

32. PIAGET, JEAN: *La Construction du Réel chez l'Enfant* (Neuchatel: Delachaux, 1937).

33. SLIOSBERG, SARAH: Zur Dynamik des Ersatzes in Spiel und Ernstsituationen, *Psychol. Forsch.*, 1934, *19*, 122–181.

34. SMITH, M. E.: An investigation of the development of the sentence and the extent of vocabulary in young children, *Univ. Iowa Stud. in Child Welf.*, 1926, *3*, No. 5.

35. SPENCER, HERBERT: *The Principles of Psychology.* 2 Vols. (London: Williams & Norgate, 1872).

36. WELLMAN, BETH L.: The development of motor coordination in young children: An experimental study in the control of hand and arm movements, *Univ. Iowa Stud. in Child. Welf.*, 1925, *3*, No. 4.

37. WELLS, F. L.: Social Maladjustment: Adaptive Regression. In Murchison, Carl, editor: *A Handbook of Social Psychology* (Worcester: Clark University Press, 1935).

VI

Field Theory and Experiment
in Social Psychology
(1939)

பாபாயாயாயாயாயாயாயாயாயாயாயா

THE sociologists, I suppose, have reason to be satisfied with the recent trends in psychology. Traditionally, most psychologists seem to have felt more or less obliged to emphasize the biological character of the individual, to believe in the reality of physical and physiological processes, but to be rather suspicious of social categories and to regard as mystic those who claimed that social facts were as real as physical ones.

Recently, however, a growing number of psychologists seem to have abandoned this view. They seem to be persuaded that social facts are equally or even more important for psychology than the so-called "physiological facts." These psychologists recognize that the child from his first day of life is objectively a part of a social setting and would die within a few days if he were to be withdrawn from it. Also, the so-called "subjective" psychological world of the individual, his life-space, is influenced in a much earlier stage by social facts and social relations than anyone would have expected a few decades ago. Already, at a few months, the child seems to react to another person's smile and voice in a rather specific way. It is probably safe to say that the child is able to perceive and to distinguish the friendliness and unfriendliness of another person at an earlier age than he is able to distinguish the pattern of physical lines in a countenance which expresses these social attitudes.

Beginning with this early age, the child's behavior is molded in every respect by his social situation. Of course, his morale, his religion, and his political values are determined by his being a part of, and reacting to, the society in which he lives. If one considers the findings of cultural anthropology and of experimental psychology, one can, I think, establish evidence that social influences enter every action of the individual, even actions which seem to have nothing to do with society.

Human behavior is either a directed action or an emotional expression. Experimental psychology has shown that the formation of goals depends directly upon the laws which govern the level of aspiration, particularly upon the effect which success or failure has in raising and lowering the level of aspiration. These experiments make it evident that the level of aspiration is greatly influenced by such social facts as the presence or absence of other persons or by the competitive or noncompetitive character of the situation. It has been shown, too, that goal-setting depends upon certain ideal goals, upon what the sociologists call the "ideology" of the person. Cultural anthropology proves that these ideologies vary extremely among different cultures. As to emotional expression, experiments have shown that, for instance, the emotional reaction to failure can be changed to a great extent by appropriate praise or change in social atmosphere. This substantiates the general thesis[1] that the management of tension by the individual depends upon his particular social and cultural setting.

From this it should be apparent that experimental psychology is instrumental in helping the sociologists to realize their most ardent dream: the demonstration of the fundamental, direct, and widespread effect of social facts on behavior.

There is a growing number of psychologists who emphasize the "historical," social side of psychological facts; and even the hard-boiled believers in a stimulus-reaction psychology show a peculiar interest in getting as much of, and as close to, social facts as they can. I believe there is no longer any need for the traditional opposition between psychologists and sociologists in this basic issue.

I

Unfortunately, this insight into the social dependency of behavior does not end the problem for the psychologist. His problems rather

[1] L. K. Frank: The management of tensions, *Am. J. Sociol.*, 1928, *33*, 705–736.

begin here. For the sociologist, too, they should begin here. Psychology, including social psychology, cannot possibly be satisfied with any "generalities" (however correct they may be). It has to judge scientific concepts and theories largely by their ability or inability to handle problems of dynamic interdependence and to handle them in a manner sufficiently specific to attack the concrete tasks of the laboratory or the clinic.

Of course, for hundreds of years the belief was prevalent that personality, will, and emotion were not subject to strict laws and that they could not be studied experimentally. A similar view is traditionally strong in sociology. In the long run, however, *dira necessitas* is bound to be stronger in both sociology and psychology than those metaphysical prejudices, and sociology seems to be ready now for important steps away from these prejudices. Psychology as a science might be said to be somewhat more advanced technically and conceptually, at least in some of its areas. However, on the whole, and particularly in regard to social psychology, it too is facing the task of developing a general approach which offers specific conceptual tools for solving the concrete problems of a vast and diversified area.

Social psychology indicates, probably better than any other part of psychology and of sociology, what is needed. Its progress depends upon overcoming certain major difficulties, which include at least the following:

a. The integrating of vast areas of very divergent facts and aspects: The development of a scientific language (concepts) which is able to treat cultural, historical, sociological, psychological, and physical facts on a common ground
b. The treating of these facts on the basis of their interdependence
c. The handling of both historical and systematic problems
d. The handling of problems related to groups as well as to individuals
e. The handling of all "sizes" of objects or patterns (social psychology has to include problems of a nation and its situation, as well as of a play group of three children and their momentary struggle)
f. Problems of "atmosphere" (such as friendliness, pressure, etc.)
g. Experimental social psychology will have to find a way to bring the large-size patterns into a framework small enough for the technical possibilities of experimentation

The variety of facts which social psychology has to treat might really seem frightening to even a bold scientific mind. They include "values" (such as religious and moral values), "ideologies" (such as conservatism or communism), "the style of living and thinking," and other so-called "cultural" facts. They include sociological problems, i.e., problems of group and group structure, their degree of hierarchy and type of organization; or such problems as the difference between a rural and an urban community, their rigidity or fluidity, degree of differentiation, etc. They also include so-called "psychological" problems, such as the intelligence of a person, his goals and fears, and his personality. They include such "physiological" facts as the person's being healthy or sick, strong or weak, the color of his hair and of his complexion. They include, finally, such "physical" facts as the size of the physical area in which the person or a group is located.

It is utterly fruitless and merely a negative scientific treatment to put these facts into classificatory pigeonholes, however accurately built and fitted they may be. It is widely accepted today that we need positive means of bringing these various types of facts together in such a way that one can treat them on one level without sacrificing the recognition of their specific characteristics. The problem of adolescence which we will discuss as an example shows, I think, particularly clearly that a way must be found to treat bodily changes, shift of ideology, and group-belongingness within one realm of scientific language, in a single realm of discourse of concepts. The question is "How can this be done?"

Behaviorism has tried to answer this question by interpreting everything as a conditioned reflex. One of the main reasons for the appeal of such an approach is the same as that which lies behind the popular appeal of the "unity of science" idea: namely, it appeared to put every problem on a "physiological" basis (although in fact it did not), and in this way it seemed to promise integration of the divergent facts on one level.

Today most research workers in sociology and social psychology will agree that the program of describing and explaining social-psychological processes by concepts and laws of physics or physiology might at best be something to talk about as a distant possibility for a speculative philosopher. But such a way would definitely not be a realistic research program for attacking the social-psychological problems of today. On the other hand, to elaborate on the "fundamental differences" between physics, sociology, and psychology and to rest satisfied with such distinctions is no help either.

To discuss these problems adequately would involve a more thorough treatment of certain questions of comparative theory of science than is possible here. As far as I can see the solution lies in the direction (a) that a science should be considered a realm of problems rather than a realm of material; (b) that the different realms of problems might necessitate different universes of discourse of constructs and laws (such as those of physics, esthetics, psychology, and sociology); and (c) that any one of them refers more or less to the same universe of material.

For any practical purpose of research—and that, after all, is what counts—sciences like sociology or psychology should feel fully free to use those types of constructs which they think most adequate for handling their problems; and they should attempt to find the integration we have discussed on their own level. They should not feel obliged to use constructs of another science merely out of philosophical reasons (e.g., because some philosophies or popular metaphysics apply "true reality" to physical entities only). On the other hand, feeling confident in their own right, those sciences do not need to be afraid of using methods or concepts (e.g., mathematical concepts) which might or might not have similarities with those of other sciences.

The field-theoretical approach is intended to be a practical vehicle of research. As is true with any tool, its characteristics can be understood fully only by the use of it in actual research. Therefore, instead of stating general methodological principles *in abstractum,* I prefer to discuss, as an illustration, the problem of adolescence and the definition of a social group. The purpose in discussing them is not the proving of certain facts or theories (which might or might not be fully correct) but to survey certain major aspects of the field-theoretical approach as applicable to social psychology. In discussing these examples I will therefore, from time to time, point to similar aspects in other problems.

II

We have chosen the problem of adolescence because the changes in behavior which are supposed to be characteristic for this period seem, at first sight, to give excellent backing to a biological view in sociology. Obviously, adolescence has something to do with sexual hormones and with certain periods of bodily growth. The more recent treatments of the problem of adolescence, however, seem to emphasize its social aspect. They point particularly to the fact that the behavior typical of this age is rather different in different societies.[2] Considerable argumentation has been advanced for and against both views.

However, it does not help much to argue whether adolescence is a biological or psychological effect. It does not help much either to try to describe, on a statistical basis, to what degree this problem is biological or psychological in nature. Even if an answer could be found, it would be of as little value as, for instance, the determining of the degree to which heredity and environment affect intelligence. We still would not have gained any insight into the way in which bodily and social factors are working together and against each other, integrating the concrete behavior of the adolescent. It would seem to be more fruitful to start with an analysis of the setting in a concrete case. This case should be chosen not so much according to the frequency of occurrence as according to the amount of insight it offers into a constellation which is typical at least for a part of the setting in question.

In regard to the problem of adolescence, it might be helpful to refer first to cases which show the so-called "typical" difficulties of adolescent behavior. A field-theoretical analysis of such a situation should give some hints as to what conditions would increase or decrease these symptoms.

The period of adolescence can be said to be a period of transition. It seems to imply, at least under certain circumstances, a more rapid or deeper shift than the period before. After the rather important changes around the age of three years, often a more stable situation

---

[2] See, for example: Luella Cole: *Psychology of Adolescence* (New York: Farrar & Rinehart, 1936); E. B. Reuter: The Sociology of Adolescence, *Am. J. Sociol.*, 1937, *43*, 414–427.

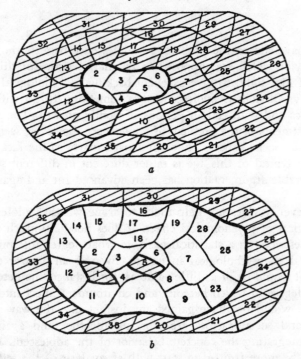

FIGURE 16. Comparison of the *space of free movement* of child and adult. The actual activity regions are represented. The accessible regions are blank; the inaccessible shaded. (*a*) The space of free movement of the *child* includes the regions *1–6*, representing activities such as getting into the movies at children's rates, belonging to a boy's club, etc. The regions *7–35* are not accessible, representing activities such as driving a car, writing checks for purchases, political activities, performance of adults' occupations, etc. (*b*) The *adult* space of free movement is considerably wider, although it too is bounded by regions of activities inaccessible to the adult, such as shooting his enemy or entering activities beyond his social or intellectual capacity (represented by regions including *29–35*). Some of the regions accessible to the child are not accessible to the adult, for instance, getting into the movies at children's rates, or doing things socially taboo for an adult which are permitted to the child (represented by regions *1* and *5*).

has arisen. Maybe minor crises have come up; but particularly in cases where the adolescence is characterized by special disturbances, a relatively quiet or stable time might have preceded it. If one tries to characterize the nature of the transition, one can point to several aspects.

a. One can view adolescence as a change in group-belongingness. The individual has been considered by himself and by others as a child. Now he does not wish to be treated as such. He is ready to separate himself from things childish and to try seriously to enter adult life in manners and in outlook on occupation, as on life in general. Any change in belongingness from one group to another is of great importance for the behavior of the person; the more central for the person this belonging is, the more important is the change. A shift in group-belongingness is a "social locomotion," that is, it changes the position of the person concerned.

It is a simple fact, but still not sufficiently recognized in psychology and sociology, that the behavior of a person depends above all upon his momentary position. Often, the world looks very different before and after an event which changes the region in which a person is located. That is the reason why, for instance, a *fait accompli* is so feared in politics. A change in position, for instance, the locomotion from one group to another, changes not only the momentary surroundings of a person but more or less the total setting: what has been a neighboring region, easily accessible from the previous position, might now be farther away or no longer accessible at all. On the other hand, different regions are now neighbors, and new ones may be accessible. The shift into the group of the adults, for instance, makes possible certain activities which previously were forbidden but which are now socially permitted. The individual might attend certain parties, have access to certain activities. On the other hand, certain taboos exist for the adults that do not exist for the child (Figure 16, *a* and *b*).

b. The change from the group of children to that of the adults is a shift to a more or less unknown position. Psychologically, it is equivalent to entering an unknown region, comparable to coming into a new town. Experiments in the field of learning, for example, give some kind of picture of the fundamental differences between a situation which is familiar to an individual and that which is unfamiliar. The unfamiliar can be represented psychologically as a cognitively unstructured region. This means that that region is not differentiated into clearly distinguishable parts. It is not clear therefore where a certain action will lead and in what direction one has to move to approach a certain goal. This lack of clearness of the direction in the field is one of the major reasons for the typical "uncertainty of behavior" to be found in unknown surroundings. Studies on social pressure and on ascendant and submissive behavior[3] clearly indicate that an individual in an unfamiliar surrounding is less ready to put up a fight or to show ascendant behavior. An unfamiliar surrounding is dynamically equivalent to a soft ground. Or, to be more specific, the lack of a cognitively clear structure is likely to make every action a conflicting one. The individual, not knowing whether

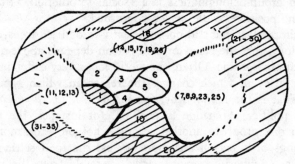

FIGURE 17.   The *space of free movement* of the *adolescent* as it appears to him. The space of free movement is greatly increased, including many regions which previously have not been accessible to the child, such as freedom to smoke, returning home late, driving a car (regions 7–9, 11–13, . . .). Certain regions accessible to the adult are clearly not accessible to the adolescent, such as voting (represented by regions 10 and 16). Certain regions accessible to the child have already become inaccessible, such as getting into the movies at children's rates, or behaving on too childish a level (region 1). The boundaries of these newly acquired portions of the space of free movement are only vaguely determined and in themselves generally less clearly and sharply differentiated than for an adult. In such cases the life space of the adolescent seems to be full of possibilities and at the same time of uncertainties.

the action will lead him closer or farther away from his goal, is necessarily uncertain as to whether or not he should carry it out.

The child's development naturally leads to an opening up of new unknown regions. Periods of transition are characterized by more than the usual impact of such new regions. Entering a new social group can mean something very similar to being thrown into a cognitively unstructured field, being forced to stand on unfirm ground and not knowing whether the "right thing" is being done. The un-

[3] L. M. Jack: An experimental study of ascendant behavior in preschool children, *Univ. Iowa Stud. Child Welf.*, 1934, 9, No. 3.

certain character of the adolescent's behavior and his conflicts can partly be explained by the lack of cognitive clarity concerning the adult's world which he is going to enter (Figure 17). It follows that this uncertainty is greater the more the individual has previously been kept out of the adult world and has been kept in the dark about it.

c. One region particularly close and important to the individual is his own body. Psychologically one's own body can be treated in some respects in the same way as one's environment. Generally the individual "knows" his body sufficiently. That means he knows what he can expect from it and how it will react under given circumstances. The time of sexual maturity brings with it changes which make the individual sometimes disturbed by his own body. More or less strange and new body experiences arise and make this part of the life space, which is so close and vital to the individual, strange and unknown. In this case the change does not mean merely the usual uncertainties of a new and strange environment; but, in addition, a region which previously appeared to be well known and reliable becomes now unknown and unreliable. This change necessarily shakes the belief of the individual in the stability of the ground on which he stands and perhaps even in the stability of the world at large. Since the region of the body happens to be very important and central for anyone, this doubting might be rather fundamental. It might lead, on the one hand, to increased uncertainty of behavior and to conflicts; on the other, to the aggressiveness of some of the adolescent reactions.

Such explanation would be in line with the findings of L. B. Murphy[4] that insecure situations lead both to highly aggressive and highly sensitive behavior. The disastrous effect which the breakdown of a previously firm ground might have is dramatically illustrated by foster-children, who discover at a late age the true facts concerning their parentage. The trauma of such a collapse of a social ground sometimes permanently destroys their belief in the world.

d. The "radicalism" which makes some adolescents flock to extreme "left" or "right" political parties and be extreme in many judgments has to deal also with a second factor. A period of radical

---

[4] L. B. Murphy: *Social Behavior and Child Personality: An Exploratory Study of Some Roots of Sympathy* (New York: Columbia University Press, 1937).

change is naturally a period of greater plasticity. The very fact that a person is in the state of moving from one region A to a new region B, and is therefore cut loose from the region A but not yet firmly established in the region B, puts him in a less stable position and makes him, as any object in *statu nascendi,* more formative.

The psychological environment has to be regarded functionally as a part of one interdependent field, the life space, the other part of which is the person. This fundamental fact is the keynote of the field-theoretical approach. In psychology it has become, in various forms, more and more recognized and can be expressed simply by the formula: Behavior = Function of person and environment = function of life space $(B = F [P,E] = F [L Sp])$. The instability of the psychological environment leads, in some respects, therefore, to greater instability of the person. "Being established" means having a well-defined position and definite relations to the many regions of a highly differentiated life space: under such circumstances any major change means a great number of steps and a shift of interrelation. In an unestablished, new situation the field is not very much differentiated, and whatever differentiation has occurred is not very firm. The shift of position of the individual from one region to another, which in the less differentiated field might be merely one step (Figure 17), would have to be considered a major change (equivalent to many steps) in a more differentiated field (Figure 16,*b*). Similarly, what in reality is a not very great and easily made shift in cognitive structure of the ideological field of the adolescent, which contains relatively few regions, appears to be a radical shift to the adult, with his highly differentiated cognitive field. The difference in cognitive differentiation is probably one of the reasons why adolescents easily go to extremes.

e. The widening of the life space into unknown regions concerns not only geographical surroundings (interest in traveling, hiking, etc.) and social surroundings (more inclusive social groups like political or occupational ones) but also the time dimension of the life space. Persons of all ages are influenced by the manner in which they see the future, that is, by their expectations, fears, and hopes.

The scope of time ahead which influences present behavior, and is therefore to be regarded as a part of the present life space, increases during development. This change in time perspective is one of the most fundamental facts of development. Adolescence seems to be a period of particularly deep change in respect to time perspective.

The change can be partly described as a shift in scope. Instead of days, weeks, or months, now years ahead are considered in certain goals. Even more important is the way in which these future events influence present behavior. The ideas of a child of six or eight in regard to his occupation as an adult are not likely to be based on sufficient knowledge of the factors which might help or interfere with the realization of these ideas. They might be based on relatively narrow but definite expectations or might have a dream- or playlike character. In other words, "ideal goals" and "real goals" for the distant future are not much distinguished, and this future has more the fluid character of the level of irreality.

In adolescence a definite differentiation in regard to the time perspective is likely to occur. Within those parts of the life space which represent the future, levels of reality and irreality are gradually being differentiated. That which is dreamed of or wished for (level of irreality in the future) becomes separated from what is expected (level of reality in the future). Vague ideas have to be replaced by more or less definite decisions in regard to preparation for future occupation. In other words, one has to "plan": to structure the time perspective in a way which is in line both with one's own ideal goals or values and with those realities which must be taken into account for a realistic structuring of the plane of expectation.

This task is characteristic for all kinds of planning. The situation of the adolescent in this respect is particular only in that he has to form the time perspective in regard to a field which is especially great and unknown. What he learns from books and adult counsel about what an individual might accomplish is full of contradiction: the adults praise the hero who has realized what seemed to be impossible, and at the same time preach the moral of "standing with both feet on the ground."

In another respect the adolescent finds the adults (the group he is to enter) full of contradiction. A variety of conflicting religious, political, and occupational values is obviously powerful within that group. A child may fail to bring to adolescence a well-established framework of values, or he may have thrown the values of his child-

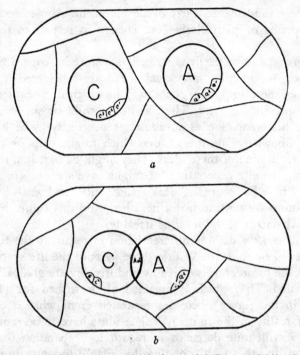

FIGURE 18. The adolescent as a *marginal man*. (*a*) During *childhood* and *adulthood* the "adults" (*A*) and "children" (*C*) are viewed as relatively separated groups, the individual child (c^1, c^2) and the individual adult (a^1, a^2) being sure of their belonging to their respective groups. (*b*) The *adolescent* belonging to a group (*Ad*) which can be viewed as an overlapping region of the children's (*C*) and the adults' (*A*) group belonging to both of them, or as standing between them, not belonging to either one.

hood away. In either case the structure of his adolescent time perspective will be unstable and undetermined, owing to the uncertainty of not only what can be done (which we have discussed previously) but also what should be done. The uncertain character of the ideals and values keeps the adolescent in a state of conflict and tension which is the greater the more central these problems are. The wish to structure these fields in a definite way (and in this manner to solve the conflict) seems to be one of the reasons behind the readiness of the adolescent to follow anyone who offers a definite pattern of values.

f. The transition from childhood to adulthood may be a rather sudden shift (for instance, in some of the primitive societies), or it may occur gradually in a setting where children and adults are not sharply separated groups. In case of the so-called "adolescence difficulties," however, a third state of affairs is often prevalent: children and adults constitute clearly defined groups; the adolescent does not wish to belong any longer to the children's group and, at the same time, knows that he is not really accepted in the adult group. In this case he has a position similar to what is called in sociology the "marginal man."

The marginal man is a person who stands on the boundary (Figure 18, *b*) between two groups, A and B. He does not belong to either of them, or at least he is not certain about his belongingness. Not infrequently this situation occurs for members of an underprivileged minority group, particularly for the more privileged members within this group. There is a strong tendency for the members of the underprivileged minority group to cut loose and to try to enter the majority group.[5] If the person is partly successful in establishing relationships with the privileged group without being fully accepted, he becomes a marginal man, belonging to both groups but not fully to either of them. The fact of being located in a social "no man's land" can be observed in very different types of minority groups—for instance, racial groups or the hard-of-hearing, which is a marginal group between the deaf and the normal group.

Characteristic symptoms of behavior of the marginal man are emotional instability and sensitivity. They tend to unbalanced behavior, to either boisterousness or shyness, exhibiting too much tension, and a frequent shift between extremes of contradictory behavior. The marginal man shows a typical aversion to the less privileged members of his own group. This can be noted in the hostile attitude of some subgroups of the Negroes or other races against members of their own race, and the hard-of-hearing against the deaf.

To some extent behavior symptomatic for the marginal man can be found in the adolescent. He too is oversensitive, easily shifted from one extreme to the other, and particularly sensitive to the shortcomings of his younger fellows. Indeed, his position is sociologically

[5] Kurt Lewin: *Resolving Social Conflicts* (New York: Harper & Brothers, 1948). See especially Chapter 11.

the same as that of the marginal man; he does not wish to belong any longer to a group which is, after all, less privileged than the group of adults: but at the same time he knows that he is not fully accepted by the adults. The similarities between the position of the members of the underprivileged minority and the adolescent, and between their behavior, seem to me so great that one might characterize the behavior of the marginal members of the minority group as that of permanent adolescence.

We might sum up our discussion of the adolescent in the following manner:

a. The basic fact concerning the general situation of the adolescent can be represented as the position of a person during locomotion from one region to another. This includes (1) the widening of the life space (geographically, socially, and in time perspective), and (2) the cognitively unstructured character of the new situation.

b. Somewhat more specifically, the adolescent has a social position "between" the adult and the child, similar to a marginal member of an underprivileged minority group.

c. There are still more specific factors involved in adolescence, such as the new experiences with one's own body, which can be represented as the baffling change of a central region of the established life space.

From this representation one can derive conceptually:

I. The adolescent's shyness, sensitivity, and aggressiveness, owing to unclearness and instability of ground (follows from a, b, and c).

II. A more or less permanent conflict between the various attitudes, values, ideologies, and styles of living (follows from b).

III. Emotional tension resulting from these conflicts (follows from a, b, and c).

IV. Readiness to take extreme attitudes and actions and to shift his position radically (follows from a, b, and c).

V. The "adolescent behavior" should appear only if the structure and dynamics of the field are such as represented by a, b, and c. The degree and particular type of behavior should depend upon the degree of realization of this structure and upon the strength of the conflicting forces. Above all, the degree of difference and of separation between adults and children which is characteristic for a particular culture is important; also, the extent to which the particular adolescent finds himself in the position of a marginal man. According to field theory, actual behavior depends upon every part of the field. It follows that the degree of instability of the adolescent should be greatly influenced also by such factors as general stability or instability of the particular individual.

III

Before I discuss the methodological aspect of our example, I wish to illustrate by an additional example one particular point, namely, the characterizations of events and objects by their interdependence rather than by their similarity or dissimilarity of appearance. In the example of adolescence, only such a procedure made possible the linking of such divergent factors as group-belongingness, bodily changes, and attitudes.

To my mind, it is hopeless to link the different problems involved in social psychology in a proper manner by using classificatory concepts of the type of the Linnean system in botany. Instead, social psychology will have to use a framework of "constructs." These constructs do not express "phenotypical" similarities, but so-called "dynamic" properties—properties defined as "types of reactions" or "types of influences." In other words, these constructs represent certain types of interdependence. The transition from phenotypical concepts to dynamic (genetic, conditional-reactive) constructs based on interdependence is, to my mind, one of the most important prerequisites for any science which wishes to answer questions of causation. Psychology is in the midst of a process of transition to this type of concept. Social psychology, and sociology too, will have to turn definitely in this direction. It is true that such a transition can be made only if and when there is a sufficient amount of phenotypical "facts" gathered and classificatory work has been done. This state, however, seems now to have been reached both in psychology and in sociology.

As an example of the type and importance of this shift to constructs based on interdependence, I might point to the definition of "social group."

The definition of the concept "group" has a somewhat chaotic history. The term is interwoven with philosophical and metaphysical considerations. One of the main points of discussion was whether or not the group has a group mind and is therefore an entity over and above the individual. Besides this, the discussion was dominated frequently by the emphasis upon the difference between *Gemeinschaft* and *Gesellschaft*, whether one has to deal merely with matters of formal organization or whether there exists something like a "natural group unity," based on such factors as empathy.

To the psychologist who has observed the historical development of the concept of "whole," or Gestalt, in psychology, most of the argumentation about the group mind sounds strangely familiar. It took psychology many steps before it discovered that a dynamic whole has properties which are different from the properties of their parts or from the sum of their parts. Even relatively recently (in the early Gestalt psychology) the statement was frequently made that "the whole is more than the sum of its parts." Today such a formulation can be considered hardly adequate. The whole is not "more" than the sum of its parts, but it has different properties. The statement should be: "The whole is different from the sum of its parts." In other words, there does not exist a superiority of value of the whole. Both whole and parts are equally real. On the other hand, the whole has definite properties of its own. This statement has lost all its magic halo and has become a simple fact of science, since it was discovered that this holds also for physical parts and wholes. In addition, psychology today recognizes that there exist wholes of all degrees of dynamic unity: there exist, on the one extreme, aggregates of independent objects; then wholes of small degrees of unity, of medium degrees of unity, of a high degree of unity; finally, at the other extreme, wholes of such a high degree of unity that it is hardly adequate to speak of parts.

Whatever has been of scientific value in the concept of group mind resolves itself into the concrete and familiar problems of dynamic wholes in sociology and social psychology.

Conceiving of a group as a dynamic whole should include a definition of group which is based on interdependence of the members (or better, of the subparts of the group). It seems to me rather important to stress this point because many definitions of a group use the similarity of group members rather than their dynamic interdependence as the constituent factor. Frequently, for instance, a group is defined as composed of a number of persons who show certain similarities, particularly a similarity of attitudes. I think one should realize that such a definition is fundamentally different from a definition of a group based on interdependence of its members. It is very possible that a number of persons have a certain similarity—for instance, of sex, of race, of economic position, of attitudes—without being a group in the sense of being interdependent parts of one social whole. Women all over the world, or unskilled workers, or farmers, may show a certain amount of similarity. It might even be possible to pick out a group of Negroes in Louisiana, poor whites in Kentucky, and peasants in China with great economic similarity. It might be proper to distinguish, in this respect, "types," or "classes."[6] However, this does not imply that these numbers of persons are interdependent to any great extent. One of the developments in modern times is for some of these economic classes to show an increasing degree of interdependence, i.e., they show trends in the direction of development to international groups.

A group, on the other hand, does not need to consist of members which show great similarity. As a matter of fact, it holds for social groups, as for wholes in any field, that a whole of a very high degree of unity may contain very dissimilar parts. Doubtless, for instance, a man, wife, and baby within one family may show much greater dissimilarity than each of the members of this group shows to other individuals (babies, men, women) outside of this group. It is typical of well-organized groups of high degree of unity to include a variety of members who are different and have different functions within the whole. Not similarity, but a certain interdependence of members constitutes a group.

One should realize that even a definition of group membership by equality of goal or equality of an enemy is still a definition by similarity. The same holds for the definition of a group by the feeling of loyalty or of belongingness of their members. However, such an equality, as well as the equality of goal or of enemy, constitutes sometimes, also, a certain interdependence of the persons who show these similarities. Therefore, if one wishes to use the feeling of belonging as the criterion of a group, one can do so if one points to the interdependence established by this feeling. However, one should realize

[6] The term "social class" is used generally to designate both an interdependent group and a number of persons who show similar properties.

that loyalty or feeling of belongingness is only one of a variety of possible types of interdependence which may constitute a group (others are economic dependence, love, living together in a certain area). The kind of interdependence of the members (what holds the group together) is equally as important a characteristic of a group as the degree of their interdependence and the group structure.

Stressing similarity or dissimilarity, rather than interdependence, is typical of the descriptive "classificatory" epoch, which can be observed in a relatively early stage of development in practically every science. It governs also, to a large degree, the everyday thinking concerning groups. The discrepancy between what people "should do, if they would be guided by their real interest," and what they actually do is frequently caused by the fact that a person feels himself belonging to those to whom he is similar or to whom he wishes to be similar. On the other hand, his "real interest" would demand that he should feel belonging to those upon whom his dependence is greatest. Thus, the behavior of persons belonging to underprivileged groups can hardly be understood without realizing that the membership in such a group is determined by actual interdependence but that many underprivileged persons feel themselves (and often are) more similar to people outside that group.

In relation to the problem of group belongingness, as well as to any other social problem, one must become sensitive to the difference between concepts based on interdependence (including similarity of interdependence) and those based on similarity without interdependence. I am persuaded that in the further development of sociology and social psychology the former will more and more pervade and guide.

Conclusions

This cursory examination of the problem of adolescence and the definition of "social group" is meant to illustrate the following general points concerning the field-theoretical approach:

a. It is possible to link in a definite manner a variety of facts of individual and social psychology which, from a classificatory point of view, seem to have very little in common (such as the process of learning and orientation, time perspective, planning, problems of individual maturation, conflicts and tension, group belongingness and the marginal man, and bodily changes).

b. This can be accomplished by the use of constructs which characterize objects and events in terms of interdependence rather than of phenotypical similarity or dissimilarity. It may seem that emphasizing interdependence will make the problem of classification even more difficult because, generally, it is more difficult to describe a fact in terms of its effect on others and its being affected by others (its conditional-genetic properties) than in terms of its appearance (phenotypical properties). However, as soon as one grasps the idea, it becomes evident that if one characterizes an object or event by the way it affects the situation, every type of fact is placed on the same level and becomes interrelated to any other fact which affects the situation. The problem of whether or not one is permitted to combine concepts of values with those of bodily weight, for example, vanishes when confronted with the simple truth that both facts influence the same situation.

The transition to constructs which express interdependence includes:

c. The systematization of facts by "classification" should gradually be replaced by an order based on "construction," "derivation," and "axiomatization" of laws.

d. It is possible to take into account "general" trends, as well as more "specific" ones, in various degrees of specificity (for instance, to link the general factor of locomotion from one region to another to the more specific one of locomotion to an unknown region, or to a locomotion from one social group to another, and finally to the state of the marginal man "between" two groups). Instead of picking out isolated facts, and later on trying to "synthesize" them, the total situation is taken into account and is represented from the beginning. The field-theoretical approach, therefore, means a method of "gradual approximation" by way of a stepwise increasing specificity. Picking out isolated facts within a situation may lead easily to a picture which is entirely distorted. A field-theoretical representation, on the other hand, can and should be essentially correct at any degree of perfection.

e. Whether or not a certain type of behavior occurs depends not on the presence or absence of one fact or of a number of facts as viewed in isolation but upon the constellation (structure and forces) of the specific field as a whole. The "meaning" of the single fact depends upon its position in the field; or, to say the same in more dynamic terms, the different parts of a field are mutually interdependent. This is of fundamental importance in social psychology. It goes a good way in explaining, for example, the effect of rural and urban surroundings and of nursery schools and orphanages on the development of intelligence, or, more generally, the effect of the state of the environment (its degree of differentiation, tension, etc.) on the state of the person, because person and environment are both parts of one dynamic field.

f. The properties of a field as a whole, such as its degree of differentiation, its fluidity, and its atmosphere, should be emphasized sufficiently.

g. The representation of social-psychological facts by dynamic constructs permits derivation of the conditions which influence behavior in one direction or the other and of the conditions under which "exceptions" should be expected. It covers the usual case as well as the exceptional one.

h. It is true that all constructs in psychology and sociology should be operational; i.e., it should be possible to coordinate to each of them observable facts or procedures. However, it is equally important that the conceptual properties of the constructs, that is, their logical-mathematical interrelations, be well determined. The latter necessity, I think, has been relatively more neglected in psychology.

One of the most important among these conceptual problems is finding a geometry which is able to represent the psychological or social field adequately.

Psychology has to deal with a multitude of coexisting facts which are interrelated and have a relative position to each other; in mathematical terms, it has to deal with a "space." Mathematics knows a variety of different types of spaces. It is an empirical question as to what kind of geometry is best suited to represent the dynamic interdependence of that realm of facts which is treated in a particular science. Since Einstein it has been known that Euclidean geometry, which previously was the only geometry applied in physics, is not best fitted for representing the empirical physical space. For psychology, a recently developed nonquantitative geometry, called "topology," can be used satisfactorily in dealing with problems of structure and position in a psychological field.[7] This space permits representation of the position inside or outside of a certain region, the relation between parts and whole, and a great number of structural characteristics. All of this is done in a mathematically exact way but does not presuppose the quantitative determination of size, which is generally not possible in a psychological field. The topological space is too "general" for representing those dynamic psychological problems which include the concept of direction, distance, or force. They can be treated with a somewhat more specific geometry, which I have called "hodological space."[8] This space permits us to speak in a mathematically precise manner of equality and differences of direction, and of changes in distance, without presupposing the "measuring" of angles, directions, and distances, which is usually not possible in a social-psychological field.

It is, I suppose, beyond question that sociology, too, deals with a "multitude of coexistent interdependent facts"—in other words, with the "empirical space."[9] The sociologists and psychologists should recognize what has been long known, that the empirical space is nothing other than a multitude of facts existing at a given time and showing certain types of interdependence. Indeed, sociology has for a long time used a great number of spatial concepts (such as social approach, change in direction of action, etc.). The popular prejudice that the physical space is the only empirical space has made sociologists regard their spatial concepts as merely an analogy. Better insight into the meaning of space in mathematics and physics should readily lead to the understanding that the social field is actually an empirical space, which is as "real" as a physical one.

Euclidean space generally is not suited for adequately representing the structure of a social field—for instance, the relative position of groups, or a social locomotion. For example, in a social field what is meant by a straight line or an angle of 20° cannot be determined

[7] Kurt Lewin: *Principles of Topological Psychology* (New York: McGraw-Hill Book Co., 1936).

[8] Kurt Lewin: The conceptual representation and measurement of psychological forces, *Contr. Psychol. Theor.*, 1938, *1*, No. 4.

[9] This does not mean that every sociological term which sounds geometrical is really a geometrical concept. The term "social distance," for instance, is probably not a geometrical concept.

(at least not at present). However, the topological and the hodological space are, as far as I can see, applicable within sociology proper as well as in social psychology. For in sociology, as in psychology, one is frequently able to determine relations of parts and whole and changes in distance or direction without being able to determine quantitative relations of size, distance, or angle. In addition, these geometries seem to be particularly suitable for representing the peculiar combination of "cognitive" and "dynamic" factors, which is characteristic of psychological and social fields, as well as a number of other fundamental properties of the social-psychological dynamic.

The use of the same kind of geometry in psychology and sociology would not imply that they are one and the same science. The question of the "unity" of both sciences could remain open. However, the task of social psychology would, of course, be greatly facilitated by such a similarity of conceptual tools.

Independent of the solution of this problem, sociology, as well as psychology, will have to decide what kind of geometry it is going to apply in representing the spatial characteristics of its field. Before this question is answered, neither sociology nor psychology can hope to produce scientific derivations more solid than the "statistical rules" based on a coordination of facts treated more or less without regard to their particular position in specific fields.

Both psychology and sociology contain "historical" and ahistorical ("systematical") problems closely interwoven. As opposed to psychology, sociology has been fighting repeatedly against too great an emphasis on the historical aspect of its problems almost from the beginning. The transition to dynamic constructs makes it necessary to see this problem as clearly as possible. It cannot be the task of sociology or psychology to eliminate the historical side of their problems. On the contrary, a field-theoretical approach cannot avoid taking into account the historical character of every fact and its specific historical setting.

Nevertheless, it should be recognized that systematic problems of interdependence are different from historical problems of origin. The question concerning the "nature" and conditions of a social process—in other words, concerning "cause and effect"—is a systematic one both in psychology and sociology. The first and main task of a field-theoretical approach can be characterized as the determination of "what situations are empirically possible and which situations are not"; this is identical with the task of finding laws. For instance, does a dictatorship necessarily suppress discussion? Does it need scapegoats? What forms of dictatorships or of democracies are possible, and how do they affect group structure, the style of living, the ideology, and individual behavior? Questions of such a systematic type of causation will have to be answered experimentally before the dynamic aspect of "historical" problems of origin can be treated satisfactorily.

j. Finally, a point concerning fact-finding should be stressed which is technical in nature but nevertheless important for a field-theoretical approach. It applies to experimental as well as to other investigations.

It has already been emphasized that the validity of social-psychological experiments should be judged not by the properties of isolated events or single individuals within the field but mainly by whether or not the properties of the social group or the social situation as a whole are adequately represented. This implies that one of the foremost tasks of fact-finding and observation in social psychology is to supply reliable data about those properties of the field as a whole.

How should this be done? Suppose, for instance, that the life of a group containing five members were to be observed during a certain period. Let us assume that five observers are available. The natural procedure might seem to be to assign one observer to each member of the group, and in this way to gather all the necessary data about the group life. Generally, however, such a procedure is hardly the best one. What the observers will bring home will be five miniature "biographies" of five individuals. It is true theoretically that if these biographies were to be perfect in securing all individual data, and if, in addition, the time indices for every action were accurate up to the second, the total group life might be "reconstructed" on the basis of such material. In reality, of course, these biographies will be neither complete nor sufficiently accurate as to time. As a rule, therefore, it will not be possible to reconstruct even such simple data about group life as: a continuous record of the size and character of subgroups, their change, and their degree of unity. Generally, this will be as impossible as to construct meaningfully the behavior and the personality of an individual from separate accounts of the history of his various muscles. Any observation necessarily means selection. The observer, confronted with the task of observing an individual, naturally will select those facts which are important for the individual even if they do not matter much for the group. He simply will not "see" facts important for the group as a whole (e.g., for its organization and atmosphere) if they do not immediately reflect strongly in the individual's behavior.

At best, the data about group properties gathered in this fashion on the basis of individual biographies are "indirectly reconstructed." They cannot claim to have the strength of direct observations. However, such direct observations about properties of the group as a whole are possible. Frequently they can be carried through as easily and as accurately as an observation on single individuals. In our example, for instance, it is possible to assign one of the five observers to direct observations of the subgrouping occurring in the group, another one to recording the kind and character of interactions. I am persuaded that, as a rule, for the study of social-psychological problems such a procedure is bound to be more fruitful and more reliable than the assignment of one observer to each individual of the group.

Of course, given the social data, specific observation of individual "biographies" may prove very valuable. I do not doubt, however, that even for the understanding of the character and the behavior of an individual the first type of observation will generally be more significant than a record of the individual without the data about his social background. Because the observation of the group will provide more and better material for the characterization of the position and the role of this individual within the group, they will determine, therefore, the meaning of his action more accurately than what could be achieved by observing him more or less as a separated entity.[10] It would be not at all surprising to me if such a sociological procedure would become a key technique even for problems of individual psychopathology.

[10] The stressing of the field-theoretical approach in regard to the technique of fact-finding in social psychology does not, of course, exclude the possibility that under certain conditions the behavior of an individual can be treated as a symptom for certain properties of the group.

VII

Problems of Research in Social Psychology
(1943-44)*

⎍⎍⎍⎍⎍⎍⎍⎍⎍⎍⎍⎍⎍⎍⎍⎍⎍⎍⎍⎍⎍⎍⎍⎍⎍⎍⎍

THE first task of science is to register objectively and describe
reliably the material one wishes to study. We have learned to
register fairly accurately the *physical* aspects of behavior. But in
regard to the *social* aspects of behavior, the task of objective scientific
description seemed for a long time insoluble. Not many years ago,
a methodological study of this problem in one of our leading uni-
versities came to the following pessimistic conclusion: Observing
the interrelation of a group of individuals, it was possible to collect
reliable data about such items as who moved his arm, turned his
head, or moved from one place to another. However, no reliable
data could be obtained about friendliness or unfriendliness or many
other social characteristics of behavior. The study seemed to lead to
the unfortunate conclusion that what can be observed reliably is
socially meaningless and what is socially meaningful cannot be
observed reliably.

Fortunately, during recent years a number of studies have shown
that, after all, the social aspect of interpersonal behavior can be
observed with high accuracy and with a degree of reliability which
satisfies fully the scientific requirements. It may be worthwhile to
examine how this methodological step forward has been accomplished.

* Editor's note: The material in the first part of this chapter (up to the section,
Experimentation in "Real Life" Settings) is taken from Kurt Lewin: Psychology
and the process of group living, *J. Social Psychol.*, 1943, *17*, 119–129. The re-
mainder of the chapter comes from Kurt Lewin: Constructs in psychology and
psychological ecology, *Univ. Iowa Stud. Child Welf.*, 1944, *20*, 23–27.

SOCIAL PERCEPTION AND INTERPRETATION

One of the fundamental difficulties is related to the distinction between "observation" and "interpretation." In all sciences, it is important to keep observation as free as possible from theories and subjective interpretation. In psychology, too, the observer has to learn to use his eyes and ears and to report what happened rather than what he thinks should have happened according to his preconceived ideas. That is not an easy task. Can it be accomplished at all in social psychology? Can a friendly or an aggressive act be observed without interpretation in the same sense as the movement of an arm can be observed?

Until recently the majority of psychologists were inclined to answer with an emphatic "no" and even today they may give that answer. Actually such an answer implies the impossibility of a scientific social psychology. If we ask the same psychologist, not as a "psychologist" but as an ordinary human being, how he gets along with his wife, he will probably be eager to tell us that—with few exceptions—he and his wife are well able to understand the social meaning of each other's behavior. If we were unable to perceive adequately and objectively the majority of social interactions with our colleagues and students, we would hardly be permitted to remain on the campus for long. Child psychology has established beyond doubt that within the first year of life social perception is well under way. Within three or four years, the child can perceive rather complicated social actions. He is not likely to be fooled by the superficial friendliness of a hostile or uninterested aunt. He is able to "see through" such a surface. Frequently he seems to perceive more clearly than an adult the character of certain social interrelations in his surroundings. This social perception has to be adequate in most of the essential cases if the child is to survive socially. Therefore, objective social observation *must* be possible and the psychologist should find a way to do in science what any normal three-year-old child does in life.

I think we would have sooner found our way if we had not been blinded by philosophical considerations. For more than fifty years psychology has grown up in an atmosphere which recognizes only physical facts as "existent" in the scientific meaning of that term.

The effect of this atmosphere can be observed in every psychological school, in the classical form of Gestalt theory as well as in behaviorism. As usual, the conservative power of philosophy—this time in the form of physicalistic positivism—did its part to keep alive an attitude which once had a function for the progress of science, but which now has outlived its usefulness.

What is needed in social psychology today is to free its methodology from speculative limitations. We do well to start again with the simple facts of everyday life for which the possibility of an adequate social observation never could be in doubt because community life is unthinkable without it. Such an empirical basis should be one basis of the methodology of social psychology. The other should be a progressively deeper understanding of the laws of "social perception."

I would like to mention a few aspects of the problems of social perception. How is it possible today to get reliable observations of social action which could not be recorded reliably yesterday?

If a biologist is to observe the growth of a leaf during a fortnight, he will never finish his job if he tries to follow the movement of the ions contained in that leaf; nor will he succeed if he watches only the tree as a whole on which this leaf grows. The first prerequisite of a successful observation in any science is a definite understanding about *what size of unit* one is going to observe at a given occasion.

This problem is of fundamental importance for social psychology. For a long time we have misinterpreted the scientific requirements of analysis and have tried to observe under all circumstances as *small* units as possible. It is true that sometimes a twinkle of the eye means the difference between acceptance or refusal of marriage. But that meaning is the result of a defined and specific setting. An observation which approaches the movement of the arm or head in isolation is missing the social meaning of the events. In other words, social observation should look toward units of sufficient size.

In addition, the observer should perceive the units in their particular setting. This again is by no means a problem specific for psychology. A physician who would cut up the X-ray picture of the broken bone into small pieces and classify these pieces according to their shades of gray would have destroyed all that he wanted to observe. To give another example, if two persons are running one behind the other, it may mean that the first is leading and the second following, or it may mean that the first is being chased by the second. There is frequently no way to distinguish between these possibilities if the observation lasts only a few seconds. One has to observe a sufficiently extended period before the meaning of an act becomes definitely clear. One does not need to be a Gestalt psychologist or be interested in field theory to recognize these facts which are well established in the psychology of perception. All that is necessary is to acknowledge that the same laws which rule the perception of physical entities also rule social perception.

Like the physician who has to read an X-ray picture, the social psychologist has to be *educated* to know what he can report as an *observation* and what he might add as a more or less valuable *interpretation*. A transition exists between observation and interpretation in the case of the X-ray picture as well as in regard to social data. But that does not weaken the importance of this distinction. Observers have to be trained; then they are able to give reliable observations where the untrained person has to resort to guesswork or interpretation. This holds for the flyer who has to learn to recognize enemy planes even under adverse conditions, for the physician studying the X-ray picture, and also for the social psychologist.

All observation, finally, means classifying certain events under certain categories. Scientific reliability depends upon correct perception *and* correct classification. Here again the observers have to be trained and trained correctly.

There has to be agreement among observers as to what is to be called a "question" and what a "suggestion," where the boundary lies between "suggestion" and a "command." Exactly where the boundary is drawn between two such categories is to a certain degree a matter of convention. However, there are certain basic facts to be learned that are not a matter of arbitrary conventions. If the teacher says to the child in a harsh, commanding voice, "*Would you close the door?*" this should not be classified under the category "question" but under the category "command." The statement of one of our native Nazis that the President's neck is well fitted for a rope is definitely not to be classified under the category "statement of facts" nor under the category "expression of opinion," in spite of its grammatical form. In the attempt to be objective, the psychologist too frequently has made the grammatical form of a sentence, or the physical form of behavior rather than its social meaning, the criterion for classification. We can no longer permit ourselves to be fooled by such superficialities, and will have to recognize that the social meaning of an act is no less objective than its grammatical meaning. There are, of course, also in psychology boundary cases which are difficult to classify; however, experience shows that the observer who is well trained to look for the social meaning of the action is able to perceive correctly and to classify reliably his data.

We should be aware that the problems of social perception have very broad theoretical and practical implications. To name but a few examples: The development of better methods for psychologically correct classifications of social actions and expressions could be of great value for the legal and political aspects of free speech. Recent experiments have shown that the training of leaders is to a high degree dependent upon the sensitizing of their social perception. The good leader is able and ready to perceive more subtle changes in social atmosphere and is more correct in observing social meaning. The good scout master knows that a joking remark or a scuffle during the ceremony of the raising of the flag is something different from the same scuffle during a teaching period or during a period of games; that it has a different meaning if the group is full of pep or all tired out; if it occurs between intimate friends or between two individuals who are enemies.

Social Units of Different Size

Observation of social behavior is usually of little value if it doesn't include an adequate description of the character of the social atmosphere or the *larger unit of activity* within which the specific social act occurs. A running account of such larger units of activity should record whether the situation as a whole has the meaning of "discussing plans" or of "working," of "playing around," or of a "free-for-all fight." It has been shown that a reliable description of the larger units of social events is possible and that the beginning and end of such periods can be determined with an astonishing degree of accuracy. The statistical treatment of the data and their evaluation must carefully take into account the position of a social action within that unit to which it actually belongs. This is as important theoretically as practically. For instance, on the average, the democratic leader will give less direct commands and will more frequently place the responsibility for decision on the members of the group. This does not mean, however, that whenever a leader gives a command he turns autocrat. In matters of routine, even an extremely democratic group might gladly accept a leader or a parliamentary whip who has to see to it that certain objectives are reached efficiently and with a minimum of bother for the members. The democratic leader who may have to be careful to avoid commands in his first contacts might be much freer in the form of his behavior after the social character of the group and his position within it are clearly established. The social meaning and the effect of a command depend upon whether this command deals with an unessential question of "execution" or an essential problem of "policy determination"; whether it is an isolated event, which as Fritz Redl says is "antiseptically" imbedded in the general social atmosphere, or whether it is one of the normal elements of this social setting. It is not the *amount* of power which distinguishes the democratic and the autocratic leader. The President of the United States always had more political power than the Kaiser in Germany. What counts is *how* this power is imbedded in the larger social unit and particularly whether in the long run the leader is responsible to the people below him. In Hitlerism, the leader on any level of the organizational hierarchy had no responsibility whatever to the people below. The leader above him was his only judge and his only source of power.

Of course, much is a question of degree. However, two points should be clear; first, that a democratic leader is neither a man without power nor a traffic policeman nor an expert who does not affect group goals and group decisions; second, that the evaluation of any social atmosphere or organization has to take into account the full spatial and temporal size of the social unit which is actually determining the social events in that group.

It is clear that observation and theory in social psychology face here a number of problems which we have barely started to attack. In physics, we are accustomed to recognize that an ion has different properties from the atom of which it is a part, that the larger molecule again has specific properties of its own, and that a macroscopic object like a bridge, too, has its specific properties as a whole. A symmetrical bridge might be composed of unsymmetrical molecules and the stability of the bridge is not identical with the stability of its molecules. These are simple facts beyond dispute. In social psychology the same facts hold: the organization of a group is not the same as the organization of the individuals of which it is composed. The strength of a group composed of very strong personalities is not necessarily greater but frequently weaker than the strength of a group containing a variety of personalities. The goal of the group is not identical with the goal of its members. Frequently, in a well-organized group, the goals of the members are different. For instance, in a good marriage the husband should be concerned with the happiness of the wife and the wife with happiness of the husband rather than the husband and wife both being concerned only with the happiness of the husband.

That a social unit of a certain size has properties of its own should be accepted as a simple empirical fact. If we refuse to see anything magical about it, we will be better prepared to perceive these units correctly and to develop methods for their scientific description.

The greatest recent progress in methodology has been made in the study of relatively small units: of the single social acts and of face-to-face groups. Some of the characteristics of group structure, such as the degree of subgrouping for work, can frequently be recorded with rather simple means. Sometimes a filming or a recording of the physical grouping of the members gives a fairly accurate picture. Beyond that, methods have been developed which, I think, are able to secure an adequate and reliable picture of the social atmosphere and the social organizations of the group. The leaders and subleaders within the group can be determined and their form of leadership can be measured accurately in a rather short time in many face-to-face groups. Such measurement makes it possible, for instance, to determine typical forms of social management of the good leader and to compare it with the typical forms of group management of the poor leader in the same organization. Such measurement is obviously of greatest importance for the training of good leaders. We should be aware of the fact that good leadership in one organization is not necessarily good leadership in another organization. Leadership should be tailor-made for the specific organization. Even the symptoms, for instance, for an autocratic leader are fairly different in different types of activities. They are different in teaching, in dancing, or playing football. They are different in recreation, in the factory, or in the army, although they all are parts of one democratic culture.

In studying and evaluating problems of leadership or other social actions, we should be careful to determine how much in that social setting is *imposed* on the life of the group by the rules of the organization or other social powers which limit the freedom of action by the members of the group. There is not much chance of distinguishing the democratic from the autocratic scout master within the opening ceremony of flag raising. The way a foreman in a factory treats his workers might be determined by a fight between union and management to such a degree that no training of the foreman in social management could affect the social relations between the foreman and the worker to any considerable degree. In this case, a change in the relation between management and union would be a prerequisite to any essential change in the foreman's behavior. Such an example shows clearly that the size of the social unit which has to be taken into account for the theoretical or practical solution of a social problem is not an arbitrary matter which can be decided by the social psychologist in one way or the other. What social unit is decisive for a given social behavior is an objective question and a problem which has to receive much consideration in any social study.

For instance, the interest which the church or the school that sponsors a Boy Scout troop has in scouting and the status which scouting has in the community might be more important for the membership and the group life of a scout troop than the behavior of the scout master. It is of prime importance in studying morale in the army to know whether the loyalty of the soldier is primarily directed toward his squad, his platoon, his regiment, or to the army as a whole.

In studying the relatively small face-to-face groups we are, I think, well on the way to measuring even such dynamic properties as the degree of group tension, the degree of cohesiveness, and, of course, its ideology. It is possible to conduct experiments, with a group as a whole, which fulfill the requirements of standardized settings to a degree not much different from what we are accustomed to require of an experiment with individuals. It is possible, also, to study empirically the question of to what degree group life, in a given case, depends upon the specific personality of its individual members.

Some properties of groups such as the degree of homogeneity of its ideology can be measured on all sizes of groups. On the whole, however, we are at present much less able to deal adequately with the properties of the social units beyond the size of a face-to-face group. One of the reasons seems to be that the time period which has to be taken into consideration for one unit of events within this larger social group is frequently of considerable extent. The action within a smaller unit—particularly if one deals with children— lies usually within the grasp of an observer who spends an hour or two watching the group. This provides him with a sufficient background to perceive the meaning of the social acts he wishes to study. However, to determine the social meaning of a foreman's conversation with a worker, a continuous observation of the foreman alone, even for weeks, might not suffice. It might be necessary for adequate observation of the foreman to attend a number of meetings of the workers, of certain committees which include management and workers, and some meetings of the management.

In studying such larger units, the interview of certain persons is one of the most essential means of investigation. It is very important to know in what position within the group one is likely to find the best "informants." The psychologist can learn much in this respect from the cultural anthropologist. The questionnaire which has been somewhat in disgrace in psychology may come back in a slightly different form for the study of group life and particularly of the ideology of a group. We are gradually giving up the idea that the answer to the questionnaires or interviews is an expression of facts. We are slowly learning to treat them as reactions to a situation which are partly determined by the question, partly by the general situation of that individual. We have to learn to treat questionnaires as we are accustomed to treat a projective technique. In short, we need most urgently a real theory of questionnairing and interviewing which offers more than a few technical rules.

One technical point seems to hold great practical promise for the future: If the views of the field-theoretical approach are correct, there is a good prospect of approaching experimentally a great number of problems which previously seemed out of reach. If the pattern of the total field is generally more important than, for instance, size, it becomes possible to study fundamental social constellations experimentally by "transposing" them into an appropriate group-size. (Gestalt psychology understands by "transposition" a change which leaves the essential structural characteristics unaltered.) If the experimenter is able to create such a transposition, he does not need to be afraid of creating "artificial," "unlifelike" situations. Experiments become artificial if merely one or another factor is realized, but not the essential pattern. In view of these considerations we should be able to investigate the properties of large groups on relatively small-scale models. We do not need, for instance, to study whole nations to find out to what degree our perception of the ideals of other persons depends on our own culture. We can study the same phenomenon in the eight- and eleven-year-old child who perceives the degree of egoism, generosity, of fairness of his surroundings according to his own degree of egoism, generosity, or fairness.

To mention another example: The morale of a group of any size seems to be stronger if its action is based on its own decision and on "accepting" its own situation. For instance, the ability of an individual to "take it" in a shock situation is much greater in persons who create this situation themselves than in persons who are pushed into the situation from without. A comparison of a lecture method with a method of group decision for changes of food habits in housewives shows that the method of group decision is much more effective.

The success of the fight for equality of an underprivileged group seems to depend greatly on finding leaders who have fully accepted, for better or for worse, their own belonging to this minority or who have joined spontaneously the underprivileged group, as it happened in the French Revolution.

EXPERIMENTATION IN "REAL LIFE" SETTINGS

Although it appears to be possible to study certain problems of society in experimentally created, smaller, laboratory groups, we shall have also to develop research techniques that will permit us to do real experiments within existing "natural" social groups. In my opinion, the practical and theoretical importance of these types of experiments is of the first magnitude. That the basic questions of sociology cannot be answered without experimenting in the strict sense of the term with groups has become clear even to persons who still believe that it will never be possible to carry out such experiments. Such experiments will be important for studying ideologies and changes of culture. They may become one of the foremost techniques for studying normal and abnormal personality and for bringing about personality changes. In other words, the group experiment lies on the intersection of experimental psychology, experimental sociology, and experimental cultural anthropology.

It is clear that experimentation within "life situations" offers particular difficulties, such as in setting up comparable control groups and keeping conditions constant during longer periods. The power and endowment of research institutions have not reached a level which would permit creating large factories or a nation-wide organization for the purpose of science. It may, therefore, be appropriate to mention certain methodological problems which usually would be classified as problems of "applied psychology."

I. CONSTANCY AND SELF-REGULATION IN GROUP BEHAVIOR

The experimenter who is accustomed in his studies of fatigue to keep the flow of material, the amount of interruptions and disturbances constant might well feel that it is hopeless to try exact experimentation in a setting such as a factory where any number of irregularities occur in the flow of material, where workers come and leave, where foreman and fellow workers change their moods and so on. Nevertheless, that a factory may for months show only minor variations in production points to a theoretically important problem. One could try to explain this steadiness of output as a result of the fact that the large social units are influenced by a multitude of strong factors and that, therefore, even relatively strong "chance variations" would be expected not to alter significantly the factory production. It seems, however, that such explanation is by no means sufficient.

Many experimental investigations of groups would hardly be possible without certain "self-regulating" processes within the group. Self-regulating processes are well known in the individual. The body, for instance, is kept at a relatively constant level by certain regulatory processes. A worker who does not feel well might compensate by a temporarily greater effort. Similarly, self-regulating processes in regard to groups as a whole seem to be characteristic of those social conglomerations which are "natural groups." For instance, if a worker is temporarily absent other workers of his team might pinch-hit for him. In other words, the constellation of forces which keeps the group life on a certain quasi-stationary level (see Chapter 9) may maintain this level in spite of disturbances. In such cases, it might well be possible to measure relatively small changes of the forces which determine this quasi-stationary equilibrium even in situations where the irregular disturbances are relatively large. Of course, self-regulation within a group as well as within an individual occurs only to a certain degree and within certain limits.

On the whole then, it seems possible to consider many groups as "natural dynamic units" or wholes which show the typical properties of these units as wholes. In this respect experimentation on a group level is not very different from experiments on the individual level as long as a *transposition* is made from smaller to larger units in regard to time as well as space. Certain social aspects of experimentation with life groups are, however, rather different from ordinary experimentation in the laboratory.

2. THE EXPERIMENTER'S POWER TO CONTROL

Experimentation in the laboratory occurs, socially speaking, on an island quite isolated from the life of society. Although it cannot violate society's basic rules, it is largely free from those pressures which experimentation with "life groups" has to face daily. In a laboratory experiment in perception or frustration the psychologist is usually in control of the situation. In other words he has the power to create the physical conditions he wants. Socially, his power is limited merely by the fact that he does not wish to harm the subject or does not get sufficient cooperation from him. By and large, then, the question of the power of the experimenter is well taken care of in individual psychology.

For experimentation with life groups, however, the power aspect is a major problem. Any organization in which the experiment might proceed has definite, practical purposes. Interference with the objectives of the organization cannot be permitted. On the other hand, to carry through an experiment, the experimenter must somehow have sufficient power to set up the necessary constellations and variations.

As a rule, the only way to acquire such power is to gain the active cooperation of the organization. There would be little chance to gain such power if it were not for the fact that many experimental studies if properly conducted have immediate or long-range practical implications. The organizational form of the existing factories, unions, political parties, community centers, associations—in short, of most groups—is based on tradition, on ideas of "a born organizer," on the nonsurvival of the unfit, or at best, on primitive methods of trial and error. Of course, much practical experience has been gathered and systematized to a degree. We know from other fields, however, that the efficiency of this procedure is far below what can be achieved with systematic scientific experimentation.

It would not be surprising, therefore, if scientific studies on group life would soon be considered as essential for the progress of any large organization as today chemical research is considered essential for the chemical factory.

3. EXPERIMENTATION AND EDUCATION

Even if the person at the helm of the organization is persuaded that certain experiments would be of potential practical value, he will still not be ready to give the experimenter unlimited freedom of action. He might be ready, however, to cooperate with the experimenter to the degree of setting up jointly an experimental procedure. This presupposes that everyone involved in the execution of the project must to some measure become familiar with scientific aspects of the problem.

A considerable amount of education is, therefore, a frequent prerequisite to research in an organization. In the beginning, each section of the organization usually shows some suspicion as a result of its particular type of insecurity; each section is afraid that its power or influence may be affected or that some unpleasant data be uncovered by the research. If the experimenter proceeds correctly, this suspicion usually diminishes the more everyone understands the nature of the problems and gets a first-hand experience of such research. Frequently, such an education can be used as an important part of a planned reorganization of the group. The very attempt to face each other's problems objectively changes attitudes to some degree. The active cooperation in fact finding opens up new horizons, creates better understanding, and often results in higher morale.

4. THEORETICAL AND APPLIED SOCIAL PSYCHOLOGY

The scientist cannot be blind to the fact that the more important the group problems which he intends to study, the more likely it is that he will face not merely technical social problems. He should be clear about his objective. This objective is fact finding in regard to what is and what would be if certain measures were adopted. Without additional premises, the scientist cannot decide whether a manager "should" prefer high production coupled with a factory atmosphere of relatively small status differences or whether he "should" prefer great status differences even if that means less production. He cannot decide what the ideal of the Scout movement "should" be. In other words, the experimenter as such is not the policy determiner of the organization. However, he can investigate what ought to be done if certain social objectives are to be reached. He can secure data which will be important for analyzing a given policy and its effect, and which will be pertinent for any rational policy determination.

In a particular way then are the methodological problems in this field of experimental social psychology interlocked with so called "applied" problems. Even experiments which are designed to solve theoretical problems presuppose close cooperation between the research worker and the practitioner, a sufficient power of the experimenter, and the recognition that any such research on groups is, to a degree, social action.

The relation between scientific psychology and life shows a peculiar ambivalence. In its first steps as an experimental science, psychology was dominated by the desire of exactness and a feeling of insecurity. Experimentation was devoted mainly to problems of sensory perception and memory, partly because they could be investigated through setups where the experimental control and precision could be secured with the accepted tools of the physical laboratory. As the experimental procedure expanded to other sections of psychology and as psychological problems were accepted by the fellow scientist as proper objects for experimentation, the period of "brass instrument psychology" slowly faded. Gradually experimental psychology became more psychological and came closer to life problems, particularly in the field of motivation and child psychology.

At the same time a countercurrent was observable. The term "applied psychology" became—correctly or incorrectly—identified with a procedure that was scientifically blind even if it happened to be of practical value. As the result, "scientific" psychology that was interested in theory tried increasingly to stay away from a too close relation to life.

It would be most unfortunate if the trend toward theoretical psychology were weakened by the necessity of dealing with natural groups when studying certain problems of social psychology. One should not be blind, however, to the fact that this development offers great opportunities as well as threats to theoretical psychology. The greatest handicap of applied psychology has been the fact that, without proper theoretical help, it had to follow the costly, inefficient, and limited method of trial and error. Many psychologists working today in an applied field are keenly aware of the need for close cooperation between theoretical and applied psychology. This can be accomplished in psychology, as it has been accomplished in physics, if the theorist does not look toward applied problems with highbrow aversion or with a fear of social problems, and if the applied psychologist realizes that there is nothing so practical as a good theory.

In the field of group dynamics, more than in any other psychological field, are theory and practice linked methodologically in a way which, if properly handled, could provide answers to theoretical problems and at the same time strengthen that rational approach to our practical social problems which is one of the basic requirements for their solution.

VIII

Psychological Ecology
(1943)

⊓⎍⊓⎍⊓⎍⊓⎍⊓⎍⊓⎍⊓⎍⊓⎍⊓⎍⊓⎍⊓⎍⊓⎍⊓⎍⊓⎍⊓⎍⊓⎍⊓⎍⊓⎍⊓

T HE relation between psychological and nonpsychological factors
    is a basic conceptual and methodological problem in all branches
of psychology, from the psychology of perception to the psychology
of groups. A proper understanding of this relationship must be
achieved before we can answer the many questions raised in efforts
to produce an integration of the social sciences. A field-theoretical
approach to these problems of "psychological ecology" suggests some
of the ways in which these questions may be answered.

The following discussion of food habits may suffice as an example
of a first step in analyzing a field for the purpose of changing cultural
habits. This analysis has the purpose of clarifying exactly where and
how psychological and nonpsychological problems overlap. Any type
of group life occurs in a setting of certain limitations to what is and
what is not possible, what might or might not happen. The nonpsychological factors of climate, of communication, of the law of the
country or the organization are a frequent part of these "outside
limitations." The first analysis of the field is done from the point of
view of "psychological ecology": the psychologist studies "nonpsychological" data to find out what these data mean for determining
the boundary conditions of the life of the individual or group. Only
after these data are known can the psychological study itself be begun
to investigate the factors which determine the actions of the group
or individual in those situations which have been shown to be
significant.

For planning to adapt the food habits of a group to the requirements of health or of changing social conditions, one obviously should know the *status quo*. But what should one consider in studying this *status quo*? In particular, how should the psychologist proceed to make a contribution toward planned changes?

THE SOCIAL TRENDS APPROACH

By studying what people have eaten during, let us say, the last decade one may hope to find certain "trends." By distinguishing more rigid and more flexible trends one then might hope to find indications as to which changes might be expected to encounter much and which little resistance.

Numerous attempts have been made to forecast the future on the basis of "social trends"; we know now that their value for prediction is very limited. Not infrequently, they are misleading.

There are several reasons why technical advice for bringing about changes cannot, as a rule, be based on the study of historical trends:

1. Even if the sampling method is perfect for securing both reliable and valid data, the prediction for the future is a probability statement which presupposes that the situation will remain stationary, or that it will change at a known rate in a known direction. The crux of the matter is that conditions frequently do change radically from one day to another.

2. There is no definite way to judge from historical trends the degree of difficulty for bringing about a change in a certain direction. A long duration of a group habit does not necessarily mean that this habit is rigid. It may mean merely that the related conditions happen not to have changed during that period. It may well be that food habits which remained rigidly upheld for a long time can be changed more easily than habits which in the past have shown a fair amount of flexibility.

3. No amount of descriptive data will settle the question of what techniques are efficient in bringing about desired changes. For instance, no amount of data about what people eat or have eaten can

tell whether advertisement, or lecture, or school education will be most effective.

THE CHILD DEVELOPMENT APPROACH

One may hope to find better means of forecast by studying the individual history. Cultural anthropology has emphasized recently that any constancy of culture is based on the fact that children are growing into that culture. They are indoctrinated and habituated in childhood in a way which keeps their habits strong enough for the rest of their lives.

This shift of approach from the history of the group to the history of the person might be viewed as a change from sociology to psychology. At the same time, it is a step toward linking the degree of resistance to change with the present state of the group members, rather than with the past conduct of the group. It is a step away from an historical and toward an ahistorical dynamic approach.

To my mind, the child development approach in present cultural anthropology is fruitful and desirable. It is very important to know what the likes and dislikes of the children at the different age levels are, what the values behind their food ideology are, and what or whom they conceive as sources of approval and disapproval. Still, one should be clear that the historical and the descriptive approach cannot answer the question of how to change food habits of groups in the desired direction.

THE FIELD APPROACH: CULTURE AND GROUP LIFE AS QUASI-STATIONARY PROCESSES

This question of planned change or of any "social engineering" is identical with the question: What "conditions" have to be changed to bring about a given result and how can one change these conditions with the means at hand?

One should view the present situation—the *status quo*—as being maintained by certain conditions or forces. A culture—for instance, the food habits of a given group at a given time—is not a static affair but a live process like a river which moves but still keeps a recognizable form. In other words, we have to deal, in group life as in individual life, with what is known in physics as "quasi-stationary" processes.[1]

Food habits do not occur in empty space. They are part and parcel of the daily rhythm of being awake and asleep; of being alone and in a group; of earning a living and playing; of being a member of a town, a family, a social class, a religious group, a nation; of living in a hot or a cool climate; in a rural area or a city, in a district with good groceries and restaurants or in an area of poor and irregular food supply. Somehow all of these factors affect food habits at any given time. They determine the food habits of a group every day anew just as the amount of water supply and the nature of the river bed determine from day to day the flow of the river, its constancy, or its change.[2]

Food habits of a group, as well as such phenomena as the speed of production in a factory, are the result of a multitude of forces. Some forces support each other, some oppose each other. Some are driving forces, others restraining forces. Like the velocity of a river, the actual conduct of a group depends upon the level (for instance, the speed of production) at which these conflicting forces reach a state of equilibrium. To speak of a certain culture pattern—for instance, the food habits of a group—implies that the constellation of these forces remains the same for a period or at least that they find their state of equilibrium at a constant level during that period.

Neither group "habits" nor individual "habits" can be understood sufficiently by a theory which limits its consideration to the processes themselves and conceives of the "habit" as a kind of frozen linkage, an "association" between these processes. Instead, habits will have to be conceived of as a result of forces in the organism *and* its life space, in the group *and* its setting. The structure of the organism, of the group, of the setting, or whatever name the field might have in the given case, has to be represented and the forces in the various parts of the field have to be analyzed if the processes (which might be either constant "habits" or changes) are to be understood scien-

[1] For the general characteristics of quasi-stationary processes see Wolfgang Koehler: *Dynamics in Psychology* (New York: Liveright Publishing Co., 1940).

[2] The type of forces, of course, is different; there is nothing equivalent to "cognitive structure" or "psychological past" or "psychological future" in the field determining the river.

tifically. The process is but the epiphenomenon, the real object of study is the constellation of forces.

Therefore, to predict which changes in conditions will have what result we have to conceive of the life of the group as the result of specific constellations of forces within a larger setting. In other words, scientific predictions or advice for methods of change should be based on an analysis of the "field as a whole," including both its psychological and nonpsychological aspects.

AN ILLUSTRATIVE STUDY

The study used here as an illustration of these general principles was conducted by a field staff at the Child Welfare Research Station of the State University of Iowa. Its primary objective was to investigate some of the aspects of *why* people eat what they eat. The method consisted of interviewing housewives. Five groups were studied; three representing economic subdivision (high, medium, and low income levels) of White American stock, and two subcultural groups, Czech and Negro.[3]

A. CHANNEL THEORY

The question "why people eat what they eat," is rather complex, involving both cultural and psychological aspects (such as traditional foods and individual preferences caused by childhood experiences), as well as problems of transportation, availability of food in a particular area, and economic considerations. Therefore the first step in a scientific analysis is the treatment of the problem of where and how the psychological and the nonpsychological aspects intersect. This question can be answered, at least in part, by a "channel theory."

Of paramount importance in this theory is the fact that once food is on the table, most of it is eaten by someone in the family. There-

---

[3] After a period of preliminary trials of various methods, the final data were collected during May and June, 1942. It should be kept in mind that the results describe the attitudes and habits of the people at that time (only sugar was rationed). The material was collected from the residents of a midwestern town with a population of about 60,000. Although surrounded by farming country, the town has a variety of industrial plants. It has employed a nutritionist for a number of years and has a good nutrition program.

For a full discussion of this study see Kurt Lewin: Forces behind food habits and methods of change, *Bulletin of the National Research Council*, 1943, *108*, 35-65.

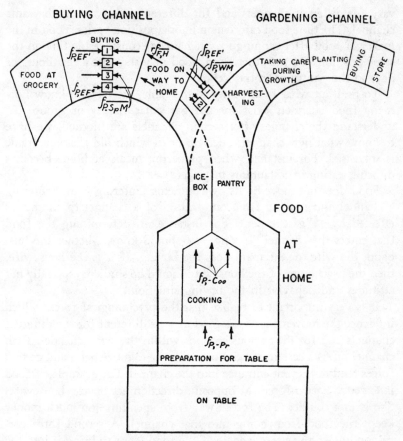

FIGURE 19. Channels through which food reaches the table.

fore one would find the main answer to the question "why people eat what they eat," if one could answer the question, "how food comes to the table and why."

Food comes to the table through various channels (Figure 19). One is buying in a store. After the food has been bought, it may be stored in a locker to be taken out later, then to be cooked and brought to the table. Another channel is gardening. There are additional channels such as deliveries, buying food in the country, baking at home, and canning.

Food moves step by step through a channel. The number of steps vary for different channels and for different foods within the same channel. The time food can remain in one position varies. Food in the locker or food after canning may remain for considerable time in the same position. On the other hand, food may stay just a few hours or days in the pantry or in the icebox.

To find out what food comes to the table, we have to know how many food channels exist for the particular family or group. To understand the changes after certain channels are blocked, we have to know what new channels open up or in which old channels traffic is increased. For instance, when preparing meals at home becomes difficult, eating in restaurants may increase.

Food does not move by its own impetus. Entering or not entering a channel and moving from one section of a channel to another is effected by a "gatekeeper." For instance, in determining the food that enters the channel "buying" we should know whether the husband, the wife, or the maid does the buying. If it is the housewife, then the psychology of the housewife should be studied, especially her attitudes and behavior in the buying situation.

It is very important to realize that the psychological forces which influence the movement of the food may be different for the different channels and for the various sections within the same channel. Each channel offers a certain amount of resistance to movement, and certain forces tend to prevent entrance into the channel. For example, if food is expensive, two forces of opposite direction act on the housewife. She is in a conflict. The force away from spending too much money keeps the food from going into that channel. A second force corresponding to the attractiveness of the food tends to bring it into the channel.

Let us assume that the housewife decides to buy an expensive piece of meat: the food passes the gate. Now the housewife will be very eager not to waste it. The forces formerly opposing each other will now both point in the same direction: the high price that tended to keep the expensive food out is now the reason why the housewife makes sure that through all the difficulties the meat gets safely to the table and is eaten.

1. *The Use of Various Channels.* In our study of a midwestern community we found that in the five groups investigated each of the

foods, except desserts, was obtained through the buying channel considerably more frequently than through any other channel.

For all groups together, it was found that about a third of the vegetables and fruits were canned at home. There seemed to be no relation between income levels and the percentage of families who can, although it was found that the *amount* of food canned was greater in the two lower income groups. A pronounced cultural difference was discovered in that all of the Czech families did some canning, and the amount of food they canned was greater than in comparable income groups in other segments of the community.

In general, the data permitted the following conclusions: To some extent financial circumstances and cultural values do influence the extent to which various food channels are used and the uses to which they are put. Thus, the lower income groups are able to effect savings by canning more of the essential foods they eat and by having more food gardens. The higher income groups are able to maintain lockers and have milk deliveries. Moreover, the lower income groups can essential foods whereas the higher income groups, by canning such foods as jams and jellies, do so for taste and possibly status. The Czech group, resourceful and strongly motivated toward self-sufficiency, does the most canning and gardening.

2. *Who Controls the Channel?* It is important to know what members of the family control the various channels, as any changes will have to be effected through those persons. In all our groups the wife definitely controls all the channels except that of gardening where the husband takes an active part. Even there, however, the husband seldom controls this channel alone. Children are never mentioned as controlling any of the channels, although they undoubtedly influence the decisions indirectly through their rejection of food put before them.

B. THE PSYCHOLOGY OF THE GATEKEEPER

To understand and influence food habits we have to know in addition to the objective food channels and objective availability, the psychological factors influencing the person who controls the channels.

The psychology of the gatekeeper includes a great variety of factors which we do not intend to cover fully. The factors might be classified under two headings, one pertaining to the cognitive structure, i.e., the terms in which people think and speak about food; and the other pertaining to their motivation, e.g., the system of values behind their choice of food.

1. *The Cognitive Structure.* The cognitive structure deals with what is considered "food," "food for us," or "food for other members of the family," with meal patterns, and with the significance of the eating situation.

a. Food Outside and Within Consideration. Physical availability is not the only factor which determines availability of food to the individual. One of the determining factors is "cultural availability." There are many edible materials which people never even consider for use because they do not think of them as food for themselves.

If we consider as food all that which some human beings actually eat and like to eat, then live grasshoppers would have to be included in the category of food. If, however, we ask what people in the United States consider as food, live grasshoppers would be excluded. In other words, the psychological area of food in our culture is only a small part of the objectively edible food, and could be conceived of as a small restricted region within the total region of all objectively edible food.

In some parts of our country peanuts or cheese are considered food for animals but not for human beings. A farm girl in Iowa refused to eat cottage cheese because it is something for the pigs. Even within the area of food in our culture, the boundary between food for human beings and food for animals varies.

Even the food that is recognized as that for human beings still may not be accepted as food for one's own family. For example, kidneys or certain viscera are considered by some as food only for poor people, or champagne a drink for the rich. In other words, only a certain part of the area recognized as "food for human beings" is recognized as "food for us." To find out what is considered "food for us" by different groups is one of the first objectives of studying food habits.

b. Food for Husbands and Children. Within the area of "food for us" one might distinguish "food for the husband" and "food for children" as special subareas. The fact that the housewife controls the channels does not mean that she is uninfluenced by the preferences of the husband, or what she thinks is good for him and the children. The indirect influence of other members of the family was demonstrated in our study in a variety of ways. The most typical husband's food was found to be meat. Meat ranked first as a husband's food for all the subgroups except the Negro group where it ranked third, with vegetables and desserts preceding it. On the other hand, the most typical children's food was vegetables, mentioned by one-third of the families having children. Vegetables ranked first as a children's food for all the groups except the Negro group where it ranked second with desserts first. Potatoes were served more frequently as a special dish for the husband than for the children.

This indirect control by other members of the family is but one of the many aspects of the psychology of the gatekeeper.

c. "Meal Patterns." Other aspects of the cognitive structure of food are the difference between breakfast food, food for lunch, and for dinner; the distinction between main dish and dessert; the concept of balanced meal and of "leftover."

Cereal, caffeins (coffee, tea), eggs, and bread or toast were found to be the most generally accepted *breakfast foods* by all the groups studied. Fruits were mentioned by three-fourths of the high and middle income groups, but by only one-fourth of the Czech, Negro, and low income groups.

As lunch foods, fruits and milk were mentioned more frequently by the high income group, and soups more often by the low income group. Salads, sandwiches, and fruits were much more characteristic of the high and middle income groups than of the others. Leftovers were used for lunch by all groups but more frequently by the Czech group. Lunch is apparently a "pick-up" meal more than either of the other meals. Whereas approximately 75 per cent of the high and middle income groups claimed to plan their lunches, only about 25 per cent of the other groups did. The others said they ate whatever happened to be in the house.

Meat, vegetables, potatoes, and dessert were commonly accepted by all groups as *foods for dinner*. Salads were mentioned much more frequently by the two upper income groups while bread was listed less often and butter not at all. The lower income groups named butter and bread much more frequently. It is likely that bread and butter were considered a real part of the dinner in these groups, and only accessories by the higher income groups.

d. The Meaning of the Eating Situation. One important point is the feeling of group belongingness created by eating in the company of others. At a banquet, eating means something very different from eating after a long period of starvation, and may be classified as a social function rather than as a means of survival. On the whole, eating is usually a more complicated function than just taking nourishment.

The psychological meaning of eating is closely related to group situations. Eating with fellow workers in a factory is something different from eating at the family table or eating in a restaurant. The "eating group" influences greatly the eating conduct and the eating ideology of the individual. One can say that every eating group has a specific eating culture.

2. *Motivation.* We will discuss the various factors in motivation under three major headings: (a) values (motives, ideologies) behind food selection, (b) food needs, and (c) obstacles to be overcome.

a. Values Behind Food Selection. There is more than one value which acts as a frame of reference for the individual choosing foods. These values have not always the same weight for the individual; they may change, as during wartime, and in addition may be different in the restaurant and at home.

At least four frames of reference may be used in evaluating foods —expense, health, taste, and status. It is important to know the relative strengths of these different frames of reference for various groups of people and also how they vary for different foods.

In regard to the system of values, three questions may be asked: (1) What are the values for this group? (2) What is the relative weight of each value? (3) How are specific foods linked with certain values?

In our investigation significant differences were found in the frequency with which various frames of reference were mentioned both between the groups and within each group. Within the groups the following differences were observed. In the high income group, health is the predominant value, with money and taste at a lower, approximately equal level. In the middle group money is the predominant frame, with health considerably lower, and taste a great deal lower. This is also true of the low income and Negro groups except that the differential between money and health is even greater, money being by far the most important consideration. The Czech group falls between the high and middle groups, in that their mention of money and health are approximately equal, with taste a great deal lower.

In order to know which food will be chosen one has to know, in addition to the general value system and the relative weight of each frame of reference, exactly where each of the foods in question stands on each of the value scales.

Fowl was found almost never to be mentioned as a dish to have when short of money, or as a most healthful, or most filling food, but it was frequently mentioned as a dish to have for a company dinner.

The position of the various foods on a taste scale was investigated by asking each housewife, "What dishes are your family especially fond of?" Meats, desserts, and vegetables were the most frequent favorites in all groups. For the Czechs, however, bread was named significantly more often than desserts. That this category, bread, was so high is probably due to the large consumption of kolatches, a Czech dish made of dough similar to bread and stuffed with meat or fruit.

Meat tended to be less mentioned as a favorite dish with decreasing income level. Vegetable dishes showed the opposite trend and were mentioned significantly more often by the low income and Negro groups than by the high income group. This finding may be interpreted as supporting the hypothesis that people like what they eat rather than eat what they like. Our data do not give support to the widely prevalent idea that favorites are generally those foods which are difficult to obtain.

Each housewife was also asked, "What foods do you think are *essential* to a daily diet?" Vegetables and milk were the most frequently mentioned essential foods in all groups. Bread was considered essential by significantly more families from the low income group, the Czechs, and the Negroes than from the high income group. Fruits were regarded as essential much more frequently in the high income groups than in the others. Similar differences were found with respect to eggs.

b. Food Needs. It is important to recognize that the relative weight of the various frames of reference changes from day to day in line with the changing needs. These needs might change because of satiation, of variation in the situation, or because of cultural forces toward diet variations.

It is in line with the basic phenomena of all needs that continued consumption of the same type of food leads to a decrease in the attractiveness of that particular food. This is a powerful determinant of daily and seasonal cycles in food choice. It affects different foods in different degrees; for instance, it is smaller for bread than for meat.

The general level of food satisfaction, too, affects the attractiveness of food and changes the relative weight of the various value scales. If less food is within reach of a person the relative weight of the taste scale tends to diminish in favor of the "essential" aspects of food. If the food basket is pretty well filled the housewife can afford to be more discriminating in her choices than when it is empty.

The situational factors are fairly obvious: When the housewife is short of money at the end of the month or when she is preparing a meal for guests, the corresponding frames of reference will increase in weight.

The continued advocation of a "rich and varied diet" during the last decade has strengthened cultural forces toward day-to-day variations·in foods.

c. Obstacles to be Overcome. The interview did not approach the problem of obstacles along the various channels in a specific way, although these problems must be taken into account in planning changes of food habits. Canned foods, for instance, are frequently preferred because of the little time necessary for preparation. The extent to which such obstacles as difficulty in transportation, lack of domestic help, time necessary for preparing and cooking influence the choice of the gatekeeper depends on his particular circumstances.

3. *Conflict.*

a. Buying as a Decision Situation. We have discussed a number of forces which act toward or away from choosing a given food. Their simultaneous presence in the actual choice situation creates conflict.

In general a conflict situation arises when there is, on the one hand, a drive to engage in a certain activity (as buying food) and on the other hand, a force opposing that activity. An increase in prices, acting as a resistance to buying the foods which people have grown accustomed to enhances the conflict in the food area for all groups. Families of low income are likely to experience more conflict in buying food than those of high income since their freedom in buying the foods they want is restricted by their limited finances. Members from the middle income group, however, may experience greater conflict than those from the low income group in so far as they are psychologically a marginal group. They strive to achieve the social status of the financially more able and at the same time fear dropping back to the level of poor people.

The degree to which a proposed change of food habits happens to touch a food area of high or low conflict is one of the factors determining the degree of emotionality with which people will react.

At the time of the study, prices of foodstuffs had gone up without a comparable rise in income and people were especially conscious of the rising cost of food. Three questions concerning food retrenchment were asked: (1) "Which foods are you *already cutting* because of the increase in the price of food?" (2) "If prices continue to rise, which foods *might* you cut?" (3) "Even if prices continue to rise, which foods are you particularly anxious *not* to cut?"

On the basis of the answers to these three questions it was possible to construct a scale of conflict in terms of which each individual could be rated.

It was assumed that there was some conflict associated with a given food if it was mentioned in answer to any one of the questions, and that the conflict would show a progressive increase (1) if the food had already been cut and might be cut still further (questions 1 and 2), (2) if the food might be cut but was one which the individual did not want to cut (questions 2 and 3), and still more (3) if the food was one which had already been cut but was one which the individual did not want to cut (questions 1 and 3).

For the total group, meat has a significantly higher conflict rating than that of any other food. Its conflict rating, however, varies considerably among the groups, being lowest for the high group and highest for the Czechs and middle income group. Vegetables and milk are second and third highest in the total group. These three foods which produce the greatest conflict are also those which are considered the most essential. At the time of this study, meat had been by far the most frequently cut food. Although it was considered an essential food, it was one of the most expensive, and cutting it could produce a greater saving than cutting any other food. From this analysis we should expect also that cutting meat would produce the greatest emotional disturbance.

C. APPLICATION TO PROBLEMS OF CHANGE

How strong the forces are which resist changes of food habits in a certain direction can be investigated finally only by actual attempts to change food habits, that is, by an experimental approach. No amount of questionnairing can be a substitute for experiments. However, much of the information gathered from interviews can be helpful in planning experiments. Two such types of information may be indicated.

1. *Substitutability of Essential Foods*. The effect of certain motivational forces toward changes in food habits will depend upon the flexibility of these habits. One factor related to flexibility is the degree to which undesirable or unattainable food can be replaced by another food.

We approached this question by asking the housewives what they would substitute for each of the foods listed as essential. In general the substitutes fall into nutritionally similar categories: oranges for lemons, fats for shortening, cheese and eggs for meat, oleomargarine for butter, another kind of vegetable for the one named, fruits for vegetables, etc. Nutritionally dissimilar substitutes were mentioned only by those in the low income group. This finding is in line with the fact that the lower the level of satisfaction of a need the greater is the range of possible consummatory actions for it.

2. *Basis of Change of Food Habits*. Changes in *availability* of food is one obvious cause of changes of food habits. The area of available food may shrink considerably, as is the case in a situation of shortages. This necessitates a change in type and frequently in amount of consumption.

A second cause of changes of eating habits is a change concerning the food *channels*. An example of shifting to more available channels in time of war is the change to gardening and canning.

A third possibility is a psychological change: a food that had been considered "*food for others, but not for us*" may become "*food for us*." Food shortages may facilitate such change. An example is the increased use of glandular meats during the rationing of meats. Whereas a housewife might heretofore have passed them by, she may now consider them seriously and buy them frequently because of their availability and low "point cost." Similar changes can occur with respect to patterns of meals. In the American culture the "food basket" has three distinct parts assigned to breakfast, lunch, dinner; many foods are considered fit for only one part. In case of food shortage this might change. Since lunch is the least structured meal there might be a greater readiness to change the content of the lunch than of the other meals.

A fourth possibility for change in food habits is to *change the potencies of the frames of reference.* This can be accomplished in one of two ways: (1) Changing the *relative potency* of the frames of reference. For example, the emphasis during the war upon nutritional eating was planned to increase the relative potency of the "health" frame of reference ("Eating well to make a strong nation"). (2) Changing the *content* of the frames of reference, that is, the foods related to them. During the first two years of the war the position of fowl undoubtedly changed from that of a "fuss" food, in the direction of an everyday substitute for other meats which were less available. It is quite possible that there was some resistance at first to using it as an "ordinary" meat for everyday meals because of its high position in the "fuss" or "company" frame of reference.

A fifth possibility for change is a change in *belongingness to "eating groups."* Increased incidence of school luncheons and eating in factories should be mentioned here.

In summary, food behavior is determined by the dynamics of the food situation which includes the channels through which food comes to the table, the gatekeeper governing the channels at various points, and the food ideology of the gatekeeper. A system of values is the basis of some of the forces which determine decisions about food and bring about conflicts of varying intensities.

GENERALITY OF THE THEORY

The kind of analysis which we have made here with special reference to changing food habits may be applied quite generally. Social and economic channels may be distinguished in any type of formalized institution. Within these channels gate sections can be located. Social changes in large measure are produced by changing the constellation of forces within these particular segments of the channel. The analytic task is approached from the point of view of psychological ecology; nonpsychological data are first investigated to determine the boundary conditions for those who are in control of various segments of the channel.

Gate sections are governed either by impartial rules or by "gatekeepers." In the latter case an individual or group is "in power" to make the decision between "in" or "out." Understanding the functioning of the gate becomes equivalent then to understanding the factors which determine the decisions of the gatekeepers, and changing the social process means influencing or replacing the gatekeeper. The first diagnostic task in such cases is that of finding the actual gatekeepers. This requires essentially a sociological analysis and must be carried out before one knows whose psychology has to be studied or who has to be educated if a social change is to be accomplished.

Similar considerations hold for any social constellation which has the character of a channel, a gate, and gatekeeper. Discrimination against minorities will not be changed as long as forces are not changed which determine the decisions of the gatekeepers. Their decisions depend partly on their ideology—that is, their system of values and beliefs which determine what they consider to be "good" or "bad"—and partly on the way they perceive the particular situation. Thus if we think of trying to reduce discrimination within a factory, a school system, or any other *organized institution*, we should consider the social life there as something which flows through certain channels. We then see that there are executives or boards who decide who is taken into the organization or who is kept out of it, who is promoted, and so on. The techniques of discrimination in these organizations is closely linked with those mechanics which make the life of the members of an organization flow in definite channels. Thus discrimination is basically linked with problems of management, with the actions of gatekeepers who determine what is done and what is not done.

We saw in our analysis of the flow of food through channels that the constellation of forces before and after the gate region is decisively different. Thus, an expensive food encounters a strong force against entering a channel but once it does enter the same force pushes it on through. This situation holds not only for food channels but also for the traveling of a news item through certain communication channels in a group, for movement of goods, and the social locomotion of individuals in many organizations. A university, for instance, might be quite strict in its admission policy and might set up strong forces against the passing of weak candidates. Once a student is admitted, however, the university frequently tries to do everything in its power to help everyone along. Many business organizations follow a similar policy. Organizations which discriminate against members of a minority group frequently use the argument that they are not ready to accept individuals whom they would be unable to promote sufficiently.

The relation between social channels, social perception, and decision is methodologically and practically of considerable significance. The theory of channels and gatekeepers helps to define more precisely how certain "objective" sociological problems of locomotion of goods and persons intersect with "subjective" psychological and cultural problems. It points to sociologically characterized places, like gates and social channels, where attitudes count most for certain social processes and where individual or group decisions have a particularly great social effect.

IX

Frontiers in Group Dynamics
(1947)

ᒐᒐᒐᒐᒐᒐᒐᒐᒐᒐᒐᒐᒐᒐᒐᒐᒐᒐᒐᒐᒐᒐᒐᒐᒐᒐᒐ

ONE of the by-products of the second World War of which society is hardly aware is the new stage of development which the social sciences have reached. This development indeed may prove to be as revolutionary as the atom bomb. Applying cultural anthropology to modern rather than "primitive" cultures, experimentation with groups inside and outside the laboratory, the measurement of socio-psychological aspects of large social bodies, the combination of economic, cultural, and psychological fact-finding—all of these developments started before the war. But, by providing unprecedented facilities and by demanding realistic and workable solutions to scientific problems, the war has accelerated greatly the change of social sciences to a new developmental level.

The scientific aspects of this development center around three objectives:

1. Integrating social sciences.

2. Moving from the description of social bodies to dynamic problems of changing group life.

3. Developing new instruments and techniques of social research.

Theoretical progress has hardly kept pace with the development of techniques. It is, however, as true for the social as for the physical and biological sciences that without adequate conceptual development, science cannot proceed beyond a certain stage. It is an important step forward that the hostility to theorizing which dominated a number of social sciences ten years ago has all but vanished. It has been replaced by a relatively widespread recognition of the necessity for developing better concepts and higher levels of theory. The theoretical development will have to proceed rather rapidly if social science is to reach that level of practical usefulness which society needs for winning the race against the destructive capacities set free by man's use of the natural sciences.

CONCEPT, METHOD, AND REALITY IN SOCIAL SCIENCE

1. DEVELOPMENTAL STAGES OF SCIENCES

For planning and executing research a clear insight into the present stage of scientific development is needed. Research means taking the next step from the known into the jungle of the unknown. To choose scientifically significant objectives and procedures it does not suffice to be acquainted with the factual knowledge available at a given stage. It is also necessary to free oneself from the scientific prejudices typical of a given developmental stage.

To gain sufficient distance from scientific details and to gain proper perspective for determining next steps the scientist may avail himself of the findings of "comparative theory of science." This discipline deals with the developmental stages of sciences, with their differences and equalities, and can sometimes provide useful yardsticks or way-posts to the empirical scientist.

The types of obstacles which have to be overcome when proceeding to a next scientific step are frequently quite different from what one may expect. Looking backwards it is often hard to understand how anyone could have been influenced by those arguments which have delayed scientific progress for considerable time.

Ernst Cassirer, who has analyzed the developmental stages of the natural sciences, and who had a great gift of viewing logical problems as they appear to the person doing research, points out that scientific progress has frequently the form of a change in what is considered to be "real" or "existing" (4).

2. THE PROBLEM OF EXISTENCE IN AN EMPIRICAL SCIENCE

Arguments about "existence" may seem metaphysical in nature and may therefore not be expected to be brought up in empirical sciences. Actually, opinions about existence or nonexistence are quite common in the empirical sciences and have greatly influenced scientific development in a positive and a negative way. Labeling something as "nonexisting" is equivalent to declaring it "out of bounds" for the scientist. Attributing "existence" to an item automatically makes it a duty of the scientist to consider this item as an object of research; it includes the necessity of considering its properties as "facts" which cannot be neglected in the total system of theories; finally, it implies that the terms with which one refers to the item are accepted as scientific "concepts" (rather than as "mere words").

Beliefs regarding "existence" in social science have changed in regard to the degree to which "full reality" is attributed to psychological and social phenomena, and in regard to the reality of their "deeper," dynamic properties.

In the beginning of this century, for instance, the experimental psychology of "will and emotion" had to fight for recognition against a prevalent attitude which placed volition, emotion, and sentiments in the "poetic realm" of beautiful words, a realm to which nothing corresponds which could be regarded as "existing" in the sense of the scientist. Although every psychologist had to deal with these facts realistically in his private life, they were banned from the realm of "facts" in the scientific sense. Emotions were declared to be something too "fluid" and "intangible" to be pinned down by scientific analysis or by experimental procedures. Such a methodological argument does not deny existence to the phenomenon but it has the same effect of keeping the topic outside the realm of empirical science.

Like social taboos, a scientific taboo is kept up not so much by a rational argument as by a common attitude among scientists: any member of the scientific guild who does not strictly adhere to the taboo is looked upon as queer; he is suspected of not adhering to the scientific standards of critical thinking.

3. THE REALITY OF SOCIAL PHENOMENA

Before the invention of the atom bomb the average physical scientist was hardly ready to concede to social phenomena the same degree of "reality" as to a physical object. Hiroshima and Nagasaki seem to have made many physical scientists ready to consider social facts as being perhaps of equal reality. This change of mind was hardly based on philosophical considerations. The bomb has driven home with dramatic intensity the degree to which social happenings are both the result of, and the conditions for the occurrence of, physical events. Gradually, the period is coming to an end when the natural scientist thinks of the social scientist as someone interested in dreams and words rather than as an investigator of facts, which are not less real than physical facts and which can be studied no less objectively.

The social scientists themselves, of course, have had a stronger belief in the "reality" of the entities they were studying. Still, this belief was frequently limited to the specific narrow section with which they happened to be familiar. The economist, for instance, finds it a bit difficult to concede to psychological, to anthropological, or to legal data that degree of reality which he gives to prices and other economic data. Some psychologists still view with suspicion the reality of those cultural facts with which the anthropologist is concerned. They tend to regard only individuals as real and they are not inclined to consider a "group atmosphere" as something which is as real and measurable as, let us say, a physical field of gravity. Concepts like that of "leadership" retained a halo of mysticism even after it had been demonstrated that it is quite possible to measure, and not only to "judge," leadership performance.

The denial of existence of a group, or of certain aspects of group life, is based on arguments which grant existence only to units of certain size, or which concern technical methodological problems, or conceptual problems.

4. REALITY AND DYNAMIC WHOLES

Cassirer (4) discusses how, periodically throughout the history of physics, vivid discussions have occurred about the reality of the atom, the electron, or whatever else was considered at that time to be the smallest part of physical material. In the social sciences it has usually been not the part but the whole, whose existence has been doubted.

Logically, there is no reason to distinguish between the reality of a molecule, an atom, or an ion, or more generally between the reality of a whole or its parts. There is no more magic behind the fact that groups have properties of their own, which are different from the properties of their subgroups or their individual members, than behind the fact that molecules have properties which are different from the properties of the atoms or ions of which they are composed.

In the social as in the physical field the structural properties of a dynamic whole are different from the structural properties of subparts. Both sets of properties have to be investigated. When one, and when the other, is important depends upon the question to be answered. But there is no difference of reality between them.

If this basic statement is accepted, the problem of existence of a group loses its metaphysical flavor. Instead we face a series of empirical problems. They are equivalent to the chemical question whether a given aggregate is a mixture of different types of atoms, or whether these atoms have formed molecules of a certain type. The answer to such a question has to be given in chemistry, as in the social sciences, on the basis of an empirical probing into certain testable properties of the case in hand.

For instance, it may be wrong to state that the blond women living in a town "exist as a group," in the sense of being a dynamic whole characterized by a close interdependence of members. They are merely a number of individuals who are "classified under one concept" according to the similarity of one of their properties. If, however, the blond members of a workshop are made an "artificial minority" and are discriminated against by their colleagues they may well become a group with specific structural properties.

Structural properties are characterized by *relations* between parts rather than by the parts or elements themselves. Cassirer emphasizes that throughout the history of mathematics and physics problems of constancy of relations rather than of constancy of elements have gained importance and have gradually changed the picture of what is essential. The social sciences seem to show a very similar development.

5. REALITY AND METHODS; RECORDING AND EXPERIMENTATION

If recognition of the existence of an entity depends upon this entity's showing properties or constancies of its own, the judgment about what is real or unreal should be affected by changes in the possibility of demonstrating social properties.

The social sciences have considerably improved techniques for reliably recording the structure of small or large groups and of registering the various aspects of group life. Sociometric techniques, group observation, interview techniques, and others are enabling us more and more to gather reliable data on the structural properties of groups, on the relations between groups or subgroups, and on the relation between a group and the life of its individual members.

The taboo against believing in the existence of a social entity is probably most effectively broken by handling this entity experimentally. As long as the scientist merely describes a leadership form he is open to the criticism that the categories used reflect merely his "subjective views" and do not correspond to the "real" properties of the phenomena under consideration. If the scientist experiments with leadership and varies its form, he relies on an "operational definition" which links the concept of a leadership form to concrete procedures of creating such a leadership form or to the procedures for testing its existence. The "reality" of that to which the concept refers is established by "doing something with" rather than "looking at," and this reality is independent of certain "subjective" elements of classification. The progress of physics from Archimedes to Einstein shows consecutive steps by which this "practical" aspect of the experimental procedure has modified and sometimes revolutionized the scientific concepts regarding the physical world by changing the beliefs of the scientists about what is and is not real.

To vary a social phenomenon experimentally the experimenter has to take hold of all essential factors even if he is not yet able to analyze them satisfactorily. A major omission or misjudgment on this point makes the experiment fail. In social research the experimenter has to take into consideration such factors as the personality of individual members, the group structure, ideology and cultural values, and economic factors. Group experimentation is a form of social management. To be successful it, like social management, has to take into account all of the various factors that happen to be important for the case in hand. Experimentation with groups will therefore lead to a natural integration of the social sciences, and it will force the social scientist to recognize as reality the totality of factors which determine group life.

6. SOCIAL REALITY AND CONCEPTS

It seems that the social scientist has a better chance of accomplishing such a realistic integration than the social practitioner. For thousands of years kings, priests, politicians, educators, producers, fathers and mothers—in fact, all individuals—have been trying day by day to influence smaller or larger groups. One might assume that this would have led to accumulated wisdom of a well-integrated nature. Unfortunately nothing is further from the truth. We know that our average diplomat thinks in very one-sided terms, perhaps those of law, or economics, or military strategy. We know that the average manufacturer holds highly distorted views about what makes a work-team "tick." We know that no one can answer today even such relatively simple questions as what determines the productivity of a committee meeting.

Several factors have come together to prevent practical experience from leading to clear insight. Certainly the man of affairs is convinced of the reality of group life, but he is usually opposed to a conceptual analysis. He prefers to think in terms of "intuition" and "intangibles." The able practitioner frequently insists that it is impossible to formulate simple, clear rules about how to reach a social objective. He insists that different actions have to be taken according to the various situations, that plans have to be highly flexible and sensitive to the changing scene.

If one tries to transform these sentiments into scientific language, they amount to the following statements: (a) Social events depend on the social field as a whole, rather than on a few selected items. This is the basic insight behind the field-theoretical method which has been successful in physics, which has steadily grown in psychology, and, in my opinion, is bound to be equally fundamental for the study of social fields, simply because it expresses certain basic general characteristics of interdependence. (b) The denial of "simple rules" is partly identical with the following important principle of scientific analysis. Science tries to link certain observable (phenotypical) data with other observable data. It is crucial for all problems of interdependence, however, that—for reasons which we do not need to discuss here—it is, as a rule, impracticable to link one set of phenotypical data *directly* to other phenotypical data. Instead it is necessary to insert "intervening variables." To use a more common language: the practitioner as well as the scientist views the observable data as mere "symptoms." They are "surface" indications of some "deeper lying" facts. He has learned to "read" the symptoms, like a physicist reads his instruments. The equations which express physical laws refer to such deeper lying dynamic entities as pressure, energy, or temperature rather than to the directly observable symptoms such as the movements of the pointer of an instrument (4).

The dynamics of social events provides no exception to this general characteristic of dynamics. If it were possible to link a directly observable group behavior, B, with another behavior, B^1 ($B = F [B^1]$ where F means a simple function), then simple rules of procedure for the social practitioner would be possible. When the practitioner denies that such rules can be more than poor approximations he seems to imply that the function, F, is complicated. I am inclined to interpret his statement actually to mean that in group life, too, "appearance" should be distinguished from the "underlying facts," that similarity of appearance may go together with dissimilarity of the essential properties, and *vice-versa*, and that laws can be formulated only in regard to these underlying dynamic entities: $k = F$ *(n, m)* where k, n, m refer not to behavioral symptoms but to intervening variables.

For the social scientist this means that he should give up thinking about such items as group structure, group tension, or social forces as nothing more than a popular metaphor or analogy which should be eliminated from science as much as possible. While there is no need for social science to copy the specific concepts of the physical sciences, the social scientist should be clear that he, too, needs intervening variables, and that these dynamic facts, rather than the symptoms and appearances, are the important points of reference alike for him and for the social practitioner.

7. "SUBJECTIVE" AND "OBJECTIVE" ELEMENTS IN THE SOCIAL FIELD; THE THREE-STEP PROCEDURE

One last point concerning conceptualization and general methodology may be mentioned. To predict the course of a marriage, for instance, a psychologist might proceed in the following way. He might start by analyzing the life space of the husband, H. This analysis would involve the relevant physical and social facts in the husband's surroundings, including the expectations and character of his wife, *W,* all represented in the way the husband, *H,* perceives them. Let us assume that this analysis is sufficiently complete to permit the derivation of the resultant forces on the husband (Figure 20, upper left diagram). This would be equivalent to a prediction of

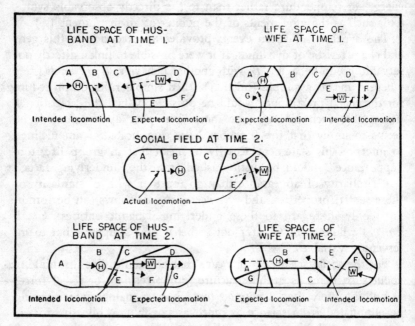

FIGURE 20. The life spaces of a husband and a wife and the social field containing them both.

what the husband actually will do as his next step. The data about the life space of the husband might be sufficiently elaborate to determine the resultant force on the wife, *W,* as he sees her. This resultant force, however, would not indicate what the wife will actually do but merely what the husband expects his wife to do.

To derive the next conduct of the wife, her life space would have to be analyzed (Figure 20, upper right diagram). Usually the wife will see the situation, including herself *W,* and her husband, *H,* somewhat differently from her husband. Let us assume she sees her husband located in an area corresponding to his own perception of himself; that she perceives her own position, however, as being in region E rather than D; and that the cognitive structure of the intermediate regions B and C are for her, too, somewhat different from what they are for her husband. Corresponding to this difference between the life spaces of the husband and wife, the resultant force on the wife, W, may point to the region F rather than to C. This means that the wife will actually move toward F rather than toward C as her husband expected.

The considerations thus far give the basis for predicting the next moves of husband and wife to the region B and F respectively (Figure 20, middle diagram): analyzing the two psychological ("subjective") fields gives the basis for predicting the actual ("objective") next step of behavior.

But how do we proceed from here if we are to answer the social problem of the fate of the marriage? Neither husband nor wife had expected their partner to behave as he or she actually did. Obviously, the next step will depend largely on how each will react to this surprise, how each will interpret the conduct of the other, or, more generally speaking, how each will "perceive" the new situation.

The husband who has expected his wife to move from D to C and now sees her moving in the opposite direction, to F, may interpret this to mean that his wife has "changed her mind." In this case he may expect her next move to proceed in the same direction, namely toward G (Figure 20, lower left diagram). Furthermore, the behavior of his wife is likely to change for him the "meaning" of C, that is, the cognitive structure of the situation. The wife who sees her husband move to B rather than G may perceive this to be an excursion to an activity which would be completed in a certain time after which he would return to A (Figure 20, lower right diagram). She therefore decides to join her husband in B, whereas her husband, having a different perception of the situation, intends to move on to F. which he perceives as being closer to his wife.

Obviously, husband and wife will soon be in trouble if they do not "talk things over," that is, if they do not communicate to each other the structure of their life spaces with the object of equalizing them.

This analysis of the history of a marriage has proceeded in a series of three steps: first, a separate analysis of the psychological situation of the husband and that of the wife, at time 1, with the purpose of deriving the next behavior of each. Second, representing the resultant sociological ("objective") situation at time 2. Third, deriving with the help of the laws of perception the resultant psychological situation for husband and wife at time 2. This would give the basis for the next sequence of three steps, starting with the analysis of the psychological situation of the persons involved to predict their actual next step.

Such a procedure looks involved, particularly if we consider groups, composed of many members. Is it possible to eliminate the "objective" or the "subjective" aspect of this analysis? Actually, social science faces here two types of question; one concerning the size of units, the other concerning the role of perception in group life. It would be prohibitive if the analysis of group life always had to include analysis of the life space of each individual member.

Analysis of group life can proceed rather far on the basis of relatively larger units. In the end, of course, the theory of small and large units has to be viewed in social science as well as in physical science as one theoretical system. But this stage can be reached only after an attack on both the larger and the smaller units.

Unfortunately, treating groups as units does not eliminate the dilemma between "subjective" and "objective" aspects of social fields. It seems to be impossible to predict group behavior without taking into account group goals, group standards, group values, and the way a group "sees" its own situation and that of other groups. Group conflicts would have quite different solutions if the various groups concerned did not perceive differently the situation existing at a given time. To predict or to understand the steps leading to war between two nations *A* and *B* it seems to be essential to refer to the group life space of *A* and to the different group life space of *B*. This means that the analysis of group interaction has again to follow a three-step procedure, moving from the separate analysis of the life space of each group to the group conduct in the total social field and from there back again to the effect on the group life space.

This procedure of analysis which swings from an analysis of "perception" to that of "action," from the "subjective" to the "objective," and back again is not an arbitrary demand of scientific methodology, nor is it limited to the interaction between groups or between individuals. The procedure mirrors one of the basic properties of group life. Any kind of group action or individual action, even including that of the insane, is regulated by circular causal processes of the following type: individual perception or "fact-finding"—for instance, an act of accounting—is linked with individual action or group action in such a way that the content of the perception or fact-finding depends upon the way in which the situation is changed by action. The result of the fact-finding in turn influences or steers action.

Certain schools in psychology, sociology, and economics have tended to eliminate the problems of perception. The analysis of all social sciences, however, will have to take into account both sections of this circular process. The following discussion of the mathematical representation of social problems should not be misunderstood as trying to minimize the importance of cognitive processes in group life. It is rather based on the conviction that field-theoretical psychology has demonstrated the possibility of including them in such a treatment.

QUASI-STATIONARY EQUILIBRIA IN GROUP LIFE AND THE PROBLEM OF SOCIAL CHANGE

Periods of social change may differ quite markedly from periods of relative social stability. Still, the conditions of these two states of affairs should be analyzed together for two reasons: (a) Change and constancy are relative concepts; group life is never without change, merely differences in the amount and type of change exist. (b) Any formula which states the conditions for change implies the conditions for no-change as limit, and the conditions of constancy can be analyzed only against a background of "potential" change.

1. CONSTANCY AND RESISTANCE TO CHANGE

It is important to distinguish two questions which are generally not sufficiently separated; the one concerns actual change or lack of change, the other concerns resistance to change. A given group may show little change during a period of, let us say, two weeks. The group may be composed of friends on an island in the middle of their vacation, or a work-team in a factory. Let us assume that the conditions under which this group lives happen to stay constant during this period: no individual leaves or joins the group, no major friction occurs, the facilities for activities or work remain the same, etc. Under these circumstances the constancy of group life—for instance, the unchanged level of production—does not require any other "explanation" than the reference to the principle: the same conditions lead to the same effect. This principle is identical with the general idea of lawfulness of group life.

The case would be different if the production level of the work-team were maintained in spite of the fact that a member of the work-team took sick or that inferior or superior material was provided. If, in spite of such changes in the group life setting, production is kept at the same level, then can one speak of "resistance" to change of the rate of production. The mere constancy of group conduct does not prove stability in the sense of resistance to change, nor does much change prove little resistance. Only by relating the actual degree of constancy to the strength of forces toward or away from the present state of affairs can one speak of degrees of resistance or "stability" of group life in a given respect.

The practical task of social management, as well as the scientific task of understanding the dynamics of group life, requires insight into the desire for and resistance to, specific change. To solve or even to formulate these questions adequately we need a system of analysis which permits the representation of social forces in a group setting. The following considerations are directed more toward the improvement of these analytical tools than toward the analysis of a particular case.

2. SOCIAL FIELDS AND PHASE SPACES

A basic tool for the analysis of group life is the representation of the group and its setting as a "social field." This means that the social happening is viewed as occurring in, and being the result of, a totality of coexisting social entities, such as groups, subgroups, members, barriers, channels of communication, etc. One of the fundamental characteristics of this field is the relative position of the entities, which are parts of the field. This relative position represents the structure of the group and its ecological setting. It expresses also the basic possibilities of locomotion within the field.

What happens within such a field depends upon the distribution of forces throughout the field. A prediction presupposes the ability to determine for the various points of the field the strength and directions of the resultant forces.

According to general field theory the solution of a problem of group life has always to be finally based on an analytical procedure of this type. Only by considering the groups in question in their actual setting, can we be sure that none of the essential possible conduct has been overlooked.

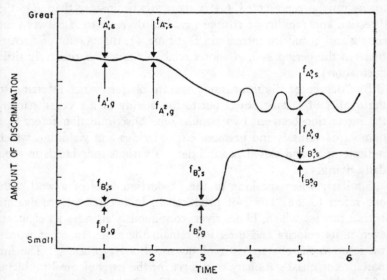

FIGURE 21. Level of equilibrium and strength of opposing forces determining the level of discrimination in two towns.

Certain aspects of social problems, however, can be answered through a different analytical device called "phase space." The phase space is a system of coordinates, each corresponding to different amounts of intensities of one "property." The phase space does not intend to represent the layout of a field composed of groups, individuals, and their ecological setting, but concentrates on one or a few factors. It represents, by way of graphs or equations, the quantitative relation between these few properties, variables or aspects of the field, or of an event in it.

For the discussion of the conditions of change we make use of such a phase space, realizing that one has finally to refer back to the actual social field.

3. SOCIAL STATES AS QUASI-STATIONARY PROCESSES

It is possible to represent the change in discrimination against Negroes in towns *A* and *B* by means of a curve in a diagram where the ordinate represents degrees of discrimination and the abscissa, time (Figure 21). In this way the level of discrimination in the two towns can be represented (*A* is more discriminatory than *B*), the direction and rapidity of change (gradual decrease in *A* between the time 2 and 3, sudden increase in *B* at time 3), the amount of fluctuation (in the period 4–6, *A* shows relatively much, *B* relatively little fluctuation).

By "degree of discrimination" we are obviously not referring to the quality of a static object but to the quality of a process, namely the interaction between two populations. Discrimination refers to a number of refusals and permissions, orderings and yieldings, which indicate open and closed possibilities for various individuals in their daily living.

Similarly when speaking of the production level of a work-team one refers to the "flow" of products. In both cases we are dealing with a process which, like a river, continuously changes its elements even if its velocity and direction remain the same. In other words, we refer to the characteristic of quasi-stationary processes. The importance of quasi-stationary equilibria for the psychological problems of individual life has been emphasized by Koehler (6).

In regard to quasi-stationary processes one has to distinguish two questions: (1) Why does the process under the present circumstances proceed on this particular level (for instance, why does the water in this river move with this particular velocity)? and (2) What are the conditions for changing the present circumstances?

4. A GENERAL ANALYTICAL TREATMENT OF QUASI-STATIONARY SOCIAL EQUILIBRIA

Concerning the relation between the character of the process and the present conditions, certain analytical statements of a rather general nature can be made.

Frequently, analytical conceptual tools (intervening variables) must be developed to a relatively elaborate stage before they are ready to be linked to observable facts. In the beginning it seems to be easier to make empirical use of secondary derivations; only gradually is one able to design experiments to test the fundamentals more directly. The concept of "force," for instance, is more fundamental than the concept "resultant of forces." It is, however, easier in psychology and sociology to coordinate an observable fact to a resultant of forces than to the components: certain aspects of behavior can be directly related to the resultant force, whereas we are able at present to determine psychological component forces only under special conditions (3). We have thought it advisable, therefore, to develop in some detail the conceptual analysis before discussing examples and specific testable theories.

a. The Level of a Quasi-Stationary Process as a Quasi-Stationary Equilibrium. In the case of discrimination, for instance, certain social forces drive toward more discrimination. The interest of certain sections of the white population to keep certain jobs for themselves is such a force; other forces correspond to ideals of the white and colored population about what is "proper" or "not proper" work, etc. Other forces act against greater discrimination: the colored population may show signs of rebellion against higher degrees of discrimination, the white may consider "too much" discrimination unfair, etc. If we indicate the forces toward greater discrimination in the community A by $f_{A,g}$ and the forces toward less discrimination by $f_{A,s}$ we may state that $f_{A,g}$ and $f_{A,s}$ are equal in strength and opposite in direction.[1]

---

[1] The notation of forces follows on the whole the notation I have used for psychological problems (8): $f_{P,g}$ means a force acting on the person P in the direction toward g. $f_{P,-g}$ indicates a force on P in the direction away from g. $rf_{P,g}$ is a restraining force against P's moving toward g. $f^{*}_{P,\,g}$ means a resultant force which has the direction toward g. The strength of the force $f_{P,g}$ is indicated by $|f_{P,g}|$.

If not the individual P but a group Gr is viewed as the point of application of the force, a force toward g is indicated as $f_{Gr,g}$ away from g as $f_{Gr,-g}$. To refer to forces acting on different groups A or group B, or on the same group in different positions A and B, we will use the notation $f_{Gr,\,A,\,g}$ and $f_{Gr,\,B,\,g}$ or the shorter notation $f_{A,g}$ and $f_{B,g}$. The reader should keep in mind, however, that if we say that a force $f_{A,g}$ exists at a position (or a level) A we mean that a force is acting on a group in the position A or that it would act on the group if the group were in that position. The concept of force field refers to such potential positions.

(1) $$f_{A,g} + f_{A,s} = 0$$

This equation does not determine the absolute strength of the forces. The strength of the opposing forces at the time 1 in town A may be smaller or greater than in town B $|f_{A,g}| > |f_{B,g,}|$ (Figure 21). The strength of the opposing forces may increase without a change of the level. For instance, before the level of discrimination has decreased in A the opposing forces may have increased:

$$|f_{A,s}|^2 = |f_{A,g}|^2 > |f_{A,s}|^1 = |f_{A,g}|^1.$$

This would imply that *group tension* has increased. A similar increase of the opposing forces may have occurred in town B at the time 3 prior to the increase in discrimination:

$$|f_{B,s}|^3 = |f_{B,g}|^3 > |f_{B,s}|^1 = |f_{B,g}|^1.$$

Social changes may or may not be preceded by an increase in the opposing forces. Under some conditions, however, social changes can be achieved much easier if the tension is previously decreased. This is important for social management and for the theory of the after effect of changes.

After the discrimination in the town A has decreased the tension may gradually decrease so that

$$|f_{A,s}|^5 < |f_{A,s}|^3.$$

In some cases, however, tension may increase: the decrease of discrimination may lead to a still stronger pressure of the suppressed toward further advances and to an increased counterpressure. After a change to a higher level of discrimination the opposing forces may decrease again or may remain permanently stronger.

On the whole, then, we can say that a quasi-stationary social state corresponds to equally strong opposing forces but that no general statement concerning their absolute strength is possible.

b. Force Fields. Quasi-stationary processes are not perfectly constant but show fluctuations around an average level L. If we assume the fluctuation to be due to the variation in the strength of an additional force and the amount n of the change of the level L to be a function of the strength of this force, we can state that a force field in the area of fluctuation around L exists which has the following characteristics: the opposing forces on all levels between L and $(L + n)$ and between L and $(L - n)$ are unequal with the stronger force pointing toward the level L.

(2)
$$|f_{(L+n),L}| > |f_{(L+n),-L}| ;$$
$$|f_{(L-n),L}| > |f_{(L-n),-L}|$$

The meaning of this statement becomes clearer if we consider the resultant force $f^*_{L,x}$ where $f^*_{L,x} = f_{L,s} + f_{L,g}$. In case of a quasi-stationary process the resultant force on the level L equals zero (Figure 22).

GRADIENTS OF RESULTANT FORCES (f*)

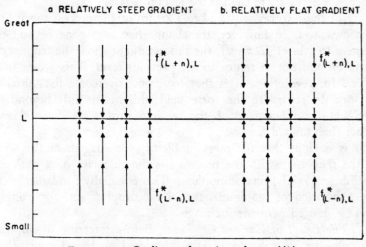

FIGURE 22. Gradients of resultant forces (f^*).

(3)
$$f^*_{L,x} = 0$$

The direction of the resultant forces at the "neighboring levels" $(L \pm n)$ is *toward* level L, their strength increasing with the distance from L. In other words, the resultant forces in the neighborhood of L have the character of a "positive central force field" (8).[2]

---

[2] A positive central force field is defined as a constellation of forces directed toward one region. In a phase space where one dimension is time, one may use this term for a constellation where all forces are directed toward one level.

(4) $$f^*_{(L\pm n),L} = F_{(n)}$$

The character of the function F determines how far, *ceteris paribus*, the social process fluctuates in a specific case.

Changes of the level of quasi-stationary processes will occur if and only if the numerical value of L changes for which the opposing forces are equal. If the resultant force field loses the structure of a central field, the social process loses its quasi-stationary character.

c. Force Field Within and Beyond the Neighborhood Range. It is important to realize that a quasi-stationary process presupposes a central structure of the force field only within a certain neighborhood area of L. The statement (4) does not need to hold for n above or below a certain value. In other words, within a certain range stronger forces are necessary to change the level to a larger extent and a weakening of these forces will lead to a return of the process toward the previous level. If, however, the change has once gone beyond this range n to a level $(L \pm m)$, the process might show the tendency to move on and not to return to the previous level. This seems to be typical for revolutions after they have once overcome the initial resistance. In regard to the force field, this means that beyond the "neighborhood range" of L the resultant forces are directed away rather than toward L.

It is obvious that for most problems of management the width of the range in which the process has the character of a stationary equilibrium is of prime importance. This is equally fundamental for the prevention of major managerial catastrophes and for bringing about a desired permanent change.

d. The Effect of Various Gradients. Before referring to empirical examples let us mention certain additional analytical conclusions. Statement (4) characterizes the structure of the neighboring force field but its gradient is not yet characterized. It might be more or less steep (Figure 22, *a* and *b*). The gradient can be different above and below L.

(5) Given the same amount of change of the strength of the resultant force $(f^*_{L,x})$, the amount of change of the level of social process will be the smaller, the steeper the gradient.

This holds for permanent changes of L as well as for periodical fluctuations.

We have thus far referred to the conduct of the group as a whole. If we consider individual differences within a group we may state:

(6) *Ceteris paribus,* individual differences of conduct in a group will be smaller the steeper the gradient of the resultant force field in the neighborhood of the group level.

Situations of different degrees of permissiveness can be viewed as examples of different steepnesses of the gradient affecting the individuals within a group. The greater range of activities permitted by the democratic leader in the experiment of Lippitt and White (14) was paralleled by greater differences of conduct among the individuals in regard to such items as suggestions to leader, out-of-club-field conversation, and attention demands to companions.

It would be important to relate quantitatively the ease of change of the group level as a whole to the individual differences within the group, although we do not expect to find this relation to be simple.

EXAMPLES OF QUASI-STATIONARY EQUILIBRIUM IN DIFFERENT AREAS OF GROUP LIFE

The following examples are not intended to prove the correctness of a theory for the given case. They are intended mainly to illustrate principles and to prepare the way for the quantitative measurement of social forces. In regard to the specific case they represent hypotheses which have to be tested experimentally.

In the absence of sufficient data on group experiments to illustrate the various analytical principles which should be discussed we have taken the liberty of using somewhat indiscriminately data concerning groups, populations that do not happen to be groups, and individuals.

I. LEVEL OF AGGRESSIVENESS IN DEMOCRATIC AND AUTOCRATIC ATMOSPHERES

Lippitt (13) and Lippitt and White (14) have compared the amount of intermember aggression of the same groups of boys in democratic and autocratic atmospheres. Since the personalities and types of activities were kept constant, the change can be attributed to the different social climate or form of leadership. They found that the group average of intermember aggressiveness in autocracy is either very high or very low; in democracy it is on a more medium level (Figure 23).

Let us assume that each of these levels of aggressiveness is a quasi-stationary equilibrium, and ask which forces tend to raise and which to lower the level. One factor is the type of activity: a wild game gives more chance for clashes than quiet work; a certain amount of fighting might be fun for boys. Forces against intergroup aggression

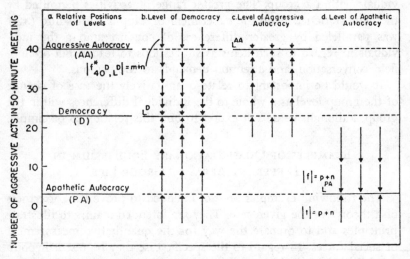

FIGURE 23.   Force fields at the different aggressiveness levels for aggressive autocracy, democracy, and apathetic autocracy.

might be: friendship between members; the presence of an adult leader; the dignified character of the setting.

The actual conduct indicates that in the democratic atmosphere these conflicting forces lead to an equilibrium $(f^*_{L^D,x} = 0)$ for $_L{}^D = 23$. This implies a resultant force field of the character indicated in Figure 23b.

If we use the force field in the democratic atmosphere as our base for comparison, the higher level of aggressiveness in aggressive autocratic *(AAGr)* $(L^{AA} = 40)$ could be explained by an increase in the strength of forces toward more aggression or by a diminishing of the forces toward less aggression. Actually both forces seem to have been altered in autocracy: the style of leadership and the irritation due to the restriction of the space of free movement increases the force toward aggressiveness

$$(\, | f_{AAGr,g} | \; > \; | f_{DGr,g} | \,);$$

Lippitt found that the we-feeling which tends to decrease intermember aggression is diminished in autocracy

$$(\, | f_{AAGr,s} | \; < \; | f_{DGr,s} | \,).$$

This would suffice to explain why the level of aggression increases in autocracy $(L^D < L^{AA})$. If there were no other changes involved, we could even derive a statement concerning the gradient of the force field in the democratic situation: if the increase of the force $f_{Gr,g}$ equals m and the decrease of the force $f_{Gr,s}$ equals n, the strength of the resultant force at level 40 would be $| f^*_{40}{}^D, {}_L{}^D | = m + n$.

How then can aggressiveness in apathetic autocracy (PA) be low $(L^{PA} = 3)$? Lippitt and White (14) found the we-feeling to be low in both types of autocracy; it is unlikely that the irritating effect of the frustrating autocratic leadership should not exist. We are inclined rather to assume that the autocratic leadership form implies an additional force $(f_{Gr,c})$ which corresponds to the higher degree of authoritarian control and which in these situations has the direction against open agression.

As a rule we can assume that this force is rather strong and is considerably greater than $m + n$ $(f_{PAGr,c} = p > (m + n))$. This autocratic control would keep open aggression very low in spite of the greater force toward aggressions. Only if this control were, out of one reason or other, sufficiently weakened so that $| f_{Gr,c} | < (m + n)$ would the increased tendency toward aggression come into the open.

From this theory one could conclude: Although the resultant force on the level L^{PA} of apathetic autocracy is of course again zero $(f^*_{L}{}^{PA},_x = O)$ the opposing components which make up the resultant forces are greater than in the case of democracy. The strength of this additional component is—compared with that in the democratic situation—*ceteris paribus* equal to the pressure of the autocratic control plus the force due to the difference in we-feeling $(\, | f | = p + n)$. In other words we would expect a *high degree of inner tension existing in apathetic autocracy in spite of its appearance of quietness* *and order.* This additional tension would correspond to opposing forces of the strength $|f| = p + n$ (Figure 23*d*).

Since an autocratic atmosphere is less permissive than the democratic atmosphere one may wonder how a high level of in-group aggression can occur in autocracy. The answer lies in the fact that the restrictive character of autocracy has two contradictory effects: (a) it leads to frustration of the group members and therefore to an increase of $f_{P,g}$ in the direction of more aggression. (b) The control aspect of restriction is equivalent to a restraining force $rf_{\overline{P,g}}$ against in-group aggression. This inner contradiction is inherent in every autocratic situation and is the basis of the higher tension level (Figure 23*d*).

From the point of view of management autocratic leadership is confronted with the task of establishing a restraining force field $(rf_{\overline{P,g}})$ of such strength and gradient that the intensity of open in-group aggression does not rise above a certain level. As a first step toward this end, usually, the autocrat tries to strengthen his operational means of control. Strengthening the police or other means of power corresponds to an increase in the "capacity" to control. If this is actually used for stronger suppression, a higher degree of conflict results. This means that a spiral has been set in motion which leads to increasingly more tension, stronger forces toward aggression and suppression.

There are two ways by which autocratic leaders try to avoid this spiral. Restrictive control creates less frustration or at least less open aggression if the individual accepts "blind obedience to the leader" as a value. Germany and Japan are examples of cultures where this attitude is relatively strong. Hitler systematically tried to decrease $f_{P,g}$ through an "education for discipline" in this sense. The second method of reducing $f_{P,g}$ is based on the fact that the tension resulting from a conflict is dynamically equivalent to a "need." Need satisfaction, in this case open aggression, decreases $f_{P,g}$ at least for a certain time. To permit open aggression, but to channel it in a way which is not dangerous for the autocrat is an old technique of social management for autocratic leaders. Another conclusion from the general theory would be that, if the autocratic control in a case of apathetic autocracy were abandoned, a high degree of open aggression should occur as the result of removal of $f_{Gr,c}$. Replacing the autocratic atmosphere with a democratic or laissez-faire atmosphere is equivalent to such a removal. Indeed Lippitt and White (11) observed marked "boiling over" in the first meeting of transition from apathetic autocracy to laissez-faire or democracy (Figure 24). It is in line with the theory that this boiling over went to a higher

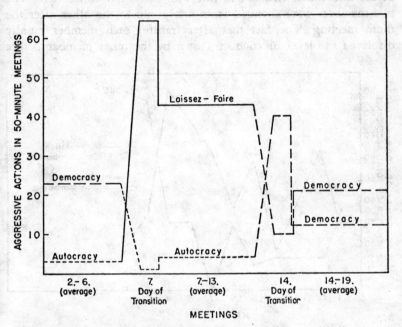

FIGURE 24. Aggression in two groups of boys in different social climates.

level in the case of transition to laissez-faire than to democracy since the general degree of control or self-control which counteracts intermember aggression is stronger in democracy than in laissez-faire.

This representation by way of a phase space takes into account only certain aspects of the actual processes in the social field. For instance, if authoritarian control weakens to the point of permitting open intermember aggression, this aggression is likely to weaken still further the level of control (unless the leader is "reacting" to the situation by a heightening of control). These circular causal processes have to be taken into account for prediction.

2. AN ATMOSPHERE AFFECTING INDIVIDUAL LEVELS OF CONDUCT

Figure 25 represents the amount of dominating behavior of a member of an aggressive autocratic group and a member of a democratic group. After an equality at the first meeting, the conduct of the individuals changed in line with the social atmosphere. The two members were changed from one group to the other after the ninth meeting. The fact that after transfer each member rapidly displayed the level of conduct shown by the other member before

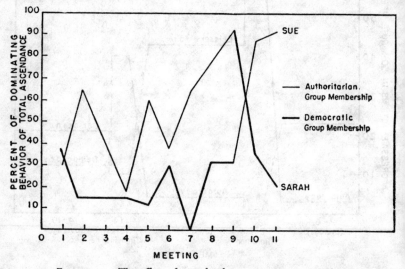

FIGURE 25. The effect of transfer from one group to another.

change indicates that the strength and the gradient of the resultant force field corresponding to the two atmospheres was approximately the same for both individuals.

3. SCAPEGOATING AND THE INTERDEPENDENCE OF LEVELS OF CONDUCT

Data regarding the amount of dominance given and received by individual members of an aggressive autocratic group can serve as an illustration for several general points concerning quasi-stationary processes.

a. Levels of Received Hostility as Equilibria. It is appropriate to consider such a *passive* property as "being attacked" as a quasi-stationary equilibrium. The amount of aggression received depends partly on the degree to which the individual provokes or invites aggression and the way he fights or does not fight back. Other factors are the aggressiveness of the other members, the social atmosphere, etc. On the whole, then, the constellation is the same as in the forces in other cases of equilibrium: the forces always depend on the characteristics of the group or the individual in question and on his relation to the surroundings.

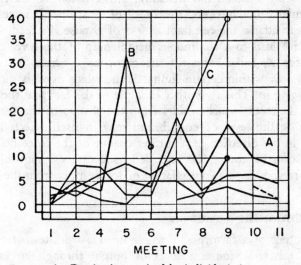

FIGURE 26. Domination received by individuals in a group.

b. Quitting and the Range of the Central Force Field. Scapegoat *B* (Figure 26) quits membership in the club on the sixth day, scapegoat *C* on the ninth day. These happenings are examples of the general fact that a sufficiently large change of the level of equilibrium leads to a basic change in the character of the total situation: too much received dominance makes the member leave.

One may be tempted to represent the tendency of the individual to leave the club after too much received hostility by means of a central force field with a definite range beyond which the resultant forces are directed away from the level of equilibrium. Such a representation could not indicate, however, that the individual leaves the club since the coordinates of the phase space refer only to time and to the amount of received dominance. To represent this fact one has either to refer to the force constellation in the actual social field or to introduce the degree of "eagerness to belong to the club" as a third dimension of the phase space.

c. Interaction and Circular Causal Processes. The scapegoats *A* and *B* who received much dominating behavior (Figure 26) themselves showed much dominating behavior. This indicates a close relation between being attacked and attacking. This relation has the character of a circular causal process: the attack of *A* against *B* increases *B*'s readiness to attack; the resultant attacks of *B* raise *A*'s readiness, etc. This would lead to a continuous heightening of the level of equilibrium for *A*, for *B*, and for the group as a whole. This holds, however, only within certain limits: if the attack of *A* is successful, *B* might give in. This is another example of the fact that the change of a social process which results from the change of the force field determining the level of equilibrium may in itself affect the total situation in the direction of a further change of the force field. This example can, of course, be regarded as a case of nonequilibrium which corresponds to a constellation of forces away from the present level.

4. PRODUCTION IN A FACTORY

The output of a factory as a whole or of a work-team frequently shows a relatively constant level of output through an extended period of time. It can be viewed as a quasi-stationary equilibrium. An analysis of the relevant forces is of prime importance for understanding and planning changes.

One of the forces keeping production down is the strain of hard or fast work. There is an upper ceiling for human activity. For many types of work the force away from the strain $f_{P,-st}$ increases faster the closer one comes to the upper limit. The force field has probably a gradient similar to an exponential curve.

The common belief views the desire to make more money $(f_{P,m})$ as the most important force toward higher production levels. To counter the gradient of the forces $f_{P,-st}$, away from fast work,

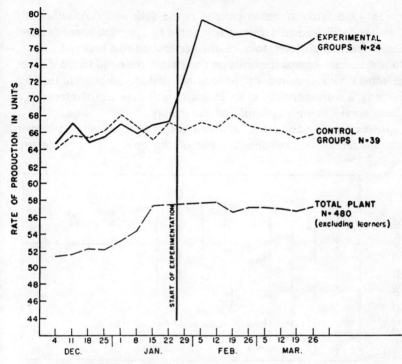

FIGURE 27. Effect of group decision and pacing cards in a sewing factory.

various incentive systems are used which offer higher rates of pay above a certain standard.

Several reasons make it unlikely that the force toward greater output is actually proportional to the unit pay rate. An increase in earning a certain amount means quite different things to different people. Some factories which moved from a northern state to the South ten years ago found it impossible for years to reach a level of production which was at all comparable to that of northern workers. One of the reasons was the fact that for the rural southern girls the weekly pay was so much above previous living standards that they did not care to make more money even for a relatively small additional effort.

The relation between the total amount of earnings and the strength and gradient of the force field differs with the subculture of the group. One fairly common pattern is the following: A sufficiently low level will lead to a very strong force $f_{P,m}$ toward more income; a sufficiently high level, to a small force toward still higher earnings. In some social groups the units on the scale correspond to ten dollars, in others to a hundred or a thousand dollars. The strength of a force $f_{P,m}$ corresponding to an incentive will depend therefore upon the general "living standards" of the group.

In teamwork one of the strongest forces is the desire to remain not too far above or below the rest of the group. This holds par-

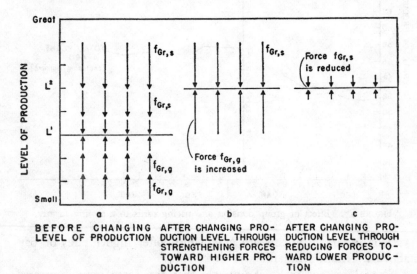

FIGURE 28. Two possible states of tension resulting from different ways of changing levels of production.

ticularly between "parallel workers" or "friends" in an assembly line (18). An important force against increase of speed may be the fear that a temporary increase of speed would bring about pressure from the supervisor or foreman permanently to keep up the higher speed.

Figure 27 presents data from experiments carried out by Bavelas. The output of the sewing factory as a whole, of the experimental population, and of a control population has a typical quasi-stationary character. After the introduction of pacing cards or group decision the experimental groups show a marked increase to a new level of equilibrium. We will not discuss here the details of the methods used. They seem to be based at least in part on procedures which reduce the forces that tend to keep production down rather than on procedures that add new forces toward higher levels.

5. TWO BASIC METHODS OF CHANGING LEVELS OF CONDUCT

It is of great practical importance for any type of social management that production levels are quasi-stationary equilibria which can

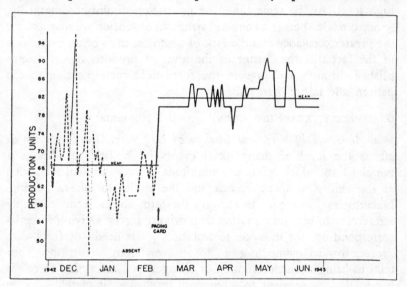

FIGURE 29. Effect of pacing cards on stability of production.

be changed either by adding forces in the desired direction or by diminishing opposing forces.

(7) If a change from the level L^1 to L^2 is brought about by increasing the forces toward L^2 (Figure 28a and b), the secondary effects should be different from the case where the same change of level is brought about by diminishing the opposing forces (Figure 28c). In the first case, the process on the new level L^2 would be accompanied by a state of relatively high tension, in the second case by a state of relatively low tension.

Since increase of tension above a certain degree goes parallel with greater fatigue, higher aggressiveness, higher emotionality, and lower constructiveness it is clear that as a rule the second method will be preferable to the high-pressure method.

Figure 29 offers a striking example of the production of a "nervous" worker which is in line with these considerations. Her average level was above the average of the group; she showed, however, extreme variations in speed and frequent absenteeism. The use of pacing cards led to an increase in production to an exceptionally high level. At the same time, the fluctuation diminished markedly.

Since restlessness is a common symptom of tension we may assume the greater constancy and the lack of absenteeism to be an expression of the fact that the change of the level of production was accomplished through a change in the force field corresponding to the pattern 28c rather than 28b.

6. CAPACITY, LEARNING CURVES, AND EQUILIBRIA

a. Ability, Difficulty, and Change of Difficulty. One factor which affects the level of many social events is "ability." Ability is a popular term which refers to a multitude of very different facts such as the ability to speak French and the ability to take a beating. Nevertheless, in regard to changes the term ability seems to imply a reference to restraining rather than driving forces. Driving forces—corresponding, for instance, to ambition, goals needs, or fears—are "forces toward" something or "forces away from" something. They tend to bring about locomotion or changes. A "restraining force" is not in itself equivalent to a tendency to change; it merely opposes driving forces.

A change in ability is equivalent to a change in the "difficulty of a task." Indeed, for the representation as forces in a phase space, both are identical. Always we deal with a relation between an individual or group and a task. The term ability or the term difficulty is used according to whether one views the subject or the activity as the variable in this relation.

Figure 30 shows the drop in work output after a worker is transferred—on the same sewing machine—to a different sewing job. Although for the two jobs the learning curve of newcomers and the production level of old hands are equal on the average, indicating

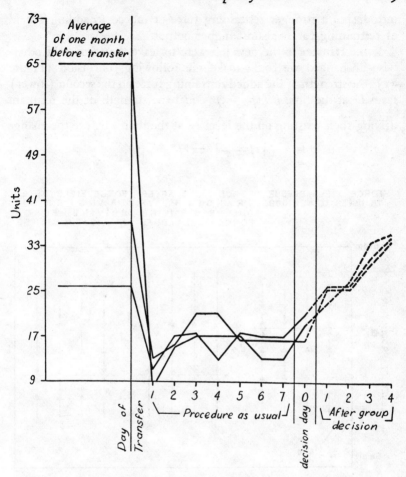

FIGURE 30. Effect of group decision on slow workers after transfer (data from Alex Bavelas).

equal difficulty of the two jobs, transferred workers were found to do less well on the new job. For a transferred worker, obviously, the new task is more difficult than the previous one.

Let us assume that the resultant force field (of the driving and restraining forces) before transfer corresponds to the central field represented in Figure 31. Introducing the new task is equivalent to introducing a stronger restraining force or indeed to adding a field of restraining forces against higher output.

If the transfer to the new job were to leave the force field otherwise unchanged we could make the following conclusion (Figure 31): the strength of the added restraining force on the second (lower) level L^2 at the time b $(rf_{L^2, g})^b$ equal the strength of the resultant driving force existing on the level L^2 at the time a before the change

$$(|rf_{L^2, g}|^b = |f^*_{L^2, g}|^a).$$

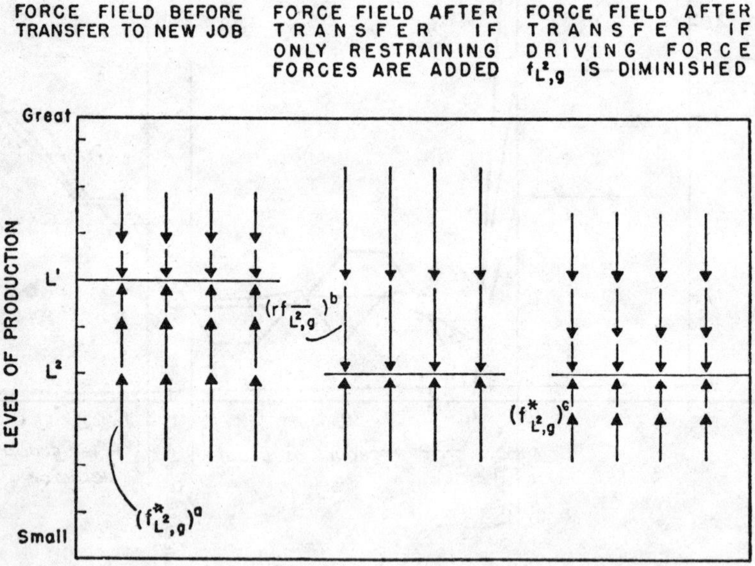

FORCE FIELD BEFORE   FORCE FIELD AFTER   FORCE FIELD AFTER
TRANSFER TO NEW JOB   TRANSFER   IF   TRANSFER   IF
                  ONLY RESTRAINING   DRIVING FORCE
                  FORCES ARE ADDED $f_{L^2, g}$ IS DIMINISHED

FIGURE 31. Force field before and after transfer to a new job.

This would mean that the lowering of the output would be accompanied by an increase in tension.

This is but another example for the theorem: that a change brought about by adding forces in its direction leads to an increase in tension. (In the previous case we had applied this theorem to a change upwards, this time to a change downwards.)

This conclusion, however, is not in line with observations. Actually, the tension after transfer seemed lower, indicating that the change to the lower production level was accompanied by a decrease in the strength of the driving forces toward higher production (Figure 31):

$$|f^*{}_{L^2, g}|^c < |f^*{}_{L^2, g}|^a$$

There are indications that the transfer in these cases is indeed accompanied by a marked lowering of work morale in the sense of drive to higher production. If this interpretation is correct, learning after transfer should be slow, and indeed it is astonishingly slow (Figure 30). Although these workers are familiar with the machines, their speed improves so slowly that it is more profitable for the factory to hire new workers than to change the job of experienced workers.

Probably, several factors combine to decrease the force $f_{L^2, g}$ after transfer: a worker in good standing who is proud of his achievement is thrown back into a state of low working status. This is likely to affect his morale and eagerness. The goal of working at a level "above standard" has been a realistic possibility before transfer; now it is "too" high, it is out of reach. The studies on level of aspiration (12) have shown that under these circumstances a person tends to "give up." This would explain the decrease in $f_{L^2, g}$. After group decision the learning curve rises, probably because the setting up of new goals brings about a resultant force toward higher levels without which learning may not take place.

b. Learning Curves as Base Line for Equilibria Considerations. There are circumstances under which equilibria must be related to a base line defined in other than absolute values. Bavelas gave special training to a person in charge of training beginners in a factory. This led to a considerable steepening of the learning curves of the beginners. After a few weeks when the specially trained trainer was withdrawn and replaced by the previously employed trainer, the learning curve promptly returned to the level it would have had without the training of the trainer. This and other cases make it probable that under certain circumstances a learning curve can be treated as the base line, that is, a line of "equal level" for determining of force fields.

The inclusion of the learning curve as a possible base could be interpreted as an expression of a general principle:

(8) Social forces should be analyzed on the basis of the relation between social processes and the ability (capacity) of the group (or individual) concerned.

If one accepts this general principle, the treatment of "absolute" standards of processes (height of production, of friendliness, etc.), as the frame of reference for analyzing the forces which determine quasi-stationary equilibria is permissible only if the capacities of the groups concerned do not change during that period.

7. THE COMBINATION OF "SUBJECTIVE" AND "OBJECTIVE" METHODS

To determine the nature of the forces which are the main variables in a given case a great variety of procedures can be used. An analysis of both the cognitive ("subjective") and behavioral ("objective") aspects of group life requires a combination of methods which lays open the subjective aspects and permits conclusions concerning conduct which can be checked. An example may illustrate the principle involved.

The Division of Program Surveys of the United States Department of Agriculture during the war carried out for the Treasury Department periodic studies of motivation for buying and redeeming war bonds. Interviews indicated the nature of some of the forces toward and away from redemption for individuals in various sections of the population.

The force toward redemption most frequently encountered was found to be financial pressure resulting from an actual emergency like sickness. Forces against redemption were the need for security which is provided by a financial reserve, patriotism, or gaining a higher interest return if bonds are kept longer.

To relate the "subjective" data about the nature of the forces to the curves representing equilibria, such "objective" data as the "capacity" of a population to redeem war bonds has to be taken into account. Since this capacity depends upon the total amount of war bonds outstanding, it is appropriate according to theorem (8) to base considerations of forces on curves which represent levels of redemption as percentages of this total.

Pearl Harbor, the official entrance of the United States in the war, was accompanied by a marked decline in the level of redemption. From interviews with the population it appears that this was due to an increase of a force against redemption (rather than a decrease of the forces for redemption), namely, a heightened patriotism. From this explanation one would expect that at the end of the war an opposite change would occur. Indeed, Figure 32 shows an increase

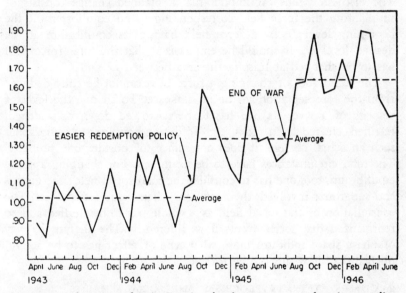

FIGURE 32. Redemptions of Series E savings bonds as percentage of total outstanding.

of the level of redemption at that time; it can be understood in part as the result of the diminished patriotic motive.

On the whole, redemption during the periods from April, 1943, to September, 1944, from October, 1944, to July, 1945, and from August, 1945, to April, 1946, seem to represent three levels of a quasi-stationary process, each period showing typical periodic fluctuations. The change from the first to the second level coincides with the establishing of an easier redemption policy by the Treasury Department corresponding to a decrease of the restraining forces against redemption.

THE CREATION OF PERMANENT CHANGES

1. CHANGE OF FORCE FIELDS

In discussing the means of bringing about a desired state of affairs one should not think in terms of the "goal to be reached" but rather in terms of a change "from the present level to the desired one." The discussion thus far implies that a planned change consists of supplanting the force field corresponding to an equilibrium at the beginning level L^1 by a force field having its equilibrium at the desired level L^2. It should be emphasized that the total force field has to be changed at least in the area between L^1 and L^2.

The techniques of changing a force field cannot be fully deduced from the representation in the phase space. To change the level of velocity of a river its bed has to be narrowed down or widened, rectified, cleared from rocks, etc. To decide how best to bring about such an actual change, it does not suffice to consider one property. The total circumstances have to be examined. For changing a social equilibrium, too, one has to consider the total social field: the groups and subgroups involved, their relations, their value systems, etc. The constellation of the social field as a whole has to be studied and so reorganized that social events flow differently. The analysis by way of phase space indicates more what type of effect has to be accomplished than how this can be achieved.

2. QUASI-STATIONARY PROCESSES AND SOCIAL "HABITS"

Influencing a population to make a change such as substituting the consumption of dark bread for white bread means trying to break a well-established "custom" or "social habit." Social habits usually are conceived of as obstacles to change. What does a social habit mean in terms of force fields and what does "breaking of a habit" mean?

If one regards a social stationary process as determined by a quasi-stationary equilibrium one will expect any added force to change the level. We know that the resultant force on a present level L is zero $(f^*_{L,\,x} = 0)$. Adding the force $|f_{L,\,n}| > 0$ should move the level in the direction of n to a different level $(L + \triangle)$. The amount of change $\triangle$ is determined by the equation

$$(9) \qquad |f^*_{(L+\ ),L}| = |f_{L,n}|$$

The idea of "social habit" seems to imply that in spite of the application of a force $f_{L,n}$ the level of the social process will change less than $\triangle$ because of some type of "inner resistance" to change. To overcome this inner resistance an additional force seems to be required, a force sufficient to "break the habit," to "unfreeze" the custom.

One could try to deny the existence of such "inner resistance to change" out of social habit.[3] Perhaps social habits merely refer to cases of such steep gradient that adding the force $f_{L,n}$ does not lead to a perceivable change. Such an interpretation hardly suffices. At best, it transforms the problem of habit into the question, why does the resultant force field show such a steep gradient in the immediate neighborhood of L?

The social habit theory answers that the historic constancy creates an "additional force field" which tends to keep up the present level in addition to whatever other forces are keeping the social process at that level. Two statements are implied in such a theory; one asserting the existence of the "additional force field," the other regarding its historical origin. We are here interested mainly in the nature of the additional force field.

Social life proceeding on a certain level leads frequently to the establishment of organizational institutions. They become equivalent to "vested interests" in a certain social level. A second possible source of social habits is related to the value system, the ethos of a group. We shall discuss this in more detail.

3. INDIVIDUAL CONDUCT AND GROUP STANDARDS

In discussing force fields we have viewed as "point of application" of the force either an individual or a group as a whole. Let us now consider the relation between the individual and the level of social processes.

An individual P may differ in his personal level of conduct (L^P) from the level which represents group standards (L^{Gr}) by a certain

---

[3] The concept "habit" has played havoc with the progress of psychology for decades. Today it can be regarded as a popular term referring to a conglomeration of various processes. It is to be exchanged for several more adequate concepts (see Chapter 4).

amount n $(|L^{Gr} - L^P| = n)$. Such a difference is permitted or encouraged in different cultures to different degrees. If the individual should try to diverge "too much" from group standards he will find himself in increasing difficulties. He will be ridiculed, treated severely, and finally ousted from the group. Most individuals, therefore, stay pretty close to the standard of the groups they belong to or wish to belong to.

In other words: the group level is not merely a level of equilibrium resulting from whatever forces $f_{L,g}$ and $f_{L,s}$ the circumstances pro-

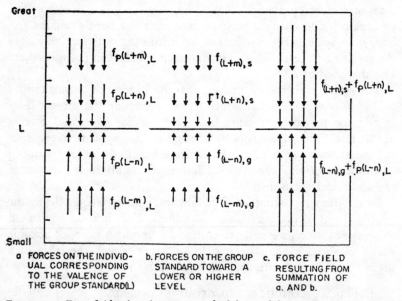

| a. FORCES ON THE INDIVIDUAL CORRESPONDING TO THE VALENCE OF THE GROUP STANDARD(L) | b. FORCES ON THE GROUP STANDARD TOWARD A LOWER OR HIGHER LEVEL | c. FORCE FIELD RESULTING FROM SUMMATION OF a. AND b. |

FIGURE 33. Force fields when the group standard does and does not have social value.

vide. Frequently this level itself acquires value. It becomes a positive valence corresponding to a central force field with the force $f_{P,L}$ keeping the individual in line with the standards of the group.

4. GROUP LEVELS WITH AND WITHOUT SOCIAL VALUE AND THE RESISTANCE TO CHANGE

Although the value character of a group level is rather common, it does not hold for all types of processes. For instance, few individuals know that the level of redemption of war bonds between April, 1943, and August, 1944, was about one per cent. The values which entered into the decisions to redeem did not include the value of keeping the rate of redemption neither above nor below that level. In this respect, the situation is quite different, for instance, from the situation of an individual who tries to keep up with a working team.

Whatever the reason that a certain level acquires or does not acquire value, the difference is important for the problem of change.

Let us assume that for two groups Gr and Gr^1 the resultant force field corresponds to Figure 33b if we do not take into account the social value of L. In the case of Gr^1, but not in the case of Gr, we assume that the level L has social value for the members. This value should correspond to the force field represented in Figure 33a. Let us assume that a force f were applied on the individual to change his conduct towards g. In Gr^1 the amount of change will be determined by the gradient of the counterforce $f_{(L+n),\,g}$, in Gr by the combined counterforces $f_{(L+n),\,g} + f_{P,\,L}$ (Figure 33c). This means:

(10) The greater the social value of a group standard the greater is the resistance of the individual group member to move away from this level.

Many cases of "social habit" seem to refer to group standards with social value, and resistance to change can frequently be explained through theorem (10) If this theory is correct certain derivations can be made in regard to the breaking of social habits.

5. INDIVIDUAL PROCEDURES AND GROUP PROCEDURES OF CHANGING SOCIAL CONDUCT

If the resistance to change depends partly on the value of the group standard for the individual, the resistance to change should be diminished if one uses a procedure which diminishes the strength of the value of the group standard or which changes the level that is perceived by the individual as having social value.

This second point is one of the reasons for the effectiveness of "group carried" changes (17) which approach the individuals in face-to-face groups. Perhaps one might expect single individuals to be more pliable than groups of like-minded individuals. However, experience in leadership training, in changing of food habits, work production, criminality, alcoholism, prejudices—all seem to indicate that it is usually easier to change individuals formed into a group than to change any one of them separately (10). As long as group values are unchanged the individual will resist changes more strongly the further he is to depart from group standards. If the group standard itself is changed, the resistance which is due to the relation between individual and group standard is eliminated.

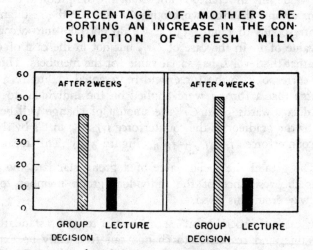

PERCENTAGE OF MOTHERS RE·
PORTING AN INCREASE IN THE CON·
SUMPTION OF FRESH MILK

AFTER 2 WEEKS   AFTER 4 WEEKS

GROUP   LECTURE   GROUP   LECTURE
DECISION   DECISION

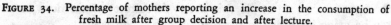

FIGURE 34. Percentage of mothers reporting an increase in the consumption of fresh milk after group decision and after lecture.

6. CHANGING AS THREE STEPS: UNFREEZING, MOVING, AND FREEZING OF GROUP STANDARDS

A change toward a higher level of group performance is frequently short lived; after a "shot in the arm," group life soon returns to the previous level. This indicates that it does not suffice to define the objective of a planned change in group performance as the reaching of a different level. Permanency of the new level, or permanency for a desired period, should be included in the objective. A successful change includes therefore three aspects: unfreezing (if necessary) the present level L^1, moving to the new level L^2, and freezing group life on the new level. Since any level is determined by a force field, permanency implies that the new force field is made relatively secure against change.

The "unfreezing" of the present level may involve quite different problems in different cases. Allport (1) has described the "catharsis" which seems to be necessary before prejudices can be removed. To break open the shell of complacency and self-righteousness it is sometimes necessary to bring about deliberately an emotional stir-up.

PERCENTAGE OF MOTHERS FOLLOWING
COMPLETELY GROUP DECISION
OR INDIVIDUAL INSTRUCTION IN
GIVING ORANGE JUICE

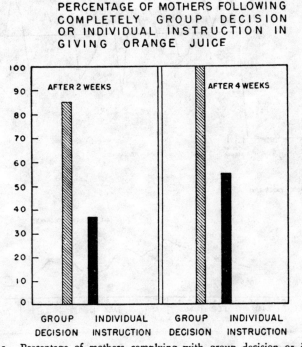

FIGURE 35. Percentage of mothers complying with group decision or individual instruction in giving orange juice.

The same holds for the problem of freezing the new level. Sometimes it is possible to establish an organizational setup which is equivalent to a stable circular causal process.

7. GROUP DECISION AS A CHANGE PROCEDURE

The following example of a process of group decision concerns housewives living in a midwestern town, some of whom were exposed

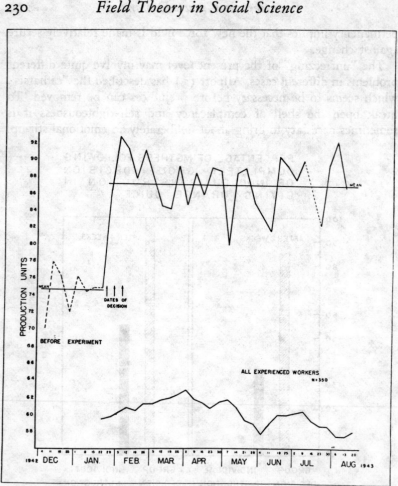

FIGURE 36. The effect of group decision on sewing machine operators.

to a good lecture about the value of greater consumption of fresh milk and some of whom were involved in a discussion leading step by step to the decision to increase milk consumption (16). No high-pressure salesmanship was applied; in fact, pressure was carefully avoided. The amount of time used was equal in the two groups. The change in milk consumption was checked after two and four weeks. Figure 34 indicates the superiority of group decision. Similar results were found in regard to evaporated milk.

The effect of individual treatment was compared with the effect of group decision among farm women who had come to the maternity ward of the State Hospital of Iowa. Before their release they received individual instruction concerning the proper formula for feeding babies and the advisability of giving them orange juice and cod liver oil. This procedure was compared with a procedure of discussion and decision carried out with six mothers as a group. In the first case the nutritionist devoted about twenty-five minutes to a single mother, in the second the same amount of time to a group of six mothers.

Figure 35 shows the superiority of the group decision procedure. At four weeks every one of the mothers in the decision group was giving to the baby the advised amount of cod liver oil. Surprisingly, after both procedures there is an improvement between the second and fourth weeks. Figure 36 presents an example of the effect of three group decisions of a team in a factory reported by Bavelas (15) which illustrates an unusually good case of permanency of change measured over nine months.

The experiments reported here cover but a few of the necessary variations. Although in some cases the procedure is relatively easily executed, in others it requires skill and presupposes certain general conditions. Managers rushing into a factory to raise production by group decisions are likely to encounter failure. In social management as in medicine there are no patent medicines and each case demands careful diagnosis. The experiments with group decision are nevertheless sufficiently advanced to clarify some of the general problems of social change.

We have seen that a planned social change may be thought of as composed of unfreezing, change of level, and freezing on the new level. In all three respects group decision has the general advantage of the group procedure.

If one uses individual procedures, the force field which corresponds to the dependence of the individual on a valued standard acts as a resistance to change. If, however, one succeeds in changing group standards, this same force field will tend to facilitate changing the individual and will tend to stabilize the individual conduct on the new group level.

Sometimes the value system of this face-to-face group conflicts with the values of the larger cultural setting and it is necessary to separate

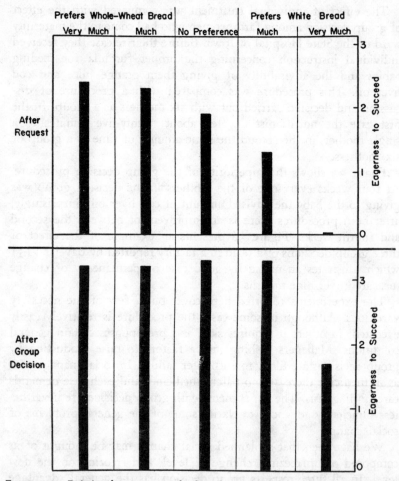

FIGURE 37.   Relation between own food preferences and eagerness to have group succeed after request and after group decision.

the group from the larger setting. For instance, during retraining of recreational leaders from autocratic to democratic patterns Bavelas (2) was careful to safeguard them from interference by the administration of the recreational center. The effectiveness of camps or workshops in changing ideology or conduct depends in part on the possibility of creating such "cultural islands" during change. The stronger the accepted subculture of the workshop and the more isolated it is the more will it minimize that type of resistance to change which is based on the relation between the individual and the standards of the larger group.

One reason why group decision facilitates change is illustrated by Willerman (9). Figure 37 shows the degree of eagerness to have the group change from the consumption of white bread to whole wheat. When the change was simply requested the degree of eagerness varied greatly with the degree of personal preference for whole wheat. In case of group decision the eagerness seems to be relatively independent of personal preference; the individual seems to act mainly as "group member."

A second factor favoring group decision has to do with the relation between motivation and action. A lecture and particularly a discussion may be quite effective in setting up *motivations* in the desired direction. Motivation alone, however, does not suffice to lead to change. That presupposes a link between motivation and action. This link is provided by the decision but it usually is not provided by lectures or even by discussions. This seems to be, at least in part, the explanation for the otherwise paradoxical fact that a process like decision which takes only a few minutes is able to affect conduct for many months to come. The decision links motivation to action and, at the same time, seems to have a "freezing" effect which is partly due to the individual's tendency to "stick to his decision" and partly to the "commitment to a group." The importance of the second factor would be different for a students' cooperative where the individuals remain together, for housewives from the same block who see each other once in a while, and for farm mothers who are not in contact with each other. The experiments show, however, that even decisions concerning individual achievement can be effective which are made in a group setting of persons who do not see each other again.

It would be incorrect to attribute the permanence of the new level entirely to the freezing effect of the decision. In many cases other factors are probably more important. After the housewife has decided to use more milk she might place a standing order with the milkman which could automatically keep milk consumption high. These questions lead to problems of reconstructurization of the social field, particularly to problems of channeling social processes.

Many aspects of social life can be viewed as quasi-stationary processes. They can be regarded as states of a quasi-stationary equilibrium in the precise meaning of a constellation of forces the structure of which can be well defined. These forces have to be identified and will have to be measured quantitatively. A sufficient conceptual analysis is a prerequisite to this step.

The scientific treatment of social forces presupposes analytical devices which are adequate to the nature of social processes and which are technically fitted to serve as a bridge to a mathematical treatment. The basic means to this end is the representation of social situations as "social fields." Some aspects of social processes can be treated by way of systems of coordinates called "phase space."

The use of a phase space for treating a social equilibrium makes it necessary to clarify certain technical questions of analysis, such as the relation between the strength of the opposing forces at a given level of the process, the structure of the force field inside and outside of the neighboring range, the formal conditions of fluctuation and of individual differences, the relation between forces and capacities, and the relation between forces and tension.

This technical analysis makes it possible to formulate in a more exact way problems of planned social changes and of resistance to change. It permits general statements concerning some aspects of the problem of selecting specific objectives in bringing about change, concerning different methods of bringing about the same amount of change, and concerning differences in the secondary effects of these methods. A theory emerges that one of the causes of resistance to change lies in the relation between the individual and the value of group standards. This theory permits conclusions concerning the resistance of certain types of social equilibria to change, the unfreezing, moving, and freezing of a level, and the effectiveness of group procedures for changing attitudes or conduct.

The analytical tools used are equally applicable to cultural, economic, sociological and psychological aspects of group life. They fit a great variety of processes such as production levels of a factory, a work-team and an individual worker; changes of abilities of an individual and of capacities of a country; group standards with and without cultural value; activities of one group and the interaction between groups, between individuals, and between individuals and groups.

The analysis concedes equal reality to all aspects of group life and to social units of all sizes. The application depends upon the structural properties of the process and of the total situation in which it takes place.

Our consideration of quasi-stationary equilibrium has been based on analytic concepts which, within the realm of social sciences, have emerged first in psychology. The concepts of a psychological force, of tension, of conflicts as equilibria of forces, of force fields and of inducing fields, have slowly widened their range of application from the realm of individual psychology into the realm of processes and events which had been the domain of sociology and cultural anthropology. From what I have been able to learn recently about the treatment of equilibria by mathematical economics, I am convinced that this treatment, although having a different origin and being based perhaps on a different philosophy, is also fully compatible with our considerations.

The ease of quantitatively measuring economic data on the one hand, and the disturbing qualitative richness of psychological and cultural events on the other, have tended to keep the methods of investigating these areas separated. Perhaps this situation has driven some mathematical economists into an attempt to develop an economics without people and without culture, much in the way that some mathematically inclined psychologists have tried to develop a theory of learning without organisms. It is possible, however, to leave the philosophical interpretation in abeyance and to regard the equations of mathematical economics as a treatment of certain aspects of events which are methodologically similar to our treatment of certain aspects of social processes by way of phase spaces; in both cases one has to realize that for prediction it is necessary to refer finally to the total social field with all its essential properties. If one is conscious of the limitation of the separate analytical treatment of certain aspects of the social field, this treatment is a useful and indeed necessary step.

Certainly, mathematical economics has developed powerful analytical tools for treating some basic aspects of group life. If our considerations are correct they mean that it is possible to join hands with mathematical economics and I see no reason why, for instance, the methods of treating economic equilibria (5, 7, 19) or the treatment of the grouping in competitive constellations (20) cannot be applied to other areas of social life.

The analytical tools of mathematical economics should be of great help for carrying through the task of measuring social forces, a task which thus far has been accomplished only in a limited area of individual psychology (3). This task implies three steps; a sufficient development of analytical concepts and theories concerning social forces, their quantification in principle through equations, and measuring concrete cases. It seems that the first step in the treatment of group life has sufficiently progressed to permit a collaboration of the various branches of the social sciences for the second and third task.

For economics the fusion implies the possibility of taking into account the cultural and psychological properties of the population involved and, therefore, of improving greatly the ability of analyzing concrete cases and making correct predictions. Economics will have to be ready to complicate its analytical procedures at certain points, particularly it will have to recognize the cognitive problems mentioned above in the discussion of the three-step procedure.

The fusion of the social sciences will make accessible to economics the vast advantages which the experimental procedure offers for testing theories and for developing new insight. The combination of experimental and mathematical procedures has been the main vehicle for the integration of the study of light, of electricity, and of the other branches of physical science. The same combination seems to be destined to make the integration of the social sciences a reality.

REFERENCES

1. ALLPORT, G. W.: Catharsis and the reduction of prejudice, *J. Social Issues,* 1945, *1*, No. 3, 3–10.
2. BAVELAS, ALEX: Morale and the training of leaders. In G. Watson (Ed.): *Civilian Morale* (Boston: Houghton Mifflin Company, 1942).
3. CARTWRIGHT, D., and FESTINGER, L.: A quantitative theory of decision, *Psychol. Rev.,* 1943, 50, 595–621.
4. CASSIRER, E.: *Substance and Function* (Chicago: Open Court, 1923).
5. HICKS, J. R.: *Value and Capital* (Oxford: The Clarendon Press, 1939).
6. KOEHLER, WOLFGANG: *The Place of Value in a World of Fact* (New York: Liveright Publishing Corporation, 1938).
7. LANGE, O.: *Price Flexibility and Employment* (Chicago: University of Chicago Press, 1945).

8. LEWIN, KURT: The conceptual representation and the measurement of psychological forces, *Contr. Psychol. Theory*, 1938, *1*, No. 4.

9. LEWIN, KURT: Forces behind food habits and methods of change, *Bull. Nat. Res. Council*, 1943, *108*, 35–65.

10. LEWIN, KURT: *Resolving Social Conflicts* (New York: Harper & Brothers, 1948, Ch. 4).

11. LEWIN, K., LIPPITT, R., and WHITE, R.: Patterns of aggressive behavior in experimentally created "social climates," *J. Social Psychol.*, 1939, *10*, 271–299.

12. LEWIN, K., DEMBO, T., FESTINGER, L., and SEARS, P.: Level of aspiration. In J. M. Hunt (Ed.): *Personality and the Behavior Disorders* (New York: The Ronald Press Co., 1944).

13. LIPPITT, RONALD: An experimental study of authoritarian and democratic group atmospheres, *Univ. Iowa Stud. Child Welf.*, 1940, *16*, 45–195.

14. LIPPITT, R. and WHITE, R.: The "social climate" of children's groups. In R. Barker, J. Kounin, and H. Wright (Eds.): *Child Behavior and Development* (New York: McGraw-Hill Book Co., 1943).

15. MAIER, N. R. F.: *Psychology in Industry* (Boston: Houghton Mifflin Company, 1946).

16. RADKE, M., and KLISURICH, D.: Experiments in changing food habits, *J. Am. Dietet. A.*, 1947, *23*, 403–409.

17. REDL, FRITZ: Clinical group work with children. In *Group Work and the Social Scene Today* (New York: Association Press, 1943).

18. ROETHLISBERGER, F. J., and DICKSON, W. J.: *Management and the Worker* (Cambridge: Harvard University Press, 1939).

19. SAMUELSON, P. A.: The stability of equilibrium: linear and non-linear systems, *Econometrica*, 1942, *10*, 1–25.

20. VON NEUMANN, J., and MORGENSTERN, O.: *Theory of Games and Economic Behavior* (Princeton: Princeton University Press, 1944).

X

Behavior and Development as a Function
of the Total Situation
(1946)

┌┐┌┐┌┐┌┐┌┐┌┐┌┐┌┐┌┐┌┐┌┐┌┐┌┐┌┐┌┐┌┐┌┐┌┐┌┐┌

IF ONE wishes to use the wealth of accumulated facts concerning
development, personality, social relations, cognition, and motivation for the purpose of understanding, guiding, or predicting the
behavior of any given individual, these data will have to be linked in
such a way that they become applicable to a particular person at a
particular time. This chapter discusses procedures and concepts which
have been found to be instrumental for this purpose. Some of the
relevant methodological questions are considered and certain problems of cognition, motivation, and development are treated as
examples.

ANALYSIS, CONCEPTS, AND THEORY

I. THE PSYCHOLOGICAL FIELD

Scientific procedure is analytical in that it tries to determine or to
"isolate" the effect of various factors. It studies, for instance, the
effect on the child of different intensities of light, of different degrees
of hunger, of failure or praise. It is widely agreed, however, that the
effect of a given stimulus depends upon the stimulus constellation
and upon the state of the particular person at that time. The perceived
form, size, and color of a visual object corresponding to the same
retinal stimulus vary widely according to the visual background and
the nature of the rest of the visual field (46). The toys and other
objects in a room may lead to very different reactions of the one-

year-old child when the mother is present and when she is not (6). In general terms, behavior (B) is a function (F) of the person (P) and of his environment (E), $B = F (P, E)$. This statement is correct for emotional outbreaks as well as for "purposive" directed activities; for dreaming, wishing, and thinking, as well as for talking and acting.

In this formula for behavior, the state of the person (P) and that of his environment (E) are not independent of each other. How a child sees a given physical setting (for instance, whether the frozen pond looks dangerous to him or not) depends upon the developmental state and the character of that child and upon his ideology. The worlds in which the newborn, the one-year-old child, and the ten-year-old child live are different even in identical physical or social surroundings. This holds also for the same child when it is hungry or satiated, full of energy or fatigued. In other words, $E = F (P)$. The reverse is also true: The state of the person depends upon his environment, $P = F (E)$. The state of the person after encouragement is different from that after discouragement (34), that in an area of sympathy or security from that in an area of tension (95), that in a democratic group atmosphere from that in an autocratic atmosphere (82). The momentary intellectual ability of a child as measured by an intelligence test (MA) is different in an atmosphere of good rapport with the examiner from what it is in one of poor rapport. In regard to the effect of the environment upon development, there is a consensus that environment may change intelligence, although opinion differs in regard to how much intelligence can be changed by environment (21, 50, 118, 119, 128). Certainly the ideology, values, and attitudes of the growing individual depend greatly upon the culture in which he is reared (38, 92) and upon his belonging to a privileged or underprivileged group (27, 80).

In summary, one can say that behavior and development[1] depend upon the state of the person and his environment, $B = F (P, E)$. In this equation the person (P) and his environment (E) have to be viewed as variables which are mutually dependent upon each other. In other words, to understand or to predict behavior, the person and

---

[1] The possibility of treating the factors determining development formally in the same way as the factors determining behavior simplifies psychological theory considerably. I owe this idea to Donald K. Adams.

his environment have to be considered as *one* constellation of inter-dependent factors. We call the totality of these factors the life space *(LSp)* of that individual, and write $B = F (P, E) = F (LSp)$. The life space, therefore, includes both the person and his psychological environment. The task of explaining behavior then becomes identical with (1) finding a scientific representation of the life space *(LSp)* and (2) determining the function *(F)* which links the behavior to the life space. This function *(F)* is what one usually calls a *law*.

The novelist who tells the story behind the behavior and development of an individual gives us detailed data about his parents, his siblings, his character, his intelligence, his occupation, his friends, his status. He gives us these data in their specific interrelation, that is, as part of a total situation. Psychology has to fulfill the same task with scientific instead of poetic means. The method should be ana-lytical in that the different factors which influence behavior have to be specifically distinguished. In science, these data have also to be represented in their particular setting within the specific situation. A totality of coexisting facts which are conceived of as mutually inter-dependent is called a *field* (31). Psychology has to view the life space, including the person and his environment, as one field.

What means are most appropriate for analyzing and representing scientifically a psychological field have to be judged on the basis of their fruitfulness for explaining behavior. In this respect, the follow-ing general points should be remembered:

1. A prerequisite for properly guiding a child or for the theoretical understanding of his behavior is the distinction between that situa-tion which the teacher, the parents, or the experimenter sees and that situation which exists for the child as his life space. *Objectivity* in psychology demands representing the field correctly as it exists for the individual in question at that particular time. For this field the child's friendships, conscious and "unconscious" goals, dreams, ideals, and fears are at least as essential as any physical setting. Since this field is different for every age and for every individual, the situation as characterized by physics or sociology, which is the same for every-body, cannot be substituted for it. It is important, however, to know the physical and social conditions because they limit the variety of possible life spaces—probably as *boundary conditions* (see Chapters 3 and 8) of the psychological field.

2. The social aspect of the psychological situation is at least as important as the physical. This holds even for the very young child.

3. To characterize properly the psychological field, one has to take into account such *specific* items as particular goals, stimuli, needs, social relations, as well as such more *general* characteristics of the field as the *atmosphere* (for instance, the friendly, tense, or hostile atmosphere) or the amount of freedom. These characteristics of the *field as a whole* are as important in psychology as, for instance, the field of gravity for the explanation of events in classical physics. Psychological atmospheres are empirical realities and are scientifically describable facts (82).

4. The concept of the psychological field as a determinant of behavior implies that everything which affects behavior at a given time should be represented in the field existing at that time, and that only those facts can affect behavior which are part of the present field (see Chapter 3).

5. To avoid unnecessary assumptions, one can represent the psychological field scientifically by the interrelation of its parts in mathematical terms without asking what the "essence behind" this field is. Such a mathematical representation of the psychological field and the equations expressing the psychological laws are all that have to be known for predicting behavior.

II. THEORIES AND CONSTRUCTS: LAW AND THE INDIVIDUAL CASE

Without theories it is impossible in psychology, as in any other science, to proceed beyond the mere collection and description of facts which have no predictive value. It is impossible to handle problems of conditions or effects without characterizing the *dynamic* properties behind the surface of the directly observable *phenotypical* properties.

The terms *need, association, conditioned reflex, excitatory tendency, gestalt, libido,* and *super-ego* are examples of theoretical constructs with which various psychological schools have attempted to characterize certain underlying dynamic or genotypical facts. It is important to distinguish those facts which are essential for prediction and explanation from their various symptoms. For instance, an emotional state such as anger can lead to a variety of such very different symptoms as noisiness and extreme politeness (25); tension can lead to aggressiveness as well as apathy (82). The same personality may manifest itself in practically opposite actions. In other words, a given state of a person corresponds to a variety of behavior and can, therefore, be inferred only from a combined determination of overt behavior and the situation. This is another way of saying that behavior *(B)* is determined by the person and the environment *(B = F (P, E))* and not by the person or the environment alone.

Psychology has never avoided, nor can it avoid, theory (16, 59, 79, 101, 123), but it can try to eliminate those speculative theories which are frequently introduced without clear intent or in a hidden way, and try instead to make use of openly stated empirical theories. The main desiderata for an efficient empirical theory are: (1) constructs which (a) are linked to observable facts (symptoms) by a so-called operational definition or by a number of operational definitions corresponding to the possibilities of observation under different circumstances; and which (b) have clearly defined conceptual properties. These properties are coordinated to certain mathematical (logical) concepts. Such a coordination is a prerequisite for logically strict derivations. (2) The laws (that is the relation between behavior, on the one hand, and the field characterized by certain constructs, on the other, or between various factors determining the field) should be verified by experiment. A law should be accepted as valid only if it is not contradicted by data in any branch of psychology. In this sense, a law should always be general.

The problems of general laws and of individual differences frequently appear to be unrelated questions which follow somewhat opposite lines. Any prediction, however, presupposes a consideration of both types of questions.

To give just one example of the linkage between the study of general laws and of individual differences: The velocity with which an activity is satiated increases, according to Karsten (68), with the degree to which the activity is psychologically central (as against peripheral). This proposition has the nature of a general law. If correct, it would explain why both agreeable and disagreeable activities are more quickly satiated than relatively neutral ones, and why fashions in women's clothes change faster than in men's clothes. By means of this law one can account for variations in the speed of satiation exhibited by the same person in different states. Certain activities, for example, are more central during menstruum than during intermenstruum and, in accordance with the general law, these activities are satiated more quickly during menstruum. When applied to age differences the law would explain why the velocity of satiation of certain activities is slower in older than in younger children. Finally, it would explain why certain types of problem children who are oversensitive reach the satiation point more quickly than the average child of that age.

This example may show that problems of individual differences, of age levels, of personality, of specific situations, and of general laws are closely interwoven. A law is expressed in an equation which relates certain variables. Individual differences have to be conceived of as various specific values which these variables have in a particular case. In other words, general laws and individual differences are merely two aspects of one problem; they are mutually dependent on each other and the study of the one cannot proceed without the study of the other. This implies that the data about the various age levels provided by child psychology have practical value for the understanding and guiding of individual children only if these data are linked with the concrete situation which is dominating the behavior of a given child at a given time.

This example concerning psychological satiation illustrates also that laws should, and usually can, be applied to all parts of psychology. One of the main functions of theories and constructs is to bind together all the various fields of psychology which otherwise would tend to fall apart into a number of unconnected disciplines.

III. MICROSCOPIC AND MACROSCOPIC UNITS IN PSYCHOLOGY

A problem where prejudices have greatly hampered progress of research is the treatment of units of different sizes. In child psychology we want to know the development of, and conditions for, the movement of the various fingers in the act of grasping (54) or the movement of the tongue (48), as well as the effect of the home background upon the school work of a child, or the effect of his childhood relations with his parents on his behavior as an adult. Child psychology is concerned with questions regarding time units of a fraction of a second ("reaction of the eyelid, eye movements in the act of reading") and with time units of many years (problems of life history, 3, 20, 26).

For instance, the investigation of stuttering involves the study of the position of a sound or syllable in a word (18), of a word in a sentence (17, 19); it involves the study of the importance of the sentence in the text of the paragraph (64); the relation of this verbal expression to the immediate social situation—speaking alone or to a small or large audience (7, 100); the effect of the family's classification of the child as a stutterer (53); the individual's position in his family—for instance, his position in the rank order of siblings (104); his position within the population at large (124); and the general atmosphere of his life space. In other words it is necessary to investigate units of action of widely different sizes and situations of widely different scope, such as the "immediate situation" and the "situation at large."

It is possible to obtain objective and reliable observations in regard to units of any size if one uses methods fitted to the various types (9, 83). The attempt to determine reliably large macroscopic units by observing microscopic units, however, is bound to fail (120) in psychology as in other sciences. It is technically impossible to describe the movement of the sun by describing the movement of every ion contained in it.

THE BEHAVIOR IN A GIVEN PSYCHOLOGICAL FIELD

I. COGNITIVE STRUCTURE OF THE LIFE SPACE

Differentiation of the Various Dimensions of the Life Space. An outstanding characteristic of the change of the life space during development is an increasing differentiation. The importance of this factor has been shown in regard to the development of language (49), knowledge (122), social interrelations (95), emotions (63), and actions (34).

The life space of the newborn child may be described as a field which has relatively few and only vaguely distinguishable areas (74). The situation probably corresponds to a general state of greater or less comfort. No definite objects or persons seem to be distinguished. No area called "my own body" exists. Future events or expectations do not exist; the child is ruled by the situation immediately at hand.

Some of the first areas which get a definite character seem to be connected with food and elimination. After as short a period as three to six days the child reacts to being prepared for nursing (88). A similar increase in size and differentiation of the life space occurs in other respects. The child studies his own body (20) and his immediate physical surroundings. Within the first few months, certain social relations develop.

The increase of the life space in regard to the psychological time dimensions continues into adulthood. Plans extend farther into the future and activities of increasingly longer duration are organized as one unit. For instance, between two and six years of age the duration of play units increases (9).

The differentiation of the life space also increases in the dimension of reality-irreality. The different degrees of irreality correspond to different degrees of fantasy. They include both the positive wishes and the fears. Dynamically, the level of irreality corresponds to a more fluid medium (15, 32) and is more closely related to the central layers of the person. This fact is particularly important for the psychology of dreams (42, 43). Play can be understood as an action on the level of reality closely related to the irreal level (116). The play technique (56), in the study of personality, makes use of the fact that the irreal level is closely related to the central layers of the person.

The level of irreality in the psychological future corresponds to the wishes or fears for the future; the level of reality, to what is expected. The discrepancy between the structure of the life space on the levels of irreality and reality is important for planning and for the productivity of the child (9). Hope corresponds to a sufficient similarity between reality and irreality somewhere in the psychological future; guilt to a certain discrepancy between reality and irreality in the psychological past. In the young child, truth and lying, perception and imagination are less distinguished than in an older child (39, 99, 116). This is partly due to the fact that the younger child has not yet developed that degree of differentiation of the life space into levels of reality and irreality which is characteristic of the adult.

The speed with which the life space increases in scope and degree of differentiation during development varies greatly. A close relation seems to exist between intelligence or, more specifically, between mental age and the degree of differentiation of the person and the psychological environment (76, 77). If this is correct, differences in IQ should be considered as different rates of increasing differentiation of the life space. Similar considerations apply to motor development (91) and to social development.

Figure 38a and b represents schematically the scope and degree of differentiation of the life space as a whole at two developmental

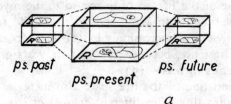

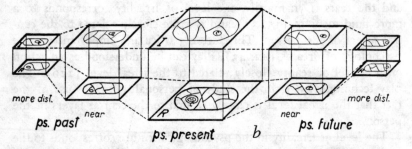

FIGURE 38. The life space at two developmental stages. The upper drawing represents the life space of a younger child. The lower diagram represents the higher degree of differentiation of the life space of the older child in regard to the present situation, the reality-irreality dimension, and the time perspective. *C*, child; *R*, level of reality; *I*, level of irreality; *Ps Past*, psychological past; *Ps Present*, psychological present; *Ps Future*, psychological future.

stages. The differentiation concerns the psychological environment as well as the person. The increasing differentiation of needs, for instance, can be represented as an increase in the differentiation of certain intrapersonal regions. The main differences between these developmental stages are: (1) an increase in the *scope* of the life space in regard to (a) what is part of the psychological present; (b) the time perspective in the direction of the psychological past and the psychological future; (c) the reality-irreality dimension; (2) an increasing *differentiation* of every level of the life space into a multitude of social relations and areas of activities; (3) an increasing *organization*; (4) a change in the general *fluidity* or *rigidity* of the life space.

Not all the areas of this life space are accessible to the child. He sees older children engaged in certain activities, which he would like to do himself, but into which he finds he cannot enter because he is

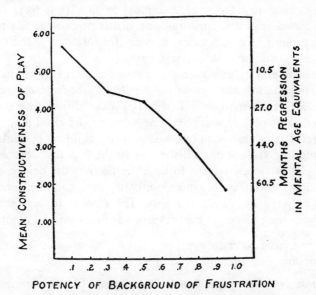

FIGURE 39. Decrease in constructiveness with a background of various degrees of frustration.[2]

not strong or clever enough. Additional limitations of his space of free movement are established by the prohibitions of the adult or by other social taboos.

The relation between accessible and inaccessible regions in the life space, the size of the space of free movement, and the precision of boundary between accessible and inaccessible areas are of great importance for behavior and development of the normal and abnormal child (78).

[2] Data presented in this Figure derive from the study by Barker, Dembo, and Lewin (9).

Regression. A change of the life space as a whole in the direction opposite to that characteristic of development may be called *regression* (see Chapter 5). Regression may include a decrease in time perspective, dedifferentiation or disorganization, leading to behavior more or less typical for children on a younger age level.

Regression may be either permanent or temporary. It is a common phenomenon and may be due, for instance, to sickness (63), frustration (9), insecurity (95), or emotional tension (25, 63). Regression, in the sense of a narrowing-down of the psychologically present area, may result from emotional tension, for instance, if the child is too eager to overcome an obstacle (75).

Regression may occur not only as a result of such frustration in the immediate situation but also as the result of a background of frustration. Barker, Dembo, and Lewin (9) have shown that the constructiveness of play of a five-and-one-half-year-old child may regress to the level of a three-and-one-half-year-old child as a result of a background of frustration. This is due to the fact that constructiveness of play is closely related to time perspective, the degree of differentiation, within an organized unit of play, and the functional relation between irreality and reality. The amount of regression increases with the potency of the background of frustration (Figure 39).

II. THE POSITION OF THE PERSON:
BEING INSIDE AND OUTSIDE A REGION

Position, Neighboringness, and Locomotion. The determination of the position of the person within the life space is the first prerequisite for understanding behavior. His social position within or outside of various groups should be known; his position in regard to various activities, in regard to his goal regions, and in regard to physical areas should be determined. This is fundamental because the region in which the person is located determines (1) the quality of his immediate surroundings, (2) what kinds of regions are adjacent to the present region—that is, what possibilities the individual has for his next step—and (3) what step has the meaning of an action toward his goal and what step corresponds to an action away from his goal.

Most behavior can be conceived of as a change of position—in other words, as a locomotion of the person. (The other cases of behavior are changes of structure.) In turn, every behavior changes the situation. We shall mention only a few examples of the effect of the region in which the person is located.

"Adaptation" to a Situation. A common phenomenon is what is usually called adaptation in the sense of "getting tuned to the present atmosphere." H. Anderson (5) found that children of preschool age reacted to an aggressive approach with aggression, to a friendly approach in a friendly manner. Lippitt's (83) study on democratic and autocratic atmospheres found similar adaptation of the children to the cultural atmosphere produced by the leader. French (41) found adaptation to group atmospheres in experiments with college freshmen. There are many indications from case studies that the tenseness of the mother easily affects the emotional state of the young child. There are indications that this occurs even during the first few months of life. It is a common observation that children who are learning bladder control may resume bed-wetting if exposed to the sound of running water.

The adaptation to the present region is frequently employed to make a child do something "against his will." A child of a few weeks may be induced to drink at the breast when he does not like to by keeping his head pressed to the breast in the position of feeding. Waring, Dwyer, and Junkin (126) describe how the child and the adult both commonly use this technique for their own purposes when they differ about the desirability of eating a certain food. The child tries to avoid the pressure of the adult by leaving the eating-situation (for instance, by going to the toilet) or by making the adult leave the eating situation psychologically (for instance, by starting conversations about noneating topics). On the other hand, the adult frequently uses one of two methods of coercion. He may lower the potency of the eating-situation (see later), and thus the resistance of the child, by "distracting his attention" from the eating (that is, by making the child enter a psychologically different region) and then slip in the food. Or he may heighten the potency of the eating-situation of his own pressure, and in this way induce the child to eat. In the latter case he frequently uses the "step-by-step method"; having the child sit at the table, then putting the food on the spoon, and so on.

J. D. Frank (37) has found, in an experiment with college students, that the step-by-step method is more efficient in coercing the person to eat than the attempt to make him go the whole way at one step. The effectiveness of the step-by-step method seems to be based on the gradual acceptance of the situation in which the person finds himself so that he resists less the making of the next step. A similar method is frequently used in domestic and international politics. People who are ready to fight against being pushed into a situation may accept the *fait accompli*.

Group Belongingness. Most social goals can be characterized as a wish to belong or not to belong to a certain group. This group may

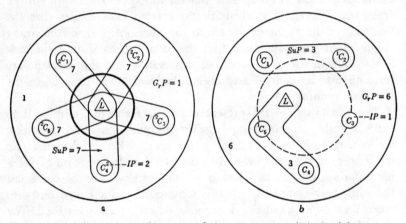

FIGURE 40. Subgrouping and potency of the group as a whole in (a) an autocratic and (b) a democratic setting.[3]

be a group of friends, an athletic organization, or a favorite subgroup within a larger group. It may be a group of only two persons, as with the friendship between mother and child. Belonging or not belonging to the group is equivalent to having a position inside or outside this group. This position determines the rights and duties of the individual and is decisive for the ideology of the individual.

The feeling of belonging to certain groups is a crucial factor for the feeling of security in children of minorities (27, 80). The tendency to enter a certain group and to keep certain children in and other children out of that group plays a great role in the behavior of

[3] This representation is derived from the theoretical analysis presented by Lippitt (83).

the nursery school child (85, 95). This tendency is important for the children's gang (113). Juveniles in the reformatory who have not fully accepted their belonging to the criminals have a tendency to name as their best friends persons outside the reformatory (73).

Lippitt (83) found that the feeling of group belongingness (as expressed, for instance, by the use of the term "we" instead of "I") is stronger in democratic than in autocratic clubs. In the autocratic situation (Figure 40) two distinct social strata exist, a higher one containing the leader *(L)* and the lower containing the children *(C)*. (The social distance between these strata is indicated in Figure 40a by the heavy black circle.) In democracy the status differences are less marked (dotted line). In the autocratic setting distinct subgroups of two exist containing one child and the leader. Therefore, if the leader is taken away, no strong bond between the members remains. In democracy the subgrouping is varying and less rigid. The potency of the group as a whole *(GrP)* is higher there than in the autocratic setting where the potency of the individual goal *(IP)* and of the subgroup *(SuP)* is relatively higher. These differences between the autocratic and democratic situations provide some of the reasons why children in the autocratic groups are more likely to be aggressive against their fellows although submissive to the leader. M. E. Wright (134) found that friendship between two children increases in certain situations of frustration partly because these situations favor a group structure in which the children see themselves opposed to the adult. Bavelas (11) found that the degree of cooperation between children in a day camp increased after their adult leaders were retrained from autocratic to democratic leadership techniques.

The difference between being inside and outside a region is basic not only for social groups but for all goal-seeking activities, and for the problem of frustration. Seeking a certain goal is equivalent to a tendency to enter a region outside of which one is located. We shall take up this question when discussing psychological forces.

III. CHANGE IN COGNITIVE STRUCTURE

The structure of the life space is the positional relations of its parts. Structure may be expressed by the topology of the life space. Locomotion of the person, that is, the change of his position from one region to another region, can be viewed as one type of change

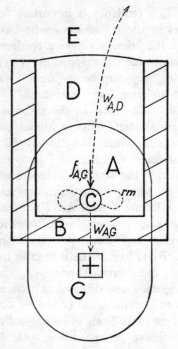

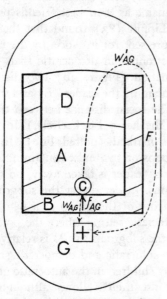

FIGURE 41. A simple detour problem as seen by a young child.

FIGURE 42. The detour problem represented in Figure 41 as seen by the older child.

in structure. Other examples are those changes which occur during "insight" or learning. The infinite variety of changes in structure may be classified roughly into (1) an increase in differentiation of a region, that is, an increase in the number of subregions; (2) a combination of separated regions into one differentiated region; (3) a decrease in differentiation, that is, a decrease in the number of subregions within a region; (4) a breaking-up of a whole, that is, previously connected subparts of a region are separated into relatively independent regions; and (5) a restructuring, that is, a change in pattern without increase or decrease of differentiation.

Detour Problems and Insight. Restructuring of certain areas of the life space can be readily observed in the solution of detour problems. The basic questions can be illustrated by a simple example: A goal *G* (Figure 41) lies behind a U-shaped physical barrier *B*. The child *C*, of a mental age of one year (this may be a chronologically young child, or an older feeble-minded child) is likely to try to reach the goal by an action toward the barrier along the path $w_{A, G}$.[4] A child of five years, under the same circumstances, will have no difficulty. It will reach the goal by way of a roundabout route along the path $w'_{A, G}$ (Figure 42). What are the difficulties of the younger child? Both children have the tendency to locomote from their present situation A toward the goal G. (As we shall see later, we can say there exists a psychological force $f_{A, G}$ acting on the child in the direction from A toward G.)

We can understand the difference in difficulties if we consider what "direction toward G" means for both children. For the young child the direction from A to G, $d_{A, G}$, is equal to the direction toward the barrier B, $(d_{A, G} = d_{A, B})$. A movement from A to D along the path $w_{A, D}$ would have, for this child, the meaning of going away from G. In other words, the direction toward D, $d_{A, D}$, is opposite to the direction toward G, $d_{A, G}$ $(d_{A, D} = d_{A, G})$. For the older child (Figure 42) the direction toward D, $d_{A, D}$ has not the character of being opposite to the direction but of being equal to the direction to G $(d_{A, D} = d_{A, G})$ because the step from A to D is seen by this child as a part of the roundabout route $w'_{A, G}$ toward G. The difference in the meaning of the direction $d_{A, G}$ toward G is due mainly to two facts:

1. For the younger child the immediate situation is less extended than for the older one (this is but one result of the fact that the life space of the younger child is smaller in many aspects than that of the older child). It includes only the regions A, B, and G (Figure 41). For the older child, a wider area is psychologically present, including, for instance, the areas D and F. As an effect of this difference in scope of the present situation, the younger child sees the areas A and G separated by the impassable barrier B. For the older child, regions A and G are connected by way of passable regions D and F.

Directions in the psychological life space are defined by certain paths as a whole. The older child sees the step from A to D as a part of the path, A, D, F, G toward G. The young child sees the

[4] A fuller discussion of the problems of direction and path in psychology may be found in Lewin (79).

step A, D, as a part of the path A, E, that is, away from G. The difference in the cognitive structure of the situation for the young and older child leads, therefore, to a different meaning of the direction toward G, and, accordingly, to a different locomotion resulting from the same tendencies of both children to reach G.

2. For the young child, the path $w'_{A, G}$ simply does not exist psychologically. For the older child two paths toward G exist psychologically, namely the roundabout route $w'_{A, G}$ and the blocked "direct" path $w_{A, G}$. The "direct" direction toward G can be interpreted, in this case, as the direction of looking toward G; the less "direct" direction as that of walking toward G. For the young child, "direction toward G" has not yet been differentiated into these two directions. (This is an example of the lesser degree of differentiation of the life space of the younger child.)

A two-year-old child placed in the same situation may at first have a cognitive structure corresponding to that of the younger child (Figure 41). After a few attempts the structure of the situation may change to that of the older child (Figure 42). These changes frequently occur as a sudden shift. They are an example of what has been called *insight* (75).

Insight can always be viewed as a change in the cognitive structure of the situation. It frequently includes differentiation and restructuring in the sense of separating certain regions which have been connected and connecting regions which have been separated. For instance, to use a branch of a tree as a stick (75) for reaching a goal behind a fence it is necessary to see the branch as a relatively separate unit instead of a part within the larger unit of the tree. In addition, it is necessary to connect this branch with the goal behind the fence.

From the theory of insight in detour problems certain conclusions in regard to factors facilitating insight can be derived. Becoming emotional leads frequently to a narrowing-down of the psychologically existing area. A state of strong emotionality should, therefore, be detrimental to finding solutions. A distance sufficient to permit a survey of the larger situation helps in the solution of intellectual problems. Katona (69) discusses the effect of various settings upon the change of the cognitive structure and the ability to find new solutions.

The principles of change in cognitive structure discussed here are as applicable to social and mathematical problems as to physical problems.

Learning and Orientation. Learning is a popular term referring to such different processes as learning to like spinach, learning to walk, and learning French vocabularies, that is, problems of changes of goals or needs, changes of posture and muscular coordination, and changes in knowledge. Therefore, no one theory of learning is possible. Problems of change in goals will be discussed later. Insight is an example of learning in the sense of change in cognitive structure. Learning, in this sense, usually involves several of those types of structural changes which we have mentioned previously, combined with a change in the degree of organization.

A change in the direction of greater differentiation takes place, for instance, when a child gets oriented in a new surrounding. Being in an unknown surrounding is equivalent to being in a region which is unstructured in the double sense that neither the quality nor the subparts of the present region, nor the immediately neighboring regions, are determined. Orientation means the structurization of the unstructured region. In this way, direction within the life space becomes determined (79). Orientation is a process which, on a smaller scale, shows significant parallels to the development of the life space of the young child.

An unstructured region usually has the same effect as an impassable obstacle. Being in unstructured surroundings leads to uncertainty of behavior because it is not clear whether a certain action will lead to or away from the goal. It is undetermined whether the neighboring regions are dangerous or friendly. Waring, Dwyer, and Junkin (126) found that children during the meals of the first nursery school day were more ready to acquiesce to the advice of the adult than later on when they felt themselves to be on better-known ground for resisting.

To conclude this section, we shall add but one remark about the relation between repetition and learning. Repetition of a certain activity may lead to differentiation of previously undifferentiated region of the life space, and to unification of previously separated activities. This is frequently the case in motor learning. However, if continued long enough, repetition may have the opposite effect, namely, a breaking-up of the larger units of actions, a dedifferentiation, unlearning, and disorganization similar to that of primitivation or degeneration. These processes are typical of psychological satiation and oversatiation.

IV. FORCE AND FORCE FIELD

A. Force and Valence. The structure of the life space determines what locomotions are possible at a given time. What change actually occurs depends on the constellation of psychological forces. The construct *force* characterizes, for a given point of the life space, the direction and strength of the tendency to change. This construct does not imply any additional assumptions as to the "cause" of this tendency. The combination of a number of forces acting at the same point at a given time is called the *resultant* force. The relation be-

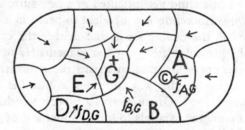

FIGURE 43.   A positive central field of forces corresponding to a positive valence.

tween force and behavior can then be summed up in the following way: Whenever a resultant force (different from zero) exists, there is either a locomotion in the direction of that force or a change in cognitive structure equivalent to this locomotion. The reverse also holds: whenever a locomotion or change of structure exists, resultant forces exist in that direction.[5]

Psychological forces correspond to a relation between at least two regions of the life space. A simple example is the force of $f_{A, G}$ acting on a child C in the direction toward a goal G (Figure 43). This force depends upon the state of the child C, particularly upon the state of his needs, and upon the nature of the region G. If the region G (which may represent an activity, a social position, an object,

[5] We are not discussing here the complicated problems of the alien factors, that is those physical and social factors which may be viewed as the boundary conditions of the life space (See Chapters 3 and 8). We keep within the realm of psychology.

or any other possible goal) is attractive to the person, it is said to have a positive valence.

Such a valence corresponds to a field of forces which has the structure of a positive central field (Figure 43). If no other valences existed, the person located in any region $A, B, D, E \ldots$ would always try to move in the direction toward G. In other words, the valence G corresponds to a force $f_{A, G}, f_{B, G}, f_{D, G}$, etc. The observation of behavior permits not only the determination of conscious goals but also of "unconscious goals," as Freud uses the term.

If the person is repulsed, we speak of a negative valence of G, corresponding to a negative central field (Figure 44), which is composed of forces $f_{A, -G}, f_{B, -G}, f_{D, -G}$, etc., away from G.

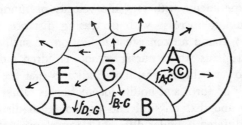

FIGURE 44. A negative central field of forces corresponding to a negative valence.

The effect of forces may be observed from earliest infancy: movements toward or away from the breast during feeding are noted in the first weeks of life. Looking toward an object (fixation) is another example of directed action. Later on, there is grasping. More elaborate directed actions presuppose a correspondingly higher differentiation of the life space. In a young child a force is more likely to affect directly every part of the child than it is at a later age. For instance, the child of six months reaching out for a toy may move both arms and legs in this direction. He may open his mouth and bend his head toward the goal. The older, more differentiated child is likely to react in a more "controlled" way with only a part of the body.

Strength of Force and Distance of Valence. We shall discuss later what factors determine a change of valence. First let us ask what effect a given valence, or distribution of valences, has on behavior.

The strength of the force toward or away from a valence depends upon the strength of that valence and the psychological distance $(e_{A, G})$ between the person and the valence $(f_{A, G} = F[Va(G), e_{A, G}])$.

Fajans (34) found that the persistence of children (ages one to six years) in trying to reach a goal from various physical distances (8 to 100 cm.) increases with decreasing distance. This may mean that, with increasing distance, either the force decreases or the child sees more quickly that the barrier is insurmountable. If the first factor is dominant, emotional tension should decrease with distance. Fajans found this to be true only for the infants. For the older children, the second factor seems to be dominant, probably because these children view the obstacle as dependent upon the will of the experimenter rather than as physical distance.

In some experiments with rats, the velocity of running toward a goal was found to increase with decreasing distance (60). H. F. Wright (133) found no consistent indication of such a speed gradient in experiments where nursery school children pulled the goal (a marble) toward themselves. This indicates that the relation between strength of force and bodily locomotion is rather complicated in psychology and that physical and psychological distance may be related quite differently under different circumstances.

As a particular example, the situation may be mentioned where the person "nearly" reaches a goal. In animals (60), as in children (133), a marked slowing-down has been observed at the last section before the goal is reached. If the force were related simply to the physical distance, there should be no sudden drop in velocity at this point. Obviously, after the individual is inside the goal region, the force $f_{A, G}$ can no longer have the direction "toward" the goal region but changes to a force $f_{G, G}$, which properly has to be interpreted as a tendency to resist being forced out of the goal region (for details see 79). Being in the goal region is frequently not equivalent to consumption of, or to bodily contact with, the goal, but it is equivalent to having the goal in one's power, to being sure of it. This is probably the reason for the slowing-down in the last section before the goal. This also explains the frequent "decrease of interest" after possession, illustrated by the following example. A nine-month-old child reaches out for two rattles lying before him.

When he gets one he does not begin to play but is interested only in the rattle he does not have.

An example of a decrease of the strength of a force with the distance from the negative valence can be found in certain eating situations (79, p. 117). For a child who dislikes his spinach, the act of eating might consist of a series of relatively separate steps, such as putting the hand on the table, taking the spoon, putting food on the spoon, etc. The strength of the force away from eating the disagreeable food and, therefore, the resistance against making the next step increases with the nearness of the step to the actual eating. After the child starts chewing, the structure of the situation in regard to this bite usually is fundamentally changed. Instead of resisting, the child tries to finish the bite. This is an example of how the direction and strength of the forces acting on the person depend upon the region in which the person is located.

The change of the strength of the force with the distance to the valence is different for positive and for negative valences. The latter usually diminishes much faster. The amount of decrease depends also upon the nature of the region which has a positive or negative valence. It is different, for example, in the case of a dangerous animal which can move about from that in the case of an immovable unpleasant object.

The effect of temporal distance on the strength of the force seems to parallel that of physical distance in some respects. E. Katz (71), in experiments with nursery school children, found that the frequency of resumption of interrupted tasks increases with the nearness of the interruption to the completion of the task, but that it drops for interruptions very close to the end. Institutionalized adolescents, like other prisoners, may attempt to escape shortly before they are eligible for release. Frequently they become rebellious (35). Their emotional tension is heightened by the temporal nearness of the goal.

B. Type of Forces. Driving and Restraining Forces. The forces toward a positive, or away from a negative, valence can be called *driving* forces. They lead to locomotion. These locomotions might be hindered by physical or social obstacles. Such barriers correspond to *restraining forces* (79). Restraining forces, as such, do not lead to locomotion, but they do influence the effect of driving forces.

The restraining forces, just as the driving forces, are due to a relation between two regions of the life space, namely, the nature of the barrier region and the "ability" of the individual. The same social or physical obstacle corresponds, therefore, to different restraining forces for different individuals.

Induced Forces, Forces Corresponding to Own Needs, and Impersonal Forces. Forces may correspond to a person's own needs. For instance, the child may wish to go to a movie or to eat certain food. Many psychological forces acting on a child do not, however, correspond to his own wishes but to the wish of another person, for instance of the mother. These forces in the life space of the child can be called *induced forces,* and the corresponding positive or negative valence "induced valence." (A force acting on the child in the direction to the goal G induced by the mother M may be written $i^M f_{G,\,G}$.)

There are forces which psychologically correspond neither to the own wish of the child nor the wish of another person, but have, for the child, the character of something "impersonal," a matter-of-fact demand. We call them *impersonal forces.* It is of great importance for the reaction of the child and for the atmosphere of the situation whether an impersonal request or the personal will of another individual is dominant.

Point of Application. Forces may act on any part of the life space. Frequently the point of application is that region of the life space which corresponds to the own person. The child may, however, experience that the "doll wants to go to bed," or that "another child wants a certain toy." In these cases the points of application of the forces are regions in the life space of a child other than his own person. Such cases are most common and play an important part, for instance, in the problems of altruism.

C. *Conflict Situations.* Definition of Conflict. A conflict situation can be defined as a situation where forces acting on the person are opposite in direction and about equal in strength. In regard to driving forces three cases are possible: The person may be located between two positive valences, between two negative valences, or a positive and negative valence may lie in the same direction. There may be, also, conflicts between driving and restraining forces. Finally, there may be conflicts between own forces and various combinations of induced and impersonal forces. The effect and the development of conflicts vary with these different constellations, although all conflicts have certain properties in common.

Conflicts Between Driving Forces. What is usually called a *choice* means that a person is located between two positive or negative valences which are mutually exclusive. The child has to choose, for example, between going on a picnic G^1 (Figure 45a) and playing with his comrades G^2. (Figure 45 and some of the later figures rep-

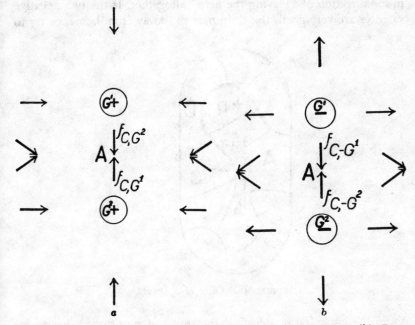

FIGURE 45.   (a) Force field corresponding to two positive valences. (b) Force field corresponding to two negative valences.

resent situations where the physical directions and distances are sufficiently important psychologically to be used as frames of reference for the life space. One can speak in these cases of quasi-physical fields.) An example of a child standing between two negative valences is a situation in which punishment G^1 is threatened if he does not do a certain disagreeable task G^2 (Figure 45b). Figure 45a and b represents the corresponding force fields. If the child is located at A and the strength of the valences are equal, he will be exposed to forces which are equal in strength but opposite in direction. In the first example, the opposing forces $f_{A, G}^1$ and $f_{A, G}^2$ are directed toward the picnic and play. In the second example, the opposing forces $f_{A, -G}^1$ and $f_{A, -G}^2$ are directed away from the task and the punishment.

From these force fields certain differences of behavior can be derived. In the case of two negative valences, there is a resultant force in the direction of "leaving the field" altogether. If the two negative valences are very great, the child may run away from home, or try to

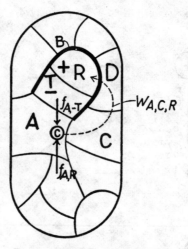

FIGURE 46. Offer of a reward.

avoid the issue. To be effective, the threat of punishment has to include the creation of a set-up which prohibits this avoidance (77), that is, the creation of a prison-like situation, where barriers B prohibit leaving the situation in any other way than by facing the task T or the punishment P. If there is a choice between two positive valences, no force in the direction of leaving the field exists. Instead, the child will try to reach both goals if possible.

An example of a conflict due to the presence of a negative and a positive valence is the promise of reward for doing a disagreeable task (Figure 46). Here a conflict is brought about by the opposition of the force $f_{A, R}$ toward the reward R and the force $f_{A, -T}$ away from the disagreeable activity T. The structure of the situation is similar to that characteristic of a detour problem. Indeed, the child frequently tries to reach the reward R along a roundabout route $w_{A, C, R}$ without passing through the disagreeable activity. The reward will be effective only if all other paths to R are blocked by an impassable barrier B which permits entrance to R only by way of T. The barriers in this case, as in the case of the threat of punishment, are usually social in nature: The child knows that the adult will prevent certain actions by social force.

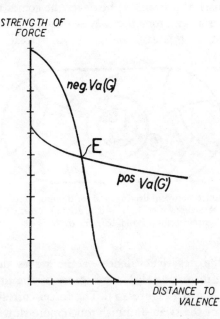

STRENGTH OF
FORCE

neg. Va(G)

E

pos Va(G')

DISTANCE TO
VALENCE

FIGURE 47. Graphical representation of the change of the strength of a force with the distance to a positive and a negative valence. E is the point of equilibrium of forces corresponding to the positive and negative valences.

The necessity for setting up a barrier around the reward indicates one of the differences between this method of making the child perform a disagreeable activity T and the methods which try to change the negative valence of T itself into a positive one. A "change of interest" in T may be brought about by imbedding the activity T (for instance, the disliked figuring) into a different setting (for instance

into playing store), so that the meaning, and consequently the valence, of T is changed for the child. Such a method makes the creation of a barrier unnecessary and secures spontaneous actions of the
child toward the previously disliked activity as a result of the newly
created positive central field.

Another example of a conflict between a positive and negative
valence can be observed in a setting where a child of three years is
trying to seize a toy swan from the waves on the seashore. Following
the forces corresponding to the positive valence of the swan, the
child will approach the swan. If, however, he comes too close to the
waves, the force away from the waves may be greater than those
toward the swan. In this case the child will retreat. The force cor-

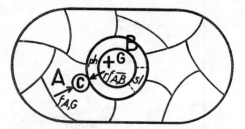

FIGURE 48. Conflict between driving and restraining forces in the case of a
physical and social obstacle to a goal. $f_{A, G}$ is a driving force. $rf_{\overline{A, B}}$ is a restraining
force. *ph* is the physical sector of the barrier, *B*. *sl* is the social sector of the
barrier.

responding to the negative valence of the waves decreases rather
rapidly with the increasing distance because of the limited range of
the effect of the waves (Figure 47). The forces corresponding to the
positive valence of the swan diminish much more slowly with the distance. There exists, therefore, an equilibrium between the opposing
forces at point E where their strengths are equal $(f_{E, s} = f_{E, -w})$.
The children may be observed wavering around this point of equilibrium until one of these forces becomes dominant as a result of
changes of circumstances or of a decision.

Conflicts between Driving and Restraining Forces. A most common type of conflict arises when a child is prevented from reaching
a goal G by a barrier B. Two basic cases may be distinguished: (1)
the child is surrounded by a barrier with the goal outside; (2) the

goal is surrounded by a barrier with the child outside. The first case is a prison-like situation which gives the child little space of free movement. In the second case, the child is free except in regard to the region *G*. Each of these cases leads to specific reactions (77). We shall now discuss in greater detail a sequence of behavior typical of the second case.

At first, a certain amount of change in structure usually occurs: The child tries to investigate the nature of the obstacle with the purpose of finding a section *s* within the barrier which will permit pas-

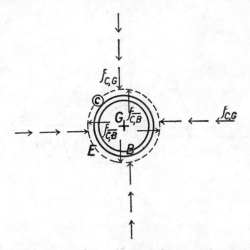

FIGURE 49.   Line of equilibrium between driving and restraining forces in the case of a circular barrier.

sage. Such a change in cognitive structure is similar to that observed in detour problems. It is very common for a child to be in situations where an obstacle could be overcome with the help of an adult. In these situations the barrier is composed of at least two sectors, one corresponding to the physical obstacle *ph* (Figure 48), the other to the social obstacle *sl*. In the experiment of Fajans, mentioned above, practically all children conceived of the barrier at first as a physical obstacle (as too great a physical distance). For the children above two years, after some time the social aspect of the situation became clear and led to social approaches toward the goal (the children asked the adult for help).

The barrier acquires a negative valence for the child after a number of unsuccessful attempts to cross it. This change is equivalent to a change in the force field from the structure represented in Figure 49 to that of Figure 50. If the barrier is an obstacle but has no negative valence, the corresponding force field does not reach much beyond the barrier (Figure 49). The restraining forces $rf_{c,\,B}$ merely hinder a locomotion in the direction of the force $f_{c,\,B}$ without driving the person away from B. The line of equilibrium E between driving and restraining force lies, therefore, close to the barrier region.

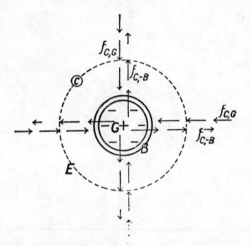

FIGURE 50.   Line of equilibrium after the barrier (the same as in Figure 49) has acquired a negative valence.

If, after failure, the barrier acquires a negative valence, the corresponding negative central force field will reach out farther (Figure 50) so that the line of equilibrium E between the force $f_{c,\,G}$ toward the goal and the force $f_{c,\,-B}$ away from the barrier is located at a greater distance.

With increasing failure, the negative valence tends to increase. This enlarges the distance between the line of equilibrium and the barrier until the child leaves the field altogether.

Fajans (34) has given a detailed report about the form and sequence of events in such a situation. Usually the child leaves the field at first only temporarily. After some time the forces toward the goal again become greater than the forces away from the barrier, and the child returns. If the new attempts are still unsuccessful, the negative valence increases again until the child leaves. On the average, these later attempts show less duration. Finally, the child leaves the field permanently; he gives up. Barker, Dembo, and Lewin (9) report similar sequences of behavior in children between two and six years in a slightly different setting of frustration.

Active children, on the average, are more persistent than passive ones (34). Some active children, however, are particularly quick to leave the situation, probably because they decide soon that the barrier is impassable. A state of equilibrium in such a conflict can lead to passive, gesture-like action toward the goal: The child stays below the goal with his arm erect but he makes no actual attempts to reach it. Children frequently leave the field psychologically without leaving the room bodily. They may try to enter a different activity, may daydream, or start self-manipulation with their clothes or their body (6, 34, 116).

A conflict between driving and restraining forces may also occur if the child is prevented by an obstacle from leaving the field of a negative valence. Such a situation exists, for instance, if a child is oversatiated with an activity but prevented from leaving it, or in any other prison-like situation. The sequence of behavior is, in many respects, similar to that discussed above. Attempts to leave are followed by the giving up of such attempts as the result of the relation between the strength of the force $f_{A, -A}$ away from the region A and the increasing negative valence of the barrier. Frequently a state of high emotional tension results.

Conflicts Between Own and Induced Forces. Every one of the conflict situations discussed above might be due to the opposition of two forces corresponding to the child's own needs, to the opposition of two induced forces, or to the opposition between an own and an induced force. Many effects of conflict situations are independent of these differences. Certain effects, however, are typical of conflicts between own and induced forces.

A force induced by a person P on a child C can be viewed as the result of the power field of that person over the child. The person having power over the child is able to induce positive and negative valences by giving orders. By a restraining command, he can change the character of a region which would be passable according to the child's own ability into an impassable barrier. In other words, "the power of P over C" means that P is able to create induced driving or restraining forces $i^P f_{C, G}$ which correspond to P's will.

A conflict between own and induced forces always permits at least one other solution in addition to those discussed above: The child may attempt to undermine the power of the other person, at least in the area of conflict. The tendency of a conflict between own and induced forces to lead to fights has been observed by Waring, Dwyer, and Junkin (126) in nursery school children in an eating situation. Dembo (25) and J. D. Frank (37) have observed similar tendencies in students. M. E. Wright (134) found an increasing aggression against the experimenter in pairs of nursery school children in a setting of frustration induced by the experimenter. The children showed greater cooperation among themselves. This might be interpreted as due partly to the tendency to increase their own power relative to the power of the experimenter. Lewin, Lippitt, and White (82) found a strong tendency toward aggression in autocratic atmospheres which are dominated much more by induced forces than by forces corresponding to the own needs of the children. This aggressiveness, however, was usually not directed against the supreme powers of the leader but diverted toward their fellows or toward material objects. If the suppressive power of the leader is too great, even this aggression ceases.

D. *Emotional Tension and Restlessness.* Emotional Tension and Strength of Conflict. If two opposing forces are equal in strength the resultant force will be zero, independent of the absolute strength of the forces. As far as changes in position are concerned, therefore, no difference should exist in the effect of conflicts between weak and between strong forces. Actually, the state of the person is quite different in a weak and in a strong conflict. One of the main differences is the intensity of emotional tension (et), which seems to be a function of the strength of the opposing forces $[et = F(\mid f_{A, G} \mid)]$. As mentioned above, greater emotionality is found in infants if the distance to an inaccessible goal is small than if it is large. This is one of the reasons why increasing incentives favor the solution of detour and other intellectual problems only up to a certain intensity level. Above this level, however, increasing the forces to the goal makes the necessary restructurization more difficult, partly because the person has to move against stronger forces, partly because the resultant emotionality leads to primitivation (regression). Barker, Dembo, and Lewin (9) found that the frequency of negative emotional behavior increased with the intensity of frustration. The same holds for the amount of regression as measured by the constructiveness of play (Figure 39, p. 247).

The Form of Restless Movement. One of the simplest expressions of emotionality is restless movements, movements which are not directed to a certain goal, but are merely an expression of tension. Actually, all combinations of undirected expression, such as restlessness and purposeless behavior, occur (25). Irwin (61) found that general activity as measured by the stabilimeter increases in infants with the time after the last feeding. This indicates that the amount of undirected activity is a good measurement of the state of tension accompanying hunger at that age level.

Restless movements are usually perpendicular to the direction of the force to the goal, or more generally, they proceed as much as possible along the line of equilibrium. In the case of the six-month-old child reaching to the goal restless movements of his arms and legs occur perpendicular to the direction of the goal. Behind a U-shaped barrier (Figure 41), the restless movements are parallel to the barrier along the line *rm*. In a constellation corresponding to Figure 49 or 50 the restless movements will follow the line *E*. This is verified in a situation where a one-and-one-half-year-old child tries to reach a toy *G* behind a circular physical barrier *B*. The restless movements of the child take the form of circling around that barrier. (For details see 79.)

The restless movement can be understood as a tendency to move away from the present situation, that is, as a movement corresponding to a force $f_{A, -A}$.

V. OVERLAPPING SITUATIONS

Frequently the person finds himself at the same time in more than one situation. The simplest example is that of divided attention: A child in the classroom listens to the teacher but also thinks about the ball game after school. The amount to which the child is involved in either of these two situations, S^1 and S^2, is called their relative potency, $Po(S^1)$ and $Po(S^2)$.

The effect a situation has on behavior depends upon the potency of that situation. In particular, the effect a force has on behavior is proportional to the potency of the related situation.

A. Overlapping Activities. Barker, Dembo, and Lewin (9) speak of secondary play, as distinguished from primary play, when the child does not give his full attention to play. The constructiveness of secondary play is decisively below that of primary play. In experiments about psychological satiation (68, 76), a person who is supposed to repeat an activity over and over again tends to perform the repetition as a secondary activity on a peripheral level. Activities such as writing may be considered as an overlapping of two activities,

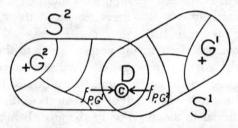

FIGURE 51. State of indecision. S^1 and S^2 are the two possibilities with their goals G^1 and G^2. D is a region of making a decision.

namely, (1) conveying a certain meaning, (2) writing symbols. The first has the nature of a steadily progressing action, the second that of a repetition. The velocity of becoming satiated depends upon the relative potency of the repetitive aspect of the activity. Writing a letter, therefore, may lead more quickly to satiation in a child for whom writing is more difficult. Similarly, walking or other activities which usually have very low potency for the adult may soon lead to satiation in the child.

B. Decision. A situation of choice can be viewed as an overlapping situation. The person being in the process of making a decision D (Figure 51) usually alternates between seeing himself in a future situation corresponding to the one and to the other possibility (S^1 and S^2). In other words, the potency of the various possibilities fluctuates. When a decision is reached, one of these situations acquires the dominant potency permanently. In a choice between activities of different degrees of difficulty, the decision is influenced by the probability of success or failure of each task. Escalona (33) has shown that this probability is equivalent to the potency of the corresponding future situation.

The decision time increases also, the more the opposing forces are equal in strength (8). B. A. Wright (132) found, in a study of altruistic and egoistic choices, that eight-year-old children whose choices were all either altruistic or egoistic arrived at a decision more quickly than those who made sometimes the one type of choice and sometimes the other. Cartwright (22), in experiments on discrimination of figures and of meaning, found the decision time to be longest if the forces in opposite directions were equal. More recently the theory has been elaborated and quantified by Cartwright and Festinger (23).

Decision time also increases with the importance of the decision (the valence of the goals). Jucknat (65), in a study of the level of aspiration with children, and Barker (8), in a study of choices between more or less agreeable or disagreeable foods, found that the choice time increased with the intensity of the conflict. The decision time is longer in choices between two negative than between two positive valences (8). This latter fact derives from the different equilibria existing in the different constellations of forces (79). Decision time shows great individual variations. Extreme decision-retardation is typical of certain types of depression (33).

C. Immediate Situation and Background. The influence which the background of a situation has on behavior can be understood as an overlapping of an immediate situation and of the situation at large (9). A background of frustration decreases constructiveness of play even if the play itself is not hampered from the outside. The amount of regression increases with increasing potency of the background of frustration (Figure 39, p. 247).

Sheffield (115) and others report cases where school work was greatly changed by a change of the home background.

D. The Effect of the Group on the Individual. The effect of group belongingness on the behavior of an individual can be viewed as the result of an overlapping situation: One situation corresponds to the person's own needs and goals: the other to the goals, rules, and values which exist for him as a group member. Adaptation of an individual to the group depends upon the avoidance of too great a conflict between the two sets of forces (79).

A child usually belongs to a great number of groups, such as his family, the school, the church, friends. Within the family he may belong to a subgroup containing him and his closest sibling. The effect of the various groups—particularly whether or not the child is ruled by the ideology and values of the one or the other—depends on the relative potency of these groups at that time. Schanck (106) has found that the influence of public or private morale is different at home and in the church. In school children, the tendency to cheat changes with the social setting (55).

Many conflicts in childhood are due to forces corresponding to the various groups to which the child belongs. Such conflicts are particularly important for children in marginal positions, that is, for children who are standing on the boundary between two groups. One example is the adolescent who no longer wants to belong to the children's group but who is not yet fully accepted by the adults. Uncertainty of the ground on which the child stands leads to an alternation between the values of the one and of the other group, to a state of emotional tension, and to a frequent fluctuation between overaggressiveness and overtimidity (see Chapter 6). The degree to which such adolescent behavior is shown depends upon the degree to which children and adolescents are treated as separate groups in that culture (13, 102).

A similar effect of marginality can be observed in regard to other types of groups. Emotional tension is high in inmates of reformatory schools as a result of the marginal position of these children between the criminal and the "honest citizen" (73). Emotional tension diminishes when the child accepts his belongingness to a definite group. A decrease in emotionality was observed in those inmates who accepted their belonging to the criminal class. Marginality is an important problem for the crippled or the otherwise handicapped child (10, 29). Shaw *et al.* (114) have shown the influence of residing in marginal sections of a city on criminality of children. Marginality raises important problems for children belonging to minority groups, such as Negroes or Jews (40, 80). The effect, in many respects, is similar to that typical of the adolescent.

FACTORS DETERMINING THE FIELD AND ITS CHANGE

In the preceding section we have discussed the results of the cognitive structure and of certain constellations of forces on behavior. We shall now discuss factors which determine the constellation of forces. This second problem is equivalent to the question of how one part or aspect of the life space depends upon other parts or aspects. Of course, both problems are interrelated since any behavior resulting from a certain situation alters the situation to some degree. We shall here limit our discussion to problems related to needs. They refer to the relation between the state of that region in the life space which represents the person and the psychological environment.

I. NEED, FORCE FIELDS, AND COGNITIVE STRUCTURE

Need and Valence. During the development of the child, needs are constantly changing in intensity and degree of differentiation. The so-called crises of development are periods of particularly important or particularly quick changes in needs. In addition, there is a change of needs in briefer periods corresponding to the states of hunger, satiation, and oversatiation.

Needs have the character of "organizing" behavior. One can distinguish a hierarchy of needs. One need or a combination of several needs may set up derived needs (quasi-needs) equivalent to specific intentions.

Needs are closely related to valences. What valence a certain object or activity $[Va(G)]$ has depends partly upon the nature of that activity (G), and partly upon the state of the needs $[t(G)]$ of the person at that time $[Va(G) = F\ (G, t(G))]$. An increase in the intensity of need (for instance, the need for recreation) leads to an increase of the positive valence of certain activities (such as going to the movies or reading a book) and to an increase in the negative valence of certain other activities (such as doing hard work). Any statement regarding change of needs can be expressed by a statement about certain positive and negative valences.

As a result of the increase in positive valence which accompanies the state of hunger of a particular need, areas of activities which are negative or on a zero level when the need is satiated acquire a positive valence. The hungrier person is usually satisfied with poorer food (70).

The valence of an activity is related to its consummatory value for satisfying the need. Not all activities, however, which have positive valence also have satisfaction value in case of consumption; on the other hand, activities with no or even negative valence may have satisfaction value. Valence and satisfaction value should, therefore, be clearly distinguished. It is surprising how frequently valence and value actually go hand in hand. D. Katz (70) reported an increase in the valence of foods which contain minerals for which deficiencies had been established in chickens. When the deficiency was removed the valence again decreased. Similar results have been claimed for children. Experience may change the valence as well as the meaning which an activity has for the child. The child has to make many important decisions (for instance, in regard to occupation) on the basis of the valence of an activity rather than on the basis of clear knowledge of its satisfaction value.

Need and Cognitive Structure. The cognitive structure of the life space is influenced by the state of the needs. Murray (96) found that faces of other people appear more malicious to children in a state of fear than normally. Stern and MacDonald (117) found that pictures without definite meanings will be seen according to the mood of the child.

The effect which a need has on the structure of the life space depends upon the *intensity of the need* and upon the fluidity of the related areas of the life space. Dembo (25) found hallucination-like wish fulfillments in highly emotional situations. If the visual field is sufficiently fluid, its structure may be considerably changed by intention (quasi-need) (51, 77). Levels of irreality, being more fluid than the level of reality, are, consequently, more easily influenced by both wishes and fears. This is the reason why dreams and daydreams mirror the needs of the child. This also explains why, in fantasy and dreams, needs may come into the open which are kept from "public life" by social taboos.

Sliosberg (116) has shown that the meaning of objects and events is more fluid in *play* than in nonplay situations. The so-called play technique (32, 56) and other projective methods (96) make use of this greater flexibility of play to study the deeper desires and suppressed wishes of children. (It should be mentioned, however, that play frequently mirrors the actual home situation rather than the wishes and fears of the child.)

Needs affect the cognitive structure not only of the psychological present, but, even more, of the psychological future and past. This is particularly important for the level of aspiration. If the effect of the needs on the psychological future is particularly great, one speaks of an unrealistic person. One form of the influence of needs on the structure of the psychological past is called *rationalization;* other forms are *repression* and *lying.* The lying of the child in the first years of life seems frequently to have the nature of an actual change of the psychological past in line with the child's needs.

There are great individual differences (24) in the way in which a child sees ink blots (Rorschach test). Unstable problem children are more likely to be carried away by wishes and fears than the average child as a result of their greater fluidity.

II. SATISFYING A NEED

A need may be satisfied either by reaching the desired goal or by reaching a substitute goal.

A. Satisfaction through Reaching the Original Goal. The intention to carry out a certain action is equivalent to the creation of a quasi-need (77). As long as that need is not satisfied, a force corresponding to the valence of the goal region should exist and lead to an action in the direction of that goal (see Chapter 1).

Ovsiankina (97) studied the resumption of interrupted activities. She found a high tendency to resume the task (about 80 per cent) if the inner goal of the person was not reached. In some cases, after resumption, the person stopped as soon as a substitute satisfaction was reached.

The frequency of resumption depends upon the nature of the task (it is high for tasks with a definite end as against continuous tasks) and upon the attitude (need) of the subject. Children between nine and eleven showed a percentage of resumption (86 per cent) similar to that of adults. Children who had the attitude of being examined and of strict obedience showed little resumption owing to the lack of involvement; they were governed mainly by induced forces. E. Katz (71), in a study of resumption of interrupted activities on nursery school children, found practically the same frequency of resumption as Ovsiankina (88 per cent). Differences of intelligence, within the normal range, did not affect the resumption significantly.

The tendency to resume is not diminished if the unfinished work is out of sight (97). On the other hand, the presence of uncompleted work of another person does not lead (or extremely seldom leads) to spontaneous completion in adults (97) or in children (2). Both results indicate that the state of the need of the child is decisive for resumption. Such a need might be instigated if the child becomes sufficiently involved through watching another person doing the work. (The results of Rosenzweig (103) with children of various ages differ somewhat from those of E. Katz and Adler and Kounin. These differences are probably due to factors peculiar to his situation.)

The forces in the direction of the goal which correspond to a need can be observed in thinking as well as in action (see Chapter 1). Zeigarnik (135) studied the effect of quasi-needs on the tendency to recall. She found the quotient of the recollection of uncompleted to completed tasks to be 1.9 for adults and 2.5 for children between five and ten years old. This quotient, like the frequency of resumption, depends on the degree of involvement of the subject. The difference between children and adults is probably due to a greater involvement of the children in the particular type of activity and to a more immediate dependence of thinking upon the valences. Zeigarnik found that certain types of unintelligent children are particularly persistent in their tendency to come back to the unfinished tasks, whereas easily distractible children show a low quotient.

Marrow (89) investigated the effect of praise and condemnation in a competitive situation on the Zeigarnik quotient. He found that in both cases it rises. This indicates that the strength of the force in the direction of spontaneous recollection is a function of the intensity of the need. When the subject was told that he would be interrupted as soon as the experimenter saw that he could complete the activity successfully, the quotient was slightly below one. The findings of Marrow and Zeigarnik show that the decisive factor for the release of the need tension is the reaching of the individual's goal rather than the finishing of the work as such. Experiments by Schlote (107), Sandvoss (105), and Pachauri (98) generally substantiate Zeigarnik's findings.

Rosenzweig (103) studied the Zeigarnik quotient under conditions where the interruption created a feeling of failure. Some children recollected more unfinished, others more finished, tasks. The latter children had a higher average rating on pride. In Rosenzweig's setting, the force in the direction of recalling a task which is due to the need tension, is counteracted by a force away from this task, which is due to the negative valence of failure. For the children who show a high rating in pride, this negative valence should be higher, thus producing Rosenzweig's results.

B. Substitute Satisfaction. The term *substitution* was introduced into psychology by Freud (43). Frequently one activity is called a substitute for another if they show similarity. However, as any two types of behavior show some kind of similarity, this terminology is misleading. Functionally, substitution can be linked either to the valence of an activity or to its satisfaction value.

Substitute Value, Similarity, and Degree of Difficulty. Lissner (86) studied the value which one activity has for satisfying a need originally directed toward another activity by a technique of resumption. The substitute value was measured by the amount of decrease in resumption of the interrupted original activity after a substitute activity has been completed. The substitute value increased (1) with the degree of similarity between the original and the substitute activity, and (2) with the degree of difficulty of the substitute activity. The latter factor seemed to be related to the higher level of aspiration corresponding to a more difficult task.

Substitution on Fantasy Level. If reaching the original goal (for instance, that of attacking another person) is hindered, frequently a substitute action on the level of fantasy or talk can be observed (28). Freud views the dream in part as such a substitute activity. Have these substitute activities substitute value?

Mahler (87), using as her subjects children six to ten years old, has studied the substitute value of finishing an interrupted activity by talking or thinking instead of acting. She, too, measured substitute value by the decrease of the frequency of resumption. On the average, the substitute value (2.3) for finishing by action was considerably higher than for finishing by talking (1.2). (Little difference was found between children and adults.) For some activities, such as figuring, however, finishing by talking had a high substitute value. According to Mahler, the same factor which determines the substitute value of actions is decisive for the substitute value of talking, namely, whether or not the individual's goal is reached. For *problem tasks* the intellectual solution is decisive; therefore, talking can have a very high substitute value. For *realization tasks* the building of a material object (such as making a box) is the goal; therefore, talking has practically no substitute value. Thinking through an activity had no measurable substitute value for realization or problem tasks. This finding indicates that frequently a condition for satisfaction value is the creation of a social fact (letting another person know). "Magic" solutions performed in a "make-believe" manner seemed to have a certain amount of substitute value, but only if the subject had accepted the magical nature of the situation. This was accepted more readily by children than by adults.

Substitute Value and Cognition. Adler (1) studied the relation between certain cognitive processes and substitute value at three age levels (seven to ten years chronological age). After interruption of the original task, the child had to finish a second task which was physically identical to the interrupted one. For the younger children, building a house for Mary had no substitute value for building a like house for Johnny, although these children were able to see the similarity of the two activities. For older children, too, the substitute value was low in a situation which favored the "concrete attitude" (that is, viewing each house as specifically related to Mary or Johnny). If, however, a *categorical attitude* (that is, if house-building as such) was stressed, the two activities showed considerable substitute value in the older children. For the younger children the substitute value was low even in the "categorical" situation.

Theoretically, the substitute value of one activity for another depends upon a communication between the two underlying need systems in such a way that satisfying the one also satisfies the other. The results of Lissner, Mahler, and Adler indicate that this communication depends partly on the cognitive similarity of the activities, and this in turn on the nature of the situation and the developmental state of the person. These results are in line with the findings that the more primitive person is more *concrete-minded* (Gelb and Goldstein's (47) work on patients with brain lesions; H. Werner's (129, 130) findings concerning the increase of "objectivation and abstraction" during development; Weigl's (127) experiments on children; common observations of feeble-minded). They support Vigotsky's (125) theory that "situational" thinking precedes the "abstract, conceptual" thinking in the development of the child. The relatively high age (ten years) at which the "categorical situation" became effective in Adler's experiment indicates, in addition, that the mere ability to see abstract similarities does not necessarily have sufficient weight to establish substitute value for needs.

Substitute Valence in Play and Non-Play Situation. If reaching a goal, that is, satisfying a need in a particular way, is hindered, spontaneous substitute goals may arise. Students who were unsuccessful in their attempts to throw rings over a bottle were found to throw them over near-by hooks (25). Such spontaneous substitute actions, according to Dembo, have frequently no permanent substitute value. Instead of satisfying, they seem only to heighten emotional state. This indicates that activities which appeal as substitutes, that is, which have substitute valence, do not need to have satisfaction value. We have mentioned a similar discrepancy between valence and value in ordinary consumption.

Sliosberg (116) studied substitute valence with children between three and six years in play and in a serious situation. In a serious situation, children would not accept make-believe candy (cardboard) for a piece of chocolate if the make-believe candy was offered after they had started to use real chocolate. If the make-believe candy was offered from the beginning, 17 per cent of three- and four-year-old children accepted it and treated it in a gesture-like way as real candy. Also, make-believe scissors were accepted (in 15 per cent of the cases) for real ones only if they were offered before the real ones.

In a play situation, the children accepted the make-believe chocolate or scissors in almost 100 per cent of the cases (some of them even started to chew the chocolate cardboard). If the make-believe object was introduced without relation to the particular play at hand, the percentage of acceptance decreased slightly to 75 per cent. The child was less ready to accept the substitute object if the related need was in a state of greater hunger.

Important for the acceptance or refusal of a substitute is the plasticity of the meaning of the object and of the situation. A toy animal has a more fixed meaning than a pebble or a piece of plasticene and is, therefore, less likely to be accepted as a substitute for something else. The acceptability of substitutes depends more on the plasticity of meaning of the substitute object than on that of the original object. That substitutes are more readily accepted in play is due to greater plasticity of play in respect to social roles, to the child's own position and goals, and to the meaning of objects.

III. CHANGES OF NEEDS AND GOALS

The emergence of a substitute valence can be viewed as one example of a change of needs or valences. How needs arise in the long-range history of a person and in momentary situations is one of the basic problems of child psychology. New needs, or, more correctly, a change in needs, may result from a great variety of circumstances (96). A child may find out that his friend thinks highly of certain actions and he then comes to value them himself. A change in social setting, such as attending a children's party, may significantly change the needs of the child in regard to his table manners. Reaching a goal, as well as not reaching it, may change the valences in a momentary or permanent way. During development, new needs may arise by way of differentiation from the previous ones. Behavior in a specific situation usually results from a combination of several needs; in this way a "derived need" for this behavior may arise. Such a derived need may be kept dependent upon the *source needs* or may become functionally autonomous (3). During various periods of the life history some needs of the individual seem to die gradually.

Generally speaking, needs may be changed by changes in any part of the psychological environment, by changes of the inner-personal regions, by changes on the reality level as well as on the irreality level (for instance by a change in hope), and by changes in the cognitive structure of the psychological future and of the psychological past (80). This is well in line with the fact that the total life space of a person has to be considered as one connected field. The problem of emergence of needs lies at the crossroad of cultural anthropology, developmental psychology, and the psychology of motivation. Its investigation has been hampered by premature speculative attempts to systematize needs into a few categories. In the following pages we shall discuss a few of the related questions.

A. *Restraining Forces Affecting Needs.* Persistenc[...] that a failure to reach a certain goal may increase the [...] of the obstacle until the constellation of forces is c[...] a way that a person will withdraw temporarily or finally. This withdrawal is frequently accompanied by an open or concealed conflict which may show itself in aggressiveness. The withdrawal can, however, go hand in hand with a full acceptance of the inaccessibility of the goal. This is equivalent to an actual giving-up: The inaccessible region ceases to be an effective part of the life space. If the child reaches a state where the inaccessibility becomes a "matter of fact," he is no longer in a state of frustration or conflict.

What is usually called persistence is an expression of how quickly goals change when the individual encounters obstacles. Fajans (34) found previous failure to decrease persistence in one- to six-year-old children when they were again confronted with the same type of difficulty. Success led to a relative increase of persistence. When the same task was repeated, a combination of success and praise increased persistence 48 per cent, a success alone 25 per cent; a substitute success led to a decrease of 6 per cent, failure to a decrease of 48 per cent. Similar effects of praise and failure were found by Wolf (131). We have seen that such a change in goals depends on the change in the cognitive structure and on individual differences which can be observed even in the infant (34). These experiments indicate that the velocity with which these goals change depends, in addition, upon the psychological past and the social atmosphere. Jack (62) and Keister (72) found that it is possible to change the reaction of nursery school children to failure through proper training. The increase of persistence and the decrease of rationalization and of emotional and destructive reactions showed a certain amount of transfer to different areas of activity.

Difficulties Intensifying Needs. H. F. Wright (133) has shown in experiments with adults and children that a difficulty may increase the need for an object behind a barrier. Children, like adults, will prefer a goal which is more difficult to reach, provided that the barrier is not too strong and that both goal objects are not fully identical. This preference is observed if the object itself has the nature of a goal, but not if it is merely a means. For instance, the child will prefer (everything else being equal) a toy which is slightly more difficult to reach. If, however, he has to choose between two tools with which to get the same object, he will prefer that tool which is easier to reach. Wright's investigations indicate that the so-called law of parsimony (using the easiest way) holds only for psychological means, but not for ends. This latter fact is closely related to the problem of the level of aspiration.

B. *Psychological Satiation.* One can distinguish in regard to all or most needs a state of hunger, of satiation, and of oversatiation. These states correspond to a positive, a neutral, and a negative valence of the activity regions which are related to a particular need. Karsten (68), in experiments with college students, has studied the effect of repeating over and over again such activities as reading a poem, writing letters, drawing, and turning a wheel. She found the main symptoms of satiation to occur in this order: (1) small variations; (2) large variations; (3) the breaking-up of larger units of action into smaller parts, loss of meaning; (4) mistakes, unlearning; (5) fatigue and similar "bodily" symptoms.

These results provide one more reason for revising the older theories which explain the genesis of larger units of actions in terms of associations between smaller units established through repetition. Repetition may lead to the combining of smaller units of action into larger ones, but sufficient repetition will break up larger units. This involves, in case of meaningful material such as poems or sentences, a destruction of the meaning. A similar disintegration may also occur for the situation as a whole.

Satiation occurs only if the activity has, psychologically, the character of an actual repetition, of marking time as opposed to making progress. If the character of making progress can be maintained, the usual symptoms of satiation will not appear.

Psychological satiation frequently leads to muscular fatigue or such bodily symptoms as hoarseness. It is frequently the main cause of "fatigue" in children. Like hysterical symptoms, these bodily symptoms cannot be eliminated by voluntary effort, although they are caused by psychological factors and may disappear with the transition to other activities even though the new activity makes use of the same muscles in practically the same way. Imbedding an activity in a different psychological whole so that its meaning is changed has practically the same effect in satiation as shifting to a different activity. The superiority of the method of learning to read and write whole sentences or words rather than single letters is based partly on the fact that the former method is less likely to lead to satiation. The good primer is careful to repeat the same words in such a way that they are imbedded in somewhat different wholes, and that a "program of meaning" rather than actual repetition occurs.

Repetition not only changes the needs related to the activity which is carried out, but usually also affects the needs related to psychologically similar activities, by way of cosatiation.

The velocity of satiation (that is, how quickly repetition leads to a change in needs) depends, according to Karsten, mainly upon (1) the nature of the activity (particularly the size of its units of action), (2) the degree of centrality, and (3) the individual character and state of the person. Pleasant as well as unpleasant activities are more quickly satiated than neutral activities which in other respects are equivalent. Giving more attention to an activity (without changing its meaning) seems merely to quicken satiation. Freund (44) found that the velocity of satiation of minute tasks is greater during menstruum. All three results can be interpreted as indicating that the velocity of satiation increases with the centrality of the activity. Frequently a person tries to avoid satiation by doing the activity in a peripheral manner. Automatic activities such as breathing or walking do not become satiated if they are not carried out consciously as mere repetition. The effect of primary and secondary aspects of an activity can be handled with the concept of relative potency.

Children, in line with their lesser degree of differentiation, are likely to be involved in an activity with their whole person. The velocity of satiation should, therefore, vary inversely with mental age. Experimental results seem to confirm this expectation, although they are not univocal (77, 131). The apparent divergence of findings is probably due to the fact that child psychology treats the problems of satiation under the title of persisting or perseverant behavior and that the term *persistence* is used to refer to dynamically rather different situations (for instance, persistence in overcoming an obstacle and persistence in carrying on an activity without an obstacle). Shacter (112) found satiation time to be longer for a complex task than for a simpler one, without much age difference between three-, four-, and five-year-old children.

Wolf (131) studied satiation in situations of praise, competition, and of no incentive with children of four and six years, making a careful analysis of the individual cases. She found the individual goal of the child to be of primary importance and this goal to depend upon the level of aspiration.

Kounin (76) compared the satiation and cosatiation of normal 7-year-old children with 12- and 30- to 40-year-old feeble-minded persons of the same mental age. He found that the velocity of satiation (drawings of different patterns) decreased with increasing age. The younger child shows greater cosatiation in spite of the small number of repetitions required for satiating an activity. In other words, the velocity of satiation and the degree of cosatiation decrease with chronological age even if mental age is kept constant. Kounin (76), and Seashore and Bavelas (110) found about the same symptoms of satiation in children which Karsten has described with adults.

The phenomena of satiation indicate (1) that there·is a close relation between activities and needs, and (2) that an activity can be viewed as a consumption which changes the underlying need and, therefore, the positive valence of the activity into a negative one. As a result of this consumption the valence of "similar activities" also becomes negative, whereas certain different types of activities acquire an increasingly positive valence.

A satiated or oversatiated need, after a lapse of time, frequently changes back into a state of hunger. The conditions of these changes need investigation.

C. *Intention.* The effect of an intention can be viewed as the setting-up of a quasi-need (77). A quasi-need is dynamically equivalent to other needs in that it tends to create actions in the direction of satisfying the need, with or without the presence of a corresponding goal object. Intentions are made, as a result of a given time perspective, to secure a certain behavior in the future which is expected to bring nearer the fulfillment of one or of several needs. The newly established quasi-need usually remains dependent on these source needs.

Experiments of Birenbaum (14) show that the tension level of such a quasi-need depends upon the tension level of the more inclusive set of needs of which this quasi-need is a part. An intention will be "forgotten," that is, not carried out, if these source needs have been satisfied in the meantime, or if the state of the person as a whole has become one of high general satisfaction.

D. *Needs as Part of More Inclusive Needs.* It has been stated that goals or other valences are closely related to needs. Changes of goals depend largely upon the interdependence of needs. Needs may be interdependent in different ways: (a) Two or more needs can be in communication so that their need tensions vary concomitantly. As we have seen, such relation is important for the problem of substitution. (b) The interdependence between needs can be one of ruling and being ruled. For instance, quasi-needs which correspond to intentions are induced by ruling needs. In both cases of interdependence, the need becomes a part of a more inclusive needs system (see Chapter 5).

We have discussed the effect of completion and noncompletion in regard to satisfying or not satisfying the need behind an action. We shall discuss now the effect of those actions on the setting-up of new goals.

Maturity of Aspiration. To a child of six months, lying on his stomach and trying to reach a rattle, it seems to make no difference whether he finally reaches the rattle as the result of his own effort or whether the rattle is brought within his reach by someone else. The child will be satisfied both ways. A child of three, trying to jump down from the third step, may refuse help. He will not be content unless he has reached certain results by his own effort. The very young child seems to know only satisfaction and dissatisfaction but not success and failure. In other words, he has needs and goals but not yet a level of aspiration.

We speak of *aspiration* in regard to an action if the result of this action is seen as an achievement reflecting one's own ability; if, in addition, different degrees of difficulty can be distinguished, we speak of a *level of aspiration.* The level of aspiration is of basic importance for the conduct of human beings and influences most of their goal-seeking. In this connection we have the paradox that the individual may prefer something more difficult to something more easy.

Fales (4) has studied the development, over a period of six months, of aspiration in two- to three-year-old children. She observed such activities as putting on and removing snow suits. Refusing help is probably the best behavioral symptom for the existence of an aspiration in regard to an activity. Such insistence on independence indicates that one's own action has become a part of the goal. Observing manipulations of various degrees of difficulty (such as opening the zipper, getting an arm out of the coat, hanging the cap on the hook), she found that children at this age have an aspiration only in regard to particular activities. One of the determining factors is the ability of the child; he will not refuse help for activities definitely beyond his reach. As he becomes older or is better trained an aspiration develops in regard to the more difficult actions. Fales also

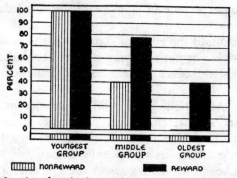

FIGURE 52. Maturity of aspiration at three age levels and amount of regression under social pressure (reward). The frequency with which the child places the missed ring on a stick or rethrows the single ring instead of finishing the series of rings is indicated.[6]

found that social situations or praise facilitate the rise of an aspiration. This indicates that a social component is important for aspiration from its earliest development.

It is possible to distinguish different degrees of "maturity of aspiration," corresponding to different types of goals and procedures in attaining them at various age levels. C. Anderson (4) developed a scale of maturity of aspiration for children between two and eight years, using activities such as throwing a series of rings over a stick and knocking down tenpins with a ball. A child of eight will consider the series of five throws as one unit and will not, therefore, rethrow single rings which miss the stick before counting his score.

[6] The data in this figure are derived from a study by C. Anderson (4).

Children of the youngest group (three years old) always pick up the single rings after missing the stick and rethrow them or place them directly on the stick. The youngest children do not hold to the rule of standing behind a given place. These and other symptoms indicate that the development of a level of aspiration, the choosing of a goal of a particular degree of difficulty, presupposes (1) that a number of goals are seen as subgoals within a larger goal structure, (2) that the action itself is conceived as a part of the goal, and (3) that the child understands the meaning of rules and is ready to keep them.

If pressure is brought to bear on a child by offering a reward, the level of aspiration (that is, the degree of difficulty chosen) will decrease. If a lowering of the level of aspiration is made impossible, the maturity of aspiration may regress (Figure 52); that is, a procedure is used which is characteristic of a younger age level. Regression of the maturity of aspiration can be observed in adults in emotional situations.

Level of Aspiration. Level of aspiration has been defined (57) as the degree of difficulty of that task chosen as a goal for the next action. One may distinguish two main problems: (1) under what condition the individual experiences success or failure, and (2) what factors influence the level of aspiration.

Conditions for the Experience of Success or Failure. The experience of success or failure depends on the level of performance within a frame of reference (81). This frame of reference can be the level of aspiration (that is, the goal which has been set for that action), the past performance, or the standards of a group. A feeling of success will prevail if a certain level, related to the dominant frame of reference, is reached. What frame of reference will be dominant depends upon a number of factors, one of which is the tendency to avoid the feeling of failure.

It has been shown (36, 52, 108) that to avoid the feeling of failure after a poor performance the frame of reference is frequently shifted. Other ways to avoid failure are various forms of rationalization (36, 57), such as blaming a poor instrument for the shortcomings of the performance. In this way the link between performance and one's own ability is cut, which is, as we have seen, one of the conditions for the phenomenon of aspiration.

Jucknat (65) distinguished different intensities of the feeling of success and failure. They are to be related to the amount of discrepancy between goal and performance. This holds, however, only within the range of difficulties which is close to the boundary level of ability. "Too easy" and "too difficult" tasks do not lead to feelings of success and failure. This may be the reason why rivalry among siblings is less frequent when there are relatively great differences of age among them (111).

The relation between the feeling of success and failure, on the one hand, and the boundary of ability, on the other, is operative only if other frames of reference, such as certain group standards, do not become dominant. The mentally retarded child might have permanently the feeling of failure in a group of children of high ability even though the tasks were actually far beyond the limit of his own ability.

Case studies (67) and experimental data (34) show that change in group status (for instance, gaining recognition or love or being rejected by an individual or a larger group) is, in many respects, equivalent to success or failure.

Factors Determining the Level of Aspiration. After the experience of success or failure the person may either quit or continue with a higher, equal, or lower level of aspiration. The difference between the level of aspiration for the new action and the level of past performance is called the "discrepancy" between level of aspiration and performance (for details see 81).

The factors determining a change in the level of aspiration are manifold. Jucknat (65) found that with children from nine to fifteen and with adults the direction and the amount of the change in the level of aspiration depended upon the degree of success and failure. In addition, within a given series of tasks, the discrepancy was smaller for the same amount of success and greater for the same amount of failure the closer the previous level of performance came to the extreme of the series of difficulties.

The level of aspiration is much influenced by social factors. In a situation of competition it might be increased (37). The knowledge of group standards may affect the level of aspiration (36). For instance, the discrepancy between aspiration and performance increased toward a higher level of aspiration if the person learned that his performance was below the standard of his own group or of a group which he considered to be lower. The discrepancy decreases if the opposite conditions obtain. The level of aspiration is affected also by the degree of realistic judgment about one's own ability (37). P. Sears (108) found the average positive discrepancy (that is, the amount by which the level of aspiration exceeds past performance) to be greater in children after failure than after success, indicating a greater degree of realism after success than after failure.

For the same individual, the direction and amount of discrepancy seem to be constant to a certain degree for a number of activities (37, 45, 108). P. Sears (37) and Jucknat (65) found the discrepancy to be greater in children of poor standing than in children of good standing in school. The degree to which the level of aspiration in one activity affects the level of aspiration in another activity depends upon their similarity and upon how well previous experience has stabilized the level of aspiration in these activities (65). The influence of success in one activity on the level of aspiration in another is slight if the child has clearly found his ability in the latter.

The level of aspiration is closely related to the time perspective with respect to both the psychological past and the psychological future. According to Escalona (33), the level of aspiration at a given time depends upon the strength of the valence of success and failure and upon the probability of success at that time. By representing this probability as the potency of the future success or failure situation, the basic facts concerning the level of aspiration can be understood (see 81).

E. *Induced Needs.* The needs of the individual are, to a very high degree, determined by social factors. The needs of the growing child are changed and new needs induced as a result of the many small and large social groups to which he belongs. His needs are much affected, also, by the ideology and conduct of those groups to which he would like to belong or from which he would like to be set apart. The effects of the advice of the mother, of the demand of a fellow child, or of what the psychoanalyst calls *super-ego*, are all closely interwoven with socially induced needs. We have seen that the level of aspiration is related to social facts. We may state more generally that the culture in which a child grows affects practically every need and all his behavior and that the problem of acculturation is one of the foremost in child psychology.

One can distinguish three types of cases where needs pertain to social relations: (1) the action of the individual may be performed for the benefit of someone else (in the manner of an altruistic act); (2) needs may be induced by the power field of another person or group (as a weaker person's obedience of a more powerful one); (3) needs may be created by belonging to a group and adhering to its goals. Actually, these three types are closely interwoven.

Sources of Ideology. Bavelas (12) studied the sources of approval and disapproval in a number of schools. He found that the frequency with which children named the teacher as a source for praise or scolding of behavior in school remained relatively constant from the fourth to the eighth grade. An individual classmate (as distinguished from the concept "children") was frequently named as source for evaluation of behavior in the fourth grade; this frequency declined to zero by the eighth grade. The school superintendent was practically never named as source by children in the fourth grade; he was named with increasing frequency later on, but mainly as a source of scolding.

Kalhorn (66) compared positive and negative values and sources of values in Mennonite and non-Mennonite children in rural areas. She found differences in the emphasis on such values as individual achievement and religion. In both groups the parents are indicated by the children to have the most dominant influence as a source of values. The same conduct may have different psychological meaning in different cultures. For instance, going to church is linked with God as the source of approval by the Mennonite children, with everyone by the non-Mennonite children. This indicates that church-going is primarily a religious affair with the former, a social affair with the latter.

Egoism and Altruism. In an experiment by Moore (94), children between the ages of two and three were asked to share orange juice with a companion who was seated beside the subject. Her results show wide individual differences and no correlation with the degree to which the child respects the rights of others as determined by other methods. Hartshorne and May (55) studied test situations in which service (altruism, cooperation) of the children could be observed. They claim that the tendency to serve is "specific" rather than "general" in children between ten and fourteen years (for a discussion of the problem of generality of traits see 3). McGrath (90), using a questionnaire technique, reports that an altruistic response to a hypothetical situation increases with age. Piaget (99) orders his findings on the moral development of children in terms of two psychologically different moralities which are an outgrowth of two types of social relations: up to seven or eight years, there exists a social relation of unilateral respect in which the child is subjected to adult authority. Gradually a relationship of mutual respect is set up in which each member has a more equal part of the control.

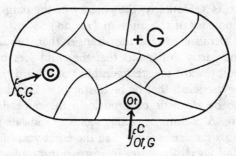

FIGURE 53. The situation of altruism. (The meaning of the various symbols is described in the text.)

B. Wright (132) studied children in a situation where they had a choice of keeping a preferred toy or giving it to someone else. The other child (who was not present) was either someone unknown or a best friend. The five-year-old child was practically always egoistic: the eight-year-old child showed considerable altruism, and more so toward the stranger (58 per cent generous choices) than to the friend (23 per cent generous choices). When acting as an umpire between a friend and a strange child in distributing the toys, the five-year-old child favored the friend more frequently than the stranger. The eight-year-old favored the stranger more frequently than the friend.

Theoretically, the altruistic or the egoistic choice can be viewed as the result of the relative strength of forces acting on different regions of the life space and of the potency of various situations. In the life space of child C (Figure 53), a force $f_{C, G}$ acts on his own person in the direction to a goal G. In addition, a force of $f^c_{Ot, G}$ exists in his life space, acting on the other child, Ot, in the direction of the same goal. (The situation permits only one person to obtain the goal.) This second force, $f^c_{Ot, G}$, corresponds to the need of the other child (as perceived by the child whose life space is represented) and the readiness of the child C to back the goal of the child Ot. Formalistically speaking, the altruistic or egoistic choice depends on the relative strength of these two forces. According to Wright, the need of the other child is not perceived by the very young child. This may be the reason for the absence of cooperative play in the young child. With increasing age, the potency of the perceived need of the other child increases. Similarly, the potency of the outgroup increases relative to the potency of the ingroup (friend).

The greater altruism toward the stranger than toward the friend seems to be due partly to the fact that the child sees himself in the position of a host toward the stranger, but not toward the friend, and that his ideology requires that he be hospitable. The children judged other people to be altruistic or egoistic to the same degree as they themselves were. A preliminary study seems to indicate that adults in a similar setting are more egoistic than the eight-year-old child.

Obedience and Social Pressure. In discussing problems of conflicts we have seen that the force acting on a person in the direction of a goal might be counteracted by induced forces corresponding to the will of another person. In view of the relation between psychological forces and psychological needs we can also speak of *induced needs*. The relation between two persons might be that of friends or that of enemies; the need of each would depend greatly on the power field of the other.

Wiehe (77) observed children between two and four years of age when a stranger entered the child's room. He found the strength of the power field of the stranger at a given moment to be influenced by the physical position of both persons. The effect of the power field on the child increases with decreasing distance. It is very high if the child is placed on the adult's lap. The power field is weaker back of the stranger, or where the child cannot be seen, than in front of the stranger. In other words, the strength of the power field of one person on another differs for different areas. J. D. Frank (37) in experiments with students, and Waring, Dwyer, and Junkin (126) in experiments with nursery school children at the dinner table, also found the effectiveness of the power field for creating induced forces to be greater if the distance between the persons is smaller.

Lippitt and White (84), in experiments with ten-year-old children, tested the effect of induced needs during the presence and the absence of the inducing power field. They found that the amount of work output in an autocratic group atmosphere dropped very decisively within a few minutes when the leader left the room. This was in contrast to a democratic group atmosphere, where the work had been chosen and planned by the group itself, and where the work output was unchanged when the leader left. C. E. Meyers (93) studied the effect of conflicting adult authority on children of nursery school age. He found that the opposing orders lower the children's constructive-ness of play very considerably (from $4\frac{1}{2}$ to $2\frac{1}{2}$ on his constructive-ness scale). The child may stop action altogether (aside from self-manipulation similar to that described by Arsenian, 6) if he does not find a way to follow the orders of both authorities. Even if the orders of both adults agree, too frequent interference with the child's play lowers his constructiveness somewhat. Negative commands were more damaging than positive commands, and vague commands more damaging than specific ones.

Induced needs which are opposite to own needs may lead to a permanent state of conflict which is more or less concealed. If such a conflict cannot be resolved by breaking the dominant power field, the child may become aggressive toward less powerful persons. Lewin, Lippitt, and White (82) found that, on several occasions, one of the children was attacked as a scapegoat in the autocratic group.

Taking Over Foreign Goals. An induced need may slowly change its character in the direction of an own need. In other words, the person not only will follow orders but also "accept" them (in the meaning of taking them over). Waring, Dwyer, and Junkin (126) have observed changes in this direction with nursery school children.

Duncker (30) studied changes in food preferences of children from two to five years of age, as affected by a story in which the hero abhorred one and enthusiastically relished the other of two kinds of food. After the story, the children preferred the hero's favorite food, although previously it had been unattractive to them. This effect decreased with time, but could still be detected after six days. Thompson (121) studied the effect of prejudicial leadership on ten-year-old children. The leader set up an underprivileged minority within a group of children who originally had equal status. After a number of club meetings the children of the privileged majority continued to treat the rest of the children as underprivileged even when the leader left the room. This discrimination, however, was not so strong as in the presence of the leader. This shows both that the presence of the power field of the leader has some influence and that the induced goals have been taken over in some measure.

Lippitt and White (84), in a study of autocratic, democratic, and laissez-faire groups, have found that the readiness of an individual to accept autocracy in the club depends partly upon the home background. A combination of a firm and warm home atmosphere seems to be most favorable to that end; that is, an atmosphere of relative autocracy which, nevertheless, by its warmness, prohibits the child from becoming independent of the family. These children are likely to adhere to "adult values" rather than "boy values." Children who follow boy values are more sociable among themselves but less obedient at school.

Horowitz (58) found no prejudices against Negroes in white children under three years. The prejudices increased between four and six years. This increase was as great in New York as in the South. It was independent of the degree of acquaintance of the children with Negro children, and of the actual status of the Negro child in the class which the white child attended. The prejudices are, however, related to the attitude of the parents of the white child. This indicates that the prejudices against the Negroes are due to an induction and gradual taking-over of the culture of the parents by the child.

A phenomenon which is probably partly due to the acceptance of originally induced needs and partly to the problems of group belongingness is the hatred against one's own group in persons belonging to an underprivileged group. This hatred against the own group is frequent among the bodily handicapped and among socially underprivileged groups (80). It means that the values and prejudices of the privileged group have been taken over by the members of the socially lower group even if they are directed against their own group. This hatred of one's own group may lead to self-hatred. It is augmented by the need of the individual to raise his status, and therefore, to separate himself from the underprivileged group.

Whether or not an induced need has changed its character and has become an own need is frequently difficult to decide. Lippitt and White (84) distinguished two types of reaction to an autocratic atmosphere: one called *aggressive autocracy,* and the other *apathetic autocracy.* In the latter case the children seem to work willingly. Signs of discontent or obstruction may be entirely absent. Particularly strict obedience may have the appearance of a voluntary action. This holds also for the behavior of children in institutions. Nevertheless, the effect of the removal of the leader in the experiment shows how great the actual difference in both situations is for the child.

Needs of a Child as a Group Member. As mentioned above, the children in the democratic group studied by Lippitt and White did not decrease the intensity of their work if the leader left. The plan for this work had been decided upon by majority vote after consideration. This shows that under these conditions a need corresponding to a group goal is more like an own need than an induced need. This problem is closely related to the difference between "we"-feeling and "I"-feeling. Lewin, Lippitt, and White (82) found "we"-feeling, as measured by the verbal expression and the attitude toward the work, to be greater in the democratic group than in the autocratic group where an egocentric attitude prevailed.

One can consider two factors to be basic for the kind and degree of influence which group goals have for the goals of the individual: (1) the degree of dependence of the person on the group; (2) the character of enmity or friendship of this dependence. According to Lippitt (83), the power fields of enemies weaken each other in areas where they overlap, whereas the power fields of friends strengthen each other. In addition, friendship as distinguished from enmity includes the readiness to accept and to back up the intention of the other person. According to M. E. Wright (134), both characteristics can be expressed by the degree of accessibility of one's own power field to the power field of the other person.

F. *Individual Differences.* We have seen that it is not possible to determine the specific characteristics of individuals by classifying them according to their overt behavior. Instead, one has to look for factors which can be inserted as constant values into the variables of the equations which represent psychological laws. In this way also the variability of behavior, that is, the difference in behavior of the same individual in different situations, becomes susceptible to treatment. This variability does not mean merely that the absolute frequency or intensity of a certain type of behavior depends upon the situation. Actually, the rank-order of individuals in regard to a certain trait may also be different in different situations. For instance, Lewin, Lippitt, and White (82) found in clubs of ten-year-old boys, that in regard to some "traits," such as "demanding attention from other club members" and "out-of-field conversation," the rank-order of the individual in different atmospheres remains rather constant ($r = .85$ and $r = .78$). In other traits, such as "dependence upon leader," there is scarcely any consistency of rank-order ($r = .02$). There are more extreme changes in the rank-order in "work-mindedness" than in "aggressiveness." The changes seem to be linked to the differences of meaning of the particular atmospheres to the particular children.

The attempts to link problems of individual differences and of general laws positively are relatively new in psychology. We shall mention but one example, which is related to differences in age, intelligence, and rigidity of the person. Lewin (77) has outlined a theory according to which differences in mental age are closely related to the degree of differentiation of the person. The variety of states which an organism can assume, and the corresponding variety of patterns of behavior, must logically be conceived of (9) as a function of the degree of the differentiation of that organism. Therefore, with increasing mental age, the individual should show an increasing flexibility, in the sense of richness, of behavior. This is in line with empirical observation of individuals of different mental age and with the peculiar pedantry and stubbornness of the young child.

The increase of flexibility with increasing mental age is somewhat counteracted by a decrease in plasticity which seems to go hand in hand with chronological age and which seems to be important for senility. A certain type of feeble-mindedness is characterized by the fact that these individuals show at the same level of differentiation (the same mental age) less plasticity (77). If this theory is correct, one should expect less cosatiation in feeble-minded persons than in normal persons of the same mental age. We have seen above that

Kounin (76) demonstrated this with individuals whose chronological ages were 7, 12, or 30, all having a mental age of 7. One can derive from the same set of premises that feeble-minded individuals should be less able to tolerate overlapping situations. One should expect, therefore, that the feeble-minded person would make fewer mistakes in case of change of habits under certain conditions, that he would show greater difference in speed of performance between overlapping and nonoverlapping situations, and that he would be less able to change the cognitive structure in a test requiring several classifications of the same group of objects. Kounin's experiments substantiate all these derivations. The results of Koepke (77) and of Gottschaldt (51) indicate that the readiness of the feeble-minded person to accept or to refuse a substitute is either very small or very great, according to the specific situation. This is in line with what should be expected from a relatively rigid individual.

The coordination of certain individual differences with differences in the degree of differentiation and rigidity of the person makes it possible to link behavior in quite a variety of fields, such as cognition, stubbornness, substitution, and satiation, and to understand apparent contradictions of behavior. A greater rigidity of the feeble-minded person also explains why his development is slower than that of the normal child (that is, the relative constancy of the IQ) and why he reaches his peak of development earlier.

It can be expected that all problems of individual differences will be linked more and more with the general psychological laws of behavior and development and that in this way a deeper understanding of both the individual differences and the general laws will be possible.

REFERENCES

1. ADLER, D. L.: *Types of Similarity and the Substitute Value of Activities at Different Age Levels.* Unpublished Ph.D. Dissertation, State University of Iowa, 1939.
2. ADLER, D. L., and KOUNIN, J.: Some factors operating at the moment of resumption of interrupted tasks, *J. Psychol.*, 1939, 7, 355–367.
3. ALLPORT, G. W.: *Personality: A Psychological Interpretation.* New York: Henry Holt and Company, 1937.
4. ANDERSON, C.: *The Development of a Level of Aspiration in Young Children.* Unpublished Ph.D. Dissertation, State University of Iowa, 1940.

5. ANDERSON, H. H.: Domination and social integration in the behavior of kindergarten children and teachers, *Genet. Psychol. Monogr.*, 1939, 21, 287–385.

6. ARSENIAN, J. M.: Young children in an insecure situation. *J. Abnorm. & Social Psychol.*, 1943, 38, 225–249.

7. BARBER, V.: Studies in the psychology of stuttering: XV. Chorus reading as a distraction in stuttering, *J. Speech Disorders*, 1939, 4, 371–383.

8. BARKER, R.: An experimental study of the resolution of conflict in children. In A. McNemar and M. A. Merrill (Eds.): *Studies in Personality*. New York: McGraw-Hill Book Company, 1942.

9. BARKER, R., DEMBO, T., and LEWIN, K.: Frustration and regression, *Univ. Iowa Stud. Child Welf.*, 1941, 18, No. 1.

10. BARTOS, A.: Die psychologischen Grundlagen der seelischen Erziehung bei Verkrüppelten, *Vers. f. Kinderforsch.*, 1932, 4, 244–253.

11. BAVELAS, A.: Morale and the training of leaders. In G. Watson (Ed.): *Civilian Morale*. Boston: Houghton Mifflin Company, 1942.

12. BAVELAS, A.: A method for investigating individual and group ideology, *Sociometry*, 1942, 5, 371–377.

13. BENEDICT, R.: *Patterns of Culture*. Boston: Houghton Mifflin Company, 1934.

14. BIRENBAUM, G.: Das Vergessen einer Vornahme, *Psychol. Forsch.*, 1930, 13, 218–285.

15. BROWN, J. F.: Über die dynamischen Eigenschaften der Realitäts—und Irrealitätsschichten, *Psychol. Forsch.*, 1933, 18, 1–26.

16. BROWN, J. F.: *Psychology and the Social Order*. New York: McGraw-Hill Book Company, 1936.

17. BROWN, S. F.: Influence of grammatical function on the incidence of stuttering, *J. Speech Disorders*, 1936, 2, 207–215.

18. BROWN, S. F.: A further study of stuttering in relation to various speech sounds, *Quart. J. Speech*, 1938, 24, 390–397.

19. BROWN, S. F.: Stuttering with relation to word accent and word position, *J. Abnorm & Social Psychol.*, 1938, 33, 112–120.

20. BÜHLER, C.: *The child and His Family*. New York: Harper & Brothers, 1939.

21. BURKS, B. S.: Mental and physical developmental pattern of identical twins in relation to organismic growth theory, *Yearbook Nat. Soc. Stud. Educ.*, 1940, 39, 85–96.

22. CARTWRIGHT, D.: Decision-time in relation to the differentiation of the phenomenal field, *Psychol. Rev.*, 1941, 48, 425–442.

23. CARTWRIGHT, D., and FESTINGER, L.: A quantitative theory of decision, *Psychol. Rev.*, 1943, 50, 595–621.

24. DAVIDSON, H. H., and KLOPFER, B.: Rorschach statistics: II. Normal children, *Rorschach Res. Exch.*, 1938, 3, 37–42.

25. DEMBO, T.: Der Ärger als dynamisches Problem, *Psychol. Forsch.*, 1931, 15, 1–144.

26. DOLLARD, J.: *Criteria for the Life History*. New Haven: Yale University Press, 1935.

27. DOLLARD, J.: *Caste and Class in a Southern Town*. New Haven: Yale University Press, 1937.

28. DOOB, L. W., and SEARS, R. R.: Factors determining substitute behavior and the overt expression of aggression, *J. Abnorm. Social Psychol.*, 1939, 34, 293–313.

29. DRESDNER, I.: Über Körperbehinderung und seelische Entwicklung, *Z. angew. Psychol.*, 1933, 44, 399–437.

30. DUNCKER, K.: Experimental modification of children's food preferences through social suggestion, *J. Abnorm. & Social Psychol.*, 1933, 33. 489–507.

31. EINSTEIN, A.: *On the Method of Theoretical Physics.* New York: Oxford University Press, 1933.

32. ERIKSON, E. H.: Studies in the interpretation of play: I. Clinical observation of play disruption in young children, *Genet. Psychol. Monogr.*, 1940, 22, 556–671.

33. ESCALONA, S. K.: The effect of success and failure upon the level of aspiration and behavior in manic-depressive psychoses, *Univ. Iowa Stud. Child Welf.*, 1940, 16, 199–307.

34. FAJANS, S.: Erfolg, Ausdauer, und Activität beim Saügling und Kleinkind, *Psychol. Forsch.*, 1933, 17, 268–305.

35. FARBER, M. L.: Imprisonment as a psychological situation, *Univ. Iowa Stud. Child Welf.*, 1944, 20, 153–228.

36. FESTINGER, L.: Wish, expectation, and group performance as factors influencing level of aspiration, *J. Abnorm. & Social Psychol.*, 1942, 37, 184–200.

37. FRANK, J. D.: Experimental studies of personal pressure and resistance: II. Methods of overcoming resistance, *J. Gen. Psychol.*, 1944, 30, 43–56.

38. FRANK, L. K.: Cultural control and physiological autonomy, *Am. J. Orthopsychiat.*, 1938, 8, 622–626.

39. FRANK, L. K.: Cultural coercion and individual distortion, *Psychiatry*, 1939, 2, 11–27.

40. FRAZIER, E. F.: *Negro Youth at the Crossways.* Washington: American Council on Education, 1940.

41. FRENCH, J. R. P., JR.: Organized and unorganized groups under fear and frustration, *Univ. Iowa Stud. Child Welf.*, 1944, 20, 229-308.

42. FRENCH, T.: Insight and distortion in dreams, *Internat. J. Psycho-Analysis*, 1939, 20, 287–298.

43. FREUD, S.: *The Interpretation of Dreams.* New York: The Macmillan Company, 1916.

44. FREUND, A.: Psychische Sättigung im Menstruum und Intermenstruum, *Psychol. Forsch.*, 1930, 13, 198–217.

45. GARDNER, J. W.: The relation of certain personality variables to level of aspiration, *J. Psychol.*, 1940, 9, 191–206.

46. GELB, A.: Colour constancy. In W. D. Ellis (Ed.): *Source Book of Gestalt Psychology.* London: Kegan Paul, 1938.

47. GELB, A., and GOLDSTEIN, K.: Über Farbennamenamnesie nebst Bemerkungen über das Wesen der amnestischen Aphasie überhaupt und die Beziehung zwischen Sprache und dem Verhalten zur Umwelt, *Psychol. Forsch.*, 1924, 6, 127–186.

48. GESELL, A., et al.: *The First Five Years of Life: A Guide to the Study of the Preschool Child.* New York: Harper & Brothers, 1940.

49. GESELL, A., and THOMPSON, H.: *Infant Behavior: Its Genesis and Growth.* New York: McGraw-Hill Book Company, 1934.

50. GOODENOUGH, F. L.: New evidence on environmental influence on intelligence, *Yearbook Nat. Soc. Stud. Educ.*, 1940, 39, 307–365.

51. GOTTSCHALDT, K.: Über dem Einfluss der Erfahrung auf die Wahrnehmung von Figuren: I. Über den Einfluss gehäufter Einprägung von Figuren auf

ihre Sichtbarkeit in umfassenden Konfigurationen., *Psychol. Forsch.*, 1926, *8*, 261–318.

52. GOULD, R.: An experimental analysis of "level of aspiration," *Genet. Psychol. Monogr.*, 1939, *21*, 3–115.

53. GRAY, M.: The X family: A clinical study and a laboratory study of a "stuttering" family, *J. Speech Disorders*, 1940, *5*, 343–348.

54. HALVERSON, H. M.: An experimental study of prehension in infants by means of systematic cinema records, *Genet. Psychol. Monogr.*, 1931, *10*, 107–286.

55. HARTSHORNE, H., and MAY, M. A.: *Studies in Service and Self-control.* New York: Macmillan Company, 1929.

56. HOMBURGER, E.: Configurations in play: Clinical notes, *Psychoanalyt. Quart.*, 1937, *6*, 139–214.

57. HOPPE, E.: Erfolg und Misserfolg, *Psychol. Forsch.*, 1930, *14*, 1–62.

58. HOROWITZ, E. L.: The development of attitude toward the Negro, *Arch. Psychol.*, N. Y., 1936, No. 194.

59. HULL, C. L.: Simple trial-and-error learning: A study in psychological theory, *Psychol. Rev.*, 1930, *37*, 241–256.

60. HULL, C. L.: The goal gradient hypothesis and maze learning, *Psychol. Rev.*, 1932, *39*, 25–43.

61. IRWIN, O. C.: The distribution of the amount of motility in young infants between two nursing periods, *J. Comp. Psychol.*, 1932, *14*, 429–445.

62. JACK, L. M.: An experimental study of ascendant behavior in preschool children, *Univ. Iowa Stud. Child Welf.*, 1934, *9*, No. 3, 7–65.

63. JERSILD, A. T.: The development of the emotions. In C. E. Skinner (Ed.): *Educational Psychology.* New York: Prentice-Hall, Inc., 1936.

64. JOHNSON, W., and KNOTT, J. R.: Studies in the psychology of stuttering: I. The distribution of moments of stuttering in successive readings of the same material, *J. Speech Disorders*, 1937, *2*, 17–19.

65. JUCKNAT, M.: Leistung, Anspruchsniveau und Selbstbewusstsein, *Psychol. Forsch.*, 1937, *22*, 89–179.

66. KALHORN, J.: Values and sources of authority among rural children, *Univ. Iowa Stud. Child Welf.*, 1944, *20*, 99–152.

67. KANNER, L.: *Child Psychiatry.* Springfield, Ill.: Charles C Thomas, 1935.

68. KARSTEN, A.: Psychische Sättigung, *Psychol. Forsch.*, 1928, *10*, 142–154.

69. KATONA, G.: *Organizing and Memorizing.* New York: Columbia University Press, 1940.

70. KATZ, D.: *Animals and Men.* New York: Longmans, Green, and Co., 1937.

71. KATZ, E.: Some factors affecting resumption of interrupted activities by pre-school children, *Inst. Child Welf. Monogr. Ser.*, No. 16, 1938, University of Minnesota Press.

72. KEISTER, M. E.: The behavior of young children in failure. In Barker, R., Kounin, J., and Wright, H. F. (Eds.): *Child Behavior and Development.* New York: McGraw-Hill Book Company, 1936.

73. KEPHART, N. C.: Studies in emotional adjustment: II. An experimental study of the "disorganization" of mental functions in the delinquent, *Univ. Iowa Stud. Child Welf.*, 1937, *15*, No. 1.

74. KOFFKA, K.: *The Growth of the Mind: An Introduction to Child Psychology.* New York: Harcourt, Brace, and Company, 1928.

75. KÖHLER, W.: *The Mentality of Apes.* New York: Harcourt, Brace, and Company, 1925.

76. KOUNIN, J.: Experimental studies of rigidity. I and II, *Character and Pers.*, 1941, *9*, 251–282.
77. LEWIN, K.: *Dynamic theory of Personality.* New York: McGraw-Hill Book Company, 1935.
78. LEWIN, K.: *Principles of Topological Psychology.* New York: McGraw-Hill Book Company, 1936.
79. LEWIN, K.: The conceptual representation and measurement of psychological forces, *Contr. Psychol. Theory*, 1938, *1*, No. 4.
80. LEWIN, K.: *Resolving Social Conflicts.* New York: Harper & Brothers, 1948.
81. LEWIN, K., DEMBO, T., FESTINGER, L., and SEARS, P.: Level of aspiration. In J. McV. Hunt (Ed.): *Handbook of Personality and the Behavior Disorders.* New York: The Ronald Press Co., 1944.
82. LEWIN, K., LIPPITT, R., and WHITE, R.: Patterns of aggressive behavior in experimentally created "social climates," *J. Soc. Psychol.*, 1939, *10*, 271–299.
83. LIPPITT, R.: An experimental study of the effect of democratic and authoritarian group atmospheres, *Univ. Iowa Stud. Child Welf.*, 1940, *16*, No. 3, 45–195.
84. LIPPITT, B., and WHITE, R.: The "social climate" of children's groups. In R. Barker, J. Kounin, and H. F. Wright. (Eds.): *Child Behavior and Development.* New York: McGraw-Hill Book Company, 1943.
85. LIPPITT, ROSEMARY: *Popularity among Preschool Children.* Unpublished Ph.D. Dissertation, University of Iowa, 1940.
86. LISSNER, K.: Die Entspannung von Bedürfnissen durch Ersatzhandlungen. *Psychol. Forsch.*, 1933, *18*, 218–250.
87. MAHLER, V.: Ersatzhandlungen verschiedenen Realitätsgrades, *Psychol. Forsch.*, 1933, *18*, 26–89.
88. MARQUIS, D. P.: Can conditioned responses be established in the newborn infant? *J. Genet. Psychol.*, 1931, *39*, 479–492.
89. MARROW, A. J.: Goal tension and recall, *J. Gen. Psychol.*, 1928, *19*, 3-64.
90. MCGRATH, M. C.: A study of the moral development of children, *Psychol. Mongr.*, 1923, *32*, No. 2, 1–190.
91. MCGRAW, M. B.: *Growth: A Study of Johnny and Jimmy.* New York: D. Appleton-Century Company, Inc., 1935.
92. MEAD, M.: *Cooperation and Competition Among Primitive Peoples.* New York: McGraw-Hill Book Company, 1937.
93. MEYERS, C. E.: The effect of conflicting authority on the child, *Univ. Iowa Stud. Child Welf.*, 1944, *20*, 31–98.
94. MOORE, E. S.: The development of mental health in a group of young children: An analysis of factors in purposeful activity, *Univ. Iowa Stud. Child Welf.*, 1931, *4*, No. 6.
95. MURPHY, L. B.: *Social Behavior and Child Personality: An Explorative Study in Some Roots of Sympathy.* New York: Columbia University Press, 1937.
96. MURRAY, H.: *Explorations in Personality.* London: Oxford University Press, 1938.
97. OVSIANKINA, M.: Die Wiederaufnahme von unterbrochener Handlungen, *Psychol. Forsch.*, 1928, *11*, 302–379.
98. PACHAURI, A. R.: A study of Gestalt problems in completed and interrupted tasks, *Brit. J. Psychol.*, 1935, *25*, 447–457.
99. PIAGET, J.: *The Moral Judgment of the Child.* New York: Harcourt, Brace, and Company, 1932.

100. PORTER, H. VON K.: Studies in the psychology of stuttering: XIV. Stuttering phenomena in relation to size and personnel of audience, *J. Speech Disorders*, 1939, *4*, 323–333.

101. REICHENBACH, H.: *Philosophie der Raum-Zeitlehere.* Leipzig: W. De Gruyter & Co., 1928.

102. REUTER, E. B.: The sociology of adolescence, *Am. J. Sociol.*, 1937, *43*, 414–427.

103. ROSENZWEIG, S.: Preferences in the repetition of successful and unsuccessful activities as a function of age and personality, *J. Genet. Psychol.*, 1933, *42*, 423–441.

104. ROTTER, J. B.: Studies in the psychology of stuttering: XI. Stuttering in relation to position in the family, *J. Speech Disorders*, 1939, *4*, 143–148.

105. SANDVOSS, H.: Über die Beziehungen von Determination und Bewusstsein bei der Realisierung unerledigter Tätigkeiten, *Arch. f. d. gès. Psychol.*, 1933, *89*, 139–192.

106. SCHANCK, R. L.: A study of a community and its groups and institutions conceived of as behaviors of individuals, *Psychol. Monogr.*, 1932, *43*, No. 2, 1–133.

107. SCHLOTE, W.: Über die Bevorzugung unvollendeter Handlungen, *Ztschr. f. Psychol.*, 1930, *117*, 1–72.

108. SEARS, P. S.: Levels of aspiration in academically successful and unsuccessful children, *J. Abnorm. & Social. Psychol.*, 1940, *35*, 498–536.

109. SEARS, R. R., and SEARS, P. S.: Minor studies in aggression: V. Strength of frustration-reaction as a function of strength of drive, *J. Psychol.*, 1940, *9*, 297–300.

110. SEASHORE, H. E., and BAVELAS, A.: A study of frustration in children, *J. Genet. Psychol.*, 1942, *61*, 279–314.

111. SEWALL, M.: Some causes of jealousy in young children, *Smith Coll. Stud. Soc. Work*, 1930, *1*, 6–22.

112. SHACTER, H. S.: A method for measuring the sustained attention of preschool children, *J. Genet. Psychol.*, 1933, *42*, 339–371.

113. SHAW, C. R.: Juvenile delinquency—a group tradition, *Bull. State Univ. Iowa, New Ser.*, 1933, No. 700.

114. SHAW, C. R., *et al.: Delinquency Areas: A Study of the Geographic Distribution of School Truants, Juvenile Delinquents, and Adult Offenders in Chicago.* Chicago: University of Chicago Press, 1929.

115. SHEFFIELD, A.: *Social Insight in Case Situations.* New York: D. Appleton-Century Company, 1937.

116. SLIOSBERG, S.: Zur Dynamik des Ersatzes in Spiel- und Ernstsituationen., *Psychol. Forsch.*, 1934, *19*, 122–181.

117. STERN, W., and MACDONALD, J.: Cloud pictures: A new method of testing imagination, *Character and Pers.*, 1937, *6*, 132–147.

118. STODDARD, G. D., and WELLMAN, B. L.: *Child Psychology.* New York: Macmillan Company, 1934.

119. TERMAN, L. M.: *The Intelligence of School Children.* Boston: Houghton Mifflin Company, 1919.

120. THOMAS, D. S.: An attempt to develop precise measurements in the social behavior field, *Sociologus*, 1932, *8*, 436–456.

121. THOMPSON, M. M.: *The Effect of Discriminatory Leadership on the Relations Between the More and Less Privileged Subgroups.* Unpublished Ph. D. Dissertation, University of Iowa.

122. TOLMAN, E. C.: *Purposive Behavior in Animals and Men*. New York: D. Appleton-Century Company, 1932.
123. TOLMAN, E. C.: Psychology versus immediate experience, *Phil. Sci.*, 1935, *2*, 356–380.
124. TRAVIS, L. E., JOHNSON, W., and SHOVER, J.: The relation of bilingualism to stuttering, *J. Speech Disorders*, 1937, *3*, 185–189.
125. VIGOTSKY, L. S.: Thought in schizophrenia, *Arch. Neurol. & Psychiat.*, 1934, *31*, 1063–1077.
126. WARING, E. B., DWYER, F. M., and JUNKIN, E.: Guidance: The case of Ronald, *Cornell Bull. Homemakers*, 1939, No. 418, 1–112.
127. WEIGL, E.: On the psychology of so-called processes of abstraction, *J. Abnorm. & Social. Psychol.*, 1941, *36*, 3–33.
128. WELLMAN, B. L.: The effect of preschool attendance upon the IQ, *J. Exp. Educ.*, 1932, *1*, 48–69.
129. WERNER, H.: *Comparative Psychology of Mental Development*. New York: Harper & Brothers, 1940.
130. WERNER, H.: Perception of spatial relationships in mentally deficient children, *J. Genet. Psychol.*, 1940, *57*, 93–100.
131. WOLF, T. H.: The effect of praise and competition on the persistent behavior of kindergarten children, *Inst. Child Welf. Monogr. Ser.*, 1938, No. 15, University of Minnesota Press.
132. WRIGHT, B. A.: Altruism in children and the perceived conduct of others, *J. Abnorm. & Social. Psychol.*, 1942, *37*, 218–233.
133. WRIGHT, H. F.: The influence of barriers upon the strength of motivation, *Contr. Psychol. Theory*, 1937, *1*, No. 3.
134. WRIGHT, M. E.: The influence of frustration upon the social relations of young children, *Character and Pers.*, 1943, *12*, 111–122.
135. ZEIGARNIK, B.: Über das Behalten von erledigten und unerledigten Handlungen, *Psychol. Forsch.*, 1927, *9*, 1–85.

Appendix

ANALYSIS OF THE CONCEPTS WHOLE, DIFFERENTIATION, AND UNITY

1. DIFFERENTIATION AND UNITY OF A WHOLE BASED ON SIMPLE DEPENDENCE

A. THE CONCEPT OF DEPENDENCE AND DEGREE OF DIFFERENTIATION OF A DYNAMIC WHOLE

Since Köhler's *Physische Gestalten* the definition of a "dynamic whole" has been based on the dependence of its parts. This definition holds good for physical, psychological, and sociological wholes.

Recently Grelling and Oppenheim have undertaken a logical analysis of the concept of functional whole. They distinguish correctly between logical and causal dependence. It is clear that we are dealing here with causal dependence. We will limit our discussion as much as possible to problems of dependence which have a bearing on the question of differentiation of a dynamic whole.

Degree of Dependence, Independence, and Interdependence. It should be clear from the outset that dependence or independence within a whole is a matter of degree. Parts within a whole are interdependent but, at the same time, they are usually independent to some degree.[1] In other words, part *a* will not be affected, as long as the alteration of part *b* is within certain limits. However, if the change of *b* surpasses this limit, the state of *a* will be affected.

More formalistically one can proceed as follows: $s^1(a)$, $s^2(a)$ may indicate the state (quality) of a region (system) *a* at the time 1 and 2;

---

[1] Grelling and Oppenheim mention occasionally that the different degrees of "empirical dependence . . . can be taken account of by introducing the notion of probability." Such a definition would, we suppose, distinguish degrees of dependence by its regularity (with correlation = 1, or "lawfulness" as the highest degree). The term, degree of dependence, in this study does not refer to the degree of regularity of dependence but to the amount of change in one part, which is without effect on the other part. We assume here strict "lawfulness" also for small degrees of dependence. See Grelling, K., and Oppenheim, P.: Der Gestaltbegriff im Licht der neuen Logik, *Erkenntnis*, 1938, 7, 211–224.

$ch(a) = s^2(a) - s^1(a)$ may indicate the change in the state of a. It may be further assumed that two regions (a and b) show the same state at the beginning: $s^1(a) = s^1(b)$. The independence of a region a from region b *(indep | a, b |)*† may then be defined as the maximum change in b which would leave the state of a unchanged, or would change it less than a small amount ϵ.

$$(13)^2 \qquad indep\ (a, b) = ch^{max}(b), \text{ which leads to } ch(a) < \epsilon$$

The degree of change of b *(ch | b |)* which does not affect a is not necessarily the same for different values of s, (for example for a low and

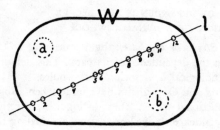

FIGURE 54. Undifferentiated whole W = whole; a, b, arbitrarily defined parts of W; l, line cutting W; $1, 2, 3, \ldots$ small regions along l.

a high tension level). To eliminate this question we may refer always to the same absolute beginning level, that is, to a definite value of $s^1(a)$.

The degree of dependence of a on b *(dep | a, b |)* can be defined as the inverse of independence.

$$(14) \qquad dep\ (a, b) = \frac{1}{indep\ (a, b)}$$

This definition of dependence and independence is not limited to neighboring regions. It can be used for any co-existing empirical regions (parts of a field).

The degree of independence of two regions a and b will usually be different for different kinds of change (change of different qualities).

† For reader's convenience, vertical lines are sometimes used in place of secondary parentheses in the Appendix. In this usage they do not indicate, as in some of Lewin's formulations, the magnitude of the conceptual element.

[2] Propositions in the appendix are numbered in sequence with those in Chapter 5.

Therefore, when comparing different cases we will always refer to the same kind of change.

The independence of two regions *a* and *b* can be different in different directions *(indep | a, b | ≠ indep | b, a |)*. We can define the degree of interdependence of *a* and *b*, *(interdep | a, b |)* in the following way if the properties of the system are such that *dep (a, b) = dep (b, a)*.

(15)   *interdep (a, b) = dep (a, b)* if *dep (a, b) = dep (b, a)*

Simple Dependence of Neighboring Regions. For the following discussion it is convenient to speak of the degree of independence of region *a* from a neighboring region *n* *(indep | a, n |)*. The region *n* is a neighbor of *a* if both regions have a common boundary and are otherwise foreign to each other.

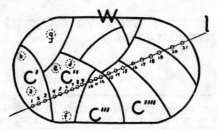

FIGURE 55. Differentiated whole. *W* = whole; *C'*, *C''*, *C'''*, . . . natural parts of *W*; *a*, *b*, *c*, . . . arbitrarily defined parts of *C*; *l*, line cutting *W*; *1*, *2*, *3*, . . . small regions along *l*.

In case we have to deal with "simple dependence," which follows the principle of proximity, and if *indep (a, n)* is equal for all neighbors of *a*, we can state *indep (a, n) ≦ indep (a, y)* where *n* is a neighbor of *a* and *y* is any other region foreign to *a*. This statement

(16)   *indep (x, n) ≦ indep (x, y)*

for any region *x* may be considered a definition of one property of simple dependence.

Definition of Natural Parts (Cells) Within a Whole and of the Degree of Differentiation of a Whole. Let us distinguish along the path *l* which cuts the whole *W* as indicated in Figure 54 and Figure 55 a sequence of points (small regions) 1, 2, 3 . . . and let us determine the degree of independence of the region 1 from every other region of this sequence *(indep | 1, 2 | ; indep | 1, 3 | ; indep | 1, 4 | ; . . .)*. A curve representing these degrees of independence might have the uniform character of Fig-

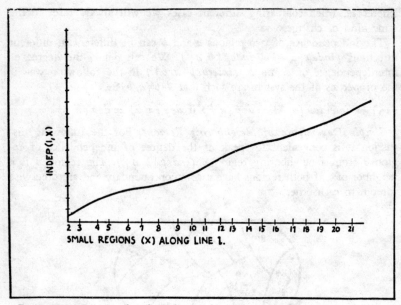

FIGURE 56. Degree of independence of regions in a whole without natural subparts. The graph refers to the whole represented in Figure 54. It indicates the degree of independence (*indep* | *1,x* |) of the region *1*, (along the line) from the regions 2, 3, 4, ...

ure 56[3] or it may show sudden changes in slope such as in Figure 57. Figure 56 corresponds to the whole represented in Figure 54. Figure 57 corresponds to Figure 55. If it is possible to make a cut through the whole in such a way that the curve of the second type results, the whole is said to be differentiated; otherwise it is undifferentiated. Regions which correspond to the same plateau within the curve we call subparts of the same "natural" part, or of the same "cell" of the whole. For instance, 1, 2, 3 belong to one cell *(c')*; 4, 5, 6, 7, 8, 9 to another cell *(c")*; 10, 11, 12 to *c'''*.

[3] We are representing wholes here by not less than two-dimensional regions without considering this to be a principal issue. To represent a whole by a zero-dimensional region (point) is not usually convenient because it is frequently required to distinguish parts within the whole. If one wishes to distinguish subparts within a part, the parts of the whole should also have more than zero dimensions. The boundary of a one-dimensional region is usually equivalent to a number of discrete points. This is an adequate representation for most psychological boundaries. In addition, one-dimensional regions are not very satisfactory for representing the forces corresponding to tension.

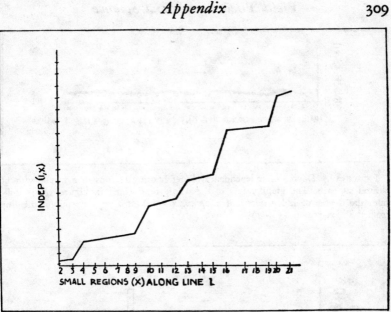

INDEP (1,x)

SMALL REGIONS (X) ALONG LINE L

FIGURE 57. Degree of independence of regions in a whole containing natural subparts. The graph refers to the whole represented in Figure 55. It indicates the degree of independence *(indep | 1,x |)* of the regions 2, 3, 4, . . . from the region 1. This curve shows definite steps not found in Figure 56.

The difference between the whole in Figure 54 and 55 can be represented in a slightly different way by referring to the degree of independence of every two consecutive points in the sequence *(indep | 1, 2 | ; indep | 2, 3 | ; indep | 3, 4 | . . .)*. For Figure 54 a curve of the type represented in Figure 58 will result; for Figure 55 a curve similar to Figure 59. If the points 1, 2, 3 . . . are properly chosen the heights of the peaks indicate the degree of independence of one cell from a neighboring cell (for instance, *indep | 3, 4 | = indep | c', c'' |*). This value may be called the "strength of the boundary" *bo (c', c'')*. (The height of the peaks in Figure 59 does not need to be the same as the height of the corresponding jumps in Figure 57.)

A third and probably the most satisfactory way to indicate natural parts mathematically is the following. If within a whole the regions *a, b, . . .* can be distinguished in such a way that the independence of any two subregions 1, 2, within each of these regions ($1^a, 2^a$), is less than a value *k* but the independence of any subregions belonging to different regions ($1^a, 1^b, . . .$) is larger than *k (indep | $1^a, 2^a$ | < k* and *indep | $1^a, 1^b$ | > k)*

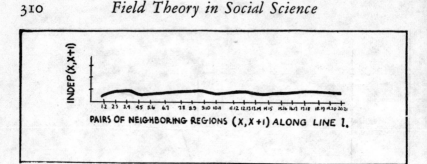

FIGURE 58. Degree of independence of neighboring regions in a whole without natural subparts. The graph refers to the whole represented in Figure 54. It indicates the degree of independence (*indep* $|x, x+1|$) of a region x along the line from the next region $(x+1)$.

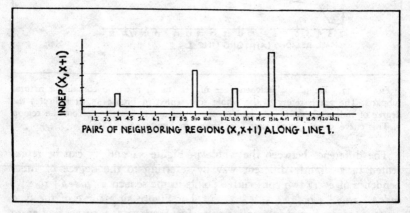

FIGURE 59. Degree of independence of neighboring regions in a whole containing natural subparts. The graph refers to the whole represented in Figure 55. It indicates the degree of independence (*indep* $|x, x+1|$) of a region x along the line from the next region $(x+1)$. The peaks on the curve correspond to boundaries between the natural cells (c^1, c^2, . . .) of the whole.

the regions a, b, . . . are "natural parts" or "cells" (c) of the whole (W). (17) The degree of differentiation of the whole $(dif^k \mid W \mid)$ is the maximum number of cells $(x, y, . . .)$ into which W can be divided so that $indep\ (x, y) \geqq k$.

The mathematical aspect of these considerations may need technical improvement. However, they suffice to characterize the relations which we have in mind and to make certain derivations possible.

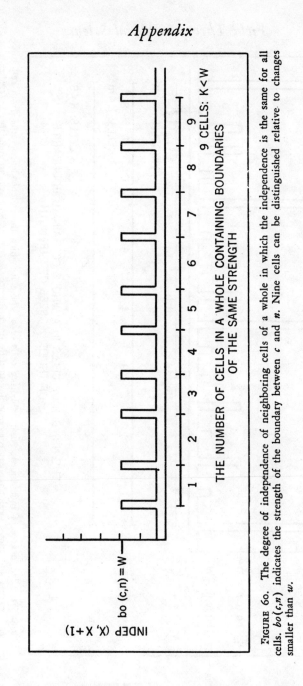

FIGURE 60. The degree of independence of neighboring cells of a whole in which the independence is the same for all cells. $bo(c,n)$ indicates the strength of the boundary between c and n. Nine cells can be distinguished relative to changes smaller than w.

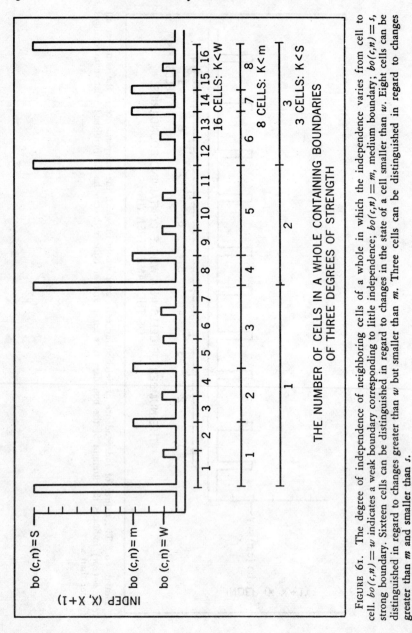

THE NUMBER OF CELLS IN A WHOLE CONTAINING BOUNDARIES
OF THREE DEGREES OF STRENGTH

FIGURE 61.   The degree of independence of neighboring cells of a whole in which the independence varies from cell to cell. $bo(c,n) = w$ indicates a weak boundary corresponding to little independence; $bo(c,n) = m$, medium boundary; $bo(c,n) = s$, strong boundary. Sixteen cells can be distinguished in regard to changes in the state of a cell smaller than w. Eight cells can be distinguished in regard to changes greater than w but smaller than m. Three cells can be distinguished in regard to changes greater than m and smaller than s.

The Relativity of Differentiation and the Macroscopic and Microscopic Functional Levels. The degree of independence of a cell c from a neighboring cell n within a whole, or as we say, the strength of its functional boundary *(bo | c, n | = indep | c, n |)* can vary widely from whole to whole and within the same whole. One may distinguish three cases in regard to the different boundaries within a whole: (a) all boundaries are equally strong; (b) a few definite degrees of strength can be distinguished; and (c) all show a great variety of strength. Using the same principle of representation as in Figure 59, we can illustrate the three cases by Figures 60, 61, and 62.

These cases help to demonstrate the relativity of the concept of differentiation. It is characteristic for a cell that its subregions are independent to a degree less than a relatively small value k. Relative to a macroscopic view certain values of k may be "small" but in relation to a microscopic detailed analysis these values may not be small. In other words, whether or not two subregions belong to the same cell depends on the value k. For a macroscopic view, a value of k which is greater than m Figure 61 might still be small. For $s > k > m$ only three cells would be distinguishable. Whereas for a microscopic view $(k < w)$ sixteen cells would be distinguishable.

From this it follows that the degree of differentiation is a decreasing function k. (10) $dif^k(W) = F(1/k)$ where F means an increasing function.

Figure 61 shows an example, however, where the degree of differentiation does not necessarily decrease continuously with increasing k. The degree of differentiation of the whole remains the same for all values of k below w. It decreases suddenly when k changes from a value below w to a value above w. The degree of differentiation again remains constant for values k above w but below m, but it drops again for a change of k to a value just above m, and finally remains the same for a value $k > m$ but $k < s$. In other words, a change in k affects the degree of differentiation *(dif^k | W |)* only if k passes the value characteristic of the boundary strength of the cells. These given boundary values, $bo(c, n) = indep(c, n)$ determine what might be called the "natural microscopic" and "natural macroscopic" view of the whole.

The example represented in Figure 60 shows nine cells for $k < bo (c, n)$. However, for $k > bo(c, n)$ the whole has to be called undifferentiated (see later).

One of the implications of the definition of differentiation is shown in Figure 63. The strength of the boundary *(bo | c,n |)* is assumed to be the same for all cells. In this case $dif^k(W) = 22$ for $k < bo(c,n)$. If k increases so that $k > bo(c,n)$

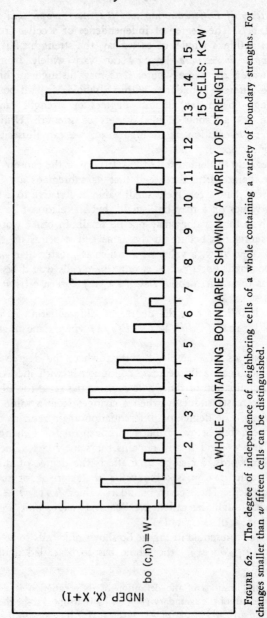

FIGURE 62. The degree of independence of neighboring cells of a whole containing a variety of boundary strengths. For changes smaller than *w* fifteen cells can be distinguished.

the whole becomes undifferentiated according to the definition because there are no regions in W which fulfill the requirements for a cell.

It is possible, however, to find seven regions in W, whose independence $> k$, if $bo\ (c,n) < k \geq 2\ bo(c,n)$ if one refers to regions which are not neighbors. With a slightly less rigid definition of cell, one can say that $dif^*(W) = 7$. The implications of such a definition have not been explored, but it may be that this definition will eventually prove to be superior. At the present time the experimental implications of the two definitions are alike.

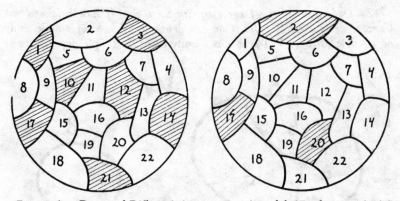

FIGURE 63. Degree of Differentiation as a Function of k. The figure at the left represents a whole W containing 22 cells $(dif^*|W| = 22)$, if the value of k is below that corresponding to the strength of the boundary $(bo|c,n|)$ between these cells. If $k > bo(c,n)$ and at the same time $k < 2bo(c,n)$, 7 cells, 1, 3, 10, 12, 14, 17, 21 can be distinguished. If k is further increased so that $2bo(c,n) < k < 3bo(c,n)$ (the right-hand figure) the number of separated cells decreases to 3 (2, 17, 20); i.e., $dif^*(W) = 3$. In the first case the diameter $dia(W) = 5$, equivalent to the maximum distance between any two cells, for instance, $e_{1,22}$; in the second case $dia(W) = 2$, equivalent to $e'_{1,14}$; in the third case $dia(W) = 1$, equivalent to $e''_{2,20}$ (see p. 321).

In Figure 62 the degree of differentiation decreases whenever k supersedes the next higher value of $bo(c, n)$; that is, the decrease is relatively continuous with increasing k.

Psychologically the person is a whole which probably has the character indicated by Figure 61, or 62.

These considerations may be instrumental for settling an old dispute. Many psychologists and philosophers have held that it is an entirely arbitrary matter as to how many parts may be distinguished within a whole. Other psychologists hold the opposite view. Our analysis indicates that both views are correct to a certain degree. The number of parts in a whole can be determined only in regard to a certain value k and this value can be arbitrarily defined. However, given this value, the number of cells are dependent on the strength of the boundary of the natural parts of the whole. What is even more important, the degree of differentiation of the whole changes only with certain values of k. These values depend entirely on the strength of the boundaries of the cells which are not arbitrarily determined.

B. THE SIMPLE UNITY AND THE DEGREE OF DIFFERENTIATION OF A WHOLE

The Definition of the Degree of Simple Unity of a Whole and the Concept of Natural Wholes. One can define the degree of simple unity of a whole *(si uni | W |)*, that is a unity based on simple dependence as

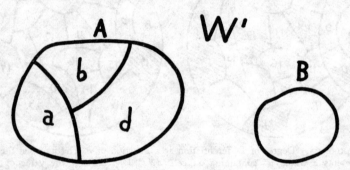

FIGURE 64. Degree of unity of natural wholes. The whole *W'* includes the regions *A* and *B*. *A* includes *a, b, d*.

characterized above, in the following way. We are comparing the degree of dependence for every pair of regions x and y in W and define:

$$(11) \qquad si\ uni\ (W) = dep^{min}\ (x, y)$$

x and y are any two regions of W. From (14) it follows that (11) is equivalent to

$$(11a) \qquad si\ uni\ (W) = \frac{1}{indep^{max}\ (x, y)}$$

For a given whole the value of $indep^{max}\ (x, y)$ may be indicated by Ch. From (11) it follows that if any part of a whole is changed by an amount greater than Ch every part of the whole will be affected.

(11b)   If $ch(x) > Ch$ then $ch(y) > \epsilon$; x and y are any two cells in W.

The definition of unity of a whole has the following implication. A whole W' may be arbitrarily determined as the totality of the regions

A and B in Figure 64. A may be composed of the highly interdependent regions, a, b, and d; $interdep(a, b) = 100$; $interdep(a, d) = 100$; $interdep(b, d) = 100$. The interdependence of B and a (or any part of A) however, may be low; for example, $interdep(B, a) = 2$. In this case the degree of unity of W' is also low: $si\ uni\ (W') = dep^{min}\ x, y = 2$. A second whole W'' may be determined as the totality of the regions A, B, C, and D, Figure 65. The interdependence of these regions with each other may also equal 2. In this case $si\ uni\ (W'') = 2$. In other words, the degree of simple unity of W' and W'' are equal. Of course, if one eliminates the region B in W' (Figure 64), the simple unity of the rest (A)

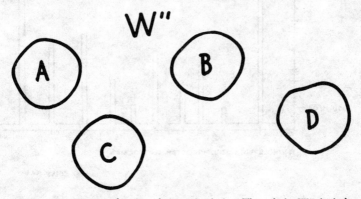

FIGURE 65. Degree of unity of natural wholes. The whole W'' includes the region a, b, d, c.

would be much higher $(si\ uni\ |\ A\ | = 100)$; whereas the elimination of the region B in W'' (Figure 65) would leave the degree of unity of the rest (A, C, D) unchanged $(si\ uni\ |\ A, C, D\ | = 2)$.

The wholes W' and W'' are examples of arbitrarily determined wholes. It would be more adequate to speak in the case of W' of two wholes $(A$ and $B)$ and in case W'' of four wholes. One can define "natural wholes" in the following way.

(18) W is called a natural whole if $dep(x, y) > dep(x, z)$ where x and y refer to any two regions within W $(x \subset W; y \supset W)$ and z to any region outside W $(Z \cdot W = 0)$.

In other words, the degree of dependence between any parts within a natural whole is greater than between any part and a region outside the whole.

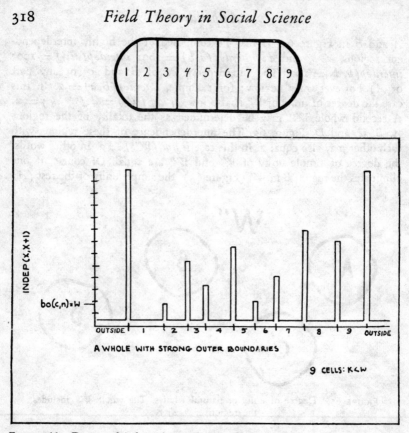

FIGURE 66. Degree of independence of cells of a natural whole from each other and from the outside.

From this it follows that the boundary of a natural whole W, and the *outside Ou* is stronger than the boundary around any arbitrary subpart p of W:

$$(18a) \qquad bo(W, Ou) > bo(p, n) \text{ where}$$

$bo(p, n)$ separates p from the rest of W.

Returning to wholes composed of natural cells we may state as a consequence from formula (10):

(19) For a natural whole, a value k can be determined so that relative to this k the whole W is undifferentiated. In other words it is possible to view a natural whole as one cell. (19) is equivalent to the statement

(19a) $bo(W, Ou) > bo(c, n)$ where $bo(c, n)$ separates any cell c from the rest of W.

The statement (19) follows from (18) but demands less than (18). For instance, the whole indicated in Figure 66 has outer boundaries which are stronger than any inner boundaries *(indep | W, Ou | > indep | c, n |)*. Therefore, k can easily be determined so that (19a) is fulfilled. Nevertheless, the sum of the strengths of the various inner boundaries may make the cells 1 and 9 less dependent of each other than the cell 9 from the outside *(dep | 1, 9 | < dep | 9, Ou |)*. In this case the whole could not be called a natural whole according to (18). [It is, however, possible to use the less demanding proposition (19a) as the definition of a natural whole. We will not discuss here the merits of such a possibility.]

The statements (18) and (19) show that the wholes indicated in Figures 60, 61, and 62 are not natural wholes. The example represented in Figure 60 can be said to be composed of nine natural wholes. The example Figure 62 is not one natural whole but can be thought of as three natural wholes.

In summary we may say: a high degree of independence from the outside is as essential for a natural whole as is the high dependence of the various parts within the whole.

The Relation between the Degree of Unity and Differentiation of a Whole. Unless it is stated differently the following discussion is limited to natural wholes where:

1. The degree of independence of each cell from its neighbor *(n)* is the same for all cells *(x)* within the whole *(indep | x, n | = const)*.
2. The independence of the subregions within the same cell is practically zero.
3. The cells have the same dynamic properties; (particularly *ch (n)* resulting from a *ch (x)* is equal for all neighbors).
4. The dependence is based on a process of spreading (simple dependence).

Under this condition the degree of unity of a whole depends mainly on two factors. Everything else being equal, the degree of unity is smaller, the greater the independence of neighboring cells. For if $indep(c, n)$ is greater $indep^{max}(x, y)$ is greater.

The second factor is related to the number and relative position of the cells. Figures 13, p. 121 illustrates the fact that two wholes W' and W'' may have the same degree of unity $[uni(W') = uni(W'') = indep(c, n + 1)$ where $n + 1$ refers to a cell which is separated by two boundaries (two steps) from c], in spite of a great difference in the number of cells $[dif\,^k(W'') = 2\,dif\,^k(W''')$, for $k < bo(c, n)]$.

The whole W'''' (Figure 67) has the same number of cells as W' (Figure 13) $(dif\,^k\,|\,W'\,| = dif\,^k\,|\,W'''\,|)$. However, the degree of unity of W'''' is definitely smaller than that of W' $[uni(W''') < uni\,(W') = dep(c, n + 1)]$. This will be understood readily if we go back to the definition of independence of cells and unity of a whole. The degree of independence of c from neighbor n $(indep\,|\,c, n\,|)$ was defined as the maximum change of n $(ch^{max}\,|\,n\,|)$ which would change c less than a small amount ϵ. In case of natural cells we called this amount of change

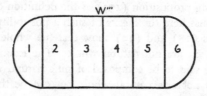

FIGURE 67. Differentiation, structure, and unity of a whole. The whole W'''' has the same degree of differentiation as the whole W' represented in Figure 13 (Chapter 5); $dif\,^k(W''') = dif\,^k(W') = 6$. However, W' has a higher degree of unity because $e_{x,y}^{max} = 1$ for W', $e_{x,y}^{max} = 5$ for W''''.

$bo(c, n)$. If the state of the cell 1 in Figure 67 was changed to this degree, this would not affect the state of the cell 3. For to affect the state of 3, the state of cell 2 would have to be changed at least to the amount $ch^{max}(n) = indep\,(3, 2) = bo(c, n)$. Whether a change of cell 1 to the amount 2 $bo(c, n)$ would suffice to affect cell 3 cannot be stated. However, we can say that the change of cell 1 must be large enough to induce in cell 2 a change equal to or greater than $indep\,(3, 2)$ before cell 3 will be affected and this change of cell 1 will be $indep(3, 1) > bo(c, n)$. A still greater change of 1 is required to affect the cells 4, 5, or 6. In other words the dependence of a cell of W'''' from cell 1 $(dep\,|\,1, y\,|)$ is smaller as more cells lie between 1 and y. As the degree of unity of a whole is the degree of dependence of the least dependent cells, it follows that $uni\,(W''') = dep(1, 6) < dep(1, 3) = uni\,(W')$.

This consideration may suffice to demonstrate that under the conditions mentioned above the degree of dependence of any two cells x and y of a whole depends upon the minimum number of boundaries crossed by a path from one of these cells to the other. This is equivalent to what in "hodological space" is called, the "distance" $(e_{x,\,y})$ between x and y. (For example, in the left-hand diagram of Figure 63 the distance of the cell 1 and 3 equals 2, $(e_{1,\ 3} = 2)$; $e_{1,\ 22} = 5$; $e_{9,\ 14} = 5$.) In other words *indep*(x, y $= F \mid e_{x,\ y} \mid$) where F means a monotonous, increasing function.

We will call $e_{x,\ y}^{max}$ the "diameter" of $W < (dia \mid W \mid)$.

(20) $$dia(W) = e_{x,\ y}^{max} ; \text{ where } x \subset W \text{ and } \jmath \subset W$$

From (11a) it follows that *si uni*(W) = $F(1/dia \mid W \mid)$ for a given value of *indep(c, n)*.

If we take both the number and position of cells in the whole and the strength of the boundaries of the cells into account we can say that the degree of unity of the whole increases with the dependence of neighboring cells and decreases with its diameter.

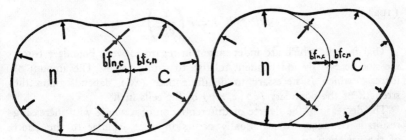

FIGURE 68. Boundary forces and resultant boundary forces. *n, c,* are neighboring cells of the whole; $bf_{n,c}$ and $bf_{c,n}$ are forces acting on the boundary between *c* and *n* in the direction toward *c* or toward *n* respectively. In the left-hand diagram, the opposing boundary forces are equal in strength, in the right-hand diagram they differ.

(12) $$si\ uni\ (W) = F \left(\frac{1}{bo(c, n),\ e_{x,\ y}^{max}} \right) = F \left(\frac{dep(c, n)}{dia\ (W)} \right)$$

This formula indicates that the unity of a whole does not depend directly on its degree of differentiation but on its "structure" (number and position of cells).

Boundary Forces, Differentiation, and Unity of a Whole. The degree of independence of cells has been defined in terms of a certain amount of change. If this change is a change of tension (and probably also if we have to do with any other kind of change) the degree of independence can be correlated to the strength of forces on the boundary of one cell which will not affect the state of another cell. More precisely, let us assume that there is a state of equilibrium, i.e., the forces at the boundary of neighboring cells $bf_{c,\ n}$ and $bf_{n,\ c}$ are equal and opposite (Figure 68, left-hand diagram). A decrease in the forces $bf_{c,\,n}$ (Figure 68, right-hand diagram) will affect the state of c as soon as the difference $|\,bf_{n,\,c}\,| - |\,bf_{c,\,n}\,|$ which we may call the resultant boundary force $bf^*_{n,\,c}$ reaches a certain value. This value of $bf^*_{n,\,c}$ will be the greater the greater the independence of these cells $(indep\,|\,c,\,n\,|\,)$. The definition of independence of neighboring cells may therefore be expressed by[4]

(13a) $$indep(c,n) = bf^{*\,max}_{n,c} \text{ for which } ch(c) < \epsilon$$

The present strength of the resultant boundary force may be indicated by bf^*. It is obvious that certain values of bf^* in formula 13a are equivalent to certain values of k in formula (17). It follows, therefore, from (10) that:

(10a)
$$dif^{bf*}(W) = F\left(\frac{1}{bf^*}\right)$$

That is, cells which are independent in regard to weak boundary forces are not necessarily independent relative to strong forces. The amount of increase which is necessary to dedifferentiate (W) depends upon the strength of the boundary $(bo\,|\,c,\,n\,|\,)$ of the cells in W.

The decrease in the degree of differentiation of a whole with increasing resultant boundary forces usually occurs in steps, similar to the effect of the variation of k.

In the case of the whole represented in Figure 61 there will be a value of $bf^*_{n,\,c}$ which corresponds to each value of $indep(n,\,c)$. Let us assume that $indep(n,\,c) = w$ corresponds to a value of $bf^*_{n,\,c} = w'$, that $indep(n,\,c) = m$ corresponds to $bf^*_{n,\,c} = m'$ and that $indep(n,\,c) = s$ corresponds to $bf^*_{n,\,c} = s'$. Then $dif^{bf*}(W) = 16$ if $bf^*_{n,\,c} < w'$. If $w' < bf^*_{n,\,c} < m'$ then $dif^{bf*}(W) = 8$ and finally if $m' < bf^*_{n,\,c} < s'$ then $dif^{bf*}(W) = 3$.

These examples may suffice to illustrate the following point: Suppose it is necessary, for some reason or other, to keep parts within a whole (e.g., an organism) independent of each other. The number of such independent parts depends on the difference in tension (the strength of the resultant boundary forces) relative to which the cells should be independent and the position of the regions in tension. How the degree of differentiation of a given whole decreases with increasing forces depends on the strength and the position of the boundaries of the natural cells within the whole. However, it is always possible to determine a strength

[4] In physics the value for $bf^{*\,max}_{n,c}$ is frequently independent of the absolute tension level. We cannot assume this to hold always. We refer therefore to a certain beginning level of $bf^*_{n,c}$.

of a resultant boundary force relative to which a natural whole is to be regarded as undifferentiated, and a certain strength relative to which the whole cannot be treated as a natural whole.[5]

The implications of these considerations become clearer when we discuss the relation between variability and differentiation (p. 328).

C. STRATIFICATION OF A WHOLE

We will limit our discussion to natural wholes where all boundaries have the same strength.

It is possible to distinguish certain groups of cells within a whole on the basis of their functional similarities. These more inclusive subparts of the whole can be called "layers." The "degree of stratification of a whole" $(stra \mid W \mid)$ can be defined as the number of its layers.

Central and Peripheral Regions. We can distinguish cells of different "degrees of centrality" $(cent \mid c \mid)$ by considering the maximum hodological distance $e_{c, y}^{max}$ of a cell c from any other cell y in a whole W.

(21a)   If $e_{c, y}^{max} = dia(W)$ then c is a peripheral cell. Its degree of centrality is zero $(cent \mid c \mid = 0)$. Or more generally:

(21)   If $e_{c, y}^{max} = dia(W) - m$ then the degree of centrality of c is m $(cent \mid c \mid = m)$.

In this way we can distinguish cells of the first, second, third . . . degree of centrality. Cells of the highest degree of centrality within a whole can be called "most central" cells.

The totality (topological sum) of cells for which the degree of centrality is m can be called the "m^{th} central layer" $(m\ cen\ lay)$.

(22) $m^{th}\ cen\ lay =$ totality of cells for which $cent(c) = m$. The layer containing the cells $cent(c) = 0$ is called the peripheral layer.

The degree of "centrality stratification" of a whole $(cen\ stra \mid W \mid)$ is one greater than the highest degree of centrality of any one of its cells. This definition makes the degree of centrality stratification equal to the number of strata.

(23) $$cen\ stra\ (W) = (cent^{max} \mid c \mid + 1)$$

[5] We cannot say that the degree of unity $(uni \mid W \mid)$ is a function of these forces. It is correct that the diameter $dia(W)$ changes with bf^* or k. However it seems to hold that $uni(W) = F\left(\dfrac{dep(c,n)}{dia(W)} \right) = const$ for a given natural W whatever the value of bf^* or k, relative to which the cell within W is defined.

One may raise the question of the relation between the diameter of a whole and the highest degree of centrality of its cells. For example, is a central layer always a connected region? We cannot attempt a detailed discussion of these questions here. However a few examples may be welcomed as illustrations.

Figure 69, left-hand diagram represents a whole containing twelve cells, which are all peripheral. The degree of centrality stratification is one. The same holds true for the whole represented in the right-hand diagram. Cell 1 and cell 2 are peripheral in spite of the fact that cell 1 is surrounded by cell 2.

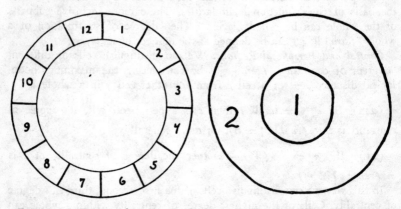

FIGURE 69.   Degree of centrality. The diagram at the left represents a whole containing 12 peripheral cells; *dif (W)* = 12; *cent (x)* = *const* = 0; *cen stra (W)* = 1; *inn stra (W)* = 1. The diagram at the right represents a whole containing 2 peripheral cells, one of them being an inner cell; *dif (W)* = 2; *cent* (1) = *cent* (2) = 0; *cen stra (W)* = 1; *inn* (1) = 1; *inn* (2) = 2; *inn stra (W)* = 2.

Figure 70, left-hand diagram represents a whole containing nineteen cells. *Cen stra (W)* = 3. The most central layer contains but two cells, namely cells 7 and 15. This is an example of a not connected central layer. If one changes the boundary of cell 3 slightly as indicated in Figure 70, the most central layer contains only cell 7. The functional difference between cells belonging to layers of various degrees of centrality may be indicated as follows: A most central cell (for instance cell 7) will be affected if in any cell the resultant boundary force bf^* takes on the value $bf^* > bf^{*max}_{n,\ c+1}$; a cell of the first degree of centrality (for instance cell 2) is affected if in any cell $bf^* > bf^{*max}_{n,\ c+2}$; a peripheral cell (for instance cell 4) is affected if in any cell $bf^* > bf^{*max}_{n,\ c+3}$ In other words, the more central a cell, the easier it is affected by changes within the whole; and the more easily a change in this cell affects all other cells of the whole.

Inner and Outer Layer. We define inner and outer layers by considering the hodological distance $e_{c,\,ou}$ of a cell c from the region (Ou) outside the whole.

We will speak of an inner cell of the degree m:

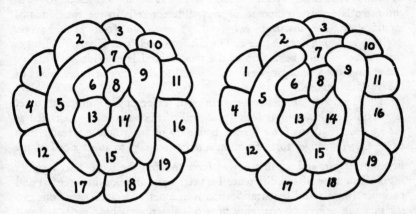

FIGURE 70. Stratified wholes. The diagram at the left shows a stratified whole in which $dif\,(W) = 19$; $dia\,(W) = e^{max}_{z,y} = 4$; $cen\,stra\,(W) = 3$; $inn\,stra\,(W) = 3$. The peripheral layer ($e^{max}_{c,y} = 4$) contains the cells, 1, 4, 10, 11, 12, 16, 19; the first central layer ($e^{max}_{c,y} = 3$) contains the cells 2, 3, 5, 6, 8, 9, 13, 14, 17, 18; the second central layer ($e^{max}_{c,y} = 2$) contains the cells 7, 15. The outer layer ($e_{c,\,out} = 1$) contains the cells 1, 2, 3, 4, 10, 11, 12, 16, 17, 18, 19; the first inner layer ($e_{c,\,out} = 2$) contains the cells 5, 7, 9, 15; the second inner layer ($e_{c,\,out} = 3$) contains the cells 6, 8, 13, 14. The diagram at the right illustrates the effect of the change of one cell upon the position of other cells of a whole. The change of the boundary between cell 3 and cell 7 eliminates cell 15 from the most central layer which contains now only cell 7.

(24) $$inn\,(c) = m,\ \text{if}\ (e_{c,\,ou}) - 1 = m.$$

If $(e_{c,\,ou}) - 1 = O$, c is called an "outer" cell. The totality of outer cells is the "outer layer" of the whole.

(25) $m^{th}\,inn\,lay =$ totality of cells for which $inn(c) = m$. The degree of "inner stratification" of a whole corresponds to the number of layers.

(26) $$inn\,stra\,(W) = (inn^{max}\,|\,c\,|) + 1$$

As an example we may discuss again Figures 69 and 70. For the whole at the left in Figure 69, *inn stra (W)* = 1; it contains only an outer layer. The whole represented at the right contains an outer and a first inner layer: *inn stra (W)* = 2, although *cen stra (W)* = 1 as we have seen above.

The whole represented at the left in Figure 70 shows the same number of central as of inner layers: *inn stra (W)* = *cen stra (W)* = 3. However, the three layers are composed of very different cells in the two kinds of stratification. For instance *cent* (cell 7) = 2, *inn* (cell 7) = 1; *cent* (cell 2) = 1, *inn* (cell 2) = 0. The change of cell 3 in Figure 70 changes the number of cells belonging to the most central layer. However, it does not change the "belongingness" of any cell to the outer or inner layers of the various degrees.

The functional difference between cells belonging to different inner layers can be illustrated as follows: A cell of the outer layer is affected as soon as the resultant force on the boundary of the whole is greater than $bf^{*max}_{Ou, W}$. A stronger force from outside is necessary to affect a cell of the first inner layer, and a still stronger force to affect the most inner layer.

As a summary of the difference between a stratification into central and peripheral layers and the stratification into inner and outer layers one can say that the degree of centrality of a cell determines how easily the cell will be affected by changes anywhere inside the whole and how easily a change in this cell will affect the rest of the whole. The position of a cell in a certain inner layer determines how easily a cell will be affected by changes outside the whole and how easily a change in this cell will affect the outside.

D. VARIETY OF PATTERNS WHICH CAN BE REALIZED IN A WHOLE

Homogeneity and Heterogeneity of a Whole. The actual state (quality) of two cells *a* and *b* can be equal $[s(a) = s(b)]$ even if both cells are highly independent. However, the maximum degree of dissimilarity of two cells depends upon their degree of independence.

$$(27) \qquad |s(a) - s(b)|^{max} = F[indep\ (a, b)]$$

One may define inhomogeneity of a whole *(inhom | W |)* as the greatest difference of the state of any cells within *W* [other definitions would be possible].

$$(28) \qquad inhom(W) = |s(x) - s(y)|^{max} \text{ at a given time}$$

This implies that *inhom(W)* = 0 if all cells are in the same state. Homogeneity can be defined:

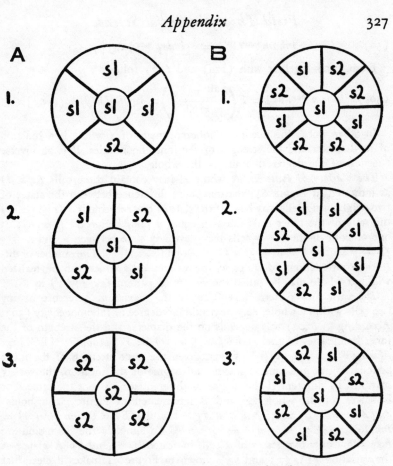

FIGURE 71. Variety of Patterns and Degree of Differentiation.

(29)
$$hom(W) = \frac{1}{inhom(W)}$$

A whole which is highly differentiated and stratified may still be fully homogeneous. In other words, it holds true for any kind of whole that $inhom(W)^{min} = 0$. The maximum inhomogeneity of different wholes, however, can be different.

We limit the discussion again to a natural whole with a constant degree of independence of neighboring cells within the whole, and to a certain absolute range of states.

From (28) and (27) follows

(30) $inhom^{max}(W) = F(indep^{max} | x, y |)$

From (30) together with (11a) and (12) follows

(30a) $inhom^{max}(W) = F\left(\dfrac{1}{si\ uni(W)}\right) = F[dia\ (W),\ bo(c, n)]$

In other words the maximum inhomogeneity of a whole is a function of its diameter and the strength of the inner boundaries. It is an inverse function of the degree of unity of the whole.

The Variety of Patterns. A whole A may contain three cells (a, b, d) as indicated in Figure 64; the maximum difference between the states of two neighboring cells may be g. If the state of one cell equals u $(s | a | = u)$ the state of the other cells can also equal u $(s | b | = u; s | d | = u)$; or one or both of these two cells may have any state between u and $u \pm g$ $(u - g \leqq s | b | \leqq u + g; u - g \leqq s | d | \leqq u + g)$. The number of different constellations of states of the various cells which can be realized within a whole may be called the variety of pattern $(var | W |)$ in W.

The variety of pattern depends upon the maximum difference of any two cells within a whole, i.e., the maximum degree of inhomogeneity (30). According to (30a) this depends on the diameter and the strength of the inner boundaries of the whole $(var | W |) = F | inhom^{max}[W] | = F[dia\ (W),\ bo\ (c, n)]$. However, given the same strength of the inner boundaries and the same diameter and degree of stratification, the variety may still be different if the degree of differentiation is not the same. For instance, for the wholes A and B represented in Figure 71 it holds: $dia(A) = dia(B) = 2$; $cen\ stra(A) = cen\ stra(B) = 2$; $inn\ stra(A) = inn\ stra(B) = 2$, $bo(c, n)^A = bo(c, n)^B$. To simplify the discussion we may allow only two states of a cell, indicated by S_1 and S_2. A glance at the variation (1), (2) and (3) shown in Figure 71 makes it clear that $var(B) > var(A)$ in spite of the equality of the factors mentioned. This means that the degree of differentiation is an important factor for the variety of possible patterns.

(31) $var(W) = F[dia\ (W),\ dif^k\ (W),\ bo(c, n)]$, where $k < bo(c, n)$

The Variety of Pattern of an Organic Whole and the Effect of Keeping Certain Parts Constant. It is possible to treat the problem of the variety of patterns in a somewhat more concrete way, if we take into consideration that the degree of change within an organism is definitely limited. If this state deviates too much from the normal state the living cell will die.

Using a scale of nine points we can indicate by $+4$ and -4 the upper and lower maxima, by 0 the normal state. To simplify the discussion we will not consider continuous changes but only states corresponding to the nine points of the scale.

Let us discuss the variety of possible patterns within a simple whole corresponding to Figure 67. The maximum difference between the states of neighboring cells may be constant and equal to one point of our scale $[\,|\,s(c)-s(n)\,|^{max}=1\,]$. The totality of possible constellations under these circumstances is $var(W) = 9\cdot3^5 - (2\cdot3^4 + 4\cdot4^3 + 6\cdot3^2 + 8\cdot3 + 10) = 1829$. Figure 72 represents these possibilities graphically by the totality of curves progressing continuously from left to right.

If for one reason or another cell 1 is kept on the normal level 0 the number of possible patterns (Figure 73, upper figure) decreases to $3^5 - 2 = 241$. If cell 1 is kept on the level ±1, ±2, ±3, or ±4 respectively, the variety of pattern decreases to 239, 230, 203 or 122[6] respectively (see Figures 73 and 74).

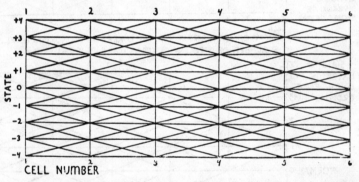

FIGURE 72. Variety of possible patterns if parts of the whole are kept constant. This figure shows the variety of possible patterns in a whole corresponding to that in Figure 67; *var (W)* = 1829.

In other words, the more the state of the cell which is kept on a constant level deviates from normal *(0)* the smaller is the variety of possible patterns. The decrease of this variety corresponding to a change from one level to the next is greater the more this level approaches the extreme.

If two cells are kept at a constant level the variety of pattern is still

[6] The general formula for a whole with this simple structure, in case cell 1 is kept constant is: $var = 3^{n-1} - (3^{n+a-1-2} + 3^{n+a-1-3} +, \ldots +3^0) - (3^{n-a-1-2} \div 3^{n-a-1-3} + \ldots + 3^0)$, where n = number of cells, $\pm a$ = difference of the state of cell 1 from "normal," and l = the greatest possible difference of the state of a cell from normal.

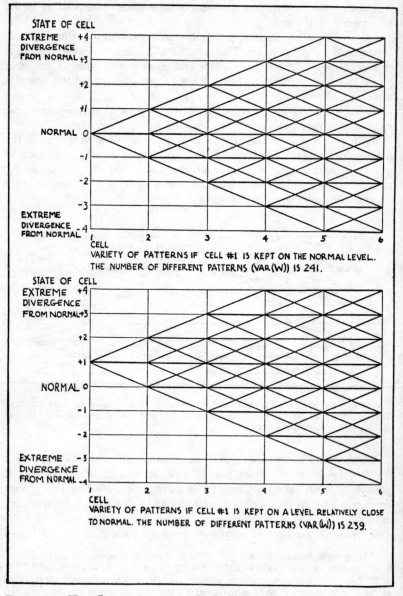

FIGURE 73. The effect on the variety of possible patterns of restricting the level of cell 1 to two different levels.

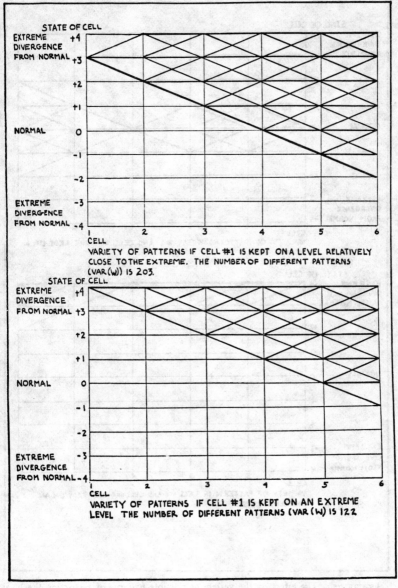

FIGURE 74. A further illustration of the effect on the variety of possible patterns of restricting the level of cell 1 to two different levels.

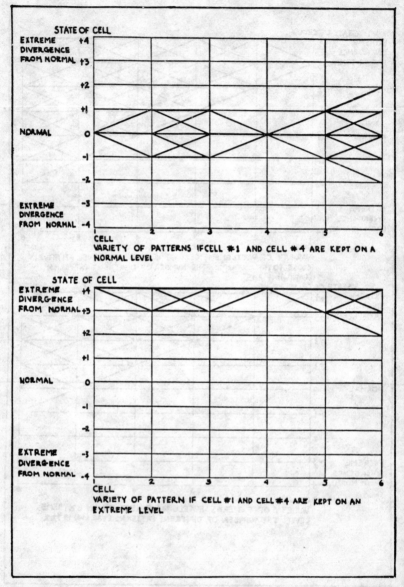

FIGURE 75. The effect on the variety of possible patterns of restricting the level of cells 1 and 4 to certain levels. In the upper figure *var* (*W*) = 63. In the lower figure *var* (*W*) = 20.

more diminished. For instance, if cells 1 and 4 are kept on the normal level (Figure 75) the variety of patterns decreases to 63. If cell 1 and 4 are kept on level ± 4 the variety decreases to 20 from the original $var(W) = 1829$ when no cell is kept constant.

It has been indicated that the state of the rest of a whole depends more on a central than on a peripheral cell. One may expect therefore that the variety of patterns should decrease more if a central cell rather than a peripheral cell is kept at a given level. This is, however, not always correct. For instance, it does not hold for the simple structure of Figure 67. Cell 4 is more central than cell 1. However, if cell 4 is kept constant on the normal level, O, the variety of remaining patterns is the same, namely 243, as if the peripheral cell 1 is kept on this level.

Nevertheless, it ordinarily holds for the more complicated wholes that the variety of pattern is more diminished if a central rather than a peripheral cell is kept at a level sufficiently different from the normal.

These examples indicate that the variety of pattern decreases with the number of cells kept in a given state, with the increasing distance from the normal state, and usually with the increasing degree of centrality of the cells kept at an extreme level. A more detailed mathematical analysis of wholes showing various structures and degree of differentiation is needed before general statements concerning the conditions for the reduction in variability can be made. This problem should be of prime importance for psychology, biology, and also for the study of the variability of various social groups.

E. VARIETY OF PATTERN AND REGRESSION

If a decrease in variety of behavior is a symptom of regression and if the variety of behavior presupposes a variety of pattern realizable in a whole, it is possible now to state certain conditions under which regression should occur.

1. Any fixation of a sufficiently large part of the whole to a constant state should lead to regression.

This decrease of variety should, however, be very slight if only one peripheral cell is held on a normal level. If the whole referred to in Figure 67 would contain twenty instead of six cells, the fixation of cell 1 to a normal level would be practically without significance for $var(W''')$. The regression should be greater the more cells are kept constant, the more central the cells are, and the more the state of the cells are removed from that of normality.

Situations where certain parts of the person are kept in a constant state occur frequently. For instance, a need which is not satisfied corresponds to a relatively constant state of tension of certain innerpersonal systems.

Pressure from the environment may keep the individual or part of him in a certain state of tension. Certain manipulations, which the person is supposed to carry out, frequently require that certain parts of the individual be kept within a definite range of states.

All or at least most of the situations in which the person is awake require that the state of a more or less extended part of the person be kept within a limited range. (In some respects this probably holds least during sleep.) However, such situations cannot be called "regression" because the person actually has never shown a higher developmental state. However, if such outside requirements are very extended, if for instance, the individual is kept busy day after day with certain routine tasks which occupy a considerable part of him (i.e., keeps that part within a definite state or sequence) he may show certain signs of regression. Nevertheless, this regression will be relatively small as long as these occupied areas are not too extensive, as long as only peripheral layers are affected, and if the degree of independence of neighboring cells (strength of inner boundaries) is sufficient.

This conclusion from our formulae is surprisingly well in line with the experiments on psychological satiation. Satiation may occur in a situation in which the same activity is repeated over and over again, that is where certain areas of the person are kept in a more or less constant state. The outstanding symptoms of oversatiation may well be called typical cases of regression. For instance, the larger units dedifferentiate into smaller and smaller parts. The experiments show that if the activity is kept sufficiently peripheral no satiation may occur. Both agreeable and disagreeable activities are more rapidly satiated than neutral ones. Indeed, in both cases, more central areas are touched and therefore larger areas of the person are kept in a fixed state. Anything else which increases centrality seems to speed up satiation. The velocity of satiation is greater in children; indeed they are less differentiated and the cells are less independent. Feeble-minded persons who show greater independence of neighboring cells (measured by co-satiation and other symptoms) show a slower satiation than younger children of the same degree of differentiation (see Chapter 10).

From our previous discussions we would expect that an increase in emotional tension should lead to marked regression when the tension has reached a certain level. This is the theory advanced in a previous investigation by Dembo[7] a theory which is well in line with the experiments and the results of the present study.

[7] Dembo, T.: Der Arger als dynamisches Problem, *Psychol. Forsch.*, 1931, 15, 116–120.

2. We should expect regression if the strength of the boundary decreases. An example may be fatigue, which, according to Zeigarnik corresponds to a more fluid state in which the person is unable to build or to preserve systems in tension. (A similar inability to keep tension has been observed in schizophrenic patients if peripheral activities are carried through.)

Of course in all of these cases other factors play a role in addition to the variety of patterns.

3. It should be noticed that the limitation of variation of patterns is based on two rather distinct groups of factors. One group has to do with the degree of differentiation, the diameter of the whole, and the strength of the boundaries of the cells. The second group deals with the scope of states which a cell may have without dying.

Both factors should be clearly distinguished particularly in view of certain developmental trends. In regard to the first factor (differentiation, boundary strength, etc.) adults show definitely greater variability than the child. In regard to the second factor, however, indications point to the fact that the cells of the young organism can differ more widely from the normal state without being destroyed and that the younger person therefore shows greater variability. Our examples indicate that a greater tolerance for deviations from the normal would have to be very outstanding (much greater than it actually seems to be) if it should counteract the increase in the variety of pattern resulting from the greater differentiation of the more mature person, its stratification and the greater strength of the boundaries of his cells.

2. Organizational Dependence and Organizational Unity of a Whole

We will limit the discussion of organizational dependence and unity to a few general considerations.

A. ORGANIZATIONAL DEPENDENCE

It does not seem to be possible to define the degree of "organizational dependence" or independence of two regions a and b in the same way as "simple dependence," namely, by referring to the amount of change which is necessary in one region to change the other region. For organizational dependence the important characteristic of a is its power to induce a change of state in b and this power seems to have no direct relation to the amount of change in a necessary to influence b. One can define the organizational dependence of a upon b *(org dep | a, b |)* as the maximum change which can be induced by b in a $(i^b ch \mid a \mid {}^{max})$.

$$(32) \qquad org\ dep\ (a, b) = i^b ch(a)^{max}$$

The difference between (32) and (13) expresses a difference between simple and organizational dependence. For the former, but not for the latter, there is a tendency for the states of dependent regions to be equal.

We have mentioned that a similar type of dependence exists in social psychology. If we refer to induced forces rather than to induced changes, we might define power of b over a *(pow b/a)* as the quotient of the maximum force which b can induce on a $(i^b f^{max}_{a, x})$, and the maximum resistance $(f^{max}_{a, \overline{x}})$ which a can offer. (x indicates the region into which a should locomote according to the will of b; $f_{\overline{a, x}}$ indicates a force in the direction opposite to $f_{a, x}$)

$$(33) \qquad \text{power } (b/a) = \frac{i^b f^{max}_{a, x}}{f^{max}_{\overline{a, x}}}$$

If one makes the reasonable assumption that there is a close relation between induced forces and induced changes (32) and (33) are probably equivalent.

B. HEAD AND TOOL

Referring to dynamic wholes, we will call a leading region a "head" *(h)*, and the led region a "tool" *(to)*. We can define head and tool by the following formula

$$(34) \qquad pow\ (h/to) > pow\ (to/h)$$

The greater the value, *pow (h/to)*, the easier it is for the head to induce such changes of the tool as desired. Let us consider, for instance, a tool containing many subregions. The ease with which the position of the subregions to each other can be changed, depends upon the strength of the forces induced by the head in comparison to the strength of the restraining forces acting on the tool opposite to the induced forces.

C. ORGANIZATIONAL UNITY

It seems possible to define the organizational unity of a whole *(org uni | W |)* in the following way:

$$(35) \qquad org\ uni\ (W) = pow\ (hh/W - hh)$$

In other words, the organizational unity of a whole is related to the power of the strongest head *(hh)* over the rest of the whole *(W-hh)*. It may be that other factors should be added. However, formula (35) may well serve as a first approximation.

If the whole is composed of cells all of which have the same power, the organizational unity of the whole is small because the power of any one cell c relative to the rest of the whole (power $c/W\text{-}c$) is small.

A simple case of high organizational unity is given if we have to deal with a whole containing *one* strong head, the rest having but little power. If the tool regions are very numerous the effective power of the head may be greater if a number of subleaders (subheads, sh) can be employed.

If the whole contains two or more independent heads, the organizational unity of the whole may be considerably reduced. It is important, of course, whether the two heads are "friends" or "enemies." However, the formula (35) is probably correct if one understands the "power of the strongest head" to be the strength of the power field of the head itself added to that of friends as far as they cooperate.

If we understand independent heads in this way, we can probably say that

$$(36) \quad org \; uni \; (W) = F\left(\frac{1}{n(h)}\right) \quad \text{where } n(h) \text{ means the number of independent heads.}$$

In other words, everything else being equal, the degree of organizational unity of a whole is inversely related to the number of independent heads.

Important individual differences seem to exist in the degree of organizational unity of the person. In some individuals one, or a few needs seem to be powerful enough to suppress the other needs. In this case a relatively high general tension level may be expected. A rather different type of unity of the person is achieved if a number of heads of relatively equal powers are organized in a more "democratic" manner. In this case, the hierarchical organization is topped by a group of heads combined into one policy-determining part (H) of the whole. If this H is considered as one region, the degree of unity of the whole is high, although no one all-powerful cell exists in the whole. It may be that the more harmonious and easy going persons show this type of inner organization.

D. ORGANIZATIONAL UNITY DURING DEVELOPMENT AND IN REGRESSION

Development involves differentiation. If this should lead to a great number of parts which have approximately the same power, the degree of organizational unity should decrease according to (35). The emergence of a head should increase the degree of organizational unity.

If the head region differentiates again into two or more independent heads h^1, h^2, h^3, each of these heads being powerful relatively to the tool regions, the value of $pow\ (h^1/W\text{-}h^1)$ should decrease very considerably and therefore according to (36) the degree of organizational unity should also decrease. We have mentioned (Chapter 5) that the increase of differentiation of the central needs during development may well lead to a decrease in the organizational unity of the person. If, however, the differentiation progresses so that one of the heads is predominant or in such a way that a new higher head *(hh)* emerges which gives to the previous heads the role of subheads, the degree of unity of the whole will increase again in accordance with (35). In this case also the degree of hierarchical organization of the whole is increasing.

Regression in the sense of disorganization should be expected if the number of opposing heads (needs) increases, because the organizational unity of the whole should then decrease in line with (36). The degree of organizational unity also decreases somewhat if the tool region becomes less fluid. That may happen if the general tension level is too high, or if the tools are governed simultaneously by conflicting forces.

Index

Abraham, K., 89

Ach, N., 5, 68, 84; concept of *determinierende Tendenz*, 27, 66

Action, mass, 105

Ad hoc theory, 8

Adams, D. K., 68, 84, 239

Adaptation, 249

Adler, D. L., 276, 278, 297

Adolescence: aggressiveness in, 139; behavior characteristics of, 98; change in group belongingness, 137; change in time-perspective, 140; conceptual analysis of, 135; conflicts in, 141; derivations of from conceptual analysis, 144; marginality in, 143; radicalism in, 139; and sexual maturity, 139; summary statement of, 144; uncertainty of behavior, 138; as unstructured regions, 137

Aggression, in democratic and autocratic atmospheres, 207

Allport, F. H., 52

Allport, G. W., 128, 229, 236, 297

Altruism, 290

Analysis in field theory, 62

Anamnesis, 49

Anderson, C., 286, 297

Anderson, H. H., 249, 298

Anthropology, cultural, 163, 172

Approximation, method of, 21

Archimedes, 193

Arsenian, J., 293, 298; (*see also* Mac-Donald)

Association: 2, 5, 7, 24, 66; execution habits, 5; experiments on, 9; laws of, 20; need habits, 5; as restraining forces, 5

Associationism, and teleology, 26

Atmosphere, psychological, 63

Atmosphere, social: 159; and individual level of conduct, 212; as quasi-stationary equilibrium, 207

Aversion, as negative force field, 40

Barker, R., xix, 35, 53, 84, 247, 248, 267, 269, 270, 271, 298

Barriers: as force field, 40; as social forces, 78; and threat of punishment, 78

Bartos, A., 298

Bavelas, A., 81, 84, 216, 221, 231, 232, 236, 251, 284, 290, 298

Behavior: as change in psychological field, 48; complexity of units, 101; complicated organization, 102; goal directed, 27; hierarchical organization, 101; unit of organization, 114

Behaviorism: 63, 67, 79; operational definition, 61, 62; and unity of science, 133

Benedict, R., 298

Bergmann, G., 84

Birenbaum, G., 128, 284, 298

Bridges, K. M., 128

Brooks, F. D., 84

Brown, J. F., 18, 298

Brown, S. F., 298

Brunswik, E.: 57, 58; role of statistics in theory, 56

Bryan, W. L., 128

Bühler, C., 128, 298

Burks, B. S., 298

Buxton, C. E., 28, 84

Cameron, N., 128

Carmichael, L., xx

Cartwright, D., xx, 28, 236, 271, 298

Cassirer, E., xv, 30, 32, 189, 191, 192, 236

Categories, objective, 16

Causation, 145

Cells, definition of, 307

Centrality: characteristics of central cell, 123

Change, resistance to, 199, 225, 226

Change, social: 186, 199; basic methods, 217; permanency of, 224; the three-

Revised December, 1967

harper 🔥 torchbooks

HUMANITIES AND SOCIAL SCIENCES

American Studies: General

LOUIS D. BRANDEIS: Other People's Money, *and How the Bankers Use It.* ‡ *Ed. with an Intro. by Richard M. Abrams* TB/3081

THOMAS C. COCHRAN: The Inner Revolution. *Essays on the Social Sciences in History* TB/1140

HENRY STEELE COMMAGER, Ed.: The Struggle for Racial Equality TB/1300

EDWARD S. CORWIN: American Constitutional History. *Essays edited by Alpheus T. Mason and Gerald Garvey* △ TB/1136

CARL N. DEGLER, Ed.: Pivotal Interpretations of American History Vol. I TB/1240; Vol. II TB/1241

A. HUNTER DUPREE: Science in the Federal Government: *A History of Policies and Activities to 1940* TB/573

A. S. EISENSTADT, Ed.: The Craft of American History: *Recent Essays in American Historical Writing* Vol. I TB/1255; Vol. II TB/1256

CHARLOTTE P. GILMAN: Women and Economics: *A Study of the Economic Relation between Men and Women as a Factor in Social Evolution.* ‡ *Ed. with an Introduction by Carl N. Degler* TB/3073

OSCAR HANDLIN, Ed.: This Was America: *As Recorded by European Travelers in the Eighteenth, Nineteenth and Twentieth Centuries. Illus.* TB/1119

MARCUS LEE HANSEN: The Atlantic Migration: 1607-1860. *Edited by Arthur M. Schlesinger* TB/1052

MARCUS LEE HANSEN: The Immigrant in American History. TB/1120

JOHN HIGHAM, Ed.: The Reconstruction of American History △ TB/1068

ROBERT H. JACKSON: The Supreme Court in the American System of Government TB/1106

JOHN F. KENNEDY: A Nation of Immigrants. △ *Illus.* TB/1118

LEONARD W. LEVY, Ed.: American Constitutional Law: *Historical Essays* TB/1285

LEONARD W. LEVY, Ed.: Judicial Review and the Supreme Court TB/1296

LEONARD W. LEVY: The Law of the Commonwealth and Chief Justice Shaw TB/1309

HENRY F. MAY: Protestant Churches and Industrial America. *New Intro. by the Author* TB/1334

RALPH BARTON PERRY: Puritanism and Democracy TB/1138

ARNOLD ROSE: The Negro in America TB/3048

MAURICE R. STEIN: The Eclipse of Community. *An Interpretation of American Studies* TB/1128

W. LLOYD WARNER and Associates: Democracy in Jonesville: *A Study in Quality and Inequality* ¶ TB/1129

W. LLOYD WARNER: Social Class in America: *The Evaluation of Status* TB/1013

American Studies: Colonial

BERNARD BAILYN, Ed.: Apologia of Robert Keayne: *Self-Portrait of a Puritan Merchant* TB/1201

BERNARD BAILYN: The New England Merchants in the Seventeenth Century TB/1149

JOSEPH CHARLES: The Origins of the American Party System TB/1049

HENRY STEELE COMMAGER & ELMO GIORDANETTI, Eds.: Was America a Mistake? *An Eighteenth Century Controversy* TB/1329

CHARLES GIBSON: Spain in America † TB/3077

LAWRENCE HENRY GIPSON: The Coming of the Revolution: 1763-1775. † *Illus.* TB/3007

LEONARD W. LEVY: Freedom of Speech and Press in Early American History: *Legacy of Suppression* TB/1109

PERRY MILLER: Errand Into the Wilderness TB/1139

PERRY MILLER & T. H. JOHNSON, Eds.: The Puritans: *A Sourcebook of Their Writings* Vol. I TB/1093; Vol. II TB/1094

EDMUND S. MORGAN, Ed.: The Diary of Michael Wigglesworth, 1653-1657: *The Conscience of a Puritan* TB/1228

EDMUND S. MORGAN: The Puritan Family: *Religion and Domestic Relations in Seventeenth-Century New England* TB/1227

RICHARD B. MORRIS: Government and Labor in Early America TB/1244

KENNETH B. MURDOCK: Literature and Theology in Colonial New England TB/99

WALLACE NOTESTEIN: The English People on the Eve of Colonization: 1603-1630. † *Illus.* TB/3006

JOHN P. ROCHE: Origins of American Political Thought: *Selected Readings* TB/1301

JOHN SMITH: Captain John Smith's America: *Selections from His Writings. Ed. with Intro. by John Lankford* TB/3078

LOUIS B. WRIGHT: The Cultural Life of the American Colonies: 1607-1763. † *Illus.* TB/3005

American Studies: From the Revolution to 1860

JOHN R. ALDEN: The American Revolution: 1775-1783. † *Illus.* TB/3011

MAX BELOFF, Ed.: The Debate on the American Revolution, 1761-1783: *A Sourcebook* △ TB/1225

RAY A. BILLINGTON: The Far Western Frontier: 1830-1860. † *Illus.* TB/3012

EDMUND BURKE: On the American Revolution: *Selected Speeches and Letters.* ‡ *Edited by Elliott Robert Barkan* TB/3068

WHITNEY R. CROSS: The Burned-Over District: *The Social and Intellectual History of Enthusiastic Religion in Western New York, 1800-1850* △ TB/1242

GEORGE DANGERFIELD: The Awakening of American Nationalism: 1815-1828. † *Illus.* TB/3061

---

† The New American Nation Series, edited by Henry Steele Commager and Richard B. Morris.
‡ American Perspectives series, edited by Bernard Wishy and William E. Leuchtenburg.
* The Rise of Modern Europe series, edited by William L. Langer.
** History of Europe series, edited by J. H. Plumb.
¶ Researches in the Social, Cultural and Behavioral Sciences, edited by Benjamin Nelson.
§ The Library of Religion and Culture, edited by Benjamin Nelson.
Σ Harper Modern Science Series, edited by James R. Newman.
° Not for sale in Canada.
△ Not for sale in the U. K.

History: Renaissance & Reformation

VESPASIANO: Renaissance Princes, Popes, and Prelates: *The Vespasiano Memoirs: Lives of Illustrious Men of the XVth Century. Intro. by Myron P. Gilmore*
TB/1111

History: Modern European

FREDERICK B. ARTZ: Reaction and Revolution, 1815-1832. * *Illus.*
TB/3034

MAX BELOFF: The Age of Absolutism, 1660-1815 △
TB/1062

ROBERT C. BINKLEY: Realism and Nationalism, 1852-1871. * *Illus.*
TB/3038

EUGENE C. BLACK, Ed.: European Political History, 1815-1870: *Aspects of Liberalism*
TB/1331

ASA BRIGGS: The Making of Modern England, 1784-1867: *The Age of Improvement* o △
TB/1203

CRANE BRINTON: A Decade of Revolution, 1789-1799. * *Illus.*
TB/3018

D. W. BROGAN: The Development of Modern France. o △
Volume I: *From the Fall of the Empire to the Dreyfus Affair*
TB/1184
Volume II: *The Shadow of War, World War I, Between the Two Wars. New Introduction by the Author*
TB/1185

J. BRONOWSKI & BRUCE MAZLISH: The Western Intellectual Tradition: *From Leonardo to Hegel* △
TB/3001

GEOFFREY BRUUN: Europe and the French Imperium, 1799-1814. * *Illus.*
TB/3033

ALAN BULLOCK: Hitler, A Study in Tyranny. o △ *Illus.*
TB/1123

E. H. CARR: German-Soviet Relations Between the Two World Wars, 1919-1939
TB/1278

E. H. CARR: International Relations Between the Two World Wars, 1919-1939 o △
TB/1279

E. H. CARR: The Twenty Years' Crisis, 1919-1939: *An Introduction to the Study of International Relations* o △
TB/1122

GORDON A. CRAIG: From Bismarck to Adenauer: *Aspects of German Statecraft. Revised Edition*
TB/1171

DENIS DIDEROT: The Encyclopedia: *Selections. Ed. and trans. by Stephen Gendzier*
TB/1299

WALTER L. DORN: Competition for Empire, 1740-1763. * *Illus.*
TB/3032

FRANKLIN L. FORD: Robe and Sword: *The Regrouping of the French Aristocracy after Louis XIV*
TB/1217

CARL J. FRIEDRICH: The Age of the Baroque, 1610-1660. * *Illus.*
TB/3004

RENÉ FUELOEP-MILLER: The Mind and Face of Bolshevism: *An Examination of Cultural Life in Soviet Russia. New Epilogue by the Author*
TB/1188

M. DOROTHY GEORGE: London Life in the Eighteenth Century △
TB/1182

LEO GERSHOY: From Despotism to Revolution, 1763-1789. * *Illus.*
TB/3017

C. C. GILLISPIE: Genesis and Geology: *The Decades before Darwin* §
TB/51

ALBERT GOODWIN, Ed.: The European Nobility in the Eighteenth Century △
TB/1313

ALBERT GOODWIN: The French Revolution △
TB/1064

ALBERT GUÉRARD: France in the Classical Age: *The Life and Death of an Ideal* △
TB/1183

CARLTON J. H. HAYES: A Generation of Materialism, 1871-1900. * *Illus.*
TB/3039

J. H. HEXTER: Reappraisals in History: *New Views on History and Society in Early Modern Europe* △
TB/1100

STANLEY HOFFMANN et al.: In Search of France: *The Economy, Society and Political System in the Twentieth Century*
TB/1219

A. R. HUMPHREYS: The Augustan World: *Society, Thought, & Letters in 18th Century England* o △
TB/1105

DAN N. JACOBS, Ed.: The New Communist Manifesto *and Related Documents. Third edition, revised*
TB/1078

LIONEL KOCHAN: The Struggle for Germany: 1914-45
TB/1304

HANS KOHN: The Mind of Germany: *The Education of a Nation* △
TB/1204

HANS KOHN, Ed.: The Mind of Modern Russia: *Historical and Political Thought of Russia's Great Age* TB/1065

WALTER LAQUEUR & GEORGE L. MOSSE, Eds.: Education and Social Structure in the 20th Century. o △ *Vol. 6 of the Journal of Contemporary History*
TB/1339

WALTER LAQUEUR & GEORGE L. MOSSE, Eds.: International Fascism, 1920-1945. o △ *Volume 1 of Journal of Contemporary History*
TB/1276

WALTER LAQUEUR & GEORGE L. MOSSE, Eds.: The Left-Wing Intellectuals between the Wars 1919-1939. o △ *Volume 2 of* Journal of Contemporary History TB/1286

WALTER LAQUEUR & GEORGE L. MOSSE, Eds.: Literature and Politics in the 20th Century. o △ *Vol. 5 of the* Journal of Contemporary History
TB/1328

WALTER LAQUEUR & GEORGE L. MOSSE, Eds.: The New History: *Trends in Historical Research and Writing since World War II.* o △ *Vol. 4 of the Journal of Conporary History*
TB/1327

WALTER LAQUEUR & GEORGE L. MOSSE, Eds.: 1914: *The Coming of the First World War.* o △ *Volume 3 of* Journal of Contemporary History
TB/1306

FRANK E. MANUEL: The Prophets of Paris: *Turgot, Condorcet, Saint-Simon, Fourier, and Comte*
TB/1218

KINGSLEY MARTIN: French Liberal Thought in the Eighteenth Century: *A Study of Political Ideas from Bayle to Condorcet*
TB/1114

ROBERT K. MERTON: Science, Technology and Society in Seventeenth Century England ¶ *New Intro. by the Author*
TB/1324

L. B. NAMIER: Facing East: *Essays on Germany, the Balkans, and Russia in the 20th Century* △ TB/1280

L. B. NAMIER: Personalities and Powers: *Selected Essays* △
TB/1186

L. B. NAMIER: Vanished Supremacies: *Essays on European History, 1812-1918* o
TB/1088

NAPOLEON III: Napoleonic Ideas: *Des Idées Napoléoniennes, par le Prince Napoléon-Louis Bonaparte. Ed. by Brison D. Gooch*
TB/1336

FRANZ NEUMANN: Behemoth: *The Structure and Practice of National Socialism, 1933-1944*
TB/1289

FREDERICK L. NUSSBAUM: The Triumph of Science and Reason, 1660-1685. * *Illus.*
TB/3009

DAVID OGG: Europe of the Ancien Régime, 1715-1783 ** o △
TB/1271

JOHN PLAMENATZ: German Marxism and Russian Communism. o △ *New Preface by the Author* TB/1189

RAYMOND W. POSTGATE, Ed.: Revolution from 1789 to 1906: *Selected Documents*
TB/1063

PENFIELD ROBERTS: The Quest for Security, 1715-1740. * *Illus.*
TB/3016

PRISCILLA ROBERTSON: Revolutions of 1848: *A Social History*
TB/1025

GEORGE RUDÉ: Revolutionary Europe, 1783-1815 ** o △
TB/1272

LOUIS, DUC DE SAINT-SIMON: Versailles, The Court, and Louis XIV. o △ *Introductory Note by Peter Gay*
TB/1250

HUGH SETON-WATSON: Eastern Europe Between the Wars, 1918-1941
TB/1330

ALBERT SOREL: Europe Under the Old Regime. *Translated by Francis H. Herrick*
TB/1121

N. N. SUKHANOV: The Russian Revolution, 1917: *Eyewitness Account.* △ *Edited by Joel Carmichael*
Vol. I TB/1066; Vol. II TB/1067

A. J. P. TAYLOR: From Napoleon to Lenin: *Historical Essays* o △
TB/1268

A. J. P. TAYLOR: The Habsburg Monarchy, 1809-1918: *A History of the Austrian Empire and Austria-Hungary* o △
TB/1187

G. M. TREVELYAN: British History in the Nineteenth Century and After: 1782-1919. o △ *Second Edition* TB/1251

H. R. TREVOR-ROPER: Historical Essays ° △ TB/1269

ELIZABETH WISKEMANN: Europe of the Dictators, 1919-1945 ** ° △ TB/1273

JOHN B. WOLF: The Emergence of the Great Powers, 1685-1715. * Illus. TB/3010

JOHN B. WOLF: France: 1814-1919: The Rise of a Liberal-Democratic Society TB/3019

Intellectual History & History of Ideas

HERSCHEL BAKER: The Image of Man: A Study of the Idea of Human Dignity in Classical Antiquity, the Middle Ages, and the Renaissance TB/1047

R. R. BOLGAR: The Classical Heritage and Its Beneficiaries: From the Carolingian Age to the End of the Renaissance △ TB/1125

RANDOLPH S. BOURNE: War and the Intellectuals: Collected Essays, 1915-1919. △ ‡ Edited by Carl Resek TB/3043

J. BRONOWSKI & BRUCE MAZLISH: The Western Intellectual Tradition: From Leonardo to Hegel △ TB/3001

ERNST CASSIRER: The Individual and the Cosmos in Renaissance Philosophy. △ Translated with an Introduction by Mario Domandi TB/1097

NORMAN COHN: The Pursuit of the Millennium: Revolutionary Messianism in Medieval and Reformation Europe △ TB/1037

C. C. GILLISPIE: Genesis and Geology: The Decades before Darwin § TB/51

G. RACHEL LEVY: Religious Conceptions of the Stone Age and Their Influence upon European Thought. △ Illus. Introduction by Henri Frankfort TB/106

ARTHUR O. LOVEJOY: The Great Chain of Being: A Study of the History of an Idea TB/1009

FRANK E. MANUEL: The Prophets of Paris: Turgot, Condorcet, Saint-Simon, Fourier, and Comte △ TB/1218

PERRY MILLER & T. H. JOHNSON, Editors: The Puritans: A Sourcebook of Their Writings
Vol. I TB/1093; Vol. II TB/1094

RALPH BARTON PERRY: The Thought and Character of William James: Briefer Version TB/1156

GEORG SIMMEL et al.: Essays on Sociology, Philosophy, and Aesthetics. ¶ Edited by Kurt H. Wolff TB/1234

BRUNO SNELL: The Discovery of the Mind: The Greek Origins of European Thought △ TB/1018

PAGET TOYNBEE: Dante Alighieri: His Life and Works. Edited with Intro. by Charles S. Singleton △ TB/1206

W. WARREN WAGAR, Ed.: European Intellectual History since Darwin and Marx TB/1297

PHILIP P. WIENER: Evolution and the Founders of Pragmatism. △ Foreword by John Dewey TB/1212

BASIL WILLEY: Nineteenth Century Studies: Coleridge to Matthew Arnold ° △ TB/1261

BASIL WILLEY: More Nineteenth Century Studies: A Group of Honest Doubters ° △ TB/1262

Law

EDWARD S. CORWIN: American Constitutional History: Essays edited by Alpheus T. Mason & Gerald Garvey TB/1136

ROBERT H. JACKSON: The Supreme Court in the American System of Government TB/1106

LEONARD W. LEVY, Ed.: American Constitutional Law: Historical Essays TB/1285

LEONARD W. LEVY: Freedom of Speech and Press in Early American History: Legacy of Suppression TB/1109

LEONARD W. LEVY, Ed.: Judicial Review and the Supreme Court TB/1296

LEONARD W. LEVY: The Law of the Commonwealth and Chief Justice Shaw TB/1309

RICHARD B. MORRIS: Fair Trial: Fourteen Who Stood Accused, from Anne Hutchinson to Alger Hiss. New Preface by the Author. TB/1335

Literature, Poetry, The Novel & Criticism

JAMES BAIRD: Ishmael: The Art of Melville in the Contexts of International Primitivism TB/1023

JACQUES BARZUN: The House of Intellect △ TB/1051

W. J. BATE: From Classic to Romantic: Premises of Taste in Eighteenth Century England TB/1036

RACHEL BESPALOFF: On the Iliad TB/2006

JAMES BOSWELL: The Life of Dr. Johnson & The Journal of a Tour to the Hebrides with Samuel Johnson LL.D.: Selections. ° △ Edited by F. V. Morley. Illus. by Ernest Shepard TB/1254

ERNST R. CURTIUS: European Literature and the Latin Middle Ages △ TB/2015

ADOLF ERMAN: The Ancient Egyptians: A Sourcebook of Their Writings. New Material and Introduction by William Kelly Simpson TB/1233

ALFRED HARBAGE: As They Liked It: A Study of Shakespeare's Moral Artistry TB/1035

STANLEY R. HOPPER, Ed: Spiritual Problems in Contemporary Literature § TB/21

A. R. HUMPHREYS: The Augustan World: Society, Thought and Letters in 18th Century England ° △ TB/1105

ARNOLD KETTLE: An Introduction to the English Novel. △
Volume I: Defoe to George Eliot TB/1011
Volume II: Henry James to the Present TB/1012

RICHMOND LATTIMORE: The Poetry of Greek Tragedy △ TB/1257

J. B. LEISHMAN: The Monarch of Wit: An Analytical and Comparative Study of the Poetry of John Donne ° △ TB/1258

J. B. LEISHMAN: Themes and Variations in Shakespeare's Sonnets ° △ TB/1259

ROGER SHERMAN LOOMIS: The Development of Arthurian Romance △ TB/1167

JOHN STUART MILL: On Bentham and Coleridge. △ Introduction by F. R. Leavis TB/1070

KENNETH B. MURDOCK: Literature and Theology in Colonial New England TB/99

SAMUEL PEPYS: The Diary of Samuel Pepys. ° Edited by O. F. Morshead. Illus. by Ernest Shepard TB/1007

ST.-JOHN PERSE: Seamarks TB/2002

V. DE S. PINTO: Crisis in English Poetry, 1880-1940 ° TB/1260

ROBERT PREYER, Ed.: Victorian Literature TB/1302

GEORGE SANTAYANA: Interpretations of Poetry and Religion § TB/9

C. K. STEAD: The New Poetic: Yeats to Eliot △ TB/1263

HEINRICH STRAUMANN: American Literature in the Twentieth Century. △ Third Edition, Revised TB/1168

PAGET TOYNBEE: Dante Alighieri: His Life and Works. Edited with Intro. by Charles S. Singleton TB/1206

DOROTHY VAN GHENT: The English Novel: Form and Function TB/1050

BASIL WILLEY: Nineteenth Century Studies: Coleridge to Matthew Arnold △ TB/1261

BASIL WILLEY: More Nineteenth Century Studies: A Group of Honest Doubters ° △ TB/1262

RAYMOND WILLIAMS: Culture and Society, 1780-1950 ° △ TB/1252

RAYMOND WILLIAMS: The Long Revolution. ° △ Revised Edition TB/1253

MORTON DAUWEN ZABEL, Editor: Literary Opinion in America Vol. I TB/3013; Vol. II TB/3014

Myth, Symbol & Folklore

MIRCEA ELIADE: Cosmos and History: The Myth of the Eternal Return § △ TB/2050

MIRCEA ELIADE: Rites and Symbols of Initiation: The Mysteries of Birth and Rebirth § △ TB/1236

THEODOR H. GASTER: Thespis: Ritual, Myth and Drama in the Ancient Near East △ TB/1281

C. G. JUNG & C. KERÉNYI: Essays on a Science of Mythology: *The Myths of the Divine Child and the Divine Maiden*   TB/2014

DORA & ERWIN PANOFSKY : Pandora's Box: *The Changing Aspects of a Mythical Symbol.* △ *Revised edition. Illus.*   TB/2021

ERWIN PANOFSKY: Studies in Iconology: *Humanistic Themes in the Art of the Renaissance.* △ *180 illustrations*   TB/1077

JEAN SEZNEC: The Survival of the Pagan Gods: *The Mythological Tradition and its Place in Renaissance Humanism and Art.* △ *108 illustrations*   TB/2004

HELLMUT WILHELM: Change: *Eight Lectures on the I Ching* △   TB/2019

HEINRICH ZIMMER: Myths and Symbols in Indian Art and Civilization. △ *70 illustrations*   TB/2005

Philosophy

G. E. M. ANSCOMBE: An Introduction to Wittgenstein's Tractatus. ° △ *Second Edition, Revised*   TB/1210

HENRI BERGSON: Time and Free Will: *An Essay on the Immediate Data of Consciousness* ° △   TB/1021

H. J. BLACKHAM: Six Existentialist Thinkers: *Kierkegaard, Nietzsche, Jaspers, Marcel, Heidegger, Sartre* ° △   TB/1002

CRANE BRINTON: Nietzsche. *New Preface, Bibliography and Epilogue by the Author*   TB/1197

MARTIN BUBER: The Knowledge of Man. △ *Ed. with an Intro. by Maurice Friedman. Trans. by Maurice Friedman and Ronald Gregor Smith*   TB/135

ERNST CASSIRER: The Individual and the Cosmos in Renaissance Philosophy. △ *Translated with an Introduction by Mario Domandi*   TB/1097

ERNST CASSIRER: Rousseau, Kant and Goethe. *Introduction by Peter Gay*   TB/1092

FREDERICK COPLESTON: Medieval Philosophy ° △   TB/376

F. M. CORNFORD: Principium Sapientiae: *A Study of the Origins of Greek Philosophical Thought. Edited by W. K. C. Guthrie*   TB/1213

F. M. CORNFORD: From Religion to Philosophy: *A Study in the Origins of Western Speculation* §   TB/20

WILFRID DESAN: The Tragic Finale: *An Essay on the Philosophy of Jean-Paul Sartre*   TB/1030

A. P. D'ENTRÈVES: Natural Law: *An Historical Survey* △   TB/1223

MARVIN FARBER: The Aims of Phenomenology: *The Motives, Methods, and Impact of Husserl's Thought*   TB/1291

MARVIN FARBER: Phenomenology and Existence: *Towards a Philosophy within Nature*   TB/1295

HERBERT FINGARETTE: The Self in Transformation: *Psychoanalysis, Philosophy and the Life of the Spirit* ¶   TB/1177

PAUL FRIEDLÄNDER: Plato: *An Introduction* △   TB/2017

J. GLENN GRAY: The Warriors: *Reflections on Men in Battle. Intro. by Hannah Arendt*   TB/1294

WILLIAM CHASE GREENE: Moira: *Fate, Good, and Evil in Greek Thought*   TB/1104

W. K. C. GUTHRIE: The Greek Philosophers: *From Thales to Aristotle* ° △   TB/1008

G. W. F. HEGEL: The Phenomenology of Mind ° △   TB/1303

F. H. HEINEMANN: Existentialism and the Modern Predicament △   TB/28

ISAAC HUSIK: A History of Medieval Jewish Philosophy   JP/3

EDMUND HUSSERL: Phenomenology and the Crisis of Philosophy. *Translated with an Introduction by Quentin Lauer*   TB/1170

IMMANUEL KANT: The Doctrine of Virtue, *being Part II of the Metaphysic of Morals. Trans. with Notes & Intro. by Mary J. Gregor. Foreword by H. J. Paton*   TB/110

IMMANUEL KANT: Groundwork of the Metaphysic of Morals. *Trans. & analyzed by H. J. Paton*   TB/1159

IMMANUEL KANT: Lectures on Ethics. § △ *Introduction by Lewis W. Beck*   TB/105

IMMANUEL KANT: Religion Within the Limits of Reason Alone. § *Intro. by T. M. Greene & J. Silber*   TB/67

QUENTIN LAUER: Phenomenology: *Its Genesis and Prospect*   TB/1169

MAURICE MANDELBAUM: The Problem of Historical Knowledge: *An Answer to Relativism. New Preface by the Author*   TB/1338

GABRIEL MARCEL: Being and Having: *An Existential Diary.* △ *Intro. by James Collins*   TB/310

GEORGE A. MORGAN: What Nietzsche Means   TB/1198

H. J. PATON: The Categorical Imperative: *A Study in Kant's Moral Philosophy* △   TB/1325

PHILO, SAADYA GAON, & JEHUDA HALEVI: Three Jewish Philosophers. *Ed. by Hans Lewy, Alexander Altmann, &Isaak Heinemann*   TB/813

MICHAEL POLANYI: Personal Knowledge: *Towards a Post-Critical Philosophy* △   TB/1158

WILLARD VAN ORMAN QUINE: Elementary Logic: *Revised Edition*   TB/577

WILLARD VAN ORMAN QUINE: From a Logical Point of View: *Logico-Philosophical Essays*   TB/566

BERTRAND RUSSELL et al.: The Philosophy of Bertrand Russell. *Edited by Paul Arthur Schilpp*   Vol. I TB/1095; Vol. II TB/1096

L. S. STEBBING: A Modern Introduction to Logic △ TB/538

ALFRED NORTH WHITEHEAD: Process and Reality: *An Essay in Cosmology* △   TB/1033

PHILIP P. WIENER: Evolution and the Founders of Pragmatism. *Foreword by John Dewey*   TB/1212

WILHELM WINDELBAND: A History of Philosophy   Vol. I: *Greek, Roman, Medieval*   TB/38   Vol. II: *Renaissance, Enlightenment, Modern*   TB/39

LUDWIG WITTGENSTEIN: The Blue and Brown Books °   TB/1211

Political Science & Government

JEREMY BENTHAM: The Handbook of Political Fallacies: *Introduction by Crane Brinton*   TB/1069

C. E. BLACK: The Dynamics of Modernization: *A Study in Comparative History*   TB/1321

KENNETH E. BOULDING: Conflict and Defense: *A General Theory*   TB/3024

CRANE BRINTON: English Political Thought in the Nineteenth Century   TB/1071

ROBERT CONQUEST: Power and Policy in the USSR: *The Study of Soviet Dynastics* △   TB/1307

EDWARD S. CORWIN: American Constitutional History: *Essays edited by Alpheus T. Mason and Gerald Garvey*   TB/1136

ROBERT DAHL & CHARLES E. LINDBLOM: Politics, Economics, and Welfare: *Planning and Politico-Economic Systems Resolved into Basic Social Processes*   TB/3037

JOHN NEVILLE FIGGIS: The Divine Right of Kings. *Introduction by G. R. Elton*   TB/1191

JOHN NEVILLE FIGGIS: Political Thought from Gerson to Grotius: 1414-1625: *Seven Studies. Introduction by Garrett Mattingly*   TB/1032

F. L. GANSHOF: Feudalism △   TB/1058

G. P. GOOCH: English Democratic Ideas in the Seventeenth Century   TB/1006

J. H. HEXTER: More's Utopia: *The Biography of an Idea. New Epilogue by the Author*   TB/1195

SIDNEY HOOK: Reason, Social Myths and Democracy △   TB/1237

ROBERT H. JACKSON: The Supreme Court in the American System of Government △   TB/1106

DAN N. JACOBS, Ed.: The New Communist Manifesto *and Related Documents. Third Edition, Revised*   TB/1078

DAN N. JACOBS & HANS BAERWALD, Eds.: Chinese Communism: *Selected Documents*   TB/3031

7

Psychology

Sociology

8